VISUAL QUICK PRO GUIDE

M000100166

Flash Professional CS5 Advanced

FOR WINDOWS AND MACINTOSH

RUSSELL CHUN

Peachpit Press

Visual QuickPro Guide
Flash Professional CS5 Advanced for Windows and Macintosh
Russell Chun

Peachpit Press
1249 Eighth Street
Berkeley, CA 94710
510/524-2178
510/524-2221 (fax)

Find us on the Web at: www.peachpit.com
To report errors, please send a note to: errata@peachpit.com
Peachpit Press is a division of Pearson Education.

Editor: Rebecca Gulick
Copy Editor: Liz Welch
Proofreader: Patricia Pane
Production Coordinator: Myrna Vladic
Compositor: David Van Ness
Indexer: Valerie Haynes Perry
Technical Reviewer: Matthew Newton
Cover Design: Peachpit Press

ISBN 13:   978-0-321-72034-4
ISBN 10:   0-321-72034-2

9 8 7 6 5 4 3 2 1

Printed and bound in the United States of America

Thank you

Bringing this book to you, as always, took the efforts of a team, to which I owe my gratitude. I want to thank my editor, Liz Welch; project editor, Rebecca Gulick; production coordinator, Myrna Vladic; compositor, David Van Ness; and proofreader, Patricia Pane. I would like to especially thank Matthew Newton, whose keen insight and detailed technical review were invaluable.

Finally, I want to thank readers like you. When I first discovered Flash, it fired up my imagination and challenged me to see how I could use the tool to deliver richer and more immersive content. Flash has come a long way since then, and despite new technologies and an evolving environment, it remains a vital part of the online experience. Readers like you will continue to push Flash forward and make the Web even more interesting by transforming your creativity into reality.

—*Russell Chun*

Contents at a Glance

Table of Contents

Introduction

Flash is one of the most pervasive technologies on the Web, delivering interactive and immersive multimedia. Leading corporate Web sites use its streamlined graphics to communicate their brands, major motion picture studios promote theatrical releases with Flash video, and online news and educational sites provide rich user experiences.

Adobe Flash Professional CS5 is the program for industry professionals to create Flash content. As a vector-based animation and authoring application, Flash is ideal for creating high-impact, low-bandwidth sites incorporating animation, text, video, sound, and database integration. With robust support for complex interactivity and server-side communication, Flash is an ideal solution for developing Internet applications as well as sophisticated Web site designs. From designer to programmer, Flash is an indispensable tool for delivering dynamic content across various browsers, platforms, and devices.

As the popularity of Flash remains high, so does the demand for designers and developers who know how to tap its power. This book is designed to help you meet that challenge. Learn how to build complex animations; integrate sophisticated interfaces and navigation schemes; and dynamically control graphics, video, sound, and text. Experiment with the techniques discussed in this book to create the compelling media that Flash makes possible. It's not an exaggeration to say that Flash has revolutionized the Web. This book will help you be a part of that revolution—so boot up your computer and let's get started!

Who Should Use This Book

This book is for designers, animators, and developers who want to take their Flash skills to the next level. You've already mastered the basics of tweening and are ready to move on to more complex tasks, such as importing video, masking, controlling dynamic sound, or detecting collisions between graphics on the Stage. You may be familiar with Flash CS4, but you are eager to explore the new features in CS5—the completely revamped text engine, the

Code Snippets panel, or the ability to add cue points to external video from the Stage. You may not be a hard-core programmer, but you're ready to learn how ActionScript can control vector and bitmap graphics, sounds, and text. You want to integrate interactivity with your animations to create more responsive environments, to create complex user interface elements like pull-down menus, and to learn how Flash communicates with outside applications such as Web browsers. If this description fits, then this book is right for you.

This book explores the advanced aspects of Flash Professional CS5 and some of the key new features, so you should already be comfortable with the basic tools and commands for creating simple Flash movies. You should know how to create and modify shapes and text with the drawing tools and be able to create symbols. You should also know how to create simple motion tweens and know how to work with shape tweens. You should know your way around the Flash interface: how to move from the Stage to symbol-editing mode to the Timeline and how to manipulate layers and frames. You should also be familiar with importing and using bitmaps and sounds, and assigning basic actions to frames for navigation. To get up to speed, review the tutorials that come with the software, or pick up a copy of *Flash Professional CS5 for Windows and Macintosh: Visual QuickStart Guide* by Katherine Ulrich (Peachpit, 2010).

Goals of This Book

The aim of this book is to demonstrate the advanced features of Flash Professional CS5 through a logical approach, emphasizing how techniques are applied. You'll learn how techniques build on each other and how groups of techniques can be combined to solve a particular problem. Each example you work through puts another skill under your belt; by the end of this book, you'll be able to create sophisticated interactive Flash projects.

For example, creating a pull-down menu illustrates how simple elements—event handlers, button-tracking options, and movie clips—come together to make more complex behaviors. Examples illustrate the practical application of techniques, and additional tips explain how to apply these techniques in other contexts.

How to use this book

The concepts in this book build on each other: The material at the end is more complex than that at the beginning. If you're familiar with some of the material, you can skip around to the subjects that interest you, but you'll find it most useful to learn the techniques in the order in which they appear.

As with other books in the Visual QuickPro Guide series, tasks are presented for you to do as you read about them, so that you can see how a technique is applied. Follow the step-by-step instructions, look at the figures, and try the tasks on your computer. You'll learn more by doing and by taking an active role in experimenting with these exercises. Many of the completed tasks are provided as FLA and SWF files on the companion Web site: Go to www.peachpit.com/flashcs5vqp to download the sample files and study how they were made.

When code is presented, it is set apart in a different font. When a line of code is meant to be typed on a single line but is forced onto a second line in this book, you'll see a small arrow like this (→) indicating the continuation of the code.

Tips follow the tasks to give you hints about how to use a shortcut, warnings about common mistakes, and suggestions about how techniques can be extended.

Occasionally, you'll see sidebars in gray boxes. Sidebars discuss related matters that aren't directly task oriented. They include interesting and useful concepts that can help you better understand how Flash works.

What's in this book

This book is organized into four parts:

- **Part I: Approaching Advanced Animation**

  Chapters 1 and 2 cover advanced techniques for graphics and animation, including motion tweening and the Motion Editor, inverse kinematics, and the new Spring option to simulate physics, as well as strategies for shape tweening, masking, and using digital video.

- **Part II: Interactivity**

  Chapters 3 though 6 introduce ActionScript 3, the scripting language Flash uses to add interactivity to a movie. You'll learn the ways in which Flash can respond to input from the viewer and how you can create complex navigation schemes with multiple timelines. You'll also see how Flash communicates with external files and applications such as Web browsers.

- **Part III: Transforming Graphics and Sound**

  Chapters 7 and 8 demonstrate how to dynamically control the basic elements of any Flash movie—its graphics and sound—through ActionScript.

- **Part IV: Working with Information**

  Chapters 9 through 12 focus on how to retrieve, store, modify, and test

information to create complex Flash environments that can respond to changing conditions. They also explore the new text engine, called Text Layout Framework, and how you can use it to create sophisticated layouts.

- **Appendix: Keyboard Key Codes**

  The appendix gives you quick access to the key code values and matching keyboard constants for the keys on your keyboard.

What's on the companion Web site

Accompanying this book is a Web site at www.peachpit.com/flashcs5vqp that contains many of the Flash source files for the tasks. You can download the files and see how each task was created, study the ActionScript, and use the ActionScript to do further experimentation. Sample media such as audio and video files are provided for your use. You'll also find a list of Web links to sites that are devoted to Flash and that showcase the latest Flash techniques and provide tutorials, articles, and advice.

Additional resources

Use the Web to your advantage. There is a thriving, active, international community of Flash developers; within it, you can share your frustrations, seek help, and show off your latest Flash masterpiece. Free forums and a significant number of Flash-related blogs exist for all levels of Flash users. Begin your search for Flash resources with the list of Web sites on the companion Web site and by choosing Help in the Flash application, which provides access to an online searchable ActionScript 3 language reference and Flash manual.

What's New in Flash Professional CS5

Whether you're a beginner or an advanced user, a designer or a programmer, a number of new features in Flash Professional CS5 will appeal to you. The following are just a few of the capabilities that make the software even more powerful, flexible, and easy to use.

New text capabilities

A completely new text engine called Text Layout Framework, or TLF, provides you with more sophisticated and nuanced control over text layouts and nearly all aspects of typography. For example, you can create text that wraps around photos or animations on the Stage for more visually appealing designs, or you can quickly make text flow in multiple columns within the same text field. TLF text comes with a host of new ActionScript classes that enable you to dynamically create, format, display, and control text. If you're into text, Flash Professional CS5 was made for you.

Video enhancements

Using Flash to download and play external video has become even easier, with more options for interactivity. New in CS5 is the ability to preview your external video on the Stage, making timing and placement of your video more precise. There are additional video skins that you can choose, and you can now add cue points directly to your video through the Properties inspector in authoring mode.

ActionScript support

ActionScript 3 continues to expand with new language elements that give you more power to build richer and more interactive applications. To help you and your team of developers create interactivity quickly and consistently, Flash Professional CS5 has added a new panel called Code Snippets. The Code Snippets panel makes adding ActionScript easy—simply select the desired interactivity from the panel and assign it to your movie. You can add your own code to the panel, and share code snippets with your team. The Code Snippets panel will save you time and even help you learn ActionScript quicker because you can study the code and its application.

Animation and drawing improvements

Inverse kinematics gets better with a new feature called the Spring option. Designed to simulate physics, the Spring option lets you create armatures that wiggle, bounce, and shimmer as they react to the effects of gravity or their own motion. Waving flags, swaying branches, or undulating underwater creatures can move more realistically with ease. The Deco tool in your Tools panel now comes with more options, with numerous new brushes for complex, expressive patterns. While not explored in this book, the Deco tool is yet one more reason to use Flash Professional CS5 to transform your creative energies into rich, interactive online content.

Building Complexity

The key to creating complex animations in Flash Professional CS5 is to build them from simpler parts. You should think of your Flash project as a collection of simpler motions, just as the movement of a runner is essentially a collection of rotating limbs. Isolating individual components of a much larger, complicated motion allows you to treat each component with the most appropriate technique, simplifies the tweening, and gives you better control with more refined results.

To animate a runner, for example, you would first consider how to simplify the animation into separate motions. Animating the entire sequence at the same time would be impossible, because the many elements making up the motion change in different ways as they move. The rotation of her legs and arms can be created with different poses using inverse kinematics. Her hair could be a shape tween that lets you show its flow, swing, and slight bouncing effect as she runs. And her entire body can move across the Stage as a motion tween.

In This Chapter

Learning to combine different techniques and break animation into simpler parts not only solves difficult animation problems but also forces you to use multiple layers and think in smaller, independent components. By doing so, you set up the animation so that it's easy to manage now and revise later.

This chapter describes some advanced approaches to basic animation techniques such as motion tweening, shape tweening, inverse kinematics, and masking.

Motion Tweening Strategies

Motion tweening lets you interpolate any of the instance properties of a symbol, such as its location, size, rotation, color, and transparency, as well as any filters that have been applied to the symbol instance. Because of its versatility, motion tweening can be applied to a variety of animation tasks, making it the foundation of most Flash projects. Because motion tweening deals with instance properties, it's a good idea to think of the technique in terms of instance tweening. Regardless of whether actual motion across the Stage is involved, changing instance properties through time requires motion tweening. Thinking of it as instance tweening will help you distinguish when and where to use motion tweening as opposed to shape tweening, inverse kinematics, or frame-by-frame animation.

The motion tween model

You should already know how to create a basic motion tween in Flash Professional CS5. This book will help you move forward and understand tweening's more advanced features. However, a quick review of the key points in the motion tween model is helpful:

- Motion tweens are object based, so tweens are applied directly to objects (rather than keyframes). The target object of a motion tween can easily be swapped with a different instance.

- Motion tweens are separated on a special layer called a tween layer in a tween span. The tween span can be selected as a single object and moved, expanded, and contracted to change its duration, or copied and pasted. Flash does not allow any drawing or other objects placed within a tween span.

- You have independent control over each property of the instance (position, scale, color effect, filter) and can change property values over time with curves in the Motion Editor panel.

- The path of the motion is part of the motion tween. The path can be directly manipulated with Bézier precision or freely scaled, skewed, rotated, or even replaced.

A Right-click (Windows) or Ctrl-click (Mac) directly on the object you want to animate, and choose Create Motion Tween.

B Motion tweens require that the object be either a symbol or text.

C A Tween layer is reserved for motion tweening.

D This instance of a star moves from left to right in a motion tween. The black triangle in the last frame of the tween span represents a keyframe for the new position.

To create a motion tween:

1. Right-click (Windows) or Ctrl-click (Mac) on an object on the Stage, and choose Create Motion Tween from the context menu that appears **A**.

   Flash may ask to convert the selected object into a symbol for it to be tweened. Click OK **B**.

   Flash automatically converts your selection to a movie clip symbol, which is saved in your Library. Flash also puts the symbol instance in a separate Tween layer and adds one second of frames so you can begin to animate the instance. Tween layers are distinguished by a special icon in front of the layer name, and the frames are tinted blue **C**. Tween layers are reserved for motion tweens, and hence, no drawing is allowed on a Tween layer.

2. Move the playhead to a desired end point on the Tween layer.

3. Move the instance to a different position on the Stage.

   Flash smoothly animates the change in positions **D**.

> **TIP** If you are more comfortable working with the older way of animating, you can do so by relying on the Classic Tween option. Create a beginning keyframe and an ending keyframe containing a symbol instance. Select the first keyframe, and then choose Insert > Classic Tween. However, many features, such as the Motion Editor, are not available for classic tweens.

Editing the path of the motion

The path that an instance moves during a motion tween is graphically shown as a stroke on the Stage. Dots along the path indicate the instance's position at each frame 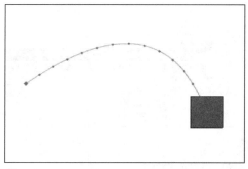. You can directly manipulate the path with a variety of tools, including the Selection tool, the Subselection tool, the Delete Anchor Point tool, the Convert Anchor Point tool, or the Free Transform tool.

To change the location of the path:

1. Click on the motion path with the Selection tool.

   The motion path becomes highlighted, indicating that the whole path is selected.

2. Click and drag the motion path to a new location on the Stage .

   The motion path is moved. The motion tween proceeds from its new location.

or

   Select the motion path and change the X and Y values in the Properties inspector under Path **G**.

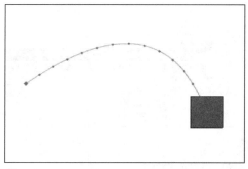

E The curved line on the Stage represents the path of motion of an object. The dots on the line represent the location of the object at each frame during the tween span.

F Move the path to move the location of the motion tween.

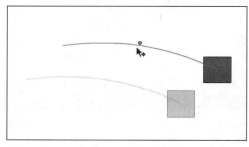

	Horizontal position of the path	Vertical position of the path

G Change the X and Y values in the Properties inspector to change the location of the motion tween.

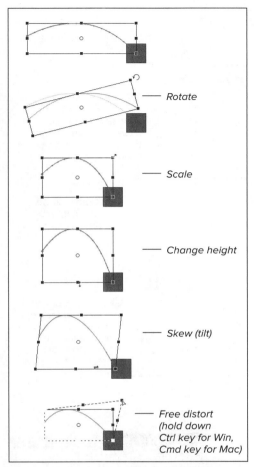

Rotate

Scale

Change height

Skew (tilt)

Free distort
(hold down
Ctrl key for Win,
Cmd key for Mac)

H Use the Free Transform tool to change the shape of the path.

To change the shape of the path:

1. Select the Free Transform tool and click on the motion path on the Stage.

   The Free Transform control points appear around the motion path.

2. Drag the Free Transform control points to change the overall shape of the motion path. The position of your mouse pointer on various control points determines the type of transformation **H**:

   On corner points. Changes the overall width and height of the path. Hold down the Shift key to constrain the proportions.

   Near corner points. Rotates the path.

   Side points. Changes either the width or the height of the path.

   Sides. Skews (tilts) the path.

or

   Select the motion path and change the W and H values in the Properties inspector under Path.

   The W and H values change the width and the height of the motion path.

TIP When using the Free Transform tool, you can move the white circle, which represents the center point around which all transformations are made. Double-click the white circle to reset its position.

To change the curvature of the path:

Choose the Selection tool and drag a portion of the motion path to change its curvature ⓘ.

or

Choose the Subselection tool and move the individual control points to new positions, or drag the control handles to change the curvature ⓙ.

or

Choose the Delete Anchor Point tool and click on a control point on the motion path.

The control point and its associated curve are deleted ⓚ.

or

Choose the Convert Anchor Point tool and click on a control point on the motion path and drag out the control handles.

The control handles change the curvature of the path at that point ⓛ.

ⓘ Drag a segment of the motion path to change its curvature.

ⓙ Move individual control points with the Subselection tool, or move the control handles to change the curvature of the motion path.

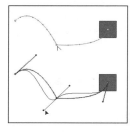

ⓚ Delete individual control points with the Delete Anchor Point tool.

ⓛ Use the Convert Anchor Point tool to click on an individual control point (top) and drag out the handles to create curves at that point (bottom).

Multiple Motion Paths

If you are designing multiple motion tweens with intersecting motion paths, it is often helpful to see all the motion paths for all the tweens simultaneously. Select a tween on the Timeline or its motion path on the Stage, and from the Properties inspector options menu, choose Always Show Motion Paths ⓜ.

Flash displays all the motion paths so you can edit one while seeing its relationship to the others ⓝ.

If you only want to see a subset of all the motion paths, simply click on the Hide Layer options in the layers that you want to hide.

ⓜ Choose Always Show Motion Paths from the Properties inspector options menu to display motion paths for all your layers.

ⓝ These three motion tweens are on separate layers, but their motion paths are displayed simultaneously.

To delete the path:

Select the path and press the Delete key on the keyboard.

The path is deleted (but the tween still exists), and the object of the motion tween remains stationary.

To reverse the path:

Right-click (Windows) or Ctrl-click (Mac) the motion path and choose Motion Path > Reverse Path.

The path remains the same; however, the target object begins at the end point and travels in the reverse direction.

To copy and paste a motion path:

1. Select a stroke on a different layer or a motion path from another tween, and copy the stroke (Edit > Copy).

2. Select the motion path and paste the stroke (Edit > Paste in Center).

   The pasted stroke replaces the motion path.

Roving and Non-roving Keyframes

Flash automatically adjusts the positions of property keyframes so that the speed of the motion is consistent throughout a tween. As you edit the motion path, the property keyframes adjust so the object moves the same distance in each frame **O**. This way of automatically adjusting keyframes is known as *roving keyframes*.

However, you may not want your motion to be consistent throughout the path. You can change the tween to *non-roving keyframes* by right-clicking (Windows) or Ctrl-clicking (Mac) the motion path and choosing Motion Path > Switch keyframes to non-roving **P**. Flash will fix the positions of the keyframes in the tween span so that any further edits to the path will increase or decrease the speed of the object in particular segments of the tween **Q**.

O Roving keyframes automatically distribute the object's position along its path equally.

Q With non-roving keyframes, this object moves along different segments on its path at different speeds.

P Roving keyframes is the default setting. Choose non-roving keyframes to prevent Flash from automatically distributing the object's position.

Using the Motion Editor

Keyframes are specific to each property of an instance. For example, a single motion tween can have keyframes for position and different keyframes for alpha. Managing these *property keyframes* may seem daunting, but fortunately you can use the Motion Editor (Window > Motion Editor) to visualize and keep track of all your property keyframes.

The Motion Editor provides a graphical representation of the changing values for all the properties of an instance in a motion tween. For example, if an object moves from left to right on the Stage, the Motion Editor shows the change in the X position values as a line on a graph ®. Learning to read and understand the Motion Editor is essential for creating more sophisticated, advanced animations.

You can add any number of keyframes along the graph for any of the properties and change their values.

To open the Motion Editor:

1. Select a tween span on the Timeline or a tweened object on the Stage.

2. Click on the Motion Editor tab behind the Timeline, or choose Window > Motion Editor.

   The Motion Editor displays the graphs for the selected motion tween ⑤.

® The Motion Editor shows the X position of this object changing from frame 1 to frame 16.

Property values   *Keyframe controls*   *Playhead*

Properties   *Timeline*   *Graphs*

Motion Editor viewing options   *Add and delete properties*

⑤ The Motion Editor displays the properties of the instance on the left and their changing values on the right.

T The graph portion of the Motion Editor has a vertical red playhead, just as the Timeline does.

Add keyframe   *Keyframe*

U Click on the diamond to add a keyframe to the currently selected property. Here, a keyframe for Alpha (transparency) has been inserted at frame 8.

V Add a keyframe directly from the context menu (right-click for Windows, Ctrl-click for Mac).

To add a property keyframe:

1. Move the playhead to the desired frame on the Timeline in the Motion Editor **T**.

2. Click the diamond icon next to the selected property.

   A keyframe at that point in time, indicated by a black square, is inserted for the property **U**.

   or

   Right-click (Windows) or Ctrl-click (Mac) on any point along the graph and choose Add Keyframe **V**.

   A keyframe at that point in time, indicated by a black square, is inserted for the property.

   or

   Ctrl-click (Windows) or Cmd-click (Mac) on any point along the graph **W**.

   A keyframe at that point in time, indicated by a black square, is inserted for the property.

W Add a keyframe by holding down the Ctrl key (Windows) or Cmd key (Mac) and clicking on the graph.

To change the value of a property keyframe:

Drag the keyframe up or down to its new value.

The value for the property keyframe changes ⓧ.

or

Drag the playhead to the selected key-frame and change the value under the Value column.

The value for the property keyframe changes ⓨ.

TIP Change the value of multiple keyframes at once by holding down the Shift key and selecting multiple keyframes and then dragging the multiple keyframes to new values. The line segment or segments between the selected keyframes will move together.

TIP Move quickly between keyframes by clicking on the left-facing or the right-facing arrowhead. The adjacent keyframes will be selected.

To remove a property keyframe:

Right-click (Windows) or Ctrl-click (Mac) on any keyframe and choose Remove Keyframe.

The selected keyframe is removed ⓩ.

or

Select a keyframe and click the yellow diamond icon.

The selected keyframe is removed.

or

Ctrl-click (Windows) or Cmd-click (Mac) on any keyframe.

The selected keyframe is removed.

ⓧ The keyframe at frame 6 for the Alpha property has been dragged down to about 92.5%. The resulting tween will show the object fade slightly from frame 1 to frame 6.

ⓨ Change the value for any keyframe directly with numerical precision. The value column for the Alpha property at this keyframe shows 92.5429%.

ⓩ Choose Remove Keyframe to delete a keyframe along the graph.

Plus button for Color Effect

AA In this example, the Brightness property is being added to the Motion Editor.

Minus button for Color Effect

BB In this example, the Brightness property is being deleted from the Motion Editor.

To reset the value of a property keyframe:

Click the Reset Values button in the upper-right corner of the property category.

The property returns to its initial value.

To add a property:

Click the plus button next to the Property category (Color Effect, Filters, or Eases) and select the desired property **AA**.

The selected property is added to the Motion Editor.

To remove a property:

Click the minus button next to the property category (Color Effect, Filters, or Eases) and select the property to remove **BB**.

The selected property is removed from the Motion Editor.

Motion Editor Display Options

There are many options you can set in the Motion Editor to help you be more comfortable accessing its information.

You can move the horizontal splitter bar that separates the Motion Editor from the Stage to increase the height of the panel. You can also expand or collapse any of the property categories by clicking on the small triangles next to the property category names. When you select a specific property, the graph expands to show more of that property.

At the bottom left of the Motion Editor, three buttons change the viewing area of the properties and their graphs **CC**. The Graph Size button changes the height of the rows of unselected properties. The Expanded Graph Size button changes the height of the row of the selected property. The Viewable Frames button changes the number of frames that are viewable along the Timeline.

Graph Size   Expanded Graph Size   Viewable Frames

CC Change the viewing options for the Motion Editor to best suit your working environment.

Easing in the Motion Editor

You can also change the curvature of the graph at any keyframe of all the properties except for X, Y, and Z. Changing the curvature affects how fast or slow the values change. A straight line represents a linear change—an equal amount of change happens throughout the tween. A curved line represents a nonlinear change known as an *ease*.

Easing shows how fast or slow the change in values happens. You could have your tween start slowly and end quickly (*ease-in*), or your tween could start quickly and gradually slow down (*ease-out*). Easing is a way to add a sense of acceleration and deceleration, which can give weight and naturalness to an otherwise mechanical animation.

Flash also provides a number of preset eases that you can apply to any property, including X, Y, and Z **DD**.

Using the preset eases is an easy way of making complex motions without explicitly defining keyframes. For example, you can quickly create bounces or shudders in a motion tween by simply applying a custom ease that moves back and forth between the values of a property keyframe.

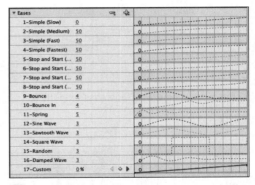

DD The Preset eases available in the Motion Editor.

EE Choose one of the Smooth options to change the curvature of the graph at any keyframe (except for the X, Y, or Z properties).

FF The handles affect the curvature of the graph at the keyframe.

To create a smooth curve:

Right-click (Windows) or Ctrl-click (Mac) a property keyframe (except for X, Y, or Z), and choose Smooth point, Smooth left, or Smooth right **EE**.

Smooth point. Control handles appear from both sides of the keyframe, which you can move to change the curvature of the graph.

Smooth left. A control handle appears from the left side of the keyframe, which you can move to change the curvature of the graph to the left of the keyframe.

Smooth right. A control handle appears from the right side of the keyframe, which you can move to change the curvature of the graph to the right of the keyframe.

or

Alt-click (Windows) or Option-click (Mac) a property keyframe (except for X, Y, or Z), and drag out the control handles to change the curvature of the graph **FF**.

To remove a curve:

Right-click (Windows) or Ctrl-click (Mac) a property keyframe (except for X, Y, or Z), and choose Corner point.

The control handles disappear from the keyframe, and the graph on both sides of the keyframe becomes a straight line.

To apply a preset ease:

1. Click the plus button on the Eases category and choose a preset ease.

   The selected preset ease appears in the Motion Editor 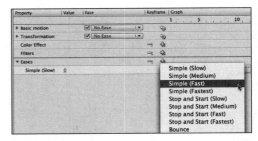.

2. Select the preset ease and change its value.

   The value of the preset ease determines the strength and direction of the ease. You can visually see the effect in the graph **HH**.

3. Choose the ease in the Ease pull-down menu next to the property you want it to affect **II**.

   The preset ease is applied to the property. The ease curve is superimposed on the graph to show how it affects the property values over time **JJ**.

TIP You can also apply ease-in and ease-out effects from the Properties inspector. In the Timeline (not the Motion Editor), select the motion tween. In the Properties inspector, enter a value for the ease between -100 (ease-in) and 100 (ease-out). Eases applied via the Properties inspector, however, will be applied globally to all the properties throughout the entire motion tween. With the Motion Editor, you have precise control over individual properties and eases between keyframes.

TIP For classic tweens, you can edit the easing profile from the Properties inspector. Select the Edit easing button to access the Custom Ease-in/Ease-out editor.

GG Choose a preset ease from the plus button next to the Ease category.

HH The Strength value of a preset ease changes its curvature.

II Apply the preset ease to a property. Here, the preset ease is applied to the Basic Motion category, so the X, Y, and Z changes of the object will be affected by the ease.

JJ The curved dotted line superimposed over the X graph shows how the preset ease affects the X property.

Interpreting the Ease Curves

The ease curves indicate how a property value changes over time. The x-axis of the graph represents time, and the y-axis represents the property value. If the change is uniform—that is, the value changes an equal amount at every frame—the graph is a straight line. If there is an upward sloping curve at the beginning and a flattening out at the end , that means that there is a greater change in the y-axis (the property value) for the frames at the beginning and a smaller change in the y-axis for the frames at the end. The result is a rapid acceleration of the property at the start and a gradual slowdown at the end.

KK A graph showing an ease-out.

The curve doesn't always have to travel in one direction only, and the curve doesn't have to end at the last property value. In fact, interesting effects can be achieved if the curve moves back and forth between property values. For example, the curve of the Spring ease moves rapidly from the beginning property value to the ending property value in the first few frames, and then moves back and forth until finally settling at a point a little more than halfway between the beginning and end values. If this ease is applied to a motion tween of position, the result would be a springing action back and forth between two points on the Stage until the object rests about halfway between.

LL The Spring ease rapidly moves from the beginning value (0) to the end value (100) and swings back and forth until settling somewhere in the middle.

The value of the ease curves determines their strength and direction. The curvature becomes more pronounced in both directions, and the result on the ease becomes more noticeable. For other ease curves, the value determines the frequency, or the number of waves or bumps in the curve .

MM This Sine Wave ease has 11 peaks and valleys.

For total control, you can choose Custom from the Ease menu NN. The Custom ease lets you create your own curve and apply it to any of the properties.

Simple (Slow)
Simple (Medium)
Simple (Fast)
Simple (Fastest)
Stop and Start (Slow)
Stop and Start (Medium)
Stop and Start (Fast)
Stop and Start (Fastest)
Bounce
Bounce In
Spring
Sine Wave
Sawtooth Wave
Square Wave
Random
Damped Wave
Custom

NN Choose the bottom option from the preset Ease menu for a custom graph.

Duplicating Motion

If you've created a motion tween that you want to duplicate with a different object, or you want to create multiple objects going through the same motion, you can easily do so with a variety of copy-and-paste and swapping options. For example, imagine that you've created a transition for the first slide of a photo slide show. Now you want to duplicate that transition with the next ten slides. You can select the motion tween of the first slide and copy all the characteristics of that tween—its rotation, scaling, position, color, or filter changes. Then you can apply the characteristics of that tween to the subsequent slides.

Copying and pasting motion and swapping out the tweened object make it easy to create complex animations with repetitive motion, such as a photo slide show or perhaps a group of fluttering leaves.

To duplicate a motion tween:

Hold down the Alt key (Windows) or the Option key (Mac) and drag a tween span to a new layer on the Timeline.

Flash duplicates the motion tween Ⓐ.

or

1. In the Timeline, right-click (Windows) or Ctrl-click (Mac) on a tween span and choose Copy Frames.

   The selected tween span is copied.

2. Right-click (Windows) or Ctrl-click (Mac) on a destination frame and choose Paste Frames.

   The copied tween is duplicated in the new location.

Ⓐ This tween span from Layer 1 is copied and pasted into Layer 2.

B The existing tween uses the square movie clip. Drag another instance from the Library onto the tween to swap instances.

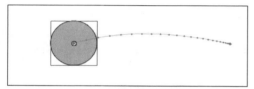

C Click OK to accept the Flash dialog warning box.

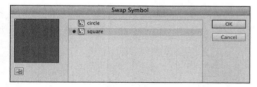

D The original tween with the square movie clip is replaced with the circle movie clip.

E Choose a different symbol in the Swap Symbol dialog box to swap for the original. The original symbol is marked with a black dot.

To swap the target object of a tween:

1. Drag a new symbol from the Library and drop it on an existing tweened object on the Stage **B**.

   A warning dialog box appears asking whether you want to replace the tweened object **C**.

2. In the dialog box, click OK.

   Flash replaces the existing object with the one you dragged out of the Library **D**.

or

1. Right-click (Windows) or Ctrl-click (Mac) on the tweened object and choose Swap Symbol.

   The Swap Symbol dialog box appears **E**.

2. In the dialog box, select your replacement symbol and click OK.

   Flash swaps the symbols, aligning their registration points.

To copy motion and apply it to another object:

1. In the Timeline, right-click (Windows) or Ctrl-click (Mac) on a tween span and choose Copy Motion.

   The selected motion of the tween span is copied.

2. On the Stage or on the Timeline, right-click (Windows) or Ctrl-click (Mac) a different symbol instance and choose Paste Motion from the context menu **F**.

   Flash duplicates the motion of the first tween and applies it to the second symbol instance **G**.

TIP Paste Motion Special (not discussed here) is for classic tweening.

Saving tweens as motion presets

If you want to save your motion tweens, perhaps to apply them in future projects or to share them with other developers, you can do so in the Motion Presets panel. The Motion Presets panel (Window > Motion Presets) is much like a library of favorite or useful tweens. The Motion Presets panel comes loaded with many basic tweens that you can use **H**.

You can also save your own tweens and share them with others. Using the Motion Presets panel will save you time and effort.

F Choose Paste Motion to apply the copied motion to a different instance.

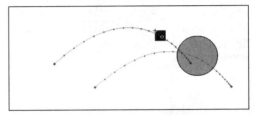

G The copied motion from the tween with the circle is pasted and applied to the square.

H The Motion Presets panel contains premade tweens and lets you save tweens that you create.

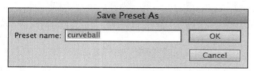

I Choose Save as Motion Preset to keep frequently used tweens.

J This tween will be saved in the Motion Presets panel as curveball.

K The tween called curveball can be applied to other instances.

Save Selection as Preset button

L You can also save a tween from the Motion Presets options menu (top) or from the Save Selection as Preset button (bottom).

To save a tween as a motion preset:

1. Right-click (Windows) or Ctrl-click (Mac) on a tween span in the Timeline or on a tweened object on the Stage and choose Save as Motion Preset **I**.

   The Save Preset As dialog box appears.

2. Enter a name to identify your tween and click OK **J**.

   Your tween is saved in the Custom Presets folder in the Motion Presets panel and is available to be applied to other objects **K**.

or

1. Select a tween span on the Timeline or a tweened object on the Stage.

2. In the Motion Presets panel, click the Save Selection as Preset button. Alternatively, choose Save from the Motion Presets options menu **L**.

   Your tween is saved in the Custom Presets folder in the Motion Presets panel and is available to be applied to other objects.

To apply a motion preset:

1. Select a symbol instance on the Stage.

2. In the Motion Presets panel, select a motion preset and click the Apply button **M**. Alternatively, right-click (Windows) or Ctrl-click (Mac) the motion preset and choose "Apply at current location."

   The motion preset is applied to your instance. The current position of the instance on the Stage is used as the initial position of the tween **N**.

   TIP If you want the selected symbol instance to be the ending position of the motion preset, choose **End at Current Location** from the Motion Presets panel options pull-down menu.

To delete a motion preset:

Select the motion preset and click the Trash icon. Alternatively, right-click (Windows) or Ctrl-click (Mac) on the motion preset and choose Remove **O**.

A dialog box appears asking you to confirm your choice. When you click Delete, Flash deletes the motion preset from the Motion Presets panel.

M Choose a preset and a preview of the tween appears in the top window.

N The preset tween is applied to your own instance.

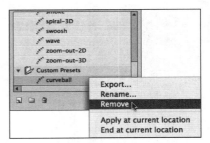

O Choose Remove to delete a tween from the Motion Presets panel.

Choose Export from the Motion Presets options menu to save a tween to an external file.

 This tween is saved as the XML document curveball.xml.

To organize your motion presets:

- Double-click the name of your motion preset to rename it. Or right-click (Windows) or Ctrl-click (Mac) and choose Rename.

- Click the New Folder icon to create a new folder to organize your motion presets.

- Double-click the name of your folder. Or right-click (Windows) or Ctrl-click (Mac) on the folder and choose Rename.

- Drag your motion presets and drop them on the highlighted folders to move them into different folders.

TIP You cannot rename, move, or delete the motion presets that are provided in the Default Presets folder.

To export a motion preset:

1. Select a motion preset.

2. In the Motion Presets panel options menu, choose Export. Or right-click (Windows) or Ctrl-click (Mac) the motion preset and choose Export **P**.

   The Save As dialog box appears.

3. Provide a name for the motion preset file. Click OK or Save **Q**.

   The file will be saved as an XML file, which you can share with fellow animators or developers.

To import a motion preset:

1. In the Motion Presets panel options menu, choose Import.

   The Open dialog box appears.

2. Choose the XML file of the motion preset. Click Open.

   The motion preset is imported into the Motion Presets panel.

Animating in 3D

Animating in 3D presents the thrill (but complication) of a third (z) axis for depth in addition to the horizontal (x) and vertical (y) axes. You can move or rotate any movie clip instance or Text Layout Framework (TLF) text (or dynamically created instances of the *DisplayObject* class, discussed in Chapter 7, "Controlling and Displaying Graphics") in three dimensions with full control over the amount of perspective distortion and the location of the vanishing point.

Use the 3D Rotation tool to rotate an object along any of its three axes and the 3D Translation tool to move an object along any of its three axes.

For example, create a *Star Wars*-style opening scrolling text screen by rotating the text along its x-axis to tilt it, and then translating it along the y- and z-axes to have it disappear in the horizon. Create confetti that realistically tumble in 3D, or develop games with cards that flip as they are dealt. Your only limit is your imagination.

To rotate an object in 3D space:

1. Begin with a movie clip instance or TLF text on the Stage.

2. Select the 3D Rotation tool and click on your object on the Stage.

   A 3D rotation display appears on your object ⓡ. The colored lines indicate the axes along which your object can move.

   Red. Drag the red line to move the object around the x-axis.

   Green. Drag the green line to move the object around the y-axis.

   Blue. Drag the blue circle to move the object around the z-axis.

   Orange. Drag the orange circle to move the object freely around all three axes.

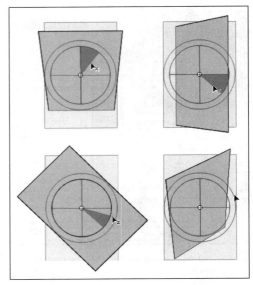

ⓡ Use the 3D Rotation tool to rotate an object in 3D space. This rectangle can be rotated along the x-, y-, or z-axis, or freely along any three of the axes.

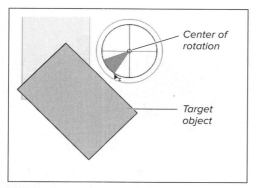

Center of rotation

Target object

 S The 3D display is moved off the object, changing its center of rotation.

 T Use the 3D Translation tool to move an object in 3D space. This rectangle can be moved along the x- (horizontal), y- (vertical), or z- (in and out) axis.

U The Transform panel shows the values for the 3D rotation and 3D center point, which you can change.

To change the center point of 3D rotation:

Move the white circle of the 3D display.

Subsequent 3D rotations will move the object relative to the new center point **S**.

To reset the center point of 3D rotation:

Double-click the white circle of the 3D display.

The 3D center point is restored.

To move an object in 3D space:

1. Begin with a movie clip instance or TLF text on the Stage.

2. Select the 3D Translation tool and click on your object on the Stage.

   A 3D translation display appears on your object **T**. The colored lines indicate the axes along which your object can move.

   Red. Drag the red line to move the object along the x-axis.

   Green. Drag the green line to move the object along the y-axis.

   Blue. Drag the blue circle to move the object along the z-axis.

TIP You can also rotate an object in 3D or change its center point in the Transform panel (Window > Transform) **U**.

Continues on next page

TIP You can also rotate or move multiple objects in 3D. Use the Shift key to select additional instances. Double-clicking the center point of the 3D display for multiple selections will place the center point between all the selected instances **V**.

TIP You can turn on or off the 3D display that appears over your objects in the General Preferences dialog box (Flash > Preferences).

TIP You cannot Edit in Place an instance that has been rotated or moved in 3D space. You must edit the instance in symbol editing mode.

TIP 3D objects are not supported in mask layers.

V These two rectangles are rotated together in 3D space using the single 3D display, which has been centered between both instances.

Global vs. Local Transformations

When you choose the 3D Rotation or 3D Translation tool, you need to be aware of the Global Transform option at the bottom of the Tools panel **W**. The Global Transform option toggles between a global option (button depressed) and a local option (button raised).

Moving an object with the global option on makes the transformations relative to the global (Stage) coordinate system. The 3D display shows the three axes in constant position, no matter how the object is rotated or moved **X**.

However, moving an object with the global option turned off makes the transformation relative to itself. The 3D display shows the three axes oriented relative to the object **Y**.

Global Transform option

W The Global Transform option is at the bottom of the Tools panel.

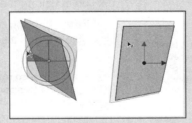

X With the Global Transform option on, the 3D rotation and 3D translation displays are always perpendicular to the Stage and remain constant.

Y With the Global Transform option off, the 3D rotation and 3D translation displays are oriented to the object, not to the Stage. Notice that the 3D Rotation tool (left) shows a globe with the three axes relative to the rectangle, and the 3D Translation tool (right) shows the z-axis pointing out from the rectangle, not from the Stage.

Z Change the Perspective angle in the Properties inspector.

1 degree

55 degrees

155 degrees

AA The perspective angle affects the degree of distortion of objects in perspective and how quickly parallel lines recede in the distance.

— *Perspective angle*

— *Vanishing point X position*

— *Vanishing point Y position*

BB Change the vanishing point in the Properties inspector.

To change the perspective:

1. Select a 3D object on the Stage.

2. In the Properties inspector, change the value of the perspective angle Z.

   The default perspective angle is 55 degrees, which is similar to a normal camera. You can change the value from 1 to 180 degrees, which determines the amount of distortion due to perspective rendering AA. The greater the angle, the more severe the objects appear to recede in the distance.

To change the vanishing point:

1. Select a 3D object on the Stage.

2. In the Properties inspector, change the value of the X and Y vanishing point positions BB.

   The default position of the vanishing point is in the middle of the Stage. The vanishing point represents the point on the horizon at which parallel lines disappear, just like the tracks of a railroad CC.

TIP Changing the perspective angle or the vanishing point changes the settings for all the 3D objects on the Stage.

Vanishing point

CC The vanishing point is represented by a horizontal and a vertical line.

Animating titles

Frequently, splash screens on Flash Web sites feature animated titles and other text-related materials that twirl, tumble, and spin until they all come into place as a complete design. Several techniques can help you accomplish these kinds of effects quickly and easily. The Break Apart command, when applied to text, breaks the text into its component parts (Classic text breaks apart into editable letters while TLF text breaks apart into drawing objects). This command lets you painlessly create separate letters that make up a word or title. You can then use the Distribute to Layers command to isolate each of those characters on its own layer, ready for motion tweening.

When you begin applying motion tweens to your individual letters or words, it's useful to think and work backward from the final design. Establish the end keyframes containing the final positions of all your characters, for example. Then, in the first keyframes, you can change the characters' positions and apply as many transformations as you like, knowing that the final resting spots are secured.

To animate the letters of a title:

1. Select the Text tool, and choose TLF Text and Read Only in the Properties inspector.

2. On the Stage, type a title you want to animate .

3. Choose Modify > Break Apart (Ctrl-B for Windows, Cmd-B for Mac).

   Flash replaces the text title with individual drawing groups of the letters .

DD Create TLF text on the Stage with the Text tool.

EE Breaking apart a block of Read Only text results in grouped drawing objects.

FF Distribute to Layers separates the selected items into their own layers.

GG Each letter has its own tween.

HH Insert a keyframe at the last frame in all the tween spans.

II The last keyframe fixes the final position for all the letters.

JJ The letters tumble and fall into place at the last keyframe.

4. Choose Modify > Timeline > Distribute to Layers (Ctrl-Shift-D for Windows, Cmd-Shift-D for Mac).

   Each selected item on the Stage is placed in its own layer below the existing layer **FF**.

5. Select each letter in turn and, choose Insert > Motion Tween, or right-click (Windows) or Ctrl-click (Mac) and choose Create Motion Tween from the context menu.

   Flash may ask to convert the selected object into a symbol for it to be tweened. Click OK.

   Flash creates a tween span for each letter in each layer and adds one second's worth of frames on the Timeline **GG**.

6. Hold down the Ctrl key (Windows) or the Cmd key (Mac) and select the last frames of all the layers.

7. Right-click (Windows) or Ctrl-click (Mac) on the selected frames and choose Insert Keyframe > All **HH**.

   A keyframe for all properties is inserted in the last frame for all the selected layers **II**.

8. In the first keyframe of each layer, rearrange and transform the letters according to your creative urges.

   Flash animates all these text elements coming together as a complete title **JJ**.

Shape Tweening Strategies

Shape tweening is a technique for inter-polating amorphous changes that can't be accomplished with instance transformations such as rotation, scale, and skew. Fill, stroke, gradient, and alpha are all shape attributes that can be shape tweened. While motion tweening is based on an object model, shape tweening still relies on a keyframe model where you establish a beginning keyframe and an end keyframe with a shape tween applied to the frames in between.

Flash applies a shape tween by using what it considers to be the most efficient, direct route. This method sometimes has unpredictable results, creating overlapping shapes or seemingly random holes that appear and merge **A**. These undesirable effects usually are the result of keyframes containing shapes that are too complex to tween at the same time.

Simplifying a complicated shape tween into more basic parts and separating those parts in layers results in a more successful interpolation. Shape hints give you a way to tell Flash what point on the first shape corresponds to what point on the second shape. Sometimes, adding intermediate keyframes helps a complicated tween by providing a transition state and making the tween go through many more manageable stages.

Using shape hints

Shape hints force Flash to map points on the first shape to corresponding points on the second shape. By placing multiple shape hints, you can control more precisely the way your shapes will tween.

To add a shape hint:

1. Select the first keyframe of the shape tween, and choose Modify > Shape > Add Shape Hint (Ctrl-Shift-H for Windows, Cmd-Shift-H for Mac).

   A letter in a red circle appears in the middle of your shape **B**.

2. Move the first shape hint to a point on your shape.

   Make sure that the Snap to Objects modifier for the Selection tool is turned on to snap your selections to vertices and edges.

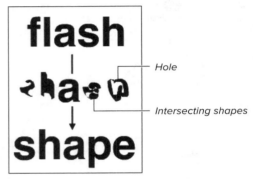

A An attempt to shape tween the word "flash" to the word "shape" all at once in a single layer has poor results. Notice the breakups between the s and the p and the hole that appears between the *h* and the *e*.

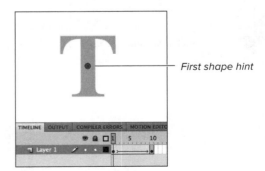

B Select the first keyframe of the shape tween, and choose Modify > Shape > Add Shape Hint. The first shape hint appears in the center of the Stage.

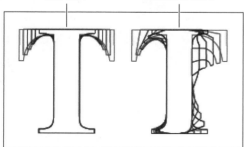

C The first shape hint in the first keyframe (top) and its match in the last keyframe (bottom).

The cross of the T is absorbed into the I

This T goes through some unnecessary changes to result in the I

D Changing from a *T* to an *I* with shape hints (left) and without shape hints (right).

3. Select the last keyframe of the shape tween, and move the matching circled letter to a corresponding point on the end shape.

   This shape hint turns green and the first shape hint turns yellow, signifying that both have been moved into place correctly **C**.

4. Continue adding shape hints, up to a maximum of 26, to refine the shape tween **D**.

To delete a shape hint:

Drag the shape hint off the Stage.

The matching shape hint in the other keyframe is deleted automatically.

To remove all shape hints:

While on the first keyframe of a shape tween, choose Modify > Shape > Remove All Hints.

TIP Place shape hints in order either clockwise or counterclockwise. Flash more easily understands a sequential placement than one that jumps around.

TIP Shape hints need to be placed on an edge or a corner of the shape. If you place a shape hint in the fill or outside the shape, the original and corresponding shape hints will remain red, and Flash will ignore them.

TIP To view your animation without the shape hints, choose View > Show Shape Hints (Ctrl-Alt-H for Windows, Cmd-Option-H for Mac). Flash deselects the Show Shape Hints option, and the shape hints are hidden.

TIP If you move your entire shape tween by using Edit Multiple Frames, you'll have to reposition your shape hints. Unfortunately, you can't move all the shape hints at the same time.

Using intermediate keyframes

Adding intermediate keyframes can help a complicated tween by providing a transition state that creates smaller changes that are more manageable. Think about this process in terms of motion tweening. Imagine that you want to create the motion of a ball starting from the top left of the Stage, moving to the top right, then to the bottom left, and finally to the bottom right. You can't create just two position keyframes—one with the ball at the top-left corner of the Stage and one with the ball in the bottom-right corner—and expect Flash to tween the zigzag motion. You need to establish the intermediate position so that Flash can create the motion in stages. The same is true with shape tweening. You can better handle one dramatic change between two shapes by using simpler, intermediate keyframes.

To create an intermediate keyframe:

1. Study how an existing shape tween fails to produce satisfactory results when tweening the letter *Z* to the letter *S* **E**.

2. Insert a keyframe (F6) at an intermediate point within the tween.

3. In the newly created keyframe, edit the shape to provide a kind of stepping stone for the final shape **F**.

    The shape tween has smaller changes to go through with smoother results **G**.

Using layers to simplify shape changes

Shape tweening lets you create complex shape tweens on a single layer, but doing so can produce unpredictable results. Use layers to separate complex shapes and create multiple but simpler shape tweens.

Intersecting shapes

E Changing a *Z* to an *S* all at once causes the shape to flip and cross over itself.

F An intermediate shape.

G The *Z* makes an easy transition to the intermediate shape (middle) from which the *S* can tween smoothly.

A hole appears at the outline of the first shape when a shape tween is applied to change an *F* to a *D*.

 The hole and the solid shapes are separated on two layers.

Gradient Transform tool control points

Rectangular shape

 Use the Gradient Transform tool from the Toolbox to change the way a gradient fill is applied to a shape.

When a shape tween is applied to change the letter *F* to the letter *D,* for example, the hole in the last shape appears at the edges of the first shape . Separating the hole in the *D* and treating it as a white shape allows you to control when and how it appears. Insert a new layer, and create a second tween for the hole. The compound tween gives you better, more refined results .

Using shape tweens for gradient transitions

It helps to think about shape tweening as a technique that does more than just *morphing,* or interpolating one amorphous contour to another. After all, shape tweening can be used on any of the attributes of a shape, such as line weight; stroke color, including its alpha or gradient; and fill color, including its alpha or gradient. You can create interesting effects just by shape tweening color gradients. For example, changing the way a gradient is applied to a particular fill using the Gradient Transform tool can be an easy way to move a gradient across the Stage; combined with changing contours, it can produce atmospheric animations like clouds or puffs of smoke.

To create a gradient transition with shape tweening:

1. Select the Rectangle tool, and draw a large rectangle on the Stage.

2. Fill the shape with a radial or linear gradient.

3. Select the Gradient Transform tool by clicking and holding down the Free Transform tool and selecting the second option. Click the rectangle on the Stage.

   The control handles for the Gradient Transform tool appear for the gradient .

Continues on next page

4. For this task, move the center point handle of the gradient to the left side of your rectangle.

5. Create a new keyframe later on the Timeline.

6. Select the last keyframe, and click the rectangle with the Gradient Transform tool.

The control handles for the Gradient Transform tool appear for the gradient in the last keyframe.

7. Move the center point handle of the gradient to the far right side of the rectangle, and change the rotation, scale, or angle of the gradient as you desire.

Your two keyframes contain the same rectangular shape, but the gradient fills are applied differently **K**.

8. Select the first keyframe and choose Insert > Shape Tween (or right-click [Windows], Ctrl-click [Mac] on the first keyframe and choose Create Shape Tween).

Flash tweens the transformation of the gradient fills from the first keyframe to the last keyframe. The actual contour of the rectangle remains constant.

9. Delete the outlines of the rectangle.

The gradient moves from left to right **L**.

TIP You can't shape tween between different kinds of gradients; that is, you can't shape tween from a radial gradient to a linear gradient, or vice versa.

Rotation handle of Gradient Transform tool

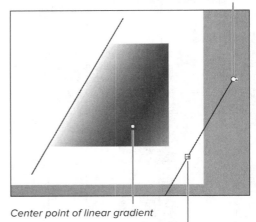

Center point of linear gradient

Width handle of Gradient Transform tool

K In the last keyframe, use the Gradient Transform tool to change the way the linear gradient fills the rectangle. Here, the linear gradient is moved to the far right side, tilted, and made narrower.

L The final shape tween makes the gradient twist, widen, and move across the rectangle.

Using Inverse Kinematics

When you want to animate an object that has multiple parts connected with joints, such as a walking person, Flash makes it easy to do so with inverse kinematics. *Inverse kinematics* is a mathematical way to calculate the different angles of a jointed object to achieve a certain configuration. You can pose your object in a beginning keyframe, and then set a different pose at a later keyframe. Flash will use inverse kinematics to figure out the different angles for all the joints to get from the first pose to the next pose.

Inverse kinematics makes animating easy because you don't have to worry about animating each segment of an object or limb of a character. You just focus on the overall poses. Flash Professional CS5 introduces a physics simulation feature for inverse kinematics called Spring. The Spring option helps make objects jiggle and move as if they were affected by the force of gravity or the force of their own motion.

There are two ways of using inverse kinematics: the first is to join together several movie clip instances, and the second is to define individual segments inside a single shape.

Inverse kinematics with movie clips

The first step when using inverse kinematics is to define the *bones* of your object. You use the Bone tool to do that. The Bone tool tells Flash how a series of movie clip instances are connected to each other. The set of connected movie clips is known as the *armature*, and each of the movie clips is known as a *node*.

To create an armature:

1. Position several movie clip instances on the Stage in roughly the layout in which you want them to be linked .

2. Select the Bone tool in the Tools panel.

3. Click on the top of the first movie clip and drag the Bone tool to the top of the second movie clip **B**.

   Your first bone is defined. Flash shows the bone as a skinny triangle with a round joint at its head and a round joint at its tail. Each bone is defined from the base of the first instance to the base of the second. For example, to build an arm, you would click on the shoulder side of the upper arm and drag it to the elbow side of the lower arm.

   Flash creates a new layer for your armature called *a pose layer*, a special layer that supports inverse kinematics. Motion tweens, shape tweens, and drawing are not allowed in pose layers.

4. Continue adding nodes to the armature by clicking on the tip of the first bone and dragging it to the base of the next object **C**.

TIP To add additional nodes to an armature, you must place the movie clips you want to add in a different layer. Then use the Bone tool to link the existing armature in the pose layer to the movie clips in the other layer. Flash will add the movie clips as additional nodes.

TIP If you want your bones to connect to the registration points of your objects, you can select the Snap to Objects option at the bottom of the Tools panel.

A Three movie clip instances are placed on the Stage, arranged end to end.

B Use the Bone tool to link the first instance to the second.

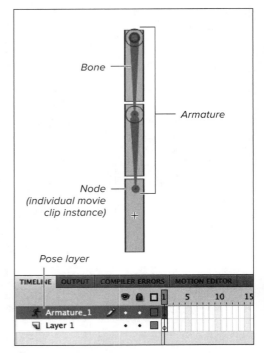

C The Bone tool links these three instances together in an armature. The armature is separated on its own layer in the Timeline.

D A new pose will be inserted in frame 20.

E In the second pose, move the armature to a new position. The connections make it easy to animate the entire object at once.

To insert a pose:

1. Select a later frame on the Timeline and right-click (Windows) or Ctrl-click (Mac) and choose Insert Pose.

   A new pose is created, which is very much like a new keyframe for the armature **D**.

2. In the second pose, move the armature into another position.

   Flash automatically animates the armature from the first pose to the second **E**.

TIP To isolate the rotation of an individual node, hold down the Shift key as you pose the armature. You'll find that making minor adjustments to the armature is easier and more exact.

To delete a pose:

Right-click (Windows) or Ctrl-click (Mac) on a pose on the Timeline and choose Clear Pose.

The selected pose on the Timeline is removed.

To move a pose on the Timeline:

Ctrl-click (Windows) or Cmd-click (Mac) to select a pose, and then drag it to a different position along the Timeline.

The selected pose moves to a different position on the Timeline.

To edit an armature:

- Use the Free Transform tool to scale, rotate, or move individual nodes.

- Hold down the Alt key (Windows) or the Option key (Mac) to drag a node to a new position.

- Select a bone and press the Delete key to remove a bone and all the bones connected to it down the chain.

Armature Hierarchy

The first bone of an armature is referred to as the parent, and the bone that is linked to it is called the child. A bone can have more than one child attached to it as well. For example, an armature of a person would have a pelvis connected to two thighs, which in turn are attached to two lower legs of their own. The pelvis is the parent, each thigh is a child, and the thighs are siblings to each other. As your armature becomes more complicated, you can use the Properties inspector to navigate up and down the hierarchy using these relationships.

When you select a bone in an armature, the top of the Properties inspector displays a series of arrows **F**.

You can click the arrows to move through the hierarchy and quickly select and view the properties of each node. If the parent bone is selected, you can click the down arrow to select the child. If a child bone is selected, you can click the up arrow to select its parent, or click the down arrow to select its own child, if it has one. The sideways arrows navigate between sibling nodes.

F Navigate through the armature hierarchy with the arrows in the Properties inspector.

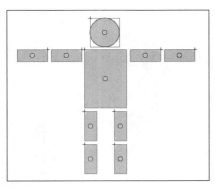

G Individual movie clips are arranged for a branching armature.

H Begin building the armature from the parent node (the body) to a child node (an upper limb).

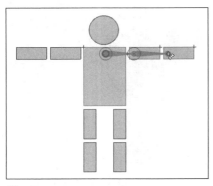

I One branch of the armature is complete.

To create a branching armature:

1. Position several movie clip instances on the Stage in roughly the layout in which you want them to be linked. This example shows a typical puppet with arms and legs branching from its central body **G**.

2. Select the Bone tool in the Tools panel.

3. Begin with the anchor movie clip, which is the body. Click on the top of the body and drag the Bone tool to the top of the upper arm **H**.

   Your first bone is defined.

4. Click on the end of the first bone and drag it to the top of the lower arm **I**.

   The armature of one arm is complete.

5. Now click on the top of the first bone in the body and drag it to the top of the other arm **J**.

   Your first branching bone is defined, which is a sibling to the bone of the first arm.

Continues on next page

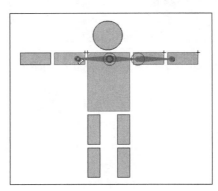

J The second branch of the armature begins from the head of an existing bone (here, from the parent node).

6. Continue extending the branch to the lower arm and create additional branches to the legs **K**.

Your completed armature has multiple nodes connected to a single central (parent) node.

Notice, however, that the limbs rotate around the head of the parent bone, which is unrealistic for this puppet **L**. To prevent the limbs from rotating freely around the head of the parent bone, you must restrict the rotation of that bone.

7. Select any of the bones in the body (the parent node), and in the Joint: Rotation section of the Properties inspector, deselect the Enable option **M**.

The selected bone and its siblings will not rotate around its head, creating a more realistic range of motion for the puppet **N**. You'll learn more about restricting joint rotation in the upcoming sections of this chapter.

K The final branching armature.

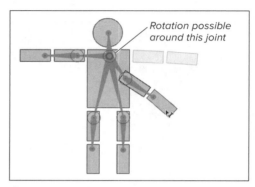

Rotation possible around this joint

L Without any constraints, the arms of this puppet rotate too freely and unrealistically.

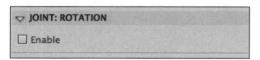

M Deselect the Enable option for Joint: Rotation in the Properties inspector for the parent bone.

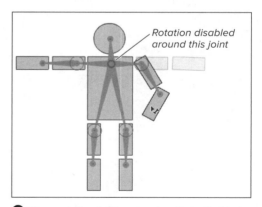

Rotation disabled around this joint

N When rotation for the parent node is disabled, only the head of the child bones can rotate, enabling the shoulders and hips to rotate from their fixed positions.

First bone   Shape

O Use the Bone tool to start an armature inside a single shape.

Bone   Shape

Pose layer   Armature

P The Bone tool creates an armature of five segments inside this rectangular shape. The armature is separated on its own layer in the Timeline.

Q In new poses, you can move any bone to change the shape around it.

Inverse kinematics with shapes

Another way you can use inverse kinematics is to define several bones inside a single shape. By providing an internal armature to a shape, you can control how the contours of the shape move and bend, somewhat like shape tweening. Use inverse kinematics with shapes to create the undulating motion of a snake or the flexing of someone's biceps.

To create an armature inside a shape:

1. Create a single shape on the Stage. The shape can be drawn in either Drawing mode or Object Drawing mode.

2. Select the Bone tool in the Tools panel.

3. Click inside the shape and drag the Bone tool a little ways inside the shape **O**.

   Your first bone is defined.

   Flash puts your armature in a *pose layer*, a special layer that supports inverse kinematics. Motion tweens, shape tweens, and drawing are not allowed in pose layers.

4. Click on the narrow end of the first bone and drag out the next bone a little farther inside the shape.

5. Continue adding bones until the armature extends throughout the shape **P**.

   Using the Selection tool, you can click and drag any of the bones to create a pose and the shape will deform to match the internal armature **Q**. Animating an armature inside a shape is the same process as animating an armature of separate movie clips (see the previous tasks in this chapter, "To insert a pose," "To delete a pose," and "To move a pose on the Timeline").

To edit the shape around an armature:

- Use the Paintbucket tool to change the fill color of the shape.

- Use the Inkbottle tool to change the stroke color and stroke height of the shape.

- Use the Subselection tool to change the contours of the shape.

- Use the Add Anchor Point tool to add new points on the contour of the shape.

- Use the Delete Anchor Point tool to delete points on the contour of the shape.

- Hold down the Alt key (Windows) or the Option key (Mac) and drag the entire shape with its armature to a new position on the Stage.

To edit the bones of the armature:

- Use the Subselection tool to move the base or the tips of the bones into new positions within the shape. You can only do this with the initial armature in the first pose.

- Select a bone with the Selection tool and press the Delete key to remove a bone and all the bones connected to it down the chain.

Refining Shape Behavior with the Bind tool

The organic control of a shape by its armature is a result of a mapping between control points along the shape and its bones. Hence, where the bones rotate, the shape follows.

You can edit the connections between the bones and their control points with the Bind tool, which is hidden under the Bone tool. The Bind tool displays which control points are connected to which bones and lets you break those connections and make new ones.

When you choose the Bind tool and select a bone, all the connected control points on the shape are highlighted in yellow ⓡ.

If you want to redefine which control points are connected to the selected bone, you can do the following:

- Shift-click to add additional associations to existing control points to the bone.
- Ctrl-click (Windows) or Cmd-click (Mac) to remove associations to control points from the bone.
- Drag a connection line between the bone and the control point.

You can also click on any control point on the shape. The selected control point is highlighted in red, and all the connected bones are highlighted in yellow ⓢ.

If you want to redefine which bones are connected to the selected control point, you can do the following:

- Shift-click to add additional bones to the control point.
- Ctrl-click (Windows) or Cmd-click (Mac) to remove bones from the control point.
- Drag a connection line between the control point and the bone.

Selected bone

Selected control point

One of four control points connected to the bone

Bone connected to control point

Bone connected to control point

ⓡ The Bind tool defines the connections between a bone and its control points on the shape. This last selected bone shows that it is associated with four control points around it.

ⓢ The Bind tool also shows the connections between a particular control point on the shape and its associated bone or bones. This selected point is associated with the last two bones of this armature.

Options for joint rotation and translation

When you build your armature, the various joints freely rotate, which may not be particularly realistic. Many armatures in real life are constrained to certain angles of rotation. For example, you can rotate your lower leg to be parallel with your thigh, but you can't rotate it past the knee (at least I hope you can't!). When working with armatures, whether they are in a shape or part of a series of linked movie clips, you can choose to constrain the rotation around the head of the joints, or even constrain the translation (side-to-side or up-and-down movement) of the joints.

To constrain the rotation of joints:

1. Click on a bone to select it.

2. In the Properties inspector, select the Constrain check box under Joint: Rotation **T**.

   The joint for the selected bone is constrained.

3. Change the values for Min and Max to set the minimum and maximum degrees of rotation for the selected joint.

   The allowable range of rotation appears on the joint on the Stage **U**. The Min and Max values are relative to the current position of the bone.

To enable joint translation:

1. Click on a bone to select it.

2. In the Properties inspector, select the Enable check box under Joint: X Translation and/or Joint: Y Translation **V**.

   The joint for the selected bone can now freely move around on the Stage.

Constrain option for joint rotation —

T Enable the Constrain option in the Properties inspector to limit the rotation of any joint.

U The middle node is constrained from its current position from 63 degrees counterclockwise to 26 degrees clockwise.

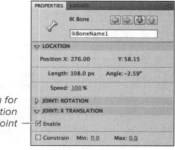

Enable option for horizontal motion of this joint —

V Choose the Enable option for Joint: X Translation or Joint: Y Translation in the Properties inspector to enable movement of the joint.

Current position
Minimum X position
Maximum X position

▽ JOINT: X TRANSLATION
☑ Enable
☑ Constrain   Min: –50.0   Max: 50.0

W The top node can move left and right, indicated by the horizontal line. It is constrained from its current position to 50 pixels to the left and 50 pixels to the right.

3. Select the Constrain check box and change the values for Min and Max to set the minimum and maximum amount of movement for the selected joint.

The allowable range of motion appears on the joint on the Stage **W**. The Min and Max values are relative to the current position of the bone.

TIP If you enable joint translation, it's a good idea to also disable joint rotation to prevent wild joint movements. An armature with both joint translation and rotation is difficult to control.

Constraining the Last Node

Joint constraints are always on the head of the selected bone. This means that the last bone in an armature can never be constrained because it is linked to the tail of the previous bone. However, you can get around this restriction by creating an "invisible" node past your last node. By setting the alpha value of this node to 0, the user never sees it, but it helps you constrain the joints of all the nodes up the hierarchy **X**.

Constrained joint
Constrained joint
Node set to 0% Alpha

X Creating an extra, invisible node at the end of an armature will let you constrain the rotation of the last visible bone.

Changing joint speed

Joint speed refers to the stickiness, or stiffness, of a joint. A joint with a low value for joint speed will be sluggish. A joint with a high value for joint speed will be more responsive. You can set the joint speed value for any selected joint in the Properties inspector.

The joint speed is apparent when you drag the very end of an armature. If there are slow joints higher up on the armature chain, those particular joints will be less responsive and will rotate to a lesser degree than the others. Changing joint speed will help you pose your armatures more realistically, but it does not affect the actual animation.

To change joint speed:

Select a bone and, in the Properties inspector, change the value of Speed **Y**.

The Speed values can range from 0% (frozen) to 100% (normal).

Controlling armature easing

Armatures do not have access to the Motion Editor and its sophisticated controls for eases. However, a few standard eases are available from the Properties inspector. Easing can make your armatures move with a sense of gravity due to acceleration or deceleration of their motion.

To control easing:

Select a pose layer and, in the Properties inspector, choose the Type of ease and change the Strength value **Z**. Type indicates the kind of easing, and Strength determines the direction and severity of the ease.

Ease-in. To start gradually and quickly come to a stop, set Type to any of the

Y A Speed value of 50 makes this joint a little more sluggish than normal.

Z Change the Type and Strength values to control the easing of your armature.

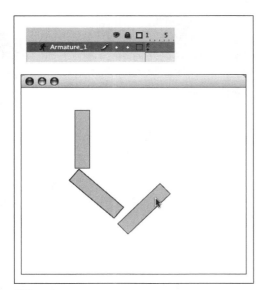

AA Choose Runtime in the Properties inspector to enable interactive control of your armature. Choose Authortime to set multiple poses along the Timeline for Flash to animate.

BB The Runtime option is only allowed when your armature has a single pose. In the Test Movie environment, viewers can move your armature interactively.

Simple options and set the Strength to a *negative* number.

Ease-out. To start quickly and gradually come to a stop, set Type to any of the Simple options and set Strength to a *positive* number.

Ease-in and Ease-out. To start gradually, speed up in the middle, and then gradually come to a stop, set Type to any of the Stop and Start options and set Strength to a *negative* number.

Ease-out and Ease-in. To start quickly, slow down in the middle, and then end quickly, set Type to any of the Stop and Start options and set Strength to a *positive* number. This setting creates an unusual motion, which you probably won't use very much.

Runtime and authortime armatures

Authortime armatures are those that you pose along the Timeline and play as straightforward animations. Runtime armatures are interactive and allow the user to move your armature. You can make any of your armatures—whether they are made with a series of movie clips or made with a shape—into an authortime or a runtime armature. Runtime armatures, however, are restricted to armatures that only have a single pose.

To make a runtime armature:

Select a pose layer and, in the Properties inspector, choose Runtime under the Options section **AA**.

A tiny armature icon appears in the pose layer to indicate the Runtime option. When you test your movie (Control > Test Movie > in Flash Professional), you can interact with the armature **BB**.

Simulating physics with the Spring option

Flash Professional CS5 adds a new feature to inverse kinematics called Spring, which simulates physics and the internal jiggling of an armature. For example, if you were to animate a small tree reacting to a strong gust of wind, you'd expect to see the tree and its branches quiver and wave in response to the wind, and continue to quiver even after the wind has stopped. The Spring option lets you set the amount of jiggling and how long the jiggling lasts.

To add Spring to an armature:

1. Select any bone in an armature **CC**. Your armature can be made of separate movie clips or be enclosed within a shape.

2. In the Properties inspector, under the Spring section, set a value for Strength **DD**.

   Strength values can range from 0 (stiff) to 100 (very loose). Each bone can have a different Strength value for its Spring, which affects the overall way an armature reacts to motion.

CC Select the bone to which you want to add some springiness.

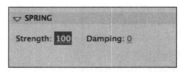

DD In the Properties inspector, set the value of Strength to determine the amount of springiness of the selected bone.

EE In a later pose, move the armature. In this example, the straight armature is moved to the right (by holding down the Alt/Option key).

FF The Spring option causes the armature to waver as it animates, simulating its reaction to the physical forces acting on the different bones.

3. Create a new pose where the armature changes pose or moves its position **EE**.

   Flash simulates the physics of a motion on the loose, springy armature **FF**.

TIP You'll see the effects of the Spring option on an armature more clearly if you have additional frames after its final pose. The extra frames give Flash time to continue jiggling the armature after its motion stops.

To dampen the Spring option:

1. Select any bone in an armature that has Spring.

2. In the Properties inspector, under the Spring section, set a value for Damping.

   Damping values can range from 0 (none) to 100 (high). The higher the Damping, the quicker the armature will cease its jiggling.

Creating Special Effects

Because Flash's drawing tools are vector based, you normally wouldn't think of incorporating special effects, such as a motion blur or color blending, which are associated with bitmap applications like Adobe Photoshop or After Effects. But using filters and blends, those special effects can be created directly in Flash. This technique can give your Flash movies more depth and richness by going beyond the simple flat shapes and gradients of vector drawings.

The following tasks demonstrate a blur effect using filters and a color-blending effect using blends.

A *blur* is an effect that occurs when the camera is out of focus. Blurs are particularly effective for transitions; you can animate a blurry image coming into sharp focus.

To create a blur-to-focus effect:

1. In Flash, create the image you want to blur using the drawing tools or by importing an image to the Stage. In this example, we use a photo.

2. Right-click (Windows) or Ctrl-click (Mac) on the image and choose Create Motion Tween.

    Flash asks whether you want to convert the selection to a movie clip symbol to begin motion tweening. Click OK.

    Flash converts the selection to a movie clip symbol and adds one second's worth of frames to the newly created tween span on the Timeline **Ⓐ**.

    In Flash, filters can only be applied to a movie clip symbol, a button symbol, or text.

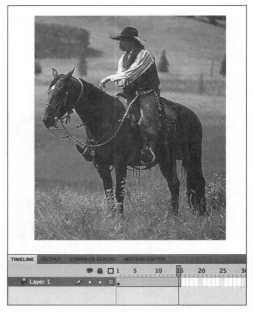

Ⓐ This imported photo is converted to a movie clip symbol and motion tweened.

Ⓑ In the Motion Editor, add the Blur filter to the Filters category.

Ⓒ Increase the value of the Blur filter to 50 pixels.

D In the last frame of the motion tween, decrease the value of the Blur filter to 0 pixels. The downward sloping graph shows the gradual transition.

E The resulting tween of the Blur filter makes an effective transition.

F The various filters are also available from the Properties inspector in the Filters section.

3. Open the Motion Editor (Window > Motion Editor).

4. Move the red playhead to the first frame of the tween.

5. Click the plus button next to Filters and choose Blur **B**.

   The Blur filter is added to the list of properties.

6. Make sure the Link icon is selected so the Blur X and Blur Y change together. Increase the values of Blur X and Blur Y to the desired blurriness **C**.

   Blur X indicates how much blurring should be applied to the object in the horizontal (x-axis). Blur Y does the same for vertical (y-axis) blur. Because these are independent values, you can create a blur in just one direction if you choose to unlink the properties.

7. Move the red playhead to the last frame of the tween.

8. Change the value of Blur X and Blur Y to 0 **D**.

   Flash animates your image's change from blurred to focused **E**.

TIP You can also access and apply the various filters from the Filters section of the Properties inspector. Choose your tweened object and, in the Properties inspector, click the Add Filter button and choose Blur **F**.

TIP The Quality property controls how smooth the blur will be. A higher-quality blur will be smoother and closer to what you might get using a Blur filter in Photoshop, but it also makes the Flash Player work harder, so it could slow down the playback of your movie.

TIP You can use any filter in this manner to create a transition. Experiment with the numerous filters to suit your movie.

TIP A movie clip instance can have more than one filter applied to it.

To blend colors from one object on another:

1. Create or import an image in a new layer.

2. Create a new layer above the first, and then create or import an image in this top layer.

   In this example, Classic static text is placed in the top layer, and a photo is imported in the bottom layer **G**.

3. Select the text in the top layer and choose Modify > Convert to Symbol (F8). Choose movie clip as the type of symbol.

   Flash converts your selection into a movie clip symbol. Blend effects from the Properties inspector can only be applied to movie clips, button instances, or TLF text.

4. Select the movie clip instance on the Stage. In the Properties inspector, choose a blending mode from the pull-down menu **H**.

   Flash blends the colors of the movie clip instance with all the images in the layers below it. The different blending modes determine how the colors interact. Some blending modes darken the colors, whereas others lighten or even reverse them. The best way to understand the blending modes is to experiment! (For more detailed information about color-blending modes and how you can control them purely with ActionScript, see the section "Blending Colors" in Chapter 7.)

TIP A movie clip instance can only have one blending effect.

TIP Blending effects cannot be motion tweened.

Movie clip instance in top layer

Photo in bottom layer

G The text is a movie clip instance in a layer above the photo.

H Choosing a Blending mode in the Properties inspector makes colors of the movie clip instance blend in different ways with the image below it.

Using Masks

Masking is a simple way to reveal portions of a layer or the layers below it. This technique requires making one layer a mask layer and the layers below it the *masked* layers.

By adding tweening to the mask layer, the masked layers, or both, you can go beyond simple, static peepholes and create masks that move, change shape, and reveal moving images. Use animated masks to achieve such complex effects as moving spotlights, magnifying lenses that enlarge underlying pictures, or "x-ray" types of interactions that show more detail within the mask area. Animated masks are also useful for creating cinematic transitions such as wipes, in which the first scene is covered as a second scene is revealed, and iris effects, in which the first scene collapses in a shrinking circle, leaving a second scene on the screen.

In the mask layer, Flash sees all fills as opaque shapes, even if you use a transparent solid or gradient. As a result, all masks have hard edges. You must use Action-Script if you want to create a mask with different alpha (transparency) levels.

Using movie clips in mask layers provides more possibilities, including multiple masks and even dynamically generated masks that respond to the user. Because dynamic masks rely on ActionScript, however, they'll be covered in detail later (in the section "Using Blending Masks" in Chapter 7) after you've learned more about Flash's scripting language.

To tween the mask layer:

1. In Layer 1, create a background image or import a bitmap.

2. Insert a new layer above the first layer.

3. Select the top layer, and choose Modify > Timeline > Layer Properties.

   or

   Double-click the layer icon in the top layer.

   The Layer Properties dialog box appears.

4. Select Layer Type: Mask.

5. Select the bottom layer, and choose Modify > Timeline > Layer Properties.

6. Select Layer Type: Masked.

   The top layer becomes the mask layer, and the bottom layer becomes the masked layer (the layer that is affected by the mask) **A**.

7. Create a tween in the mask layer (the top layer) and insert sufficient frames in the masked layer (the bottom layer) to match **B**.

   You can create a motion tween, a classic tween, a shape tween, or even inverse kinematics in the mask layer. (However, 3D objects are not supported in mask layers).

8. Lock both layers to see the effects of your animated mask on the image in the masked layer **C**.

Mask layer (will affect the masked layer)

Masked layer

A Layer 2 is the mask layer, and Layer 1 is the masked layer.

Diver in Layer 1   Shape tween in Layer 2

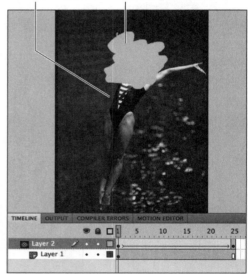

B A shape tween of a growing shape created with the Paintbrush tool is on the mask layer. The diver image is on the masked layer.

C The shape tween uncovers the image of the diver. Only the part of the photo that is under the mask is revealed.

D The moving spotlight in the mask layer (spotlight) uncovers the stained-glass image in the masked layer (bitmap). A duplicate darker image resides in the bottom, normal layer (dark bitmap).

E The mask layer contains a large motion tween that covers the entire Stage. This technique creates a cinematic wipe between an image in the masked layer (image 1) and an image in the bottom, normal layer (image 2).

TIP Use two images that vary slightly, one in the masked layer and one in a normal layer under the masked layer. This technique makes the animated mask act as a kind of filter that exposes the underlying image. For example, add a bright image in the masked layer and a dark version of the same image in a normal layer under the masked layer. The mask creates a spotlight effect on the image **D**.

TIP Place a tween of an expanding box in the mask layer that covers the Stage to simulate cinematic wipes between images **E**.

To tween the masked layer:

1. Beginning with two layers, modify the top to be the mask layer and the bottom to be the masked layer.

2. Draw a filled shape or shapes in the mask layer (the top layer) .

   This area becomes the area through which you see your animation on the masked layer.

3. Create a shape tween or a motion tween in masked layers (the bottom layers) that pass under the shapes in the mask layer. You can have as many masked layers as you want under a single mask layer **G**.

4. Lock both layers to see the effects of your animated masked layers as they show up behind your mask layer **H**.

F The windshield shapes are in the mask layer called windshields. The drawing of the car interior is in a normal layer above the windshields layer.

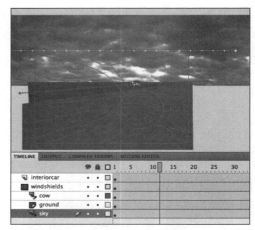

G Several motion tweens in masked layers (cow and sky) move under the windshield shapes in the mask layer.

H The images of the cow, ground, and sky show under the mask, creating the illusion of the car's forward motion.

I The fuse of a bomb shortens.

Mask   Shrinking rectangle in fuse fill layer

J The bomb's fuse is a thin shape in the mask layer. The rectangle is a motion tween in the masked layer that shrinks, making the fuse appear to be shortening.

This layer will not work as a mask layer

K Layer 1 and Layer 2 are both defined as mask layers, but only Layer 2 affects Layer 3—the masked layer.

L Two independent spotlights moving, each uncovering portions of the image.

TIP This approach is a useful alternative to using shape tweens to animate borders or similar types of objects that grow, shrink, or fill in. Imagine animating a fuse that shortens to reach a bomb **I**. Create a mask of the fuse, and animate the masked layer to become smaller slowly, making it look like the fuse is shortening **J**. Other examples that could benefit from this technique include trees growing, pipes or blood vessels flowing with liquid, text that appears as it's filled with color, or drawing a pathway on a map. Just remember that Flash doesn't recognize strokes in the mask layer; if you want to create thin lines in the mask layer, use fills only.

Creating multiple masks

Although Flash allows multiple masked layers under a single mask layer, you can't have more than one mask layer affecting any number of masked layers **K**. To create more than one mask, you must use movie clips. Why would you need multiple masks? Imagine creating an animation that has two spotlights moving independently on top of an image **L**. Because the two moving spotlights are tweened, they have to be on separate layers. The solution is to incorporate the two moving spotlights into a movie clip and place the movie clip on the mask layer.

You'll learn much more about movie clips in Chapter 5, "Controlling Multiple Timelines." If you'd like, skip ahead to read about movie clips and return when you feel comfortable.

To create multiple masks:

1. Create a mask layer and a masked layer.

2. Place your image on the masked layer (the bottom layer).

3. Choose Insert > New Symbol (Ctrl-F8 for Windows, Cmd-F8 for Mac).

   The Create New Symbol dialog box appears.

4. Enter a descriptive name, and choose Movie Clip 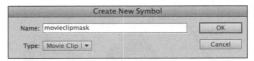; then click OK.

   Flash creates a movie clip symbol, and you enter symbol-editing mode for that symbol.

5. Create two motion tweens of spotlights moving in different directions on the Timeline of your movie clip symbol .

6. Return to the main Stage, and drag an instance of your movie clip symbol into the mask layer (the top layer) .

7. Choose Control > Test Movie > in Flash Professional to see the effects of the movie clip mask.

   The two motion tweens inside the movie clip both mask the image on the masked layer.

> **TIP** To see what your masks are uncovering, use a transparent fill or choose the View Layer as Outlines option in the Layer Properties dialog box.

> **TIP** To prevent the animation inside the movie clip from looping constantly, add a keyframe to its last frame and add a `stop ()` action.

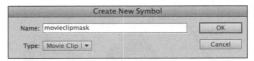

M Choose Movie Clip to create a new movie clip symbol.

N The two moving spotlights are motion tweens inside a movie clip.

O An instance of the movie clip is in the top (mask) layer, and the image of the bikers is in the bottom (masked) layer.

Working with Video

Flash is the most popular method of delivering video on the Web. Video-sharing sites like YouTube, news sites like the New York Times, and entertainment sites like Hulu use Flash to play video for its image quality, compression, and wide compatibility and penetration. This chapter explores the exciting possibilities of integrating video in your Flash project. Flash makes working with video easy with the Import Video wizard, which takes you step by step through the process, and Adobe Media Encoder, a stand-alone application that converts your video to the proper format and gives you options for editing, cropping, resizing, and setting levels of compression.

There are two main ways to use video in Flash. One way is to embed video directly within your Flash movie, and the other is to keep video separate and stream it to play through Flash. When you embed video into Flash, it's easy to integrate other Flash elements and interactivity. For playback of external video, you can embed cue points, which are special markers in the video that you can use to trigger other events.

Preparing Video for Flash

Whether you embed video into Flash or play back external video, you need to format your video correctly. The appropriate video format for Flash is Flash Video, which uses the extension .flv or the extension .f4v. F4V is the latest Flash Video format that supports the H.264 standard, a modern video codec that delivers high quality with remarkably efficient compression. A codec stands for *compression-de*compression, and it is a method for the computer to compress a video file to save space, and then decompress it to play it back. FLV is the standard format for previous versions of Flash and uses an older codec, On2 VP6.

You have several ways to acquire digital video. You can shoot your own footage using a video camera and transfer it to your computer. Alternatively, you can use copyright-free video clips that are available on a CD or DVD, or on the Web from commercial image stock houses. Any way you go, adding digital video is an exciting way to enrich a Flash Web site.

TIP Flash can actually play back any video encoded in H.264, so your video file doesn't have to have the .f4v extension. For example, a video with a .mov extension encoded by QuickTime Pro with H.264 is compatible with Flash.

What Makes a Good Video?

We all know a good video when we see one. But how do you create and prepare digitized videos so they play well and look good within Flash? Knowing a little about the video compression that is built into Flash will help.

The various codecs compress video both spatially and temporally. *Spatial compression* happens within a single frame, much like JPEG compression on an image. *Temporal compression* happens between frames, so the only information that is stored is the differences between two frames. Therefore, videos that compress well contain localized motion or very little motion (such as a talking head), because the differences between frames are minimal. (In a talking-head video, only the mouth is moving.) For the same reasons, transitions, zooms, and fades don't compress or display well—stick with quick cuts if possible.

Using Adobe Media Encoder

You can convert your video files into the proper FLV or F4V format using Adobe Media Encoder CS5, a stand-alone application that comes with Flash Professional CS5. You can convert single files or multiple files (known as batch processing) to make your workflow easier.

Several popular formats for digital video are QuickTime (MOV), MPEG, AVI, and DV. Fortunately, Adobe Media Encoder supports all of them.

To add a video file to Adobe Media:

1. Launch Adobe Media Encoder, which comes installed with Adobe Flash Professional CS5.

The opening screen has a window that lists any current video files that have been added for processing. The window should be empty **A**.

2. Choose File > Add or click the Add button on the right.

A dialog box opens for you to select a video file.

3. Navigate to your video file and click Open (Windows) or OK (Mac).

The selected video file is added to the display list and is ready for conversion to an FLV or F4V format **B**.

TIP You can also add video files to Adobe Media Encoder by simply dragging your video file from your desktop and dropping it in the display list.

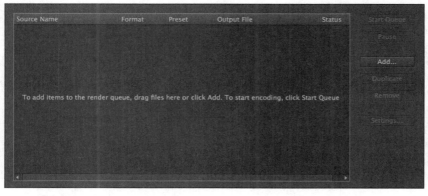

A Adobe Media Encoder prepares videos in the correct format for Flash. The large central window is the display list, which lists the videos that you want to encode. The display list is currently empty.

B This display list in Adobe Media Encoder contains one video that has been added.

To remove a video file from Adobe Media Encoder:

1. In the display list, select the video file.

2. Click the Remove button.

   A dialog box appears asking you to confirm whether you want to remove the selected video and its settings. Click Yes to remove the video file from the display list.

   TIP You can select multiple files for removal by holding down the Ctrl key (Windows) or Shift key (Mac) and selecting multiple video files in the display list.

To convert a video file to Flash Video:

1. In the display list, select the FLV | F4V option for Format **C**.

2. Under the Preset options, choose your desired encoding profile **D**.

   You can choose one of many of the standard preset options from the menu. The options determine the format (either the newer F4V or the older FLV) and the size of the video. In parentheses, Flash indicates the minimum Flash Player version required to play the selected video format.

   Choose Match Source Attributes if your source video is already sized to the correct dimensions that you desire.

C Choose FLV | F4V from the Format pull-down menu to select the encoding format.

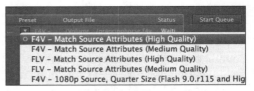

D Choose your desired setting from the Preset pull-down menu. Choose F4V Match Source Attributes or FLV Match Source Attributes if your video is already at your desired dimensions.

3. Click on the Output File.

You can choose to save the converted file in a different location on your computer and choose a different filename. Your original video will not be deleted or altered in any way.

4. Click Start Queue.

Adobe Media Encoder begins the encoding process **E**. The Media Encoder displays the settings for the encoded video, shows the progress, and shows a preview of the video. When the encoding process finishes, a green check in the display window indicates that the file has been converted successfully.

TIP If you have multiple video files to encode to F4V or FLV format, you can do so with Adobe Media Encoder all at once easily in a process known as batch processing. Each file can even have its own settings. Click the Add button to add additional videos to the display list. Choose a different format for each file, if desired. Click Start Queue to begin the batch processing.

TIP You can change the status of individual files in the queue by selecting the file in the display list and choosing Edit > Reset Status or Edit > Skip Selection. Reset Status will remove the green check from a completed file so it can be encoded again, whereas Skip Selection will make Adobe Media Encoder skip that particular file in the batch processing.

Message: Encoding item 1 of 1
Video: 360x240, Same as source fps, Progressive
Audio: AAC, 128 kbps, 44.1 kHz, Stereo
Bitrate: VBR, 1 Pass, Target 0.42 Mbps, Max 0.51 Mbps

Encodin...ancinghorse.mov" (Pass 1 of 1)   Elapsed Time: 00:00:03   Estimated Remaining: 00:00:03

Elapsed Queue Time: 00:00:05

E During the encoding process, Adobe Media Encoder shows the progress, the output specifications, and a preview of the video. The process may take seconds or several minutes, depending on the length and size of your video. This may be a good time to get yourself a cup of coffee.

Understanding Encoding Options

You can customize many settings in the conversion of your original video to the Flash Video format.

In some situations, you may want to crop the edges of a video to remove unsightly background or to display your video in an unconventional format. Or, you may decide to use just a portion of the video rather than all of it. Using Adobe Media Encoder, you can make the necessary adjustments to crop the video frame, resize the video, change the starting and ending points of the video, adjust the type of compression and the compression levels, or even apply filters to the video.

To display encoding options:

Click on the Preset selection in the display window.

or

Choose Edit > Export Settings.

or

Click the Settings button.

The Export Settings dialog box appears **A**. A summary of the current output specifications is listed on the upper-right corner, cropping and trimming options are on the left, and advanced options for video and audio compression are on the bottom right.

Output tab   Preset menu   Save, Import, and Delete Presets

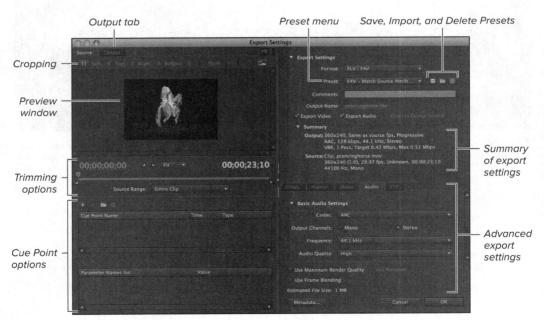

A The Export Settings dialog box contains options for customizing, cropping and resizing, trimming video length, adding cue points, and changing the video and audio compression levels.

Crop button   *Selected area*

B Select the Crop button to select only a portion of your video. Drag the sides or corners of the selection to cut unwanted material from the edges of the video. Enter numeric values in the Left, Top, Right, and Bottom fields for pixel-level precision.

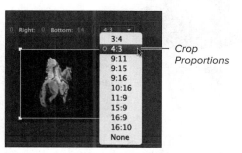

Crop
Proportions

C Constrain the crop with the Crop Proportions pull-down menu. A 4:3 proportion is the traditional aspect ratio for standard-definition video. A 16:9 proportion is the aspect ratio for high-definition video and cinematic presentations.

To crop your video:

1. Click the Crop button at the upper-left corner of the Export Settings dialog box.

   The cropping box appears over the video preview window **B**.

2. Drag the sides inward to crop from the top, bottom, left, or right.

   The grayed-out portions outside the box will be discarded. Adobe Media Encoder displays the new dimensions next to your cursor. You can also use the Left, Top, Right, and Bottom settings above the preview window to enter exact pixel values.

3. If you want to keep the crop in a standard proportion, click the Crop Proportions menu and choose a desired ratio **C**.

   The cropping box will be constrained to the selected proportions.

4. To see the effects of the crop, click the Output tab.

5. Change the Crop Setting pull-down menu to your desired output.

   Scale to Fit. Maintains the final output size but enlarges the final crop to fit the dimensions. Your video may lose quality if you enlarge beyond the resolution of the source.

   Continues on next page

Black Borders. Maintains the final output size and adds black to the areas that are cropped.

Change Output Size. Changes the final output size to the dimensions of the crop.

The preview window shows how your final video will appear **D**.

6. Click OK to accept the crop settings.

   or

   Exit the Crop tool without accepting the crop settings by clicking the Crop button again under the Source tab.

To adjust the video length:

1. Click and drag the playhead (top marker) to scrub through your video to preview the footage. Place the playhead at the desired beginning point of your video.

   Time markers indicate the number of seconds that have elapsed **E**.

Crop Setting pull-down menu

Crop selection over original video

Scale to Fit

Black Borders

Change Output Size

D The Output tab shows the final cropped appearance. Choose the options under the Crop Setting pull-down menu to determine the relationship between the crop and the output size.

Time indicator

Playhead

E Move the playhead to the point at which you want the video to begin.

Set In Point

In point marker

F Click the Set In Point icon to mark the beginning of the video.

Set Out Point

Out point marker

G Click the Set Out Point icon to mark the end of the video.

Resize video option   *Video tab*

H Click the Video tab to resize your video.

Constrain width/height

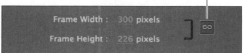

I The Resize video option lets you set how your video's size will be scaled. Click the Constrain button to keep the dimensions of your video proportional.

2. Click the Set In Point icon.

The In point moves to the current position of the playhead **F**.

3. Drag the playhead to the desired ending point of your video.

4. Click the Set Out Point icon.

The Out point moves to the current position of the playhead **G**.

5. You can also simply drag the In and Out markers to bracket the desired video segment.

6. Click OK to accept the new settings to trim the length of your video.

TIP When the playhead is selected, you can use the left or right arrow key on your keyboard to move back or ahead frame by frame for finer control.

TIP You can double-click the time marker to enter an exact numerical value for the time.

To resize your video:

1. Click the Video tab on the right side of the screen under the Export Settings **H**.

2. Select the Resize Video check box.

3. Change the values for Frame Width and Frame Height to change the dimensions of your video.

If you want to maintain the original aspect ratio of your video, click the Constrain box **I**.

4. Click OK to accept the new resize settings.

To select your own video compression settings:

1. Click the Format tab on the right side of the screen under the Export Settings.

2. Choose either the FLV format or the newer F4V format **J**.

   Embedding video into Flash requires the FLV format. To download external video, you can use either the FLV or the F4V format.

3. Click the Video tab. Choose the video settings that will give the best trade-off between video file size and image quality for your movie. Depending on the format that you've chosen in step 2, you will be presented with different options:

   Codec. If you've selected the FLV format, Flash uses the On2 VP6 codec to compress your video, which requires Flash Player 8 or later. The codec is lossy, meaning some (usually less important or less visible) video information is discarded to make the file smaller. The compressed movie appears similar to the original but not exactly the same **K**.

   Encode Alpha Channel. If your video has an alpha channel (transparent background), select this option. Alpha channels are only supported in the FLV format with the On2 VP6 codec.

   Resize Video. You can change the width and height or constrain the proportions for the new width and height. Refer to the task "To resize your video," earlier.

   Frame rate. Lets you choose whether to match the frame rate of your video to the frame rate of your Flash movie. For embedded video, you'll want to choose the same frame rate of your Flash

J Choose FLV if you want to embed your video in Flash. Choose either FLV or F4V if you want to play back external video from Flash.

K On2 VP6 is the codec for the FLV format, which requires Flash Player 8 or later.

If you plan to embed video into Flash, you must set the frame rate of your video to be identical to the frame rate of your Flash movie. Choose "Same as source" only if you want to play back external video from Flash.

 The Bitrate Settings determine the bandwidth required to download the video.

movie. This choice ensures that an embedded video plays at its intended speed even if its frame rate is different than that of the Flash document. With the "Same as source" setting, a video shot at 30 frames per second (fps) and brought into a Flash movie running at 15 fps will last twice as long (and play twice as slowly) as the original source video. You should choose "Same as source" only when encoding for playback of external video .

Bitrate Settings. Determines the *bitrate*, which is the quality of video based on download speeds measured in kilobits per second (kbps). Flash may alter the quality of individual frames to keep the download at a consistent speed. Remember, the higher the kilobits per second of your chosen setting, the higher the quality of your video but the larger the file size. The higher the bitrate, the higher quality of the video .

Advanced Settings. Select the Set Key Frame Distance option to change the keyframe distance. The *keyframe distance* is how frequently complete frames of your video are stored. The frames between keyframes (known as *delta frames*) store only the data that differs between the delta frame and the preceding keyframe. A keyframe interval of 24, for example, stores the complete frame every twenty-fourth frame of your video. If your video contains the action of someone raising his hand between frames 17 and 18, only the portion of the image where the hand is being raised is stored in memory until frame 24 when the full frame is stored. The lower you set the

Continues on next page

keyframe interval, the more keyframes are stored and the larger the file. For video where the image doesn't change much (such as a talking head in front of a solid background), a higher keyframe interval works well. For video with lots of movement and changing images, a lower keyframe interval is necessary to keep the image clear 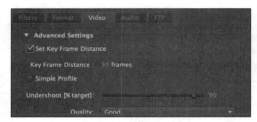.

4. Click OK to accept your custom video settings.

To select your own audio compression settings:

1. Select the Export Audio option under Export Settings if you want audio exported with your video. Deselect the option if you just want to export video with no audio .

2. Click the Audio tab on the right side of the screen under Export Settings.

3. Choose the audio settings that will give the best trade-off between file size and audio quality for your movie. Depending on the format you've chosen (FLV or F4V), you will be presented with different audio options .

   Codec. AAC is a high-quality audio compression scheme for the F4V format. MP3 is the older audio compression scheme for the FLV format.

   Output Channels. Choose Mono for a single channel or Stereo for two channels (left and right).

   Frequency. The higher the frequency, the higher quality the sound. Select 44.1 kHz for CD-quality sound.

   Bitrate Settings. The higher the bitrate, the higher quality the sound.

4. Click OK to accept your custom audio settings.

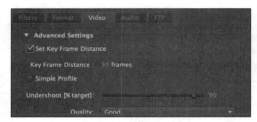

N Adjust the Key Frame Distance option based on how often significant visual changes occur in your video. A higher Key Frame Distance setting means there are fewer keyframes, so less information is recorded.

Export Audio option

O Select the Export Audio check box if you want to keep audio in your video. Deselect the check box if you only want to export video.

Audio settings for FLV format

Audio settings for F4V format

P There are different audio settings, depending on if you've chosen the FLV format or the F4V format. Bitrate and Frequency determine the audio quality (the higher the number, the better the quality).

Save Preset

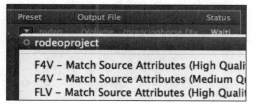

Q You can save your custom Export Settings to apply to other videos.

R Provide a name for your custom setting.

Preset	Output File	Status
▼ rodeo	/Volume /brancingborse f4v	Waiti
○ **rodeoproject**		
F4V – Match Source Attributes (High Quali		
F4V – Match Source Attributes (Medium Q		
FLV – Match Source Attributes (High Quali		

S Your custom setting is available under the Preset pull-down menu.

To save your custom encoding options:

1. In the Export Settings dialog box, click the Save Preset button **Q**.

2. In the dialog box that opens, provide a descriptive name for the video and audio options. Click OK **R**.

3. Return to the queue of videos. You can apply your custom setting to additional videos by simply choosing it from the Preset pull-down menu **S**.

Embedding Video into Flash

Everybody loves movies. So when you can add video to your Flash Web site, you'll likely create a richer and more compelling experience for your viewers.

You can embed an FLV file into Flash (but not F4V), and then add effects such as graphics, animation, masking, and interactivity; you can even apply motion tweens to your embedded video. Embedding video is the simplest way to add video and an easy way to integrate video with other Flash elements on your Timeline. However, embedding video has several limitations. Embedded video is only good for short video because Flash cannot maintain audio synchronization beyond about 2 minutes. There is also a maximum length of 16,000 frames for embedded movies. Another drawback is the increase in file size of your

Flash movie. Embedding video puts the video file inside your Flash document, so be aware of the longer download times for your audience and the more tedious testing and authoring sessions for you.

To embed a video in Flash:

1. From the File menu, choose Import > Import Video.

   The Import Video wizard appears **Ⓐ**.

2. Click the Browse button; in the dialog box that appears, select the FLV file you want to embed and click Open.

3. Back in the Import Video wizard, choose "Embed FLV in SWF and play in timeline" **Ⓑ**. Click Next (Windows) or Continue (Mac).

   If you have not yet converted your video to the FLV format, you can launch Adobe Media Encoder by clicking the Launch Adobe Media Encoder button.

Ⓐ The Import Video wizard guides you through the process of integrating video with your Flash projects. The first step is to tell Flash where to find your video.

Ⓑ Choose "Embed FLV in SWF and play in timeline" to embed your video.

C The Embedding step lets you choose different options for embedding your video.

Embedded video on the Stage | Embedded video in the Library

D The embedded video is placed on the Stage and Flash adds frames to the Timeline to accommodate the video. The video is stored in the Library.

E For videos with an alpha channel (transparency), choose FLV for the format and select the Encode Alpha Channel option (top). This allows you to embed video with transparent backgrounds (bottom), such as a weatherperson in front of a weather map.

4. The next screen of the Import Video wizard presents the Embedding options. Set the Symbol type to Embedded video; select the options "Place instance on stage," "Expand timeline if needed," and "Include audio" **C**. Click Next/Continue.

5. The Import Video wizard proceeds to the final screen, summarizing your video embedding settings.

6. Click Finish.

Flash embeds the video in your document, putting a video symbol in your Library and an instance of the video on the Stage in the active layer **D**.

TIP When embedding an FLV into Flash, remember to encode the FLV at the same frame rate as your Flash file. This is an important step to keep the frame rate of your video consistent with the frame rate of your Flash movie. This ensures your video plays at its intended speed.

TIP Flash can't display the soundtrack of embedded FLVs, so if your original video file has sound, you won't hear it within the Flash authoring environment. When you publish your Flash movie or test it by choosing Control > Test Movie > in Flash Professional, the sound will be audible.

TIP If you do not have sound, check your source video clip. Sometimes a QuickTime file uses an audio compression scheme that Flash doesn't recognize. You may have to export your video with a different audio compression from another application.

TIP If you have video with a transparent background (an alpha channel), you can import it into Flash and still preserve the transparency. In Adobe Media Encoder, click the Video tab and select the Encode Alpha Channel option **E**. Alpha channels are only supported with the On2 VP6 video codec (Flash Player 8 and later).

To swap an embedded video:

1. Double-click the video icon or the preview window in your Library.

   or

   Click the video symbol in the Library; then, from the Library window's Options menu, choose Properties ⓕ.

   The Video Properties dialog box appears showing the symbol name and the original video file's location ⓖ.

2. Click Import.

3. Choose a new FLV file and click Open.

   Flash swaps the existing FLV video with the newly selected FLV.

4. Click OK.

   The new FLV replaces the old FLV in the Library and on any existing instances on the Stage ⓗ.

ⓕ Select the video in your Library and choose Properties from the Options menu.

ⓖ The Video Properties dialog box shows the name of the symbol and the location of the original video file, as well as the properties of the compressed video (dimensions, time, and size).

ⓗ The newly selected video replaces the previous one in the Library.

Playback of External Video

So far, you've learned how to encode your videos and embed them in Flash. However, embedded video has a length restriction (16,000 frames, or approximately 8.5 minutes of 30 fps video). Also, embedded video begins to lose synchronization with its audio after about 2 minutes. Most important, embedded video significantly increases the file size of your Flash movie. You can bypass these problems by loading an external video file with a Flash playback component. This means that Flash dynamically loads video that is kept separate from the Flash file.

Playback of external video requires that your video be in the FLV or F4V file format.

Flash provides a special component known as a *skin* to give you control over the playback of your external video. Chapter 6, "Managing External Communication," looks at more advanced ways to load and control external video just using ActionScript.

Refer to **Table 2.1** for a summary comparison of embedded video and external playback.

TABLE 2.1 Embed vs. External Playback

	Embed	External Playback
Video length	Under 2 min with audio, or 16,000 frames total	No restriction
Flash Player	Versions 6 and later	Versions 7 and later
Usage	Short, small (320 x 240) video clips that need to be synchronized to other Flash elements on the Timeline	Longer, larger (720 x 580) video clips that do not need to be synchronized to other Flash elements on the Timeline
Video frame rate	Must be the same frame rate as Flash	Can be at a different frame rate than Flash
File size	Increases because video is contained within SWF	No effect, but FLV/F4V must accompany your SWF (or your SWF must be given the correct path to find the FLV/F4V)
Interface	None	Ready-made interfaces, or "skins," are available to control the playback of the video. Flash Player skins are small SWF files that are also kept external to your main Flash movie and must accompany your SWF.
Editability	Edit video and reimport into Flash	Edit video and convert to FLV/FV without opening Flash

To play back external video:

1. Choose File > Import > Import Video to open the Import Video wizard.

2. Use the Browse button to select the video file that you want **Ⓐ** and click Next/Continue. Your video *must* be an FLV or an F4V formatted video.

   If you have not yet converted your video to the FLV/F4V format, you can launch Adobe Media Encoder by clicking the Launch Adobe Media Encoder button.

3. Select "Load external video with playback component" **Ⓑ**. Click Next/Continue.

4. On the Skinning screen, choose a player skin and a color for your video player from the menu **Ⓒ**. Click Next/Continue.

   The player skin provides a viewing window and playback controls for your video. From the pull-down menu, choose a skin that includes different playback controls and from the adjacent color chip choose a color (or a transparency level). In the preview window you can see how your skin will appear. Note that some skins add the controls over the video, and some add the controls under the video.

   If you do not want any playback controls for your video, choose None from the top of the menu **Ⓓ**.

Ⓐ The Import Video wizard. The first step is to tell Flash where your video is located. Flash keeps track of the path to your external video relative to the location of your Flash file.

Ⓑ After you've selected your video file, choose the first option, "Load external video with playback component."

Ⓒ Select a video player skin from the pull-down menu. Click the color chip to change the color and transparency of the skin. The preview window shows you how the controls will appear with your video.

Ⓓ Choose the top option, None, to present your video without controls.

E The video playback component is placed on the Stage with a preview of your video. The video playback component is also added to your Library.

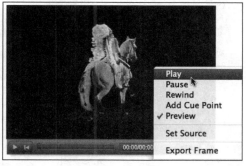

F You can preview your video on the Stage by using the controls of the skin or right-clicking (Windows) or Ctrl-clicking (Mac) the video and using the contextual menu.

G For playback of external video to work properly, your Flash movie (SWF) must be able to find and access the video file (FLV/F4V). If you are using a skin, the SWF file for the skin must also accompany your Flash movie. All three of these files are required to play.

5. On the final screen, review the summary of settings, and then click Finish.

A video playback component appears on the Stage and in the Library **E**. This component controls the playback of your external FLV/F4V file. Position the component anywhere on the Stage and at the keyframe at which you want the video to begin playing.

6. To see your video, click on the controls on your skin. If you don't have a skin on your video, right-click (Windows) or Ctrl-click (Mac) on the video and choose Play, Pause, or Rewind **F**.

Flash plays the external FLV/F4V file with the video playback component and the skin that you chose.

7. Choose Control > Test Movie > in Flash Professional.

Flash publishes a SWF for you to preview your movie. In addition to your project SWF, Flash generates a small SWF for your skin and saves it in the same folder as your Flash document. Keep the skin SWF together with your project so Flash can find it and display it correctly **G**.

TIP If you don't see a preview of your video on the Stage in the playback component, right-click (Windows) or Ctrl-click (Mac) and make sure the Preview option is checked.

Changing video playback options

You can change the way your video plays within Flash by changing the options in the video playback component. The video playback component is simply the player for the external video. By changing the options in the Parameters panel, you can change the "skin," or the appearance, of the player as well as other playback features.

To change the skin of the video playback component:

1. Click the video playback component on the Stage to select it.

   Parameters for the video playback component appear in the Properties inspector under the Component Parameters section .

2. Find the skin parameter (in the first column) and click the current value (in the second column). Click the pencil icon **I**.

   The Select Skin dialog box appears.

3. Choose a different skin and/or color for your player **J**. Click OK.

   Your newly selected skin appears on your video. Once you test (Control > Test Movie > in Flash Professional) or publish your Flash movie, a new skin SWF will be generated in the same folder as your Flash document.

H The Component Parameters section of the Properties inspector lets you set options for your video player skin. The first column is the parameter, and the second column is the value for that parameter.

I The "skin" parameter determines which playback interface to use.

J Set a new skin.

Skin transparency (0 to 1.0)   Skin color

K Set a new skin color and transparency directly in the Property inspector.

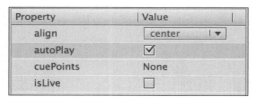

L Select skinAutoHide to hide the interface. Be careful when hiding the interface because users won't necessarily know how to access the controls.

Property	Value
align	center ▾
autoPlay	☑
cuePoints	None
isLive	☐

M Select autoPlay to make the video play automatically. Deselect it to pause the video at the first frame.

4. In the Properties inspector, find the parameters for skinBackgroundAlpha and skinBackgroundColor. Click the current value (in the second column) to change the transparency of the skin or the background color of the skin **K**.

5. In the Properties inspector, find the parameter for skinAutoHide. Click the empty check box (in the second column) to change whether or not the interface is always visible **L**.

   ▸ Select skinAutoHide to keep the interface hidden until the mouse pointer moves over the video.

   ▸ Deselect skinAutoHide to have the interface be visible all the time.

To change the playback of the external video:

1. Click the video playback component on the Stage to select it.

   Parameters for the video playback component appear in the Properties inspector under the Component Parameters section.

2. Find the autoPlay parameter (in the first column) and click the empty check box (in the second column) **M**.

   ▸ Select autoPlay to have the video automatically begin playing.

   ▸ Deselect autoPlay to have the video paused at the first frame.

To change the path to the external video:

1. Click the video playback component on the Stage to select it.

2. In the Properties inspector, find the source parameter (in the first column) and click the current value (in the second column). Click the pencil icon.

   The Content Path dialog box appears 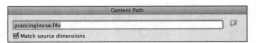.

3. Click the folder icon to browse to the new location of your FLV/F4V file.

   Flash changes the path to your video file in the Parameters panel so that the video playback component can find the file and play it.

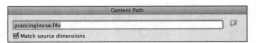

N Change the source value to modify the name or location of the file that the video player loads.

Video playhead

Ⓐ The video playhead in this example is placed at 5 seconds into the video.

Add Cue Point button

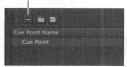

Ⓑ The cue point called "Cue Point" is added at the 5-second mark for this video.

Delete Cue Point button

Ⓒ Use the Delete Cue Point button to remove a cue point from the list.

Adding Cue Points to External Video

Although external video plays independently of the Timeline, you can synchronize external video with other Flash elements by using cue points. Cue points are special markers that you add to your video that Flash can detect and respond to with ActionScript.

There are three kinds of cue points: *Navigation* cue points allow you to jump to a particular point in the video. *Event* cue points allow you to trigger other elements from a particular point in the video. Both Navigation and Event cue points are embedded in the video during the encoding process with Adobe Media Encoder. *ActionScript* cue points are added to an already encoded video through Action-Script, or through the Properties inspector.

To add embedded cue points from Adobe Media Encoder:

1. In the Export Settings dialog box, move the yellow video playhead to the point when you want a cue point **Ⓐ**.

2. Click the Add Cue Point button.

   A cue point is added to the video **Ⓑ**.

3. Click the name of the cue point to rename it or click the time to change its time.

4. Choose Event or Navigation for the Type.

To delete cue points from Adobe Media Encoder:

Select a cue point in the Properties inspector and click the Delete Cue Point button **Ⓒ**.

To add ActionScript cue points from the Properties inspector:

1. Move the video playhead or pause the video at the point when you want a cue point **D**.

2. In the Properties inspector, in the Cue Points section, click the Add Action-Script Cue Point button.

   A cue point is added to the video **E**.

3. Click the name of the cue point to rename it or click and drag the time to change its time.

TIP Double-click the cue point in the Type column to quickly jump to that point in time in your video.

To delete cue points from the Properties inspector:

Select a cue point in the Properties inspector and click the Delete ActionScript Cue Point button.

or

Right-click (Windows) or Ctrl-click (Mac) on a cue point in the Properties inspector and choose Delete **F**.

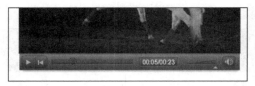

D In this example, the video is paused at 5 seconds.

Add Cue Point button

E In the Properties inspector, the cue point called "Cue Point" is added at the 5-second mark for this video.

Delete Cue Point button

F Use the Delete Cue Point button or right-click (Windows) or Ctrl-click (Mac) to remove a cue point from the list.

To add ActionScript cue points with ActionScript:

1. Select the video playback component and give it an instance name in the Properties inspector **G**.

   In this example, the video playback component is called **myvideo**.

2. Select the first frame of the Timeline and open the Actions panel.

3. Enter the instance name of the video playback component, a dot, and then the method, **addASCuePoint()**.

4. The method **addASCuePoint()** can take either an object as a single parameter or two parameters—time (in seconds) and the cue point name. For example:

   ```
   myvideo.addASCuePoint({time:5,
   → name:"mycuepoint",
   → type:"actionscript"})
   ```

   creates a cue point with an object as its single parameter. The object has three properties: **time**, **name**, and **type** **H**. (The curly braces are a shorthand way of creating an object and defining its properties all at once).

   The method **myvideo.addASCuePoint (5, "mycuepoint");** creates a cue point at 5 seconds with the name **mycuepoint** **I**.

   TIP In general, cue points added via ActionScript are less accurate than those embedded in videos during the encoding process. ActionScript cue points are accurate to a tenth of a second.

   TIP You cannot change or delete embedded cue points with ActionScript, but you can add new ones to existing embedded cue points.

   TIP Cue point information is wiped out when you set the **source** property of a video playback component. Be sure to set the source property first, and then add cue points.

G Name the video playback component on the Stage. Do not use spaces or punctuation, or begin your name with a number.

H This ActionScript code adds a cue point called **mycuepoint** at 5 seconds to the video on the Stage.

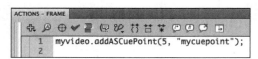

I Similar ActionScript code to add a cue point called **mycuepoint** at 5 seconds to the video on the Stage.

Detecting and Responding to Cue Points

Cue points can be used as chapter points—for example, you can make buttons that navigate to different sections of a video. Or cue points can be used to trigger Flash elements that are synchronized to the video. For example, as a speaker in the video mentions a product, an ad for that product could pop up next to the video.

Detecting and responding to cue points requires ActionScript and an understanding of event listeners. You can jump ahead to Chapter 3, "Getting a Handle on Action-Script," and Chapter 4, "Advanced Buttons and Event Handling," and return when you're more comfortable with coding.

To detect cue points:

1. Select the video playback component and make sure it has an instance name in the Properties inspector **A**.

   In this example, the video playback component is called **myvideo**.

2. Select the first frame of the Timeline and open the Actions panel.

3. Enter an **import** statement that imports the necessary ActionScript classes for the video playback component **B**:

   import fl.video.*

   The asterisk is a wildcard symbol that means all the classes in the **fl.video** package are imported.

A Name the video playback component on the Stage. Do not use spaces or punctuation, or begin your name with a number.

B The **import** statement provides the ActionScript that isn't normally included.

4. On the next line, create an event listener for your video playback component that listens for the **MetadataEvent. CUE_POINT** event. This particular event happens when Flash encounters a cue point in a video. Your code should look similar to this:

```
myvideo.addEventListener
⇢ (MetadataEvent.CUE_POINT,
⇢ cuepointfound);
```

5. Add the function that responds to the event; in this example, it's called **cuepointfound**. Within the function, you can add a conditional statement that checks the name of the cue point that was encountered, as shown here:

```
function cuepointfound
⇢ (e:MetadataEvent):void {
   if (e.info.name=="mycuepoint") {
      //respond to cue point
   }
}
```

In this example **C**, when a cue point is encountered during the video playback, the function called cuepointfound is triggered. The function checks whether the cue point's name matches mycuepoint, and if it does, it will execute any of the commands within the curly braces of the **if** statement. The event, in this example, is referred to with the variable **e**.

▸ **e.target** refers to the video playback instance.

▸ **e.info.name** refers to the cue point's name.

▸ **e.info.time** refers to the cue point's time.

```
import fl.video.*;

myvideo.addEventListener(MetadataEvent.CUE_POINT, cuepointfound);
function cuepointfound(e:MetadataEvent):void {
     if (e.info.name=="mycuepoint") {
           //respond to cuepoint
     }
}
```

C This ActionScript code detects a cue point in the video called **myvideo**, and includes a conditional statement that checks whether the cue point's name matches **mycuepoint**.

To jump to a navigation cue point:

Use the method **seekToNavCuePoint()**, which takes the name of the cue point as its parameter, for example:

myvideo.seekToNavCuePoint
→ **("mycuepoint");**

In this statement, Flash will make the video jump to the cue point named mycuepoint in the video playback component named myvideo .

```
myvideo.seekToNavCuePoint("mycuepoint");
```

D This ActionScript code makes the video component called **myvideo** jump to the navigation cue point called **mycuepoint**.

Using the Code Snippets Panel

Flash Professional CS5 contains a new panel called the Code Snippets panel that you'll learn more about in the next chapter. The Code Snippets panel makes it easy for you to add ActionScript code for common interactive tasks. For example, if you want to detect a cue point in an external video, you can use the Code Snippets panel rather than write the code yourself, as you've done in this section. You still have to add and edit some of the code to tailor it for your own project, but it can make the job easier and it can help you learn ActionScript.

To access the Code Snippets panel, choose Window > Code Snippets. The snippets are grouped in different folders. Open the Audio and Video folder to find the snippets for cue points. Select your video playback component on the Stage and double-click On Cue Point Event **E**. ActionScript code that detects cue points in your video automatically gets added to your Timeline. Follow the directions in the Actions panel to add and modify the code to fit your own needs.

If you want to add code that jumps to a navigation cue point, select your video playback component on the Stage and double-click Click to Seek to Cue Point **F**. Follow the directions in the Actions panel to add and modify the code to fit your own needs.

E The Code Snippets panel provides a quick way to add ActionScript for different tasks. Choose On Cue Point Event to detect cue points in your video.

F In the Code Snippets panel, choose Click to Seek to Cue Point to jump to a cue point in your video.

Getting a Handle on ActionScript

ActionScript is Flash's programming language for adding interactivity to your project. You can use ActionScript to create anything from simple navigation within your Flash movie to complex interfaces that react to the location of the viewer's pointer, arcade-style games, and even full-blown e-commerce sites with dynamically updating data. In this chapter, you'll learn how to write ActionScript to create effective Flash interaction. Think of the process as learning the grammar of a foreign language: First, you must learn how to put nouns and verbs together and integrate adjectives and prepositions; then you can expand your communication skills and have meaningful conversations by building your vocabulary. This chapter will give you a sound ActionScript foundation upon which you can build your Flash literacy.

If you're familiar with object-oriented programming languages such as Java, C++, or JavaScript, you'll recognize the similarities in ActionScript. Although there are slight differences, the basic syntax and the handling of objects—reusable pieces of code—remain the same.

In This Chapter

Even if you don't have any programming experience, you'll see in this chapter that Flash provides ways to help you write script, such as code hinting as you compose code, or tools to quickly add script, such as the new Code Snippets panel.

What Is ActionScript 3?

Like any language, ActionScript evolves over time. Introduced in Flash CS3, Action-Script 3 is the latest version of the Flash programming language that lets you control graphics, animation, sound, and interactivity. ActionScript 3 is significantly different from the previous version of the language, ActionScript 2, so be aware of which version you're dealing with, whether you're searching the Web for help or talking with a client about a new project. Major differences between the languages include:

- A different model for detecting and responding to events (like a mouse click or a keyboard input).

- A display list in ActionScript 3, which manages the dynamic display of all kinds of graphics on the Stage.

- Less dependence on the movie clip symbol as the main actor in advanced Flash projects. ActionScript 3 provides different objects that are more specific to the task rather than relying on the movie clip for a wide variety of purposes.

- Changes in the actual language, so users familiar with ActionScript 2 will have to relearn commands (**getURL** is instead **navigateToURL**, **_root** is **root**, properties like **_x** are simply **x**).

You'll begin your study of ActionScript 3 with its basic building blocks: objects and classes.

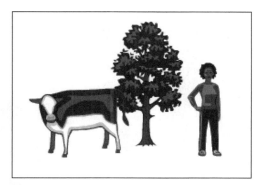

Ⓐ Objects in the real world include things like a cow, a tree, and a person.

Human class

Adam   Betty   Zeke

Ⓑ Adam, Betty, and Zeke are three objects of the Human class. Flash doesn't have such a class, but this analogy is useful for understanding objects.

About Objects and Classes

At the heart of ActionScript are objects and classes. *Objects* are specific pieces of data—such as sound, graphics, text, and numeric values—that you create in Flash and use to control the movie. A date object, for example, retrieves information about the time and the date, and an array object manipulates data stored in a particular order.

All the objects you use and create are generated from blueprints known as *classes*. Flash provides certain classes for you to use in your movie. These built-in classes handle a wide range of Flash elements such as data (**Array** class, **Math** class) and sound and video (**Sound** class, **Video** class).

Learning to code in ActionScript centers on understanding the capabilities of objects and their classes, and using them to interact with one another and with the viewer.

In the real world, you're familiar with objects such as a cow, a tree, and a person **Ⓐ**. Flash objects range from visible things, such as a movie clip of a spinning ball, to more abstract concepts, such as the date, pieces of data, or the handling of keyboard inputs. Whether concrete or abstract, however, Flash objects are versatile because after you create them, you can reuse them in different contexts.

Before you can use objects, you need to be able to identify them, and you do so by name just as you do in the real world. Say you have three people in front of you: Adam, Betty, and Zeke. All three are objects that can be distinguished by name. All three are made from a blueprint called *humans*. You can also say that Adam, Betty, and Zeke are all *instances* of the Human class **Ⓑ**. In ActionScript, *instances* and *objects* are synonymous, and the terms are used interchangeably in this book.

About Methods and Properties

Each object of a class (Zeke of the humans, for example) differs from the others in its class by more than just its name. Each person is different because of several defining characteristics, such as height, weight, gender, and hair color. In object-oriented programming, you say that objects and classes have *properties*. Height, weight, sex, and hair color are all properties of the Human class **A**.

In Flash, each class has a predefined set of properties that lets you establish the uniqueness of the object. The **Sound** class has many properties, one of which is **length**, which measures the duration of a sound in milliseconds. The **MovieClip** class, on the other hand, has different properties, such as **height**, **width**, and **rotation**, which are measures of the dimensions and orientation of a particular movie clip object. By defining and changing the properties of objects, you control what each object is like and how each object appears, sounds, and behaves.

Objects also do things. Zeke can run, sleep, and talk. The things that objects can do are known as *methods*. Each class has its own set of methods. The **MovieClip** class, for example, has a **gotoAndStop()** method that sends the Flash playhead to a particular frame on its Timeline, and the **Date** class has a **getDay()** method that retrieves the day of the week. When an object does something by using a method, you say that the method is *called* or that the object *calls* the method.

Understanding the relationships between objects, classes, properties, and methods is important. Putting objects together so that the methods and properties of one

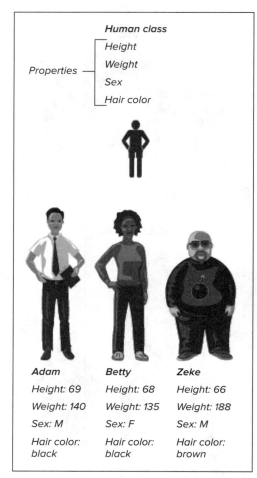

A Adam, Betty, and Zeke are human objects with different properties. Names and properties differentiate objects of the same class.

influence the methods and properties of another is what drives Flash interactivity. The key to building your ActionScript vocabulary is learning the properties and methods of different classes.

TIP It helps to think of objects as nouns, properties as adjectives, and methods as verbs. Properties describe their objects, whereas methods are the actions that the objects perform.

Betty.weight=135   *Zeke.weight=188*

Ⓐ The hypothetical **weight** property describes Betty and Zeke. In Flash, many properties of objects can be both read and modified with ActionScript.

Symbols and Classes

Symbols aren't classes. Symbols aren't even objects. It's true that most types of symbols (like movie clips, buttons, bitmaps, and video) have an associated class, which is perhaps the source of some confusion. For the most part, symbols that appear in the Library aren't objects or classes because they don't have methods and properties that you can control with ActionScript.

Symbols are simply reusable assets created in or imported to the Library. You create instances, or copies, of the symbols to use in your movie. When you place an instance of certain symbols, such as a button or a movie clip, on the Stage and give it a name, it becomes an instance of the corresponding class (**SimpleButton** or **MovieClip**) that you can manipulate using ActionScript.

Writing with Dot Syntax

As with other foreign languages, you must learn the rules of grammar to put words together. *Dot syntax* is the convention that ActionScript uses to put objects, properties, and methods together into statements. You connect objects, properties, and methods with dots (periods) to describe a particular object or process. Here are two examples:

```
Zeke.weight = 188

Betty.weight = 135
```

The first statement assigns the value **188** to the weight of Zeke. The second statement assigns the value **135** to the weight of Betty. The dot separates the object name (**Zeke**, **Betty**) from the property (**weight**) **Ⓐ**.

In this statement, the object **Betty** is linked to the object **shirt**:

```
Betty.shirt.color = "gray"
```

The object **shirt**, in turn, has the property **color**, which is assigned the value **gray**. Notice that with dot syntax you use multiple dots to maintain object hierarchy. When you have multiple objects linked in this fashion, it's often easier to read the statement backward. So you could read it as "Gray is the color of the shirt of Betty."

Continues on next page

Now consider the following statement:

`Zeke.run()`

This statement causes Flash to call the method `run()` on the object **Zeke**, which causes him to do something. The parentheses after `run` signify that `run` is a method, not a property. You can think of this construction as noun-dot-verb . Methods often have *parameters* (also called arguments) within the parentheses. These parameters affect how the method is executed.

For example, both of these statements will make the **Zeke** and **Adam** objects perform the `run()` method, but because each method contains a different parameter, the way the run is performed is different—Zeke runs fast, and Adam runs slowly:

`Zeke.run("fast")`

`Adam.run("slow")`

Each method has its own set of parameters that you must learn. Consider the basic Flash action `gotoAndPlay(20, "Scene1")`. The method `gotoAndPlay()` belongs to the **MovieClip** class. The parenthetical parameters, `(20, "Scene1")`, refer to the frame number and the scene, so calling this method makes the playhead of the object jump to Scene1, frame 20, and begin playing. Some parameters may require quotation marks, while others may require none—you'll learn the reason when you learn about data types later in this chapter.

Mouse.hide()

Adam.run()

B Dot syntax lets you make objects call methods. Just as the hypothetical method `run()` could make the **Adam** object begin to jog, the real Flash method `hide()`, when applied to the **Mouse** object, makes the pointer disappear.

More on Punctuation

Dot syntax allows you to construct meaningful processes and assignments with objects, properties, and methods. Additional punctuation symbols let you do more with these single statements.

The semicolon

To terminate individual ActionScript statements and start new ones, you use the semicolon (;). The semicolon functions as a period does in a sentence—it concludes one idea and lets another one begin. Here are two examples:

```
myMovieClip.stop();
myMovieClip.rotation = 45;
```

The semicolons separate the statements so that the object called **myMovieClip** stops playing, and then it is rotated 45 degrees. Each statement is executed in order from the top down, like a set of instructions or a cookbook recipe.

TIP Flash will still understand ActionScript statements even if you don't use semicolons to terminate each one. It's good practice, however, to include them in your scripts.

Curly braces

Curly braces ({}) are another kind of punctuation that ActionScript uses frequently. Curly braces group related blocks of ActionScript statements. When you assign actions to respond to an event, for example, those actions appear within curly braces in a statement called a *function*:

```
function doThisAfterButtonClick () {
    myMovieClip.stop();
    myMovieClip.rotation = 45;
}
```

In this case, both the **stop** action and the change in **rotation** are executed when this function is called. Notice how the curly braces are separated on different lines to make the related ActionScript statements easier to read.

Commas

Commas (**,**) separate the parameters of a method. A method can take many parameters. The **gotoAndPlay()** method, for example, can take two: a frame number and a scene name. With commas separating the parameters, the ActionScript code looks like this:

```
gotoAndPlay(20, "Scene 1");
```

Some methods may have three, four, or perhaps even ten parameters, but as long as you separate the parameters with commas, Flash knows how to handle the code.

Capitalization

ActionScript 3 is case sensitive. That is, it knows the difference between lowercase letters and uppercase letters, so you must be very careful and conscientious about capitalization in all your code.

Colons

Colons (:) identify the type of object. When you first encounter Zeke, for example, you can identify him with the statement, **Zeke:Human** because Zeke is an instance of the Human class. Colons are important whenever new instances are introduced so that Flash knows what kind of data to associate with the object. You'll learn more about colons and the process of *strict typing* later in this chapter.

The Actions Panel

The Actions panel is a Flash dialog box that lets you access all the actions that control your Flash movie. The Actions panel provides Script Assist, a mode in which you are guided through the process of writing code by using a fill-in-the-blanks style to write commands. However, writing ActionScript code directly is far more efficient and in the long run the better way to learn because you won't spend your time hunting for a command buried deep within menus. This book will not show you how to write code with Script Assist.

However, don't worry that you'll be left alone in your code writing. As you write your own ActionScript, the Actions panel provides hints as you enter code and also automates some of the formatting. The Actions panel can also check for errors and give you access to the ActionScript Reference Guide.

To open the Actions panel:

From the Window menu, choose Actions (F9 on Windows, Option-F9 on the Mac).

or

Alt-double-click (Windows) or Option-double-click (Mac) a keyframe in the Timeline.

or

Right-click (Windows) or Ctrl-click (Mac) a keyframe in the Timeline and choose Actions at the bottom of the context menu.

or

Select a keyframe and click the Actions icon on the top-right corner of the Properties inspector .

Open Actions panel

A In the Properties inspector, click the icon with the arrow to open the Actions panel.

Collapse or expand

B The Actions panel, as well as the other panels, can be viewed as icons or icons and text by clicking the double-headed arrow at the top-right corner.

To undock the Actions panel:

Grab the Actions panel by its tab and drag it out of its current location.

The Actions panel undocks with its panel set and becomes a free-floating window.

To redock the Actions panel:

1. Grab the Actions panel by its tab or top horizontal bar and drag it over the different panels on your desktop.

   The different panels will highlight, indicating that you can dock the Actions panel in that location.

2. Drop the Actions panel.

   The Actions panel docks with the highlighted panels.

TIP You can choose to view your Actions panel, as well as all your other panels, as icons and text, thus freeing up more of your screen. Choose the double-headed arrow icon at the top-right corner of the Actions panel to collapse or expand it **B**.

TIP The Actions panel can be minimized just like other windows by clicking on the top light-gray horizontal bar. Expand the panel by clicking on the light-gray horizontal bar again.

TIP Resize the Actions panel by clicking and dragging the bottom-right corner.

Actions panel layout

The Actions panel features several sections and multiple ways to enter Action-Script statements **C**. The Actions toolbox on the left side displays all the available commands, organized by *packages*, which are groups of related classes. At the bottom of the categories colored in yellow, an index lists all the ActionScript commands in alphabetical order. You can use the Script navigator in the lower-left portion of the Actions panel to navigate to different scripts within your Flash movie. In the right section, your completed script appears in the Script pane. This part of the Actions panel also offers additional functions when the panel is in the special Script Assist mode. At the top, a row of buttons and an options pop-up menu provide additional features.

Plus button adds statements

Buttons to help write and check script

Options pop-up menu

Help button

Actions toolbox contains actions organized in categories

Script pane

Script navigator

Pin or Unpin Script button

C The Actions panel.

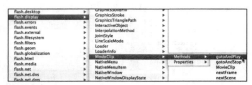

D Add an action by choosing a statement from the Actions toolbox. Here, the action **gotoAndPlay( )** has been added to the Script pane, and Flash indicates that there is still code missing before it.

E Add an action by choosing it from the plus button's pull-down menus.

Adding ActionScript

Now that you know where the Actions panel is located, how do you add Action-Script code? You must first select a keyframe on the Timeline in which you want to add ActionScript. This tells Flash when to carry out those instructions. Most often, ActionScript is put on the very first keyframe of your Flash movie.

Next, open the Actions panel and add code by directly typing in the Script pane or by choosing code from the categories or menus provided.

To add an action in the Script pane:

1. Select the keyframe on the Timeline where you want to assign an action.

2. In the Script pane of the Actions panel, begin typing the desired action.

   or

   Open a category from the left toolbox of the Actions panel and double-click the desired action or drag it into the Script pane.

   The action appears in the Script pane. The action may be incomplete, and Flash tells you what additional elements need to be provided to complete the statement **D**.

   or

   Click the plus button above the Script pane and choose the action from the pull-down menus **E**.

   The action appears in the Script pane.

TIP While making your selection in the Actions toolbox, you can use the arrow keys, the Page Up and Page Down keys, or the Home and End keys to navigate through the list. Press Enter or the spacebar to open or close categories or to choose an action to put in the Script pane.

To edit actions in the Script pane:

Highlight the action, and then click and drag it to a new position in the Script pane.

or

Highlight the action and use Copy, Cut, or Paste from the keyboard (Ctrl-C, Ctrl-X, or Ctrl-V on Windows; Cmd-C, Cmd-X, or Cmd-V on the Mac) or from the context menu (right-click on Windows, Ctrl-click on the Mac). Don't use Copy, Cut, or Paste from the Edit menu because those commands only affect the objects on the Stage.

To remove an action from the Script pane:

Highlight the action and use the Delete key to remove it from the Script pane.

To modify the Actions panel display:

Drag or double-click the vertical splitter bar, or click the arrow button that divides the Actions toolbox and Script pane, to collapse or expand an area **F**.

or

Drag or double-click the horizontal splitter bar, or click the arrow button that divides the Actions toolbox and Script navigator, to collapse or expand an area **G**.

To show earlier versions of ActionScript:

If you are authoring for earlier versions of the Flash Player and need to use commands from ActionScript 1 or 2, click the pull-down menu above the Actions toolbox and select a different version **H**.

The categories in the Actions toolbox change to only show actions that you can use for that version.

Moving the vertical splitter bar

F Resize the Script pane by dragging or clicking the vertical splitter bar that separates it from the Actions toolbox.

Moving the horizontal splitter bar

G Resize the Actions toolbox by dragging or clicking the horizontal splitter bar that separates it from the Script navigator.

H Choose an ActionScript version from the top pull-down menu.

Other Places for ActionScript

The Timeline isn't the only place you can put ActionScript. More advanced coders often will create their own ActionScript classes or extend the functionality of Flash's preexisting classes. In those cases, ActionScript is written in a separate text file (the filename is identical to the custom class name with the extension *.as* to indicate that it is ActionScript). The text file is saved in the same directory as the Flash file. When you create your own classes this way, you must use the **import** statement in the script to use the preexisting classes to build upon.

Actions panel options

The Actions panel provides many features that can help you write reliable code quickly and easily. Chapter 12, "Managing Content and Troubleshooting," explains many other debugging tools in detail.

When you're writing ActionScript in the Script pane, you can use *code hints*, which appear as you type. Code hints recognize what kind of action you're typing and offer choices and prompts on how to complete it. Flash makes it easy to be an expert! You can also customize the format options so that your code looks just the way you want it for ease of reading and understanding.

Coding help is always available in the Actions panel. The Help button, for example, calls up the Help site on the Adobe Flash Web site and sends you directly to the description and usage of any action selected in the Actions toolbox in case you have trouble remembering what a particular action does or how it's used.

If you want to keep an ActionScript visible as you select other elements in your Flash movie, you can do so by pinning your script. *Pinning* makes your script "stick" in the Script pane until you unpin it. This technique is useful if you've forgotten the name of a text box or a movie clip and need to reference it in an ActionScript statement. You can pin your current script, and then go look for your text box or movie clip. Your script remains in place so that you can make the necessary edits.

To use code hints:

1. Enter an object target path and then a period or a colon.

   Flash anticipates that you will enter a method or property after a period or a data type after a colon. A menu-style code hint appears to guide you .

2. Choose the appropriate term from the menu.

   Flash fills in your choice, completing that part of your code.

or

1. Enter an action in the Script pane, and then type the opening parenthesis.

   Flash detects the action and anticipates that you will enter its parameters. A code hint appears to guide you 🔵.

2. Enter the first parameter and then a comma.

   The bold in the code hint advances to highlight the next required parameter 🔵.

3. Continue entering the required parameters and type a closing parenthesis to finish the action.

   The code hint disappears 🔵.

🔵 A code hint guides you as you enter ActionScript. The scrolling menu lists code appropriate for the preceding object.

🔵 The **play()** method requires a parameter in between its parentheses. The first required parameter is the frame.

🔵 After you enter the first parameter (the frame), the code hint directs you to the next parameter. The next parameter for this action is the scene.

🔵 When you enter the closing parenthesis, the code hint disappears.

Show Code Hint button

M The Show Code Hint button is above the Script pane.

N In the Preferences dialog box, you can change the time that it takes for code hints to appear or turn off that feature completely.

TIP Dismiss a code hint by pressing the Esc key or clicking a different place in your script.

TIP Navigate the menu-style code hints by using the arrow keys, the Page Up and Page Down keys, or the Home and End keys. You can also start typing, and the entry that begins with the letter you type will appear in the code hint. Press Enter or the key that will follow the method or property (for example, a space, comma, or parenthesis) to choose the selection.

TIP You can call up code hints manually by pressing Ctrl-spacebar or by clicking the Show Code Hint button above the Script pane when your pointer is in a spot where code hints are appropriate **M**.

TIP Change the delay time for code hints to appear or turn off code hints by choosing Preferences from the Actions panel's Options menu. When the Preferences dialog box appears, change your preferences in the ActionScript options category **N**.

TIP Code hinting can also work with custom classes. If you create your own ActionScript classes and save them as external .as files in your Flash's source path (where it looks for external ActionScript), Flash will automatically detect and display code hints for those classes.

To set formatting options:

1. From the Actions panel's Options menu, choose Preferences.

   The Flash Preferences dialog box appears.

2. Choose the Auto Format category.

Continues on next page

3. Set the different formatting options and specify the way a typical block of code should appear ⓞ; then click OK.

4. Choose Auto Format from the Actions panel's Options menu (Ctrl-Shift-F for Windows, Cmd-Shift-F for Mac), or click the Auto Format button above the Script pane ⓟ.

Flash formats your script in the Script pane according to the preferences you set in the Auto Format category of the Flash Preferences dialog box (step 3).

To get information about an action:

Select an ActionScript term in the Actions toolbox or in the Script pane, and then click the Help button above and to the right of the Script pane ⓠ.

or

Right-click (Windows) or Ctrl-click (Mac) an action in the Actions toolbox or in the Script pane and select View Help from the context menu that appears.

The Adobe Help application opens (which mirrors the content in the Help section of the Adobe Web site) with information on the selected ActionScript term. The typical entry in the Help site contains information about usage and syntax, lists parameters and their availability in various Flash versions, and shows sample code.

To pin or unpin a script in the Script pane:

With ActionScript visible in the Script pane, click the Pin Active Script button at the bottom of the Actions panel ⓡ.

To unpin the script, click the button again.

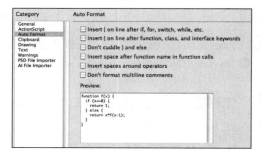

ⓞ The Auto Format category in the Flash Preferences gives you a preview of how a typical block of code will look with the selections you make.

Auto Format button

ⓟ The Auto Format button is above the Script pane.

ⓠ Make liberal use of the Help button to access ActionScript references.

Pin Active Script button

Close Pinned Script button

ⓡ The Pin Active Script button (top) toggles to Close Pinned Script (bottom).

Editing ActionScript

When the code in the Script pane of the Actions panel becomes long and complex, you can check, edit, and manage it using the Options menu of the Actions panel. There are menu options for searching and replacing words, importing and exporting scripts, and printing your scripts, as well as for different ways to display your script, such as using word wrap 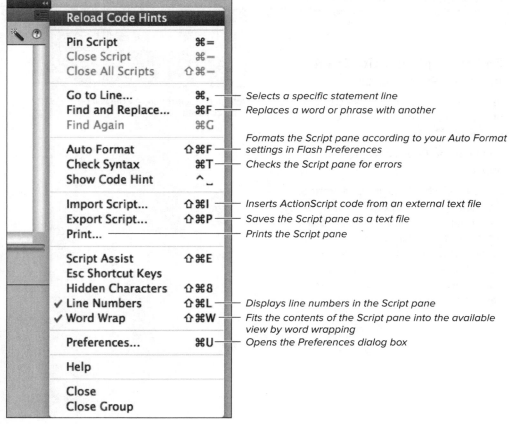.

You can use the Find and Replace functions in the Actions panel to quickly change variable names, properties, or even actions. For example, if you create a lengthy script involving the variable **redTeamStatus** but change your mind and want to change the variable name, you can replace all instances of **redTeamStatus** with **blueTeamStatus**. You can find all the occurrences of the property **height** and replace them with **width**, or you can locate all the occurrences of the action **gotoAndStop** and replace them with **gotoAndPlay**.

The Import Script and Export Script functions of the Actions panel let you work with external text editors.

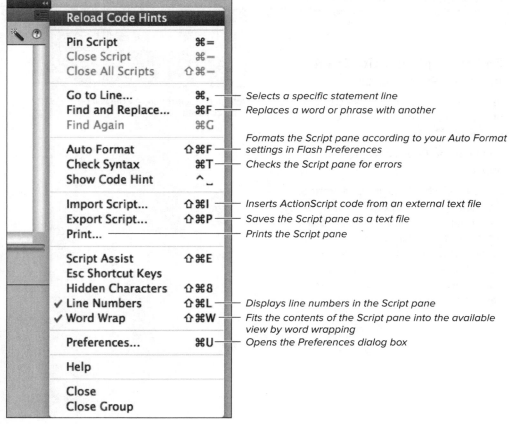

Reload Code Hints		
Pin Script	⌘=	
Close Script	⌘−	
Close All Scripts	⇧⌘−	
Go to Line...	⌘,	Selects a specific statement line
Find and Replace...	⌘F	Replaces a word or phrase with another
Find Again	⌘G	
Auto Format	⇧⌘F	Formats the Script pane according to your Auto Format settings in Flash Preferences
Check Syntax	⌘T	Checks the Script pane for errors
Show Code Hint	^ ␣	
Import Script...	⇧⌘I	Inserts ActionScript code from an external text file
Export Script...	⇧⌘P	Saves the Script pane as a text file
Print...		Prints the Script pane
Script Assist	⇧⌘E	
Esc Shortcut Keys		
Hidden Characters	⇧⌘8	
✓ Line Numbers	⇧⌘L	Displays line numbers in the Script pane
✓ Word Wrap	⇧⌘W	Fits the contents of the Script pane into the available view by word wrapping
Preferences...	⌘U	Opens the Preferences dialog box
Help		
Close		
Close Group		

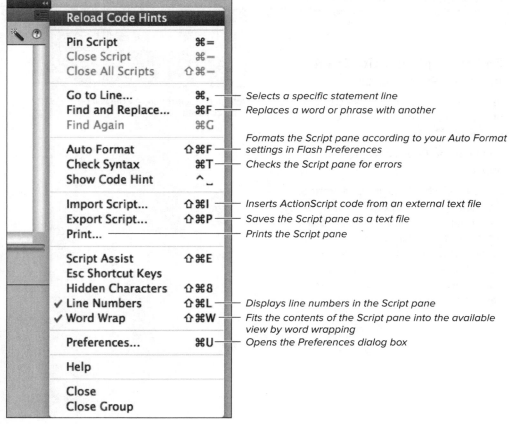 The Options menu of the Actions panel contains editing functions for the Script pane.

To check the syntax in the Script pane:

In the Actions panel, choose Options > Check Syntax (Ctrl-T for Windows, Cmd-T for Mac).

or

Click the Check Syntax button above the Script pane 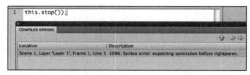.

Flash checks the script in the Script pane for errors in syntax. It reports any errors in a Compiler Errors window, which tells you the location and description of each error **C**.

TIP Check Syntax only reports the errors in the current Script pane, not for the entire movie.

To find and replace ActionScript terms in the Script pane:

1. In the Actions panel, choose Options > Find and Replace (Ctrl-F for Windows, Cmd-F for Mac).

   The Find and Replace dialog box appears.

2. In the Find what field, enter a word or words that you want Flash to find. In the Replace with field, enter a word or words that you want the found words to be replaced with. Select the Match Case check box to make Flash distinguish between uppercase and lower-case letters **D**.

Check Syntax button

B The Check Syntax button is the check-mark icon above the Script pane.

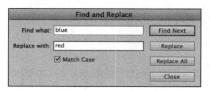

C The compiler error for a bad script. The Script pane (top) contains an extra closing parenthesis. Flash notifies you of the nature and location of the error in the Compiler Errors window (bottom).

D Every occurrence of **blue** will be replaced with **red**.

3. Click Replace to replace the first instance of the found word, or click Replace All to replace all instances of the found word.

TIP The Find and Replace dialog box replaces all the occurrences of a particular word or phrase only in the current Script pane of the Actions panel. To replace every occurrence of a certain word in the whole movie, you need to go to each script and repeat this process.

To import an ActionScript:

1. Select Options > Import Script (Ctrl-Shift-I for Windows, Cmd-Shift-I for Mac).

2. In the dialog box that appears, choose the text file that contains the ActionScript you want to import and click Open.

   Flash inserts the ActionScript contained in the text file into the current Script pane at the insertion point.

To export an ActionScript:

1. Select Options > Export Script (Ctrl-Shift-P for Windows, Cmd-Shift-P for Mac).

2. Enter a destination filename and click Save.

   Flash saves a text file that contains the entire contents of the current Script pane. The recommended extension for external ActionScript files is .*as*, as in myCode.as.

Using Objects

Now that you know what objects are and how to operate the Actions panel, you can begin to script with objects and call their methods or evaluate and assign new properties.

Flash provides existing classes (grouped in packages) that reside in the Actions toolbox. These Flash classes have methods and properties that control different elements of your Flash movie, such as graphics, sound, data, time, and mathematical calculations. You can also build your own classes or extend the functions of an existing class, a topic that we won't delve into in this book.

Variables, data types, and strict typing

In ActionScript, like most programming languages, you access and manipulate objects using variables. *Variables* are containers that hold information. You can create, change the contents of, and discard variables at any time. In ActionScript 3, it's necessary to define the existence of a variable, which is known as *declaring* the variable, before you use it. To declare a variable, you use the ActionScript keyword **var** followed by the name of the variable, which is followed in turn by a colon and the type of information the variable will be used to store. The different kinds of information that variables can contain are known as *data types*.

Examples of typical types of variables are a user's score (**Number** data type), an Internet address (**String** data type), a date object (**Date** data type), and the on/off state of a toggle button (**Boolean** data type). In ActionScript 3, you specify the data type of your variable when you create it; Flash will allow only values of that data type to be stored in the variable. This is called *strict typing*. Strict data typing prevents you from accidentally assigning the wrong type of data to a variable, which can cause problems during the playback of your movie. Strict data typing involves adding a colon (:) and the data type after the name of your variable. For example, if you want to create a variable called **myScore** to hold a number, you write **var myScore:Number**.

TABLE 3.1 Some Data Types

Data Type	Description Example	Example
Number	A numeric value	`var myTemp:Number = 98.6`
int	An integer (whole number)	`var myGolfScore:int = -4`
uint	An unsigned integer (a non-negative whole number)	`var myZipCode:uint = 11215`
String	A sequence of characters, numbers, or symbols. A string is always contained within quotation marks.	`var yourEmail:String =` `→ "johndoe@domain.com"`
Boolean	A value of either true or false. The words aren't enclosed in quotation marks.	`var buttonPressed:Boolean =` `→ true`
Object	A generic object to which you can add properties or methods. Used in cases where a simple object is needed.	`var myObj:Object =` `→ new Object()`
Any of the Flash classes	An object type	`var myMusic:Sound =` `→ new Sound()`

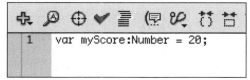

A Variables can be initialized to hold different kinds of information. The word **var** indicates that **myScore** is a variable, the colon and word **Number** indicate that the variable can only hold numbers, and the equals sign assigns the numerical value 20 to the variable.

TIP It's good practice to initialize your variables in the first frame of your Timeline. That way, you keep them all in the same place and can edit their initial values easily.

TIP When you assign a value that is one of the intrinsic data types (**Number**, **String**, **Boolean**) to a variable, even if you're assigning to one variable the value in another, Flash determines the value and puts it in your variable at that moment. If the property or the referenced variable subsequently changes, the value of your variable won't change unless you reassign it. Consider this example: **var xPosition:Number = mouseX;**. When you initialize the variable called **xPosition** in the first frame of your movie, it holds the x-coordinate of the pointer. As you move the pointer around the screen, the property **mouseX** changes but the variable **xPosition** does not. The variable **xPosition** still holds the original x-coordinate from when it was initialized.

Table 3.1 lists the most basic data types that variables can hold. However, a variable can be declared with any ActionScript class as its data type, including any of the built-in classes and classes you create yourself.

Once you declare a variable, you initialize it, or put information into the variable for the first time. Initializing a variable in the Actions panel involves using the equals sign (=), which assigns a value to a variable. The name of the variable goes on the left side of the equals sign, and a value to be assigned goes on the right side. This point is crucial: the expression **a = b** is not the same as **b = a**. So you can put a number in your **myScore** variable like this: **myScore = 20**. It's common to merge the declaration and initializing in a single line like so: **var myScore:Number = 20**. When you initialize a variable at the same time you declare the variable, it's clear which part of the statement is the variable and which part is the new value.

To declare and initialize a variable:

1. Select the first frame of the Timeline and open the Actions panel.

2. In the Script pane, enter the keyword **var**.

3. Next, enter a descriptive name for your variable.

   Your variable name should follow certain rules. See the sidebar "The Rules of Naming" for more information.

4. Type a colon and then the data type of the variable.

5. Type the equals sign (=) and then the initial value that you want the variable to hold.

   The value on the right side of the equals sign is assigned to the variable on the left side **A**.

The Rules of Naming

Although you're free to make up descriptive names for your objects, you must adhere to the following simple rules. If you don't, Flash won't recognize your object's name and will likely give you an error:

- Don't use spaces or punctuation (such as slashes, dots, and parentheses), because these characters often have a special meaning to Flash.

- You can use letters, numbers, and underscore characters, but you must *not* begin the name with a number.

- You can't use certain words for variable names because they are reserved for special functions or for use as keywords in ActionScript. If you try to use them as variables, Flash will display an error message when you test your movie. For example, you can't name your variable "function" because that word is part of the ActionScript language.

Those are the only three rules. Some additional general naming strategies, however, can make your scripts easier to understand, debug, and share:

- Variable names should describe the information that the variables hold. The variable names **playerScore** and **spaceshipVelocity**, for example, are appropriate and will cause fewer headaches than something like **xyz** or **myVariable**.

- Use a consistent naming practice. A common method is to use multiple words to describe an object and to capitalize the first letter of every word except the first. The names **spinningSquare1**, **spinningSquare2**, and **leftPaddle**, for example, are intuitive, descriptive, and easy to follow in a script. Remember that ActionScript 3 is case sensitive! Using a consistent naming practice will help you avoid mismatches between your object name and your ActionScript code due to capitalization.

- It sometimes helps to add suffixes to names to describe the object type. Using the standard suffix **_mc** for movie clips and **_btn** for buttons readily identifies the objects. Although strict typing makes Flash recognize all variable names and their associated data type for code hinting in the Actions panel, adding suffixes, especially to generic variable names, often makes the code more understandable.

```
var myArea:Number = myLength * myWidth;
var dogYears:Number = 7 * Age;
var myProgress:Number = currentFrame / totalFrames;
```

B Some examples of expressions. The variable names are on the left side of the equals signs, and the expressions are on the right.

TABLE 3.2 Common Escape Sequences

Sequence	Character
\b	Backspace
\r	New line
\t	Tab
\"	Quotation mark
\'	Single quotation mark
\\	Backslash

Expressions and strings

Using expressions and using strings are two important ways to describe and manipulate data. An *expression* is a statement that may include variables, properties, and objects, and must be resolved (figured out) before Flash can determine its value. Think of an expression as being an algebraic formula, like $a^2 + b^2$. The value of the expression has to be calculated before it can be used **B**.

A *string,* on the other hand, is a statement that Flash uses *as is* and considers to be a collection of characters. The string "$a^2 + b^2$" is literally a sequence of seven characters (including the spaces around the plus sign but not the quotation marks). When you initialize a variable with a literal string value, you must enclose the characters in straight quotation marks.

Expressions and strings aren't mutually exclusive—that is, sometimes you can have an expression that includes strings! For example, the statement **"Current frame is " + currentframe** is an expression that puts together a string and the frame number of the main Timeline. You'll learn more about this kind of operation, called *concatenation*, in Chapter 11, "Manipulating Information."

TIP If quotation marks always surround a string, how do you include quotation marks in the actual string? You use the backslash (\) character before including a quotation mark. This technique is called *escaping* a character. The string "The line \"Call me Shane\" is from a 1953 movie Western" produces the following result: *The line "Call me Shane" is from a 1953 movie Western.* Table 3.2 lists a few common escape sequences for special characters.

Creating objects

The first step to add interactivity with Flash objects is to create a new instance of a class. You do this by using the keyword **new** and then the name of the class and a pair of parentheses: **new Human()**. This creates a new Human object. However, the new Human object needs a name. So you give the object a name by declaring a variable and assigning the new object to it.

var Zeke:Human = new Human();

You've just created Zeke! The variable **Zeke** is strictly typed to hold a Human type object, and with the variable name, you can reference all the properties and methods of the Human class. The process is the same as creating an instance of, or *instantiating*, a symbol on the Stage, but here you do it purely with ActionScript.

Consider the following example:

var myData:Array = new Array();

This statement makes a new **Array** instance called **myData**. The statement on the right side of the equals sign is called a *constructor*. Most classes have a constructor method, a special method that creates new instances of that class.

The following task demonstrates how to create an instance of the **Date** class, but the general technique works for instantiation of all objects.

C The finished statement creates an object called **myDate** from the **Date** class.

Movie clip instance on the Stage *Movie clip symbol in Library* *Movie clip instance name in Properties inspector*

D Instantiation of a movie clip symbol from the Library to the Stage involves naming it in the Properties inspector.

To instantiate an object:

1. Select the first frame on the main Timeline and open the Actions panel.

2. In the Script pane, type **var**.

3. Enter a space and then a name for your new object.

4. ActionScript 3 requires strict typing, so enter a colon and then the object type. In this example, use **Date**.

5. Type an equals sign (=) and then the constructor, **new Date()**.

   The full statement creates a new **Date** object with the name you entered. Your **Date** object is instantiated and ready to use **C**.

Creating instances on the Stage

A few types of ActionScript objects, such as movie clips, buttons, and text fields, are unique because you can create them visually by adding an instance from the Library (for button and movie clip symbols) or using the drawing tools (for text). Instantiation of these objects involves two steps: placing an instance on the Stage and naming that instance in the Properties inspector. These two steps accomplish the same task that the constructor function performs for other Flash classes **D**. The result is the same: A named object, or an instance, of a class is created. You can manipulate that object by calling its methods or evaluating its properties.

Later in the book, you'll learn how to create **SimpleButton** instances (Chapter 4, "Advanced Buttons and Event Handling"), **MovieClip** instances (Chapter 7, "Controlling and Displaying Graphics"), and **TLFTextField** instances (Chapter 10, "Controlling Text"), and place them on the Stage using only code.

To name a movie clip instance or a button instance:

1. Create a movie clip symbol or a button symbol.

2. Drag an instance of the symbol from the Library to the Stage.

3. Select the instance.

4. At the top of the Properties inspector, enter a unique name for your instance **E**.

   Now you can use this name to refer to your movie clip instance or your button instance with ActionScript.

TIP The name of your symbol (the one that appears in the Library) and the name you give it in the Properties inspector are two different identifiers **F**. The name that appears in the Library is a symbol property and basically is just an organizational reminder. The name in the Properties inspector is more important because it's the actual name of the object and will be used in targeting paths. End your movie clip instance name with _mc and your button instances with _btn so that the Actions panel can identify the object type.

Calling methods

Often, the next step after creating a new object involves calling the object's methods. You can call a method by using an object's name followed by a period and then the method with its parameters within parentheses. All the methods of a particular class can be found in the Methods category of that class category in the Actions toolbox.

When you call an object's method, the code in the Script pane will look something like this:

`myShape.startDrag();`

This statement calls the method `startDrag()` of the object called `myShape`, and as a result, the graphic called `myShape` will follow the mouse pointer.

E The Properties inspector for a selected movie clip. The name of this movie clip object is `myCircle_mc`.

Movie clip symbol name   *Movie clip instance name*

F The name of the movie clip symbol appears in the Library (**Symbol 1**), and the name of the movie clip instance appears in the Properties inspector (`myCircle_mc`).

```
1    var myDate:Date = new Date();
2    trace(myDate.getDate());
```

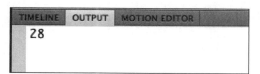 The **Date** object called **myDate** retrieves the
current date from your computer's internal clock,
and the **trace()** command displays it when you
test the movie.

TIMELINE	OUTPUT	MOTION EDITOR	
28			

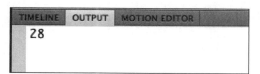 The Output panel displays the results of the
trace. When this movie was tested, it was the 28th
day of the month.

Sometimes when you call an object's
method, a value is returned. Essentially,
the object does something and then
comes back to you with an answer. In that
case, it's useful to put that answer or result
in another variable so you can store it and
analyze it. Your ActionScript would look
something like this:

```
var currentDate:Number =
→ myDate.getDate();
```

This statement calls the method **getDate()**
from the **myDate** object and puts the information it retrieves into the variable called
currentDate.

The following task continues the task "To
instantiate an object" and calls a method
of your newly created **Date** object. Later
chapters introduce specific classes,
provide more information about the **Date**
class, and show you how to use methods
to control your Flash movie.

To call a method of an object:

1. Continuing with the task "To instantiate
   an object," open the Actions panel and
   start a new line of code.

2. Enter a **trace()** statement so you
   can see the results of the method in
   this example. Between the parentheses of the **trace()** statement, enter
   myDate.getDate() 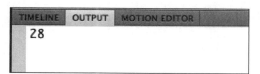.

   The **trace()** statement is a debugging
   tool that outputs messages in the Output panel. See the sidebar, "Using the
   trace() Statement."

3. Test your movie by choosing Control >
   Test Movie > in Flash Professional.

   Flash instantiates a **Date** object (from
   the earlier task) and then calls the
   getDate() method. The returned value
   (the day of the month) is displayed in
   the Output window 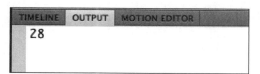.

Assigning properties

You can change the properties of objects simply by assigning new values on the right side of an equals (=) symbol. For example, this statement changes the **alpha** property of the object called **myShape** so it becomes 50 percent transparent: **myShape.alpha = .5;**.

Sometimes properties are read-only, which means they can't be changed, but you can still use them in expressions to test certain conditions.

To assign a value to a property:

1. In the Script pane, enter the object name and then a dot.

    The code hint pull-down menu appears, displaying a list of choices available to the particular object.

2. Select the desired property.

    The statement consisting of the object name, a dot, and the property appears.

3. Enter an equals (=) symbol and then a value.

    A new value is assigned to the property .

`mybox.rotation=45;`

❶ Assigning a value to a property. The value of 45 is assigned to the **rotation** property of the object called **mybox**, which results in the object rotating 45 degrees.

Using the trace() Statement

The first bit of ActionScript you should learn as you forge ahead with objects, methods, and properties is the **trace()** statement. The **trace()** statement gives you feedback by displaying messages in the Output panel, a panel that only shows up in the Flash authoring environment.

Enter a string or an expression within the parentheses of the **trace()** statement, and the results are displayed when you test your movie. Traces are for debugging, and they won't show up in your final, published SWF file. You'll often use the **trace()** statement to track the value of variables at different points of your movie to see whether or not your code is working correctly.

For example, in the Actions panel, enter

`trace(stage.stageWidth);`

J The **trace()** statement displays the width of the Stage in the Output panel when you test the movie (Control > Test Movie > in Flash Professional).

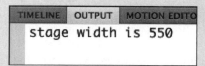

K Add text to your **trace()** statement to make it more understandable.

When you test your movie, the Output panel appears and displays the value that represents the width of your current Stage, in pixels **J**.

You can have multiple parameters within the **trace()** statement, separated by a comma. The Output panel will display the multiple results separated by a space.

You can also combine strings to make the output easier to understand. For example, the statement **trace("stage width is "+stage.stageWidth)** appends the string before the stage width so you know what the number in the Output panel refers to **K**.

About Functions

If objects and classes are at the heart of ActionScript, functions must lie in the brain. Functions are the organizers of Action-Script. Functions group related Action-Script statements to perform a specific task. Often, you need to write code to do a certain thing over and over. Functions eliminate the tedium of manually duplicating the code by putting it in one place where you can call on it to do its job from anywhere, at any time, as many times as necessary. You'll see in Chapter 4, "Advanced Buttons and Event Handling," that functions are essential for building responses to events—creating true interactivity.

As you learned earlier in this chapter, the objects **Adam**, **Betty**, and **Zeke** can perform certain tasks called methods. If these objects were to put on a dinner party, they could organize themselves and do the following:

```
Adam.answerDoor();
Betty.serveDinner();
Zeke.chitChat();
```

But every Friday night when they have a dinner party, you'll have to write the same three lines of code—not very efficient if these objects plan to entertain often. Instead, you can write a function that groups the code in one spot:

```
function dinnerParty() {
    Adam.answerDoor();
    Betty.serveDinner();
    Zeke.chitChat();
}
```

Now, every Friday night you can invoke the function by name and write the code **dinnerParty()**. The three statements inside the function's curly braces will be executed.

Building functions

To create a function, start the line of code with the word **function**, then insert a space, and then give your function a name. The rules of naming functions are the same as those for variables. Add a pair of parentheses and curly braces. Your statement may look something like this:

```
function doExplosion() { }
```

Add actions within the curly braces. Then, when you need the function, call it by name, like this: **doExplosion()**.

The following task builds a function that loads a new Web site. Doing so requires that you do two things: create an object that holds the Web-site address, called a **URLRequest** object, and then call the **navigateToURL()** method. Consolidating these statements into a single function helps organize your code. You'll learn more communicating with the Web in Chapter 6, "Managing External Communication," so for now focus on how the function works.

```
1    function loadwebsite() {
2        var mywebsite:URLRequest = new URLRequest();
3        mywebsite.url="http://www.adobe.com";
4        navigateToURL(mywebsite);
5    }
6    loadwebsite();
```

A When the function **loadwebsite()** is called, all the statements between the function's curly braces are executed, and the Adobe Web site opens in a browser (bottom).

To build and call a function:

1. Select the first keyframe of the main Timeline and open the Actions panel.

2. Enter the following code:

   function loadwebsite(){ }

   The function called **loadwebsite** is created. Statements within the curly braces will be executed when the function is called.

3. Create a blank line between the curly braces and enter the following code:

   var mywebsite:URLRequest =
   → new URLRequest();
   mywebsite.url =
   → "http://www.adobe.com";
   navigateToURL(mywebsite);

   The first line within the function creates a new object from the **URLRequest** class. The second line assigns a Web address to its **url** property, and the last line loads the site.

4. On a new line outside the function, call the function by entering the following:

   loadwebsite();

   Test your movie by choosing Control > Test Movie > in Flash Professional **A**. As soon as your movie plays, a browser automatically opens and loads the specified Web site.

Accepting parameters

When you define a function, you can tell it to perform a certain task based on parameters that you provide, or *pass*, to the function at the time you call on it. This approach makes functions much more flexible because the work they do is tailored to particular contexts. For example, in the previous task, your function only loads the Adobe Web site. But by enabling your function to accept a parameter, you can have your function load any Web address.

To build a function that accepts parameters:

1. Continuing with the file you used in the preceding task, select the first keyframe and open the Actions panel.

2. With your pointer between the parentheses of the function statement, enter:

   whatsite:String

   The variable **whatsite** is the parameter, and it is strictly typed to hold a string value.

3. Change the second line of the function body so that it reads:

   mywebsite.url = whatsite;

   The parameter is used in one or more of the function statements.

4. Change the call to the function with this:

   loadwebsite(
   →"http://www.peachpit.com");

5. Test your movie by choosing Control > Test Movie > in Flash Professional 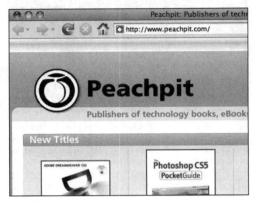.

   The value that you provide in the initial call (**"http://www.peachpit.com"**) is passed to the function. The function uses that parameter to customize its set of actions. You can call the function many times with different parameters.

Parameter   *Data type of parameter*

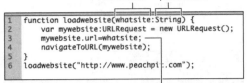

```
1  function loadwebsite(whatsite:String) {
2      var mywebsite:URLRequest = new URLRequest();
3      mywebsite.url=whatsite;
4      navigateToURL(mywebsite);
5  }
6  loadwebsite("http://www.peachpit.com");
```

Parameter used to customize the URL

B This function requires a parameter, which is used to customize the Web site that opens (below).

TIP When you define a function's parameters, they should also be strictly typed. So after the parameter name, be sure to include a colon and the parameter's data type.

Scope

Variables that are created inside a function only exist within that function. This is the consequence of a variable's *scope*. Scope refers to the area of code where your variable "belongs" (you can think of it as its home) and where you can access its contents. If you declare a variable outside a function, it is a *global* variable, which is accessible from all parts of the code. If you declare a variable inside a function, it is a *local* variable, which is only accessible from within that function.

For example, in the example presented in the tasks in this section, the variable **mywebsite** only exists within the function called **loadwebsite**, and cannot be referenced outside the function.

Returning a value

When you pass parameters to a function, you often want to know the results of a particular calculation. To make your function report a resulting calculation, use the **return** statement. The **return** statement, which you use within your function's body (between the curly braces), indicates that the value of an expression should be passed back when the function is called.

In the following task, you'll build a simple function that adds two numbers together and returns the result.

To build a function that returns a value:

1. Select the first keyframe of the main Timeline and open the Actions panel.

2. Enter the word **function**, then a space, and then enter a name for your function followed by open and closed parentheses.

3. Between the parentheses of the function, enter the following parameters:

   `a:Number, b:Number`

4. After the parentheses, add a colon, and then the data type **Number**.

5. Add an open and closed curly brace.

6. Between the curly braces for the function, enter the word **return**, followed by an expression to add the two parameters. The full function code should look like this:

   ```
   function simpleAdd(a:Number,
   → b:Number):Number {
   return (a + b);
   }
   ```

Continues on next page

7. On a new line outside the function, call the function inside a **trace()** action like so: **trace(simpleAdd(3, 5));**

8. Test your movie by choosing Control > Test Movie > in Flash Professional .

The two values (3 and 5) pass to the function, where they're processed. The function returns a value back to where it was called. The returned value is displayed in the Output panel. Use the **return** statement whenever you need to receive a value from a function.

> **TIP** The returned value of a function should also be strictly typed. After the closing parenthesis of the function, enter a colon and then the data type of the returned value. If the function doesn't return a value, you should use the keyword **void**.

```
1   function simpleAdd(a:Number, b:Number):Number {
2       return (a + b);
3   }
4   trace(simpleAdd(3, 5));
```

OUTPUT

8

 This function requires two parameters and returns a number. The **trace()** statement displays the returned value in the Output panel when you test the movie (below).

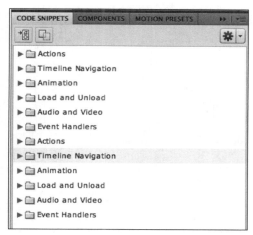

A The Code Snippets panel organizes common interactivity in folders.

Using Code Snippets

Understanding the structure of ActionScript and writing code yourself is essential for your future success in Flash, especially for more sophisticated projects. However, if you don't want to write code, or you just need to quickly add some interactivity without learning too much about what's behind the code, the new Code Snippets panel can help. The Code Snippets panel provides ActionScript code for common interactive functions. For example, if you want to make an object "drag-and-droppable," you can add the interactivity from the Code Snippets panel with just a few clicks.

The code snippets are saved in an external XML document, which makes it easy to edit, save your own version, or import one from another developer.

To add interactivity from the Code Snippets panel:

1. Open the Code Snippets panel (Window > Code Snippets, or click the Code Snippets button in the Actions panel).

   The Code Snippets panel organizes the snippets in different folders, according to their function **A**. Click the triangles in front of the folders to expand or collapse them.

   Continues on next page

2. Select a code snippet and double-click it.

or

Select a code snippet and then click on the "Add to current frame" button.

or

Right-click (Windows) or Ctrl-click (Mac) on a code snippet and choose "Add to frame."

Flash automatically adds ActionScript to a layer named Actions in the currently selected keyframe, and then opens the Actions panel. If the code references an object or instance, Flash will warn you and ask that you select one on the Stage. Flash will automatically convert selections to movie clip symbols and give them instance names, if necessary **B**.

3. View the ActionScript code in the Actions panel.

The code is heavily commented (see the next section to learn about comments) to explain what the code does and how you can customize it to fit your situation. You may have to change a few parameters to make it work in your project **C**.

B Some actions like the one selected here, Drag and Drop, requires a selected object, and Flash provides a warning.

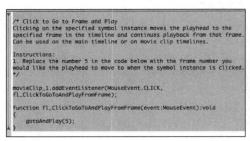

C The ActionScript code that is automatically inserted in the Actions panel provides instructions on how to customize it. In this example, the number 5 is a placeholder that should be replaced.

D Choose Create New Code Snippet to save your own code snippet.

E A simple code snippet that simply traces the words "hello friend."

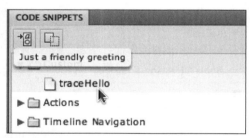

F Your custom code snippet appears in the Code Snippets panel.

G Choose Delete Code Snippet to delete a code snippet.

To save code in the Code Snippets panel:

1. In the Code Snippets panel, from the Options menu choose Create New Code Snippet **D**.

   The Create New Code Snippet dialog box opens **E**.

2. Enter a name in the Title field, a description in the Tooltip field, and your ActionScript code in the Code field. Click Autofill if you've already selected the desired code in the Actions panel.

3. Select the option "Automatically replace instance_name_here when applying code snippet" if you want Flash to replace **instance_name_here** in the code with the actual selected instance on the Stage. Click OK.

   The title appears in the Code Snippet panel under a Custom folder, and the tooltip appears when you move your mouse over the title **F**.

To delete a code snippet:

- Select a code snippet and, from the Options menu, choose Delete Code Snippet **G**.

   or

   Right-click (Windows) or Ctrl-click (Mac) a code snippet and choose Delete Code Snippet.

   The selected snippet is deleted from the Code Snippets panel.

To edit a code snippet:

1. In the Code Snippets panel, from the Options menu choose Edit Code Snippets XML.

   An XML file opens that contains all the code for each code snippet entry .

2. Edit the ActionScript code or the desired XML code and choose File > Save when you're done.

3. In the Code Snippets panel, from the Options menu choose Refresh ❶.

   Flash updates the Code Snippets panel to reflect the edits you made to the XML file.

To revert to the default Code Snippets panel:

In the Code Snippets panel, from the Options menu choose Reset to Default XML.

To export the code snippets:

1. In the Code Snippets panel, from the Options menu choose Export Code Snippets XML.

2. In the dialog box that appears, choose a filename with an .xml extension and save it in a location of your choosing.

   The XML file that is saved contains the contents of your Code Snippets panel; you can share these contents with other Flash developers.

To import code snippets:

1. In the Code Snippets panel, from the Options menu choose Import Code Snippets XML.

2. In the dialog box that appears, choose your XML file containing your desired code snippets and click Open.

```
CodeSnippets.xml
1   <?xml version="1.0" encoding="UTF-8"?>
2   <CodeSnippets>
3   <!--
4   This file determines which code snippets appear in the
5
6   isBranch attribute - Set to "false" for snippets.
7   title - The name of the snippet to display in the Code
8   description - The description of the snippet to display
9   requiresSymbol - Set to true if snippet requires an obj
10  code - The code to insert.  Actual code should be place
11  minPlayerVersion - Require FLA file to meet a minimum P
12  maxPlayerVersion - Require FLA file to be less than or
13  minASVersion - Require FLA file to meet a minimum Actio
14  maxASVersion - Require FLA file to be less than or equa
15
16  To create your own code snippets copy the following emp
17
18      <snippet isBranch="false">
19          <title>Custom Snippet</title>
20          <description>This is an example of a custom code
21          <requiresSymbol>true</requiresSymbol>
22          <code><![CDATA[
23  // Code goes here
24  trace("A custom code snippet");
25          ]]></code>
26      </snippet>
27  -->
28  <snippets>
```

❶ Code snippets are saved as an external XML file, which you can easily edit and share with others. It may look complicated, but the XML structure is logical and straightforward. Edit the contents between the opening (**<code>**) and closing (**</code>**) XML tags.

Create New Code Snippet

Edit Code Snippets XML

Delete Code Snippet

Refresh

Reset to Default XML

Show All Warning Dialogs

❶ Make sure you choose Refresh from the Code Snippets Options menu so your edits show up in the Code Snippets panel.

```
//
// building a function example
// create a function that takes one parameter, a string
//
function loadwebsite(whatsite:String) {
    var mywebsite:URLRequest = new URLRequest();
    mywebsite.url=whatsite; // the parameter is used as the url
    navigateToURL(mywebsite);
}
//
// call the function and pass a web address to the function
//
loadwebsite("http://www.peachpit.com");
```

Ⓐ Comments interspersed with ActionScript statements help make sense of the code.

Line comment button

Ⓑ The Line comment button lets you insert comments on a single line.

Using Comments

After you've built a strong vocabulary of Flash actions and are constructing complex statements in the Actions panel, you should include remarks in your scripts to remind you and your collaborators of the goals of the ActionScript. Comments help you keep things straight as you develop intricate interactivity and relationships among objects Ⓐ.

To create a line comment:

Click the Line comment button at the top of the Script pane, and then enter your comments Ⓑ.

or

In the Script pane, manually type two slashes (**//**) followed by your comments.

Comments appear in a different color than the rest of the script, making them easy to locate.

To create a block comment:

Click the Block comment button at the top of the Script pane, and then enter your comments between the /* and the */ **C**.

Block comments can span multiple lines as long as they lie between the slash-asterisk and the asterisk-slash.

or

In the Script pane, manually type a slash and an asterisk (**/***) followed by your comments. Close your comment with an asterisk and slash (***/**).

TIP Don't worry about creating too many comments. Comments aren't included when you publish your final project, so they won't bog down performance. Also, because they aren't included in the exported SWF file, they don't increase the final file size.

TIP The slash convention for creating comments in ActionScript is the same for creating them in keyframes. When you choose Comment in the Label type pull-down menu in the Properties inspector, the name in the <Frame Label> field automatically begins with two slashes (**//**). You can also enter two slashes manually to begin a frame comment **D**.

Block comment button

C The Block comment button lets you insert multiline comments.

D In the Properties inspector, double slashes indicate a comment in a frame label.

Advanced Buttons
and Event Handling

Creating graphics and animation in Flash is only half the story. The other half is interactivity, which involves giving the viewer control of those graphics and animation. What makes a movie interactive? It's the back-and-forth communication between the user and the movie. Mouse movements, button clicks, or keypresses are examples of things that happen, called events. Events form the basis of interactivity. There are many kinds of events—some are user driven whereas others are not. You'll learn to make Flash listen for and respond to these events (*event handling*).

This chapter first introduces events, listeners, and functions used to respond to events. Next, it explores the simplest class for creating interactivity: the `SimpleButton` class. You'll learn about invisible buttons, animated buttons, and more complex buttons. You'll also learn about the classes and events that are involved in keyboard input and the context menu. Additionally, you'll learn an important event known as the `ENTER_FRAME` event, which you'll rely on to create continuously running actions. Understanding these classes and event

handling is essential to creating Flash interactivity because these elements are the scaffold on which you'll hang virtually all your ActionScript.

Listening for Events

Events are things that happen that Flash can recognize and respond to. A mouse click is an event, as are mouse movements and keypresses. Events can also be things that the user doesn't initiate. The completion of a sound, for example, is an event. Anytime an event happens, an object of the **Event** class is created. When the mouse button is clicked, a **MouseEvent** object (a subclass of the **Event** class) is created. When a key on the keyboard is pressed, a **KeyboardEvent** object (another subclass of the **Event** class) is created. It may seem a little strange that an object represents an event, but remember Flash objects can be very abstract!

With all these events happening, you need a way to detect and respond to them. You detect an event by creating an event handler. An event handler simply tells Flash what to do when a specific kind of event happens. Creating an event handler is a two-part operation: first, you add, or "register," a listener to detect the event and trigger a function, and second, you create the function that tells Flash how to respond. (It doesn't matter if you register the listener first or create the function first. As long as they are both in the same block of code, the event handler will work.)

For example, if you want to listen for a mouse click on top of a particular button, you add an event listener to that object as follows:

```
myButton_btn.addEventListener(
→ MouseEvent.CLICK, reportClick);
```

The **addEventListener()** method takes two parameters. The first is the specific kind of event that you want to detect. All the event objects have properties (like **MouseEvent.CLICK**), which give more specificity to the event. The second parameter is the name of your function, which is triggered when the event is detected.

Next, add a function as the response to the event. Create the function with a parameter strictly typed to the **MouseEvent** object, like so:

```
function reportClick(
→ myevent:MouseEvent):void {
    // do something in response
}
```

Between the curly braces of the function, you add actions as the response. The word **myevent** in this example is the parameter name that you make up that refers to the event.

The actual object that receives the event (in this example, it is the button called **myButton_btn**) can be referenced in the function by using the property **target**. In the preceding example, the expression **myevent.target** references **myButton_btn**.

When you no longer need to listen for an event, you can delete the listener with the method **removeEventListener()**. The method takes two parameters, which are identical to the ones in the **addEventListener()** method.

Event Flow

Event handling is a little more involved than what is described here. When an event occurs and an **Event** object is created, the **Event** object systematically moves through other objects on the Flash Stage in a process known as the event flow. There are three parts to the event flow: a capture phase, a target phase, and a bubbling phase. Imagine that a mouse click happens on a button that is inside a movie clip on the Stage **A**. The **MouseEvent** object is created, is dispatched from the Stage, and flows down to the movie clip and to the button inside the movie clip. That downward flow through those objects is the capture phase. The target phase involves the time the **MouseEvent** object is at the target (the button). Then the **MouseEvent** object proceeds to bubble, or flow, up the hierarchy to the main Stage **B**. This round-trip flow is important because it lets you put a listener at any point along its path and still detect the event. In other words, the listener doesn't have to be tied to the object where the event occurs.

However, many events don't proceed through all three phases of the event flow. Some events, such as the **Event.ENTER_FRAME** object, are dispatched directly to the target object and don't participate in a capture or bubbling phase. Consult the Adobe ActionScript 3.0 Language Reference to learn more about each particular kind of event.

A Events traverse the display list, which are the objects on the Stage. This example shows the main Stage with a movie clip on it. Inside the movie clip is a button, where a mouse click occurs.

B When a mouse click occurs on a target (shown here as the button), a **MouseEvent** is dispatched and travels from the Stage down to the event target, and then bubbles upward back to the Stage. Listeners are usually put on the event target, but it is not required. For example, a listener could be put on the movie clip, and it would detect events happening on the movie clip or on objects inside the movie clip.

Mouse Detection

Mouse events such as a button click, double-click, or simply moving the mouse are handled by the **MouseEvent** class. Since the mouse is one of the primary means through which a user interacts with a Flash movie, it's important to understand how to listen and respond to mouse events.

The simplest event is the button click, which happens when the user presses and then releases the mouse button. You can detect and respond to a button click by first attaching a listener to the main Stage (referred to as **stage**) and using the property **MouseEvent.CLICK** as follows:

```
stage.addEventListener(
→ MouseEvent.CLICK, reportClick);
```

Next, create a function with a **MouseEvent** parameter:

```
function reportClick(
→ myevent:MouseEvent):void {
    // do something in response
}
```

If you want to detect a click on a particular object, use the object's name instead of the word **stage**. Flash can listen for a mouse event on any object of the **InteractiveObject** class displayed on the Stage (button, text field, **Loader**, **Sprite**, movie clip, or the Stage).

Table 4.1 details the specific properties that describe the events of the **MouseEvent** object.

TABLE 4.1 MouseEvent Properties

Property	Description
CLICK	Happens when the mouse button is clicked
DOUBLE_CLICK	Happens when the mouse button is clicked twice in rapid succession
MOUSE_MOVE	Happens when the mouse pointer moves
MOUSE_DOWN	Happens when the mouse button is pressed
MOUSE_UP	Happens when the mouse button is released
MOUSE_OVER	Happens when the mouse moves from a nontarget area over a target area
MOUSE_OUT	Happens when the mouse moves from a target area out of the target area
MOUSE_WHEEL	Happens when the mouse wheel is rotated

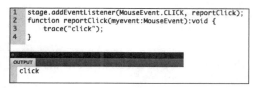

```
1  stage.addEventListener(MouseEvent.CLICK, reportClick);
2  function reportClick(myevent:MouseEvent):void {
3      trace("click");
4  }
```

```
OUTPUT
click
```

A The event handler in the Actions panel (above) makes the Output panel display "click" in the test movie mode whenever the mouse button is clicked (below).

To detect a mouse click on the Stage:

1. Select the first frame of the main Time-line, and open the Actions panel.

2. Assign a listener to the main Stage with the following code:

   ```
   stage.addEventListener(
   → MouseEvent.CLICK, reportClick);
   ```

   When the **MouseEvent.CLICK** event is detected on the main Stage, the function called **reportClick** is triggered.

3. On the next available line, enter the following function:

   ```
   function reportClick(
   → myevent:MouseEvent):void {
       // do something in response
   }
   ```

   Between the curly braces, enter actions as a response.

4. Choose Control > Test Movie > in Flash Professional.

   Whenever you click the mouse button, Flash performs the actions listed within the **reportClick** function **A**. The function name **reportClick** and Event name **myevent** are names that you make up yourself, as long as they follow the standard naming rules laid out in Chapter 3, "Managing External Communication."

   TIP The MouseEvent.DOUBLE_CLICK requires an additional bit of code to work properly. The property doubleClickEnabled for the button instance must be set to true for double-click events to be captured.

   TIP The MouseEvents have shortcuts that you can use instead of entering the full MouseEvent class name and particular event. For example, instead of MouseEvent.CLICK, you can use "click", and instead of MouseEvent.MOUSE_UP, you can use "mouseUp". Check the Flash Help Action-Script Language Reference for the full list of shortcuts.

To detect a mouse movement on the Stage:

1. Select the first frame of the main Time-line, and open the Actions panel.

2. Assign a listener to the main Stage with the following code:

```
stage.addEventListener(
→ MouseEvent.MOUSE_MOVE,
→ reportMove);
```

When the **MouseEvent.MOUSE_MOVE** event is detected on the main Stage, the function called **reportMove** is called.

3. On the next available line, enter the fol-lowing function:

```
function reportMove(
→ myevent:MouseEvent):void {
    // do something in response
}
```

Between the curly braces, enter actions as a response.

4. Choose Control > Test Movie > in Flash Professional.

Whenever you move the mouse, Flash performs the actions listed within the **reportMove** function **B**.

The mouse wheel

The mouse wheel is a third button that is nestled between the left and right mouse buttons and spins forward or backward like a wheel. By listening for the **MouseEvent.MOUSE_WHEEL** event, you can respond to the mouse wheel motion and direction. For example, you can connect the forward or backward motion of the mouse wheel to the up or down scrolling of text or to the selection of items in a pull-down menu.

The **MOUSE_WHEEL** event has the property **delta**, which is a number that indicates how quickly and in what direction the user

```
stage.addEventListener(MouseEvent.MOUSE_MOVE, reportMove);
function reportMove(myevent:MouseEvent):void {

}
```

B The full code that detects whenever the mouse cursor moves over the Stage.

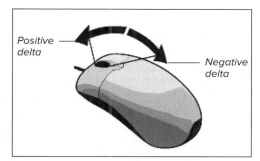

Positive delta

Negative delta

C The mouse wheel returns a positive delta when it rolls forward and a negative delta when it rolls backward.

Movie clip called myRocket_mc

Negative delta subtracts from its x-position

Positive delta adds to its x-position

D The movie clip on the Stage moves to the right if the **delta** property is positive and moves to the left if the **delta** property is negative.

```
stage.addEventListener(MouseEvent.MOUSE_WHEEL, moveRocket);
function moveRocket(myevent:MouseEvent):void{
    myRocket_mc.x+=myevent.delta;
}
```

E The full code for responding to the mouse wheel on the Stage. When the mouse wheel rolls forward, the movie clip moves to the right. When the mouse wheels rolls backward, the movie clip moves to the left.

spins the mouse wheel. A positive (+) delta refers to a forward motion (away from the user) of the mouse wheel **C**. A negative (–) delta refers to a backward motion (toward the user). The values of **delta** typically range from –3 to 3. You can use the **delta** property within the function of your event handler to respond according to the direction of the mouse wheel.

Although you can author the **MOUSE_WHEEL** event handler on either a Macintosh or Windows, the playback functionality is only available on Windows.

To detect mouse wheel motion:

1. Select the first frame of the main Timeline, and open the Actions panel.

2. Add the listener to the stage:

```
stage.addEventListener(
→ MouseEvent.MOUSE_WHEEL,
→ moveRocket);
```

3. On the next available line, create the function that will respond to the **MouseEvent**. Between the curly braces of the function, incorporate the **delta** property of the **MouseEvent** object to reflect the forward or backward roll of the mouse wheel:

```
function moveRocket(
→ myevent:MouseEvent):void {
    myRocket_mc.x += myevent.delta;
}
```

In this event handler, the movement of the mouse wheel adds or subtracts from the horizontal position of the movie clip called **myRocket_mc** **D**.

4. Choose Control > Test Movie > in Flash Professional on a Windows computer.

As you move the mouse wheel backward or forward, the movie clip on the Stage changes its position **E**.

To target an object to respond to mouse wheel motion:

1. Continue with the previous task.

2. Select the first frame of the main Timeline, and open the Actions panel.

3. Change the **addEventListener()** method to target the movie clip **myRocket_mc** instead of the **stage** **F**.

4. Choose Control > Test Movie > in Flash Professional on a Windows computer.

   Now the listener only detects the **MOUSE_WHEEL** event over the movie clip instance. When you move the mouse wheel over the movie clip on the Stage, the movie clip changes its position **G**.

> **TIP** Multiline Classic or TLF text fields (discussed in Chapter 10, "Controlling Text") automatically scroll in response to the mouse wheel. You can, however, disable the mouse wheel with the text field property mouseWheelEnabled. Set the mouseWheelEnabled property of any text field to false like this:
>
> myTF_txt.mouseWheelEnabled = false;
>
> The text field called myTF_txt will no longer respond automatically to the mouse wheel.

```
myRocket_mc.addEventListener(MouseEvent.MOUSE_WHEEL, moveRocket);
function moveRocket(myevent:MouseEvent):void{
    myRocket_mc.x+=myevent.delta;
}
```

F To detect the mouse wheel event just on the target, add the listener to the target instead of the Stage.

G The movie clip called **myRocket_mc** will change its x-position only when the user rolls the mouse wheel when it is over the movie clip.

Ⓐ The four keyframes of a button symbol.

Button instance
on the Stage

Button instance name in
the Properties inspector

Ⓑ The button instance is named **mybutton_btn** in the Properties inspector.

The SimpleButton Class

In the previous section, you were able to listen for a mouse click on the Stage. But more often than not, you'll want to detect a mouse click when it happens on a specific object on the Stage, like a button, movie clip, or a text field. The **SimpleButton** class handles the visual objects that interact with the mouse pointer. Flash lets you define four special keyframes of a button symbol that describe how the button looks and responds to the mouse: the **Up**, **Over**, **Down**, and **Hit** states. The **Up** state shows what the button looks like when the pointer isn't over the button. **Over** shows what the button looks like when the pointer is over the button. **Down** shows what the button looks like when the pointer is over the button with the mouse button pressed. And **Hit** defines the actual active, or *hot*, area of the button Ⓐ.

It's important to realize that events can target many kinds of objects, not just buttons. Buttons just give you a convenient way to create graphics that provide visual feedback when the mouse is interacting with them.

To detect a mouse event on a button:

1. Create a button symbol (Insert > New Symbol), and drag an instance of the newly created button symbol from the Library onto the Stage.

2. Select the button instance, and enter a descriptive name in the Properties inspector. Add the suffix **_btn** to the name. In this example, the button name is **mybutton_btn** Ⓑ.

Continues on next page

This name is the name of your button object; you'll use it to reference the button from ActionScript. This name is *not the same one that appears in your Library.*

3. Select the first frame of the main Time-line, and open the Actions panel.

4. In the first line of the Script pane, assign a listener to your button. The target should be the name of your button, like so:

```
mybutton_btn.addEventListener(
→ MouseEvent.CLICK, reportClick);
```

When the **MouseEvent.CLICK** event happens on the button, the function **reportClick** is called.

5. On the next available line, enter the following function:

```
function reportClick(
→ myevent:MouseEvent):void {
    // do something in response
}
```

The function name **reportClick** and parameter name **myevent** can be any name of your own choosing as long as they conform to the standard naming practice. In between the curly braces, enter actions as a response **G**.

6. Choose Control > Test Movie > in Flash Professional.

Whenever you click the mouse button on the button instance, Flash performs the actions listed within the **reportClick** function **D**.

```
mybutton_btn.addEventListener(MouseEvent.CLICK, reportClick);
function reportClick(myevent:MouseEvent):void {
    stop();
}
```

G The event handler is a function that is tied to an object via the **addEventListener** method. In this example, the movie will stop when the button is clicked.

D When the mouse click occurs over this button, named **mybutton_btn**, the actions in the function are executed.

TIP As described in Chapter 3, "Getting a Handle on ActionScript," it's recommended that you end all instance names for buttons with _btn so that Flash can provide the appropriate code hints in the Script pane. This technique also makes it easier to read your code.

TIP When you create your event handler on the main Timeline, your button must be present on the Stage at the same time so Flash knows what object it references. If you create the event handler in keyframe 1, for example, but your button doesn't appear until keyframe 10, Flash will give you a compile error.

```
mybutton_btn.addEventListener(MouseEvent.MOUSE_OVER, reportClick);
function reportClick(myevent:MouseEvent):void {
    // do something
}
```

E Change the **MouseEvent** properties (highlighted here) to listen for different kinds of mouse events.

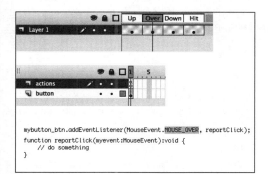

```
mybutton_btn.addEventListener(MouseEvent.MOUSE_OVER, reportClick);
function reportClick(myevent:MouseEvent):void {
    // do something
}
```

F The keyframes of a button symbol (top) provide the visual feedback to mouse interaction, and the ActionScript code on the Timeline (bottom) tells Flash what to do when an event happens.

To select different mouse events:

1. Highlight the existing first parameter of the **addEventListener()** method, and press the Delete key.

2. Type in the name of a different event that should trigger the function (such as **MouseEvent.MOUSE_MOVE**, **MouseEvent.MOUSE_OVER**, and so on) **E**.

TIP You can add more than one listener to the same object. A MouseEvent.MOUSE_DOWN may trigger one event handler, whereas a MouseEvent.MOUSE_UP may trigger another, like so:

```
myobject.addEventListener(
→ MouseEvent.MOUSE_DOWN,
→ downFunction);
myobject.addEventListener(
→ MouseEvent.MOUSE_UP, upFunction);
```

TIP Don't confuse the MouseEvent.MOUSE_OVER event with the Over keyframe of your button symbol. Both involve detecting when the pointer is over the hit area. But the Over state describes how your button appears when the mouse is over the hit area, whereas the MouseEvent.MOUSE_OVER event triggers the function for that event. The keyframes of a button symbol define how it looks, and the event handler defines what it does **F**.

Mouse Events in ActionScript 2

So far, you've seen only one way to manage event handling: by creating a function and using the method **addEventListener()** to detect an event. However, if you're authoring under a previous ActionScript version, you should use the older way of handling mouse clicks. First, in the Properties inspector, name the button or movie clip on the Stage. Then, in the Actions panel, target the button or movie clip and assign a function to the first keyframe on the Timeline, like so:

```
myButton_btn.onRelease=function(){
    // do a response
};
```

There is an even older technique for handling events that involves attaching the event-handler code directly to a button instance by selecting the button before typing in the code. You use a special event-handler syntax, as in the following:

```
on (release) { //do a response }
```

It's best to avoid the third way of handling events because your code becomes scattered among individual buttons on the Stage. As your movie becomes more complex and you have more buttons to deal with, you'll find it difficult to isolate and revise button events. Putting the event handler on the main Timeline is standard practice and the recommended route.

A An invisible button symbol has only its Hit keyframe defined.

Two instances of the same invisible button symbol cover different spots on this map to make those areas interactive.

B Two invisible button instances over a map.

Invisible Buttons

You can exploit the flexibility of Flash button symbols by defining only particular states. If you leave empty keyframes in all states except for the **Hit** state, you create an invisible button **A**. An invisible button is not visible to the audience, yet still maintains a clickable hot spot. Invisible buttons are extremely useful for creating generic hotspots to which you can assign actions. By placing invisible button instances on top of graphics, you essentially have the power to make any area on the Stage react to the mouse pointer. For example, you can place several invisible buttons over a map graphic to create hidden hotspots **B**.

When you drag an instance of an invisible button onto the Stage, you see the hit area as a transparent blue shape, which allows you to place the button precisely. When you choose Control > Enable Simple Buttons (Ctrl-Alt-B for Windows, Cmd-Option-B for Mac), the button disappears to show you its playback appearance.

To create an invisible button:

1. Choose Insert > New Symbol (Ctrl-F8 for Windows, Cmd-F8 for Mac).

   The Create New Symbol dialog box appears.

2. Type the symbol name of your button, choose Button as the Type, and click OK.

   A new button symbol is created in the Library, and you enter symbol-editing mode.

3. Select the **Hit** keyframe.

4. Choose Insert > Timeline > Keyframe (F6).

   A new keyframe is created in the **Hit** state.

Continues on next page

5. With the **Hit** keyframe selected, draw a generic shape that serves as the hotspot for your invisible button 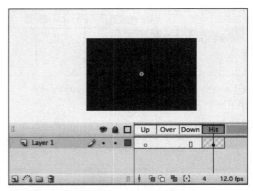.

6. Return to the main Timeline.

7. Drag an instance of the symbol from the Library onto the Stage.

   A transparent blue shape appears on the Stage, indicating the **Hit** state of your invisible button .

8. Move, scale, and rotate the invisible button instance to cover any graphic.

   When you choose Control > Enable Simple Buttons, the transparent blue area disappears, but your pointer changes to a hand to indicate the presence of a button.

9. Give the button instance a name in the Properties inspector and assign an event listener for it in the Actions panel as described in the previous tasks.

C An invisible button symbol. The rectangle in the Hit keyframe defines the active area of the button.

Invisible button instance on the Stage

D An invisible button, when placed from the Library onto the Stage, will display a transparent blue area that is identical to its Hit keyframe.

The butterfly movie clip instance resides in one frame of the main Timeline.

All ten frames of the movie clip symbol still play.

A Movie clips have independent timelines.

Comparing a Movie Clip Instance with a Graphic Instance

How does a movie clip instance differ from a graphic instance? If you create the same animation in both a movie clip symbol and a graphic symbol and then place both instances on the Stage, the differences become clear. The graphic instance shows its animation in the authoring environment, displaying however many frames are available in the main Timeline. If the graphic symbol contains an animation lasting ten frames and the instance occupies four frames of the main Timeline, you see only four frames of the animation. Movie clips, on the other hand, don't work in the Flash authoring environment. You need to export the movie as a SWF file to see any movie clip animation or functionality. When you export the movie (you can do so by choosing Control > Test Movie > in Flash Professional), Flash plays the movie clip instance continuously regardless of the number of frames the instance occupies and even when the movie has stopped.

Animated Buttons and the Movie Clip Symbol

Animated buttons display an animation in any of the first three keyframes (**Up**, **Over**, and **Down**) of the button symbol. A button can spin when the pointer rolls over it, for example, because you have an animation of a spinning graphic in the **Over** state. How do you fit an animation into only one keyframe of the button symbol? Use a movie clip.

A movie clip is a special kind of symbol that allows you to have animations that run regardless of where they are or how many actual frames the instance occupies. This feature is possible because a movie clip's Timeline runs independently of any other Timeline, including other movie clip Timelines and the main movie Timeline in which the movie clip resides. This independence means that as long as you establish an instance on the Stage, a movie clip animation plays all its frames regardless of where it is. Placing a movie clip instance in a single keyframe of a button symbol makes the movie clip play whenever that particular keyframe is displayed. That is the basis of an animated button.

An animation of a butterfly flapping its wings, for example, may take ten frames in a movie clip symbol. Placing an instance of that movie clip on the Stage in a movie that has only one frame still lets you see the butterfly flapping its wings **A**. This functionality is useful for cyclical animations that play no matter what else may be going on in the current timeline. Blinking eyes, for example, can be a movie clip placed on a character's face. No matter what the character does—whether it's moving or static in the current timeline—the eyes blink continuously.

To create a movie clip:

1. Choose Insert > New Symbol.

   The Create New Symbol dialog box appears.

2. Type a descriptive name for your movie clip symbol, choose Movie Clip as the Type, and click OK **B**.

   You now enter symbol-editing mode.

3. Create the graphics and animation on the movie clip timeline **C**.

   Notice how the navigation bar above the Timeline tells you that you're currently editing a symbol.

4. Return to the main Stage.

   Your movie clip is stored in the Library as a symbol, available for you to bring onto the Stage as an instance **D**.

TIP New instances of movie clips begin playing automatically from the first frame.

B Create a new movie clip symbol by naming it and selecting the Movie Clip Type.

C The `pondRipple` movie clip symbol contains two shape tweens of an oval getting bigger and gradually fading.

Movie clip instance (on Stage)   Movie clip symbol (in Library)

D Bring an instance of a movie clip symbol onto the Stage by dragging it from the Library.

E A simple button symbol with ovals in all four keyframes.

F The Over state of the button symbol. Place an instance of the `pondRipple` movie clip in this keyframe to play the pond-ripple animation whenever the pointer moves over the button.

G The completed animated button. When the pointer passes over the button, the `pondRipple` movie clip plays.

H A new layer in the button symbol timeline helps organize the animation.

To create an animated button:

1. Create a movie clip symbol that contains an animation, as described in the preceding task.

2. Create a button symbol, and define the four keyframes for the **Up**, **Over**, **Down**, and **Hit** states **E**.

3. In symbol-editing mode, select either the **Up**, **Over**, or **Down** state for your button, depending on when you would like to see the animation.

4. Drag your movie clip symbol from the Library to the Stage **F**.

   The movie clip instance is inside the button symbol.

5. Return to the main movie Timeline, and drag an instance of your button symbol to the Stage.

6. Choose Control > Test Movie > in Flash Professional.

   Your button instance plays the movie clip animation continuously as your pointer interacts with the button **G**.

TIP Stop the continuous cycling of your movie clip by placing a `stop()` action in the last keyframe of your movie clip symbol. Because movie clips have independent timelines, they respond to frame actions. Graphic symbols don't respond to any frame actions.

TIP To better organize animated buttons, it's useful to create a new layer in the timeline of your button symbol and reserve it specifically for the animation **H**.

Complex Buttons

You can use a combination of invisible buttons, animated buttons, and movie clips to create objects with complex behaviors such as pull-down menus. The pull-down (or pop-up) menu is a kind of button that is common in operating systems and Web interfaces, and is useful for presenting several choices under a single heading. The functionality consists of a single button that expands to show more buttons and collapses when a selection has been made .

To build your own pull-down menu, one effective strategy is to nest symbols inside each other. A simple way is to place buttons inside a movie clip. The buttons specify which frames within the movie clip timeline to play. Whether the menu is expanded or collapsed is determined within the movie clip. Placing an instance of this movie clip on the Stage allows you to access either the expanded or collapsed state independently of what's happening in your main movie.

To create a simple pull-down menu:

1. Create a button symbol that will be used for the top menu button as well as the choices in the expanded list.

2. Add a filled rectangle to the **Up**, **Over**, **Down**, and **Hit** keyframes .

3. Create a new movie clip symbol.

   Enter symbol-editing mode for the movie clip.

4. Insert a new keyframe at a later point in the movie clip Timeline.

   You now have two keyframes inside your movie clip symbol. The first one will contain the collapsed state of your menu, and the second one will contain its expanded state .

A Typical pull-down menus: a Mac OS system menu (left) and a Web menu (right). You can build similar menus in Flash with movie clips.

B A generic button with the four keyframes defined.

C The pull-down menu movie clip timeline contains two keyframes: one at frame 1 and another at frame 9.

D The two states of your pull-down menu. The collapsed state is in the first keyframe (top); the expanded state is in the second keyframe (bottom). The expanded state contains the initial button plus four button instances that represent the menu choices.

5. Drag one instance of your button symbol into the first keyframe, and add text over the instance to describe the button.

   This is the collapsed state of your menu.

6. Drag several instances of your button symbol into the second keyframe, align them with one another, and add text over these instances to describe the buttons.

   This is the expanded state of your menu.

7. Add a new layer, and place frame labels to mark the collapsed and expanded keyframes **D**.

   In the Frame Label field of the Properties inspector, enter **collapsed** for the first keyframe and **expanded** for the second keyframe.

   The frame labels let you see clearly the collapsed and expanded states of your movie clip, and let you use the **gotoAndStop()** action with frame labels instead of frame numbers.

8. Select the button instance in the first keyframe, and give it an instance name.

9. Add a new layer; select the first keyframe in that layer, and open the Actions panel.

10. In the first line of the Script pane, add the action **stop()**.

    Without this **stop()** in the first frame of your movie clip, the menu would open and close repeatedly because of the automatic cycling of movie clips. The **stop()** action ensures that the movie clip stays on frame 1 until you click the menu button **E**.

    Continues on next page

11. On the next line of the Script pane, add an event listener for the button that is on the first keyframe of your movie clip:

```
pick_btn.addEventListener(
→ MouseEvent.CLICK, expandmenu);
```

This listener listens for a mouse click on the button called `pick_btn` **F**.

12. On the next available line of the Script pane, add a function that goes to the expanded keyframe of the movie clip, like so:

```
function expandmenu(
→ myevent:MouseEvent):void {
   this.gotoAndStop("expanded");
}
```

When this function is called, the current timeline is targeted (with the keyword **this**) and the playhead goes to the frame labeled **expanded**. Make sure that the frame label is within quotation marks.

13. Select the first button instance on the last keyframe, and give it an instance name.

14. In the layer with your ActionScript, select the frame above the **expanded** keyframe, and add a new keyframe.

In this keyframe, you'll add the code for the buttons in the expanded menu.

You have to put more code here because you can't add event-handler code to buttons until they're present on the Stage. Otherwise, Flash won't find the button instances and can't reference them from the code **G**.

15. With your new keyframe selected, open the Actions panel and add an event listener for the first button in the **expanded** keyframe:

```
pick2_btn.addEventListener(
→ MouseEvent.CLICK, collapsemenu);
```

This listener listens for a mouse click on the button called `pick2_btn`.

stop() action

E The movie clip timeline for the pull-down menu. A **stop()** action is assigned to the first frame in the top layer.

New keyframe with actions for buttons that show up here

G When buttons appear on a later frame (frame number 9), add a new keyframe at the same frame number with event-handler code for those buttons.

```
pick2_btn.addEventListener(MouseEvent.CLICK, collapsemenu);
apple_btn.addEventListener(MouseEvent.CLICK, collapsemenu);
banana_btn.addEventListener(MouseEvent.CLICK, collapsemenu);
blueberry_btn.addEventListener(MouseEvent.CLICK, collapsemenu);
orange_btn.addEventListener(MouseEvent.CLICK, collapsemenu);
function collapsemenu(myevent:MouseEvent):void{
    gotoAndStop("collapsed");
}
```

H The ActionScript for the buttons in the expanded keyframe sends the Flash playhead to the frame labeled collapsed and stops there.

Movie clip in collapsed keyframe   Movie clip in expanded keyframe

I The two states of the pull-down menu work independently of the main Timeline.

TIP Use edit commands such as Copy and Paste to create similar blocks of code such as event handlers for several buttons. Once you paste in a copy of the code, don't forget to change the name of the targets and functions to which the event handler is assigned.

TIP When you understand the concept behind the simple pull-down menu, you can create menus that are more sophisticated by adding animation to the transition between the collapsed state and the expanded state. Instead of having the expanded state suddenly pop up, for example, you can create a tween that makes the buttons scroll down gently. Change the body of the function on the first keyframe of your movie clip to `gotoAndPlay()` instead of `gotoAndStop()` to see the tweens.

16. Next, add a function that goes back to the **collapsed** keyframe, like so:

```
function collapsemenu(
→ myevent:Mouse Event):void {
    this.gotoAndStop("collapsed");
}
```

17. Assign instance names to each of the remaining button instances on this keyframe, and repeat step 15 to add event-handler code for each of them **H**.

18. Return to the main movie Timeline, and place an instance of your movie clip on the Stage.

19. Choose Control > Test Movie > in Flash Professional to see how your pull-down menu works.

When you click the first button, the buttons for your choices appear because you direct the playhead to go to the **expanded** keyframe on the movie clip timeline. When you click one of the buttons in the expanded state, the buttons disappear, returning you to the **collapsed** keyframe of the movie clip timeline. All this happens independently of the main movie Timeline, where the movie clip instance resides **I**.

At this point, you've created a complex button that behaves like a pull-down menu but doesn't actually do anything (except modify itself). In Chapter 5, "Controlling Multiple Timelines," you'll learn how to make timelines communicate with one another, which enables you to create complex navigation systems.

Button-tracking Options

You can define a button instance in the Properties inspector in one of two ways: Track as Button or Track as Menu Item . These two tracking options determine whether button instances can receive a button event even after the event has started on a different button instance. The Track as Menu Item option allows this to happen; the Track as Button option doesn't. The default option, Track as Button, is the typical behavior for buttons; it causes one button event to affect one button instance. More complex cases, such as pull-down menus, require multiple button instances working together.

Imagine that you click and hold down the menu button to see the pop-up choices, drag your pointer to your selection, and then release the mouse button. You need Flash to recognize the `MouseEvent.MOUSE_UP` event in the expanded menu even though the `MouseEvent.MOUSE_DOWN` event occurred in the collapsed menu for a different button instance (in fact, in a different frame altogether). Choosing Track as Menu Item allows these buttons to receive these events and gives you more flexibility to work with combinations of buttons and events.

(A) The button-tracking options in the Properties inspector.

```
stop();
pick_btn.addEventListener(MouseEvent.MOUSE_DOWN, expandmenu);
function expandmenu(myevent:MouseEvent):void {
    gotoAndStop("expanded");
}
```

B The collapsed-menu button listens for the
MOUSE_DOWN event.

```
pick_btn2.addEventListener(MouseEvent.MOUSE_UP, collapsemenu);
apple_btn.addEventListener(MouseEvent.MOUSE_UP, collapsemenu);
banana_btn.addEventListener(MouseEvent.MOUSE_UP, collapsemenu);
blueberry_btn.addEventListener(MouseEvent.MOUSE_UP, collapsemenu);
orange_btn.addEventListener(MouseEvent.MOUSE_UP, collapsemenu);
function collapsemenu(myevent:MouseEvent):void{
    gotoAndStop("collapsed");
}
```

C The expanded-menu buttons listen for the
MOUSE_UP event.

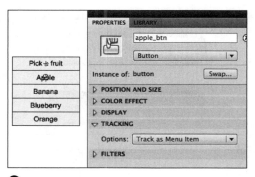

D You need to change the setting to Track
as Menu Item for each button instance in the
expanded section of the Timeline.

To set Track as Menu Item
for a pull-down menu:

1. Continue with the pull-down menu, as
   described in the preceding task.

2. Go to symbol-editing mode for the
   movie clip.

3. Select the keyframe on frame 1 containing the event handler for the button
   instance, and change the mouse event
   to **MouseEvent.MOUSE_DOWN** **B**.

4. Select the keyframe containing the
   ActionScript for the expanded section. Replace all the **MouseEvent.CLICK**
   events with **MouseEvent.MOUSE_UP** **C**.

5. Select each button instance in the
   expanded keyframe.

6. In the Properties inspector, choose
   Track as Menu Item **D**.

   The button instances in the
   expanded menu will now trigger a
   MouseEvent.MOUSE_UP event even
   if the **MouseEvent.MOUSE_DOWN** event
   occurs on a different instance.

7. Return to the main Timeline, and test
   your movie.

   You now click and hold down the
   mouse button to keep the menu open,
   and then release the mouse button
   when you've made your selection.

   TIP When you set Track as Menu Item for
   this pull-down menu, the expanded button
   instances display their Down state as you
   move your pointer over them. This display
   occurs because your mouse button is, in fact,
   pressed, but that event occurred earlier on a
   different instance.

Changing Button Behavior

Because the buttons you create are objects of the **SimpleButton** class and objects of the larger class **InteractiveObject**, you can control their properties by using dot syntax. Many button properties control the way a button looks (such as its width, height, and rotation) as well as the way the button behaves (such as its button tracking). In Chapter 7, "Controlling and Displaying Graphics," you will explore the ways to manipulate graphics, including buttons. Here, you will learn to change properties that affect a button's behavior.

To disable a button:

Set the **mouseEnabled** property to false.

If you name your button instance **mybutton_btn**, enter the following statement:

```
mybutton_btn.mouseEnabled = false;
```

Your button will no longer interact with the mouse pointer and will no longer display its **Over** or **Down** keyframes. In addition, mouse events won't be captured on this button.

To remove an event listener:

Use the **removeEventListener()** method with its two parameters set identical to the ones used in the **addEventListener()** method.

If you name your button instance **mybutton_btn**, enter the following statement:

```
mybutton_btn.removeEventListener(
→ MouseEvent.CLICK, myfunction);
```

Although your button will still interact with the mouse pointer, the listener will no longer detect a mouse click and call on the function called **myfunction**.

To disable the hand pointer:

Set the **useHandCursor** property to false .

If you name your button instance **mybutton_btn**, enter the following statement:

```
mybutton_btn.useHandCursor =
→ false;
```

A When the normal hand pointer (above) is disabled, only the arrow pointer will show up (below).

Button instance   Yellow rectangular border

B When you use the Tab key, buttons show their focus with a yellow rectangular border in their Over state.

1   2   3
4
5
6

C The automatic order of button focusing with the Tab key is by position. The numbers show the order in which the buttons will receive focus.

TIP Some browsers intercept keypresses, so you may have to click the Flash movie in your browser window before you can use the Tab key to focus on buttons.

Changing button focus with the Tab key

The button focus is a way of selecting a button with the Tab key. When a Flash movie plays within a browser, you can press the Tab key and navigate between buttons, text fields, and movie clips. The currently focused button displays its **Over** state with a yellow rectangular border **B**. Pressing the Enter key (or Return key on the Mac) is equivalent to clicking the focused button. Several properties of the `InteractiveObject` class (of which the `SimpleButton` is a subclass)—`focusRect`, `tabEnabled`, and `tabIndex`—deal with controlling the button focus. The property `focusRect` determines whether the yellow rectangular border is visible. If `focusRect` is set to `false`, a focused button displays its **Over** state but doesn't display the yellow rectangular highlight. The property `tabEnabled`, if set to `false`, disables a button's capability to receive focus from the Tab key.

The order in which a button, movie clip, or text field receives its focus is determined by its position on the Stage. Objects focus from left to right and then from top to bottom. So, if you have a row of buttons at the top of your movie and a column of buttons on the left side below it, the Tab key will focus each of the buttons in the top row first and then focus on each of the buttons in the column **C**. After the last button receives the focus, the tab order begins again from the top row.

You can set your own tab order with the property `tabIndex`. Assign a number to the `tabIndex` for each button instance, and Flash will organize the tab order using the `tabIndex` in ascending order. Take control of the tab order to create more helpful forms, allowing the user to use the Tab and Enter keys to fill out multiple text fields and click multiple buttons.

To hide the yellow rectangular highlight over focused buttons:

Set the **focusRect** property to **false**.

If you name your button instance **mybutton_btn**, for example, use the statement **mybutton_btn.focusRect = false**;

To disable focusing with the Tab key:

Set the **tabEnabled** property to **false**.

If you name your button instance **mybutton_btn**, for example, use the statement **mybutton_btn.tabEnabled = false**;

To change the tab order of button focus:

1. Give each button instance a name in the Properties inspector.

2. Select the first frame of the main Timeline, and open the Actions panel.

3. In the Script pane, enter your first button's instance name followed by a dot.

4. Type **tabIndex** after the dot.

5. For the value, you must indicate where in the tab order this object should be when the user presses the Tab key. Enter an equals symbol (=) and then a value **D**.

   This button instance will be in the tab order in the specified index.

6. Repeat steps 3–5 for each of your button instances. Continue to assign numbers in sequence to the **tabIndex** property of each button instance **E**.

7. Choose File > Publish Preview > Default to view your movie in a browser.

   Click on the Flash movie in the browser to give it focus. When you press the Tab key, Flash follows the **tabIndex** in ascending order for button focusing **F**.

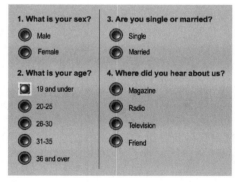

D The button called **male_btn** will receive the first focus with the Tab key.

```
male_btn.tabIndex = 1;
female_btn.tabIndex = 2;
age19_btn.tabIndex = 3;
age20_btn.tabIndex = 4;
age26_btn.tabIndex = 5;
age31_btn.tabIndex = 6;
age36_btn.tabIndex = 7;
single_btn.tabIndex = 8;
married_btn.tabIndex = 9;
magazine_btn.tabIndex = 10;
radio_btn.tabIndex = 11;
television_btn.tabIndex = 12;
friend_btn.tabIndex = 13;
```

E This block of code assigns the **tabIndex** properties for 13 different buttons.

F Control the order of button focusing to provide easier tab navigation through forms and questionnaires. This movie focuses buttons in columns to follow the question numbers rather than relying on Flash's automatic ordering.

Creating Buttons Dynamically

If you want to create a button dynamically—that is, during runtime while your Flash movie is playing—you can do so with the constructor **new SimpleButton()**. Creating buttons on the fly allows you to respond to your user and a changing environment and not rely on buttons that have been created in advance. After creating a new button from the **SimpleButton** class, you define its four keyframes, the **Up**, **Over**, **Down**, and **Hit** states, by assigning other objects to the properties **upState**, **overState**, **downState**, and **hitTestState**.

The **upState**, **overState**, **downState**, and **hitTestState** properties can take any kind of display object such as a loaded JPEG image, a movie clip, text field, or a dynamically drawn shape or sprite. In Chapter 7, "Controlling and Displaying Graphics," you'll learn to create and manage the graphics on the Stage. In this example task, you'll create four shapes dynamically with the **new Shape()** constructor, and then assign those shapes to the keyframes of a newly created button.

To create a button dynamically:

1. Select the first frame of the Timeline, and open the Actions panel.

2. In the Script pane, enter the following code that creates a new **Shape** object and then draws a filled circle:

```
var myup:Shape = new Shape();
myup.graphics.beginFill(0xff4000);
myup.graphics.
drawCircle(100,100,10);
```

Continues on next page

The new **Shape** object called **myup** is created. The **beginFill()** method defines the color of the fill, and the **drawCircle()** method defines its location and size.

3. Create three more new shapes with different colors in the same manner Ⓐ.

   These four shapes will be assigned to the four keyframes of the new button.

4. In the next line, instantiate a new button from the **SimpleButton** class, like so:

   ```
   var mybutton:SimpleButton =
   → new SimpleButton();
   ```

5. Next, assign the four shapes to the properties of your new button as in the following code:

   ```
   mybutton.upState = myup;
   mybutton.overState = myover;
   mybutton.downState = mydown;
   mybutton.hitTestState = myhit;
   ```

6. To see the new button on the Stage, you must add it to the Stage to be displayed with the following code:

   ```
   stage.addChild(mybutton);
   ```

   To see any dynamically generated graphic, you always need to use the method **addChild()**. The full Action-Script code can be seen in Ⓑ.

7. Test your movie by choosing Control > Test Movie > in Flash Professional Ⓒ.

```
var myup:Shape = new Shape();
myup.graphics.beginFill(0xff4000);
myup.graphics.drawCircle(100,100,10);

var mydown:Shape = new Shape();
mydown.graphics.beginFill(0x004000);
mydown.graphics.drawCircle(100,100,10);

var myover:Shape = new Shape();
myover.graphics.beginFill(0xf34283);
myover.graphics.drawCircle(100,100,10);

var myhit:Shape = new Shape();
myhit.graphics.beginFill(0xf34004);
myhit.graphics.drawCircle(100,100,10);
```

Ⓐ Four circles are created dynamically. Each circle is an object of the **Shape** class.

```
var myup:Shape = new Shape();
myup.graphics.beginFill(0xff4000);
myup.graphics.drawCircle(100,100,10);

var mydown:Shape = new Shape();
mydown.graphics.beginFill(0x004000);
mydown.graphics.drawCircle(100,100,10);

var myover:Shape = new Shape();
myover.graphics.beginFill(0xf34283);
myover.graphics.drawCircle(100,100,10);

var myhit:Shape = new Shape();
myhit.graphics.beginFill(0xf34004);
myhit.graphics.drawCircle(100,100,10);

var mybutton:SimpleButton=new SimpleButton();

mybutton.upState = myup;
mybutton.overState = myover;
mybutton.downState = mydown;
mybutton.hitTestState = myhit;

stage.addChild(mybutton);
```

Ⓑ A button is created dynamically, and the four shapes are assigned to the button's **upState**, **overState**, **downState**, and **hitTestState** (highlighted lines).

Ⓒ The circle shape appears on the Stage and behaves as a button.

TABLE 4.2 KeyboardEvent Properties

Property	Description
KEY_UP	Happens when a key is released
KEY_DOWN	Happens when a key is pressed

Keyboard Detection

The keyboard is just as important an interface device as the mouse, and Flash lets you detect events occurring from keystrokes, both the downward keypress and the upward key release. This ability opens the possibility of having navigation based on the keyboard (using the arrow keys or the number keys, for example) or having keyboard shortcuts that duplicate mouse-based navigation schemes. Flash even lets you control live text that the viewer types in empty text fields in a movie; these text fields merit a separate discussion in Chapter 10, "Controlling Text." This section focuses on single or combination keystrokes with modifiers (like the Ctrl or Shift key) that trigger a response.

Just as a **MouseEvent** object is created when the user does something with the mouse, a **KeyboardEvent** object (another subclass of the **Event** class) is created when the keyboard is used.

You can detect and respond to the **KeyboardEvent** object by first attaching a listener to the main Stage (or another object like a text field) using the **addEventListener** method as follows:

```
stage.addEventListener(
↦ KeyboardEvent.KEY_DOWN, detectText);
```

Next, create a function with a **KeyboardEvent** parameter:

```
function detectText(
↦ myevent:KeyboardEvent):void {
    // do something in response
}
```

Table 4.2 details the specific properties that describe the events of the **KeyboardEvent** object.

Key code values

The **KeyboardEvent** object is dispatched whenever any key on the keyboard is pressed. But to determine which particular key has been pressed, you have to use key code values. Key code values are specific numbers associated with each key (see Appendix A, "Keyboard Key Codes"). You use these codes to construct a conditional statement to determine a match. The key code for the spacebar, for example, is 32. So to see if the **KeyboardEvent** object's **key code** matches 32, you write the following:

```
if (myevent.keyCode==32){
    // spacebar was pressed
}
```

In this example, **myevent** is the name of the **KeyboardEvent** object and **keyCode** is a property whose value is the key code of the key that was pressed. This conditional statement checks if the key code of the key that was pressed matches the code for the spacebar.

Fortunately, you don't have to use clumsy numeric key codes all the time. The most common keys are conveniently assigned as properties of another class, the **Keyboard** class. These properties are constants that you can use in place of the key codes. The statement **Keyboard.SPACE**, for example, is the number 32. Appendix A also lists all the matching **Keyboard** constants for the key codes.

Two properties of the **KeyboardEvent** object, **shiftKey** and **ctrlKey**, can be used to test whether the Shift or the Ctrl key is being held down. These properties are either **true** or **false**.

To detect a keypress:

1. Select the first keyframe in the Timeline, and open the Actions panel.

2. In the Script pane, add a listener to the Stage with the **addEventListener** method, as follows:

```
stage.addEventListener(
→ KeyboardEvent.KEY_DOWN,
→ detectText);
```

When this listener detects a keypress, it triggers the function called **detectText**.

3. On the next available line, write a function with the **KeyboardEvent** object as a parameter, like so:

```
function detectText(
→ myevent:Keyboard Event):void {
    myarrow_mc.x += 5;
}
```

Between the curly braces of the function, put actions you want as a response. In this example, any keypress makes a movie clip called **myarrow_mc** move 5 pixels to the right.

4. Choose File > Publish Preview > Default to test your movie **Ⓐ**.

TIP In the Flash testing mode (Control > Test Movie > in Flash Professional), some keypresses may be interpreted as shortcut commands for the Flash tools, so use Choose File > Publish Preview > Default to test in the browser.

```
stage.addEventListener(KeyboardEvent.KEY_DOWN, detectText);
function detectText(myevent:KeyboardEvent):void {
    myarrow_mc.x += 5;
}
```

A When the ActionScript code (below) detects a keypress, it moves the movie clip called **myarrow_mc** (above) to the right.

```
stage.addEventListener(KeyboardEvent.KEY_DOWN, detectText);
function detectText(myevent:KeyboardEvent):void {
    if (myevent.keyCode == Keyboard.RIGHT) {
        myarrow_mc.x += 5;
    }
}
```

B If the right arrow key is pressed, Flash moves the movie clip to the right.

To detect a specific keypress:

1. Continue with the file you created in the previous task.

2. Select the first frame of the Timeline, and open the Actions panel.

3. Select the code in between the curly braces of the function and replace it with a conditional statement like this:

   ```
   if (myevent.keyCode ==
   → Keyboard.RIGHT) {
       myarrow_mc.x += 5;
   }
   ```

   The double equals symbol (==) checks the equivalence of the items on either side. If they are equivalent, the actions within the curly braces of the **if** statement are executed.

4. Choose File > Publish Preview > Default.

   When you press a key, Flash dispatches a **KeyboardEvent** object and calls the function. Within the function, Flash checks to see if the key that was pressed matches the right-arrow key. If so, the actions are carried out. In this example, a movie clip called **myarrow_mc** is moved 5 pixels to the right **B**.

To detect keystroke combinations:

1. Continue with the file you created in the previous task.

2. Select the first frame of the Timeline, and open the Actions panel.

3. Change the code in between the parentheses of the **if** statement so that the statement reads

```
if (myevent.keyCode ==
→ Keyboard.RIGHT &&
→ myevent.shiftKey == true) {
    myarrow_mc.x += 5;
}
```

The logical *and* operator *(&&)* joins two statements so that both must be true for the entire statement to be true.

4. Choose File > Publish Preview > Default.

The **if** statement will perform the action within its curly braces only if both the right-arrow key and the Shift key are pressed at the same time **C**.

TIP **The property ctrlKey maps to the Ctrl key on Windows and the Command (or Apple) key on the Macintosh.**

```
stage.addEventListener(KeyboardEvent.KEY_DOWN, detectText);
function detectText(myevent:KeyboardEvent):void {
    if (myevent.keyCode == Keyboard.RIGHT && myevent.shiftKey == true) {
        myarrow_mc.x += 5;
    }
}
```

C If the right arrow key and the Shift key are both pressed, Flash moves the movie clip to the right. The operator **&&** connects two statements, requiring both to be true.

Keyboard Events in ActionScript 2

If you are authoring for Flash Player 8 and must use ActionScript 2, you need to resort to the older way of handling keyboard input. In the previous version of ActionScript, you also create listeners, but they are constructed from the generic **Object** class. The syntax and methods for detecting a particular keypress look like this:

```
var myListener:Object = new Object();
myListener.onKeyDown = function() {
    if (Key.isDown(Key.SPACE)) {
        //Spacebar pressed
    }
};
Key.addListener(myListener);
```

In this example, the **isDown()** method returns a **true** value if its parameter is the key code of the key that was pressed. So you can enter a key code for its parameter or use a constant (**Key.SPACE**). The last line is needed to register the listener to the **Key** class.

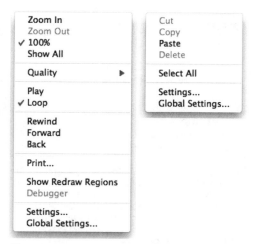

Zoom In		Cut
Zoom Out		Copy
✓ 100%		**Paste**
Show All		Delete
Quality	▶	**Select All**
Play		**Settings...**
✓ Loop		**Global Settings...**
Rewind		
Forward		
Back		
Print...		
Show Redraw Regions		
Debugger		
Settings...		
Global Settings...		

A The standard contextual menu (left), and the edit contextual menu that appears over selectable text fields (right).

TABLE 4.3 builtInItems Properties

Property	Value	Menu Items
forwardAndBack	**true** or **false**	Forward, Back
save	**true** or **false**	Save
zoom	**true** or **false**	Zoom in, Zoom out, 100%, Show all
quality	**true** or **false**	Quality
play	**true** or **false**	Play
loop	**true** or **false**	Loop
rewind	**true** or **false**	Rewind
print	**true** or **false**	Print

The Contextual Menu

In the playback of any Flash movie, a contextual menu appears when you right-click (Windows) or Ctrl-click (Mac) on the movie. There are different types of contextual menus, including a standard menu that appears over any part of the Stage and an edit menu that appears over text fields **A**. You can customize, to a certain extent, the items that appear in the standard and edit menus through the **ContextMenu** class. You can disable certain items or create your own custom items with the related **ContextMenuItem** class. You can even make different contextual menus appear over different objects like buttons, movie clips, or text fields.

Manipulating the contextual menu first requires that you instantiate a new object of the **ContextMenu** class, like so:

```
var myMenu:ContextMenu =
    new ContextMenu();
```

After you have a new **ContextMenu** object, you can call its methods or set its properties to customize the items that appear. All the default menu items are properties of the object **builtInItems**. Setting each property to **true** or **false** enables or disables that particular item in the menu. For example, the following statement disables the print item in the **ContextMenu** object called **myMenu**:

```
myMenu.builtInItems.print = false;
```

See **Table 4.3** for the **builtInItems** properties of the **ContextMenu** class.

Finally, you must associate your **ContextMenu** object with the **contextMenu** property of another object, such as the main Stage, a text field, or a specific movie clip, like so:

```
myObject_mc.contextMenu = myMenu;
```

Continues on next page

If you associate your **ContextMenu** object with a specific button or movie clip, your custom contextual menu will appear when the user activates the contextual menu only while the mouse pointer is over that object. For example, a map can have the Zoom item in its contextual menu enabled, whereas other objects may have the Zoom item in their contextual menu disabled.

To disable the contextual menu:

1. Select the first frame of the main Timeline, and open the Actions panel.

2. On the first line of the Script pane, instantiate a new **ContextMenu** object:

   ```
   var myMenu:ContextMenu =
   → new ContextMenu();
   ```

   A new **ContextMenu** object is named and created.

3. On the next line of the Script pane, call the **hideBuiltInItems()** method of your **ContextMenu** object, like so:

   ```
   myMenu.hideBuiltInItems();
   ```

   This method sets all the properties of the **builtInItems** object of **myMenu** to **false**, which hides the items of the contextual menu.

4. On the third line of the Script pane, assign your **ContextMenu** object to the **contextMenu** property of the Stage as follows:

   ```
   this.contextMenu = myMenu;
   ```

   The **ContextMenu** object now becomes associated with the main Timeline, so the default items of the main Timeline's contextual menu are hidden. The only items that remain are Settings, Show Redraw Regions, and Global Settings **B**.

```
var myMenu:ContextMenu = new ContextMenu();
myMenu.hideBuiltInItems();
this.contextMenu = myMenu;
```

Show Redraw Regions
Debugger

Settings...
Global Settings...

B By using the **hideBuiltInItems()** method, you disable all built-in (default) items of the contextual menu. The final code (top) hides all the default items except for the Settings and Global Settings (bottom). The Show Redraw Regions item appears only in debugger versions of the Flash Player and won't appear for regular users.

To associate custom contextual menus with different objects:

1. Continue with the preceding task. Starting on the next available line in the Script pane, declare another **ContextMenu** object and instantiate the object using the constructor function, **new ContextMenu()**.

   A second **ContextMenu** object is named (in this example, called **myZoomMenu**) and created **C**.

2. Add a call to the **hideBuiltInItems()** method for your new **ContextMenu** instance.

```
var myMenu:ContextMenu = new ContextMenu();
myMenu.hideBuiltInItems();
this.contextMenu = myMenu;

var myZoomMenu:ContextMenu = new ContextMenu();
```

C A new **ContextMenu** object named **myZoomMenu** has been created.

The items of your second **ContextMenu** object, like the first, are disabled.

3. Assign a **true** value to the **zoom** property of the **builtInItems** object of your second **ContextMenu** object, like so:

   myZoomMenu.builtInItems.zoom = → true;

   This enables the Zoom item in your second **ContextMenu** instance.

4. On the next line of the Script pane, assign your second contextual menu to the **contextMenu** property of an object on the Stage, like so:

   map_mc.contextMenu = myZoomMenu;

   In this example, the completed statement associates the second **ContextMenu** object with the movie clip instance called **map_mc D**.

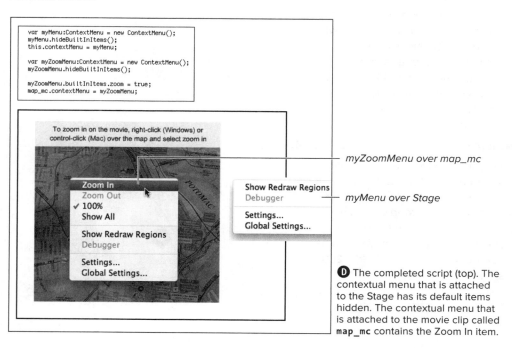

```
var myMenu:ContextMenu = new ContextMenu();
myMenu.hideBuiltInItems();
this.contextMenu = myMenu;

var myZoomMenu:ContextMenu = new ContextMenu();
myZoomMenu.hideBuiltInItems();

myZoomMenu.builtInItems.zoom = true;
map_mc.contextMenu = myZoomMenu;
```

myZoomMenu over map_mc

myMenu over Stage

D The completed script (top). The contextual menu that is attached to the Stage has its default items hidden. The contextual menu that is attached to the movie clip called **map_mc** contains the Zoom In item.

Creating new contextual menu items

You can add your own items in the contextual menu by creating new objects from the **ContextMenuItem** class. Each new item requires that you instantiate a separate **ContextMenuItem** object with a string parameter, as in the following code:

```
var myFirstItem:ContextMenuItem =
→ new ContextMenuItem("First Item");
```

The parameter represents the text that will be displayed for the item in the contextual menu. Because it's a string, use quotation marks around the enclosed text. There are certain size and content restrictions on new menu items—see the sidebar "Custom Item Restrictions" for details.

Next, you must add your new **ContextMenuItem** object to the **customItems** property of your **ContextMenu** object. However, the **customItems** property is different from the **builtInItems** property you learned about in the preceding section. The **customItems** property is an array, which is an ordered list of values or objects. (You can learn more about arrays in Chapter 11, "Manipulating Information.") To add your new **ContextMenuItem** object to the **customItems** array, use the array method **push()**, as in the following code:

```
mymenu.customItems.push(myFirstItem);
```

Finally, you have to create an event handler to respond when the user selects your new contextual item. The **Event** object that is dispatched when an item on the contextual menu is selected is a **ContextMenuEvent** object. You can use **ContextMenuEvent.MENU_ITEM_SELECT** as the specific event type.

Custom Item Restrictions

The contextual menu has a maximum of 15 custom items, and each item can't be more than 100 characters long and must fit on a single line.

Items that are identical to any built-in menu item or another custom item will be ignored.

The following words can't be used in custom items at all: Adobe, Macromedia, Flash Player, Settings.

The following words can't be used alone but can be used in conjunction with other words: Save, Zoom In, Zoom Out, 100%, Show All, Quality, Play, Loop, Rewind, Forward, Back, Movie Not Loaded, About, Print, Show Redraw Regions, Debugger, Undo, Cut, Copy, Paste, Delete, Select All, Open, Open in New Window, Copy Link.

```
var mymenu:ContextMenu = new ContextMenu();
mymenu.hideBuiltInItems();
var myFirstItem:ContextMenuItem = new ContextMenuItem("Flip");
mymenu.customItems.push(myFirstItem);
picture_mc.contextMenu = mymenu;
```

E A new **ContextMenuItem** object called **myFirstItem** is created with one parameter: the name of the item (**"Flip"**). The **ContextMenuItem** called **myFirstItem** is put into the **customItems** array.

To create a new item for the contextual menu:

1. Select the first frame of the main Timeline, and open the Actions panel.

2. In the Script pane, create a new **ContextMenu** object as in previous tasks. The completed code looks like this:

   ```
   var mymenu:ContextMenu =
   → new ContextMenu();
   ```

3. Starting on the next line, hide the default items in the contextual menu:

   ```
   mymenu.hideBuiltInItems();
   ```

4. Next, instantiate a new **ContextMenuItem** object for your first item:

   ```
   var myFirstItem:ContextMenuItem =
   → new ContextMenuItem("Flip");
   ```

   A new **ContextMenuItem** is instantiated. Be sure to enclose the parameter, which represents the title of your item, in quotation marks.

5. On the next line, add a call to the **Array** class's **push()** method with the name of your **ContextMenuItem** as its parameter:

   ```
   mymenu.customItems.push(
   → myFirstItem);
   ```

   The completed statement adds your **ContextMenuItem** object to the **customItems** array of your **ContextMenu** object.

6. On the following line, assign the **ContextMenu** object to the **contextMenu** property of an object on the Stage:

   ```
   picture_mc.contextMenu = mymenu;
   ```

   In this example, your contextual menu now becomes associated with the movie clip called **picture_mc** **E**.

   Continues on next page

7. You're not done yet! Finally, you must create the event handler. Add the listener:

```
myFirstItem.addEventListener
→ (ContextMenuEvent.
→ MENU_ITEM_SELECT, selectFlip);
```

Note that the listener goes on the **ContextMenuItem** object, not on the object on the Stage or on the **ContextMenu** object.

8. Next, create a function with the **ContextMenuEvent** object as its parameter, like so:

```
function selectFlip(
→ myevent:ContextMenuEvent):void {
    picture_mc.rotation += 180;
}
```

The actions that should happen when the user selects your custom item in the contextual menu go in between the function's curly braces.

The completed code **F** attaches a custom item to the contextual menu. When the user right-clicks on the object called **picture_mc** and selects Flip, the object rotates 180 degrees.

TIP Custom items always appear above the built-in items and are separated from the built-in items by a horizontal bar.

TIP If you have many custom items, you can group them by adding another horizontal bar **G**. Use the property `separatorBefore` and set it to `true` for any `ContextMenuItem` to add a horizontal bar before the item in the list, like so:

`myFirstItem.separatorBefore = true;`

TIP You can also use the property `caption` to define the title of a new item. For a new `ContextMenuItem` called `myFirstItem`, you can use the statement `myFirstItem.caption = "Flop"`.

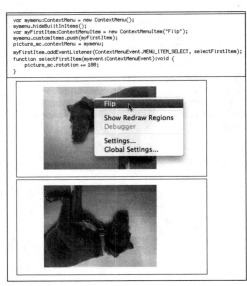

```
var mymenu:ContextMenu = new ContextMenu();
mymenu.hideBuiltInItems();
var myFirstItem:ContextMenuItem = new ContextMenuItem("Flip");
mymenu.customItems.push(myFirstItem);
picture_mc.contextMenu = mymenu;
myFirstItem.addEventListener(ContextMenuEvent.MENU_ITEM_SELECT, selectFirstItem);
function selectFirstItem(myevent:ContextMenuEvent):void {
    picture_mc.rotation += 180;
}
```

F The final code (top) makes the custom item show up at the top of the contextual menu when right-clicked over **picture_**mc (middle). When the custom item is selected, the **MENU_ITEM_SELECT** event occurs and Flash responds by rotating the picture 180 degrees (bottom).

G The custom item called Third Item has been defined with a horizontal divider above it.

Creating Continuous Actions

So far, you've learned ways to execute an action in response to events that happen when the user does something—whether it's a mouse click or a keyboard press. But on many occasions, you'll want to perform an action continuously. An **if** statement, for example, often needs to be performed continuously to check whether conditions in the movie have changed. Another example is if you want to continuously change a property of an object to create an animation.

The **Event.ENTER_FRAME** event happens continuously. The event is triggered at the frame rate of the movie, so if the frame rate is set to 24 frames per second, the **ENTER_FRAME** event is triggered 24 times per second . Even when the Timeline is stopped, the event continues to happen. This setup is an ideal way to make actions run on automatic pilot; they will run as soon as the event handler is established and stop only when the event handler is removed or the object on which it is defined is removed.

A The ENTER_FRAME event happens at the frame rate of the movie, which you can change in the Properties inspector. Typical frame rates for online playback are between 12 and 24 frames per second.

To create continuous actions with the ENTER_FRAME event:

1. Select the first frame of the main Timeline, and open the Actions panel.

2. In the Script pane, assign the **addEventListener()** method to the Stage or to an object:

   ```
   car_mc.addEventListener(
   → Event.ENTER_FRAME, movecar);
   ```

   In this example, the listener is added to the movie clip object and will detect the **ENTER_FRAME** event, which happens continuously at the frame rate of the Flash movie.

3. On the next line, create a function with the **Event** object as its parameter:

   ```
   function movecar(
   → myevent:Event):void {
      car_mc.y -= 5;
   };
   ```

   In this example, when the function is called, the movie clip called **car_mc** will move 5 pixels upward **B**.

4. Create a movie clip symbol and place an instance of it on the Stage. In the Properties inspector, name it **car_mc** to match the ActionScript code.

5. Choose Control > Test Movie > in Flash Professional.

   At the frame rate of the Flash movie (24 times a second if the frame rate is 24 fps), the **ENTER_FRAME** event occurs and your function is called, moving the movie clip on the Stage upward continuously **C**.

TIP Be careful of overusing the ENTER_FRAME event handler, because it can be processor intensive. After you no longer need the event handler, it's good practice to use removeEventListener() to remove the listener.

```
car_mc.addEventListener(Event.ENTER_FRAME, movecar);
function movecar(myevent:Event):void {
    car_mc.y -= 5;
    if (car_mc.y < 100) {
        car_mc.removeEventListener(Event.ENTER_FRAME, movecar);
    }
}
```

B Flash continuously moves the movie clip called **car_mc** 5 pixels up the Stage. An **if** statement has been added to check if the movie clip has moved beyond a certain point and, if so, removes the event listener.

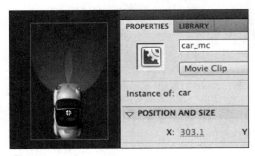

C The movie clip named **car_mc** is put on the Stage.

Using timers

The **ENTER_FRAME** event, although easy to use and effective for creating continuous actions, is restricted to the frame rate of your Flash movie. If you want to perform an action on a continuous basis and do so at an interval that you specify, you should use the **Timer** class instead.

When you create an object from the **Timer** class, the new object dispatches a **TimerEvent** event at regular intervals. You specify how long those intervals are (in milliseconds) and how many intervals there will be. You can then add an event handler to listen and respond to each event.

The **TimerEvent** has two specific events: a **TimerEvent.TIMER** event that happens at each interval and a **TimerEvent.TIMER_COMPLETE**, which happens at the end of the timer.

To create continuous actions with a timer:

1. Select the first frame of the main Timeline, and open the Actions panel.

2. Instantiate a new **Timer** object. The constructor takes two parameters—the first is a number (in milliseconds) for the timer interval, and the second is the number of intervals. The second parameter is optional, and if left out, your timer will run forever until stopped.

   ```
   var myTimer:Timer =
   → new Timer(10,1000);
   ```

   The function will be called every 10 milliseconds (1/100th of second). There will be 1,000 intervals, so this timer lasts 10 seconds.

   Continues on next page

3. On the next line, call the **start()** method to begin the timer:

```
myTimer.start();
```

The two lines of code so far create a **Timer** object and start it **D**.

4. Next, add an event handler to detect the **TimerEvent.TIMER** events that are being dispatched every 10 milliseconds:

```
myTimer.addEventListener(
→TimerEvent.TIMER, movecar);
function movecar(
→myevent:TimerEvent):void{
    car_mc.y -= 5;
};
```

This listener detects the **TimerEvent.TIMER** event and calls the function called **movecar**, moving the movie clip upward continuously until the timer stops.

5. On the Stage, add a movie clip instance called **car_mc**. Test your movie by choosing Control > Test Movie > in Flash Professional **E**.

TIP Add the command **updateAfterEvent** to your function if you're modifying graphics at a smaller interval than your movie frame rate. This method forces Flash to refresh the display, providing smoother results. The updateAfterEvent command is called on the Event object, so in this task, the code for the function would be

```
function movecar(myevent:TimerEvent)
:void{
    car_mc.y -= 5;
    myevent.updateAfterEvent();
};
```

```
var myTimer:Timer = new Timer(10,1000);
myTimer.start();
```

D A new Timer object called myTimer is created and started.

```
var myTimer:Timer = new Timer(10,1000);
myTimer.start();
myTimer.addEventListener(TimerEvent.TIMER, movecar);
function movecar(myevent:TimerEvent):void {
    car_mc.y -= 5;
}
```

E At each 10-millisecond interval for 1,000 intervals, a TIMER event happens. Each time it happens, the movie clip called **car_mc** moves 5 pixels up the Stage, animating the graphic.

To detect the end of a timer:

Add an event handler to detect the **TimerEvent.TIMER_COMPLETE** event. The following code is an example:

```
myTimer.addEventListener(
→ TimerEvent.TIMER_COMPLETE,
→ stoptimer);
function stoptimer(
→ myevent:TimerEvent):void {
   // do something
};
```

The function called **stoptimer** is called only after the timer called **myTimer** has completed all of its intervals.

A Summary of Events

Table **4.4** lists the many basic events discussed in this chapter. You'll learn about many more events in the chapters that follow. For more on the **Event** class and its subclasses, see Flash Help > Action-Script 3.0 Reference for the Adobe Flash Platform > flash.events.

TABLE 4.4 Events

Event	Description
MouseEvent.CLICK	Mouse click
MouseEvent.DOUBLE_CLICK	Mouse double-click
MouseEvent.MOUSE_MOVE	Mouse move
MouseEvent.MOUSE_DOWN	Mouse button pressed
MouseEvent.MOUSE_UP	Mouse button released
MouseEvent.MOUSE_OVER	Mouse pointer moves over the target
MouseEvent.MOUSE_OUT	Mouse pointer moves off of the target
MouseEvent.MOUSE_WHEEL	Mouse wheel moves forward or backward
KeyboardEvent.KEY_DOWN	Key pressed
KeyboardEvent.KEY_UP	Key released
ContextMenuEvent.MENU_ITEM_SELECT	Contextual menu item selected
Event.ENTER_FRAME	Happens at the frame rate of the Flash movie (not user controlled)
TimerEvent.TIMER	Happens at every interval defined by the **Timer** object
TimerEvent.TIMER_COMPLETE	Happens when the **Timer** object finishes all of its intervals

Controlling Multiple Timelines

By default, the Flash playhead moves
forward on the Timeline from beginning
to end. The playhead displays what is on
the Stage at any moment and triggers
any actions attached to keyframes that
it encounters. With ActionScript, you can
control the position of the playhead on the
main Timeline as well as the playheads
of any movie clips that are on the Stage.
Controlling multiple timelines enables you
to organize your content into objects that
behave independently for more sophisticated interactivity. You should already be
familiar with the basic navigation methods
such as **gotoAndPlay()**, **gotoAndStop()**,
play(), and **stop()**. These methods that
navigate the main Timeline are the same
ones used to navigate the timelines of
other movie clips. Your main Timeline can
control a movie clip's timeline; a movie
clip's timeline can, in turn, control the main
Timeline. You can even have the timeline
of one movie clip control the timeline of
another. Handling this complex interaction
and navigation between timelines is the
subject of this chapter.

In This Chapter

Navigating Timelines with Movie Clips

The independent timelines of movie clip symbols make more complicated navigation and interactivity possible. While the main Timeline is playing, other timelines of movie clips can be playing as well, interacting with one another and specifying which frames to play or when to stop. In fact, it's quite common to have multiple movie clips on the Stage, all being controlled in a single frame on the main Timeline. Driving all this navigation between timelines is, of course, ActionScript. The basic actions used to navigate within the main Timeline (**gotoAndStop()**, **gotoAndPlay()**, **stop()**, **play()**, **nextFrame()**, and **prevFrame()**) can also be used to navigate the timeline of any movie clip. To control a particular timeline, you give the movie clip an instance name in the Properties inspector. When an instance is named, you can target it with ActionScript and give instructions specifying where you want to move its playhead.

Insert Target Path button in Actions panel

Insert Target Path dialog box

Available objects

Target field

A The Insert Target Path dialog box displays objects on the Stage in a visual hierarchy. You can click on objects and Flash will automatically construct the target path, but it's best if you enter the target path in the Script pane yourself.

Target Paths

A *target path* is essentially an object name, or a series of object names separated by dots, that tells Flash where to find a particular object. To control movie clip timelines, you specify the target path for a particular movie clip followed by a dot and then the method you want to call. The target path tells Flash which movie clip instance to look at, and the method tells Flash what to do with that movie clip instance. The methods of the **MovieClip** class that control the playhead are **gotoAndStop()**, **gotoAndPlay()**, **play()**, **stop()**, **nextFrame()**, and **prevFrame()**. If you name a movie clip instance **myClock_mc**, for example, and you write the ActionScript statement **myClock_mc.gotoAndStop(10)**, the playhead within the movie clip instance called **myClock_mc** will move to frame 10 and stop there. **myClock_mc** is the target path, and **gotoAndStop()** is the method.

To target a movie clip instance from the main Timeline:

1. Create a movie clip symbol and place an instance of it on the Stage.

2. In the Properties inspector, give the instance a name **B**.

3. Select the first keyframe of the main Timeline, and open the Actions panel.

   You'll assign an action on the main Timeline that will control the movie clip instance.

4. Enter the instance name of your movie clip in the Script pane (this is your target path).

5. After the target path, enter a period and then an action for the movie clip, like assigning a new value to one of its properties:

   ```
   square_mc.rotation = 45;
   ```

   This statement changes the angle of the movie clip (called **square_mc**).

6. Test your movie (Control > Test Movie > in Flash Professional).

   The action you assign on the main Timeline targets your movie clip and changes its rotation to 45 degrees **C**.

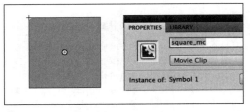

B This movie clip instance on the Stage is named **square_mc** in the Properties inspector.

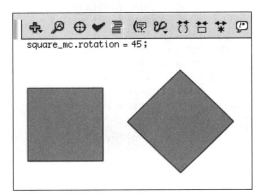

C The target path is **square_mc**, and the command is to assign the value 45 to the **rotation** property. The original movie clip instance (left) is rotated 45 degrees (right).

D There are two movie clip symbols in the Library, a clock face and one arm of the clock (which is currently selected).

Movie clip instance called bighand_mc inside the symbol of the clock face

E Place an instance of the child movie clip inside the parent movie clip. In this example, the clock arm is placed inside the symbol of the clock face, and the name of the instance is **bighand_mc**.

F The movie clip of the clock face is put on the Stage and named **clock_mc**.

Target paths for nested movie clips

You can have a movie clip within another movie clip, or as you saw in the previous chapter with pull-down menus, you can have buttons within a movie clip. The outer movie clip is the parent, and the object that's nested inside it is the child. Because the child is part of the parent, any graphical transformations you do to the parent also affect the child. To control the timeline or properties of a child object from the main Timeline, use the parent name followed by the child name separated by a period to form a hierarchical target path. In the following task, the parent movie clip is the clock (**clock_mc**), and the child movie clip is its hand (**bighand_mc**).

To target a movie clip within a movie clip:

1. Create the child movie clip symbol and the parent movie clip symbol **D**.

2. Go to symbol-editing mode for the parent movie clip, and drag an instance of your child movie clip to the Stage.

3. In the Properties inspector, give the child movie clip instance a name **E**.

   You now have a named child movie clip nested within the parent movie clip.

4. Exit symbol-editing mode, and return to the main Stage.

5. Drag the parent movie clip from the Library to the Stage and give it an instance name in the Properties inspector **F**.

Continues on next page

6. Select the first keyframe in the main Timeline, and open the Actions panel.

7. Enter the target path to the nested movie clip (parent.child), a period after the target path, and then an action. This example uses

   ```
   clock_mc.bighand_mc.rotation = 30;
   ```

8. Test your movie (Control > Test Movie > in Flash Professional).

   The action you assign on the main Timeline targets the nested movie clip called **bighand_mc** and assigns a new value to its rotation property .

```
clock_mc.bighand_mc.rotation = 30;
```

clock_mc movie clip

bighand_mc movie clip inside clock_mc movie clip

G The ActionScript statement on the main Timeline tells the **bighand_mc** movie clip inside the **clock_mc** movie clip to rotate 30 degrees.

Absolute and Relative Paths

There are two types of target paths: relative and absolute. In the preceding example, the method `clock_mc.bighand_mc.gotoAndStop(20)` originated from the main Timeline. When Flash executes that method, it looks within its own timeline for the object called `clock_mc` that contains another object called `bighand_mc`. This is an example of a relative path. Everything is relative to where the ActionScript statement resides—in this case, the main Timeline. An alternative way of inserting a target path is to use an absolute path, which has no particular frame of reference. You can think of relative target paths as directions given from your present location, as in "Go two blocks straight; then turn left." Absolute target paths, on the other hand, are directions that work no matter where you are, as in "Go to 555 University Avenue."

Using this, root, and parent

In relative mode, the current timeline is called `this`. The keyword `this` means *myself.* All other timelines are relative to the `this` timeline.

In absolute mode, the path starts with the main movie Timeline and you drill down to the timeline you want to target. To target the main movie Timeline, you can use the keyword `root`, but you must explicitly tell Flash that you are using `root` to reference a timeline. Timelines are a feature of the `MovieClip` class, so you can reference the main movie Timeline by using the statement `MovieClip(root)`.

Continues on next page

You may find that you want to target a movie clip that is above the current timeline. In that case, you can use the relative term **parent**. However, just as in the case of **root**, you must tell Flash that you want to refer to a timeline, so use the full statement **MovieClip(parent)**. For example, **MovieClip(parent).stop()** would stop the playhead of the parent's timeline.

Table 5.1 and summarize the ways you can use absolute and relative paths with the keywords **this**, **MovieClip(root)**, and **MovieClip(parent)** to target different movie clips.

TIP Using **this** or an absolute path to target a movie clip's own timeline is unnecessary, just as it's unnecessary to use **this** or **MovieClip(root)** when navigating within the main Timeline. It's understood that actions residing in one timeline pertain, or are scoped, to that particular timeline.

Ⓐ A representation of a movie with multiple movie clips. The main Timeline (scene 1) contains the square movie clip and the circle movie clip. The circle movie clip contains the triangle movie clip. These names represent instances rather than symbol names. Table 5.1 summarizes the absolute and relative target paths for calls made from the circle movie clip (you are here).

TABLE 5.1 Absolute vs. Relative Target Paths

To Target... (From Circle)	Absolute Path	Relative Path
Scene 1	MovieClip(root)	MovieClip(parent)
square	MovieClip(root).square	MovieClip(parent).square
circle	MovieClip(root).circle	this
triangle	MovieClip(root).circle.triangle	triangle

Scope

You've learned that to direct an Action-Script statement to affect a different timeline, you need a target path that defines the *scope*. Without a target path, the ActionScript would affect its own timeline. An ActionScript statement belongs, or is *scoped*, to a particular timeline or a particular object where it resides. Everything you do in ActionScript has a scope, so you must be aware of it. You could be giving the correct ActionScript instructions, but if they aren't scoped correctly, nothing—or, worse, unexpected things—could happen.

When you assign ActionScript to a frame on the main Timeline, the statement is scoped to that timeline. When you assign ActionScript to a frame of a movie clip timeline, the statement is scoped to that movie clip timeline.

Using the **with** Action to Target Objects

An alternative way to target movie clips and other objects is to use the action **with**. Instead of creating multiple target paths to the same movie clip, you can use the **with** action to target the movie clip only once. Imagine creating these statements to make the **bighand_mc** movie clip inside the **clock_mc** movie clip stop and shrink 50 percent:

```
clock_mc.bighand_mc.stop();
clock_mc.bighand_mc.scaleX = .5;
clock_mc.bighand_mc.scaleY = .5;
```

You can rewrite those statements using the **with** statement like this:

```
with (clock_mc.bighand_mc) {
    stop();
    scaleX = .5;
    scaleY = .5;
}
```

This **with** action temporarily sets the scope to clock_mc.bighand_mc so that the method and properties between the curly braces affect that particular target path. When the **with** action ends, any subsequent statements refer to the current timeline.

To target objects using the **with** action:

1. Open the Actions panel.

2. Enter the code as follows with the target path within the parentheses of the **with** action:

```
with (clock_mc.bighand_mc) {
}
```

In this example, the target path is clock_mc.bighand_mc.

3. Between the curly braces of the **with** action, create your statements for the targeted object.

Note that you don't need to specify a target path or put a dot before the method or property name **A**.

```
with (clock_mc.bighand_mc) {
    rotation = 30;
    scaleX = .5;
    scaleY = .5;
}
```

A A **with** statement is an alternative to writing out a target path in front of objects. The scaleX and scaleY properties change the vertical and horizontal dimensions, and the rotation property changes the angle of clock_mc.bighand_mc.

stop() action   Movie clip timeline

Main Timeline

A The movie clip as a container. This figure represents a main Timeline (scene 1) with a movie clip on its Stage. The movie clip has a **stop()** action in its first keyframe. The other labeled keyframes can contain buttons, graphics, animations, or any other kind of Flash information, which you can access by targeting the movie clip and moving its playhead to the appropriate keyframe.

stop() action

B The pull-down-menu movie clip contains both collapsed and expanded states.

Movie Clips as Containers

So far in this chapter, you've learned how to name your movie clip objects, target each one, and navigate within their timelines from any other timeline in your movie. But how does the ability to control movie clip timelines translate into meaningful interactivity for your Flash project? The key is to think of movie clips as containers that hold stuff: animation, graphics, sound, and text. By moving the playhead back and forth or playing certain parts of a particular movie clip timeline, you can access those items whenever you want, independently of what else is going on **A**.

For example, movie clips are commonly used to show objects with different states that toggle from one to the other; the different states are contained in the movie clip's timeline. When you built pull-down menus in Chapter 4, "Advanced Buttons and Event Handling," you used movie clips to serve that purpose. The pull-down menu is essentially a movie clip object that toggles between a collapsed state and an expanded state. The buttons inside the movie clip control which of those two states you see **B**.

Another example is a radio button. A radio button is a kind of interactive element that toggles between an "on" state and an "off" state. Radio buttons are often used to provide the reader a number of exclusive choices, when only one choice is acceptable. To answer the question of what your favorite color is, you could display several radio buttons next to color choices—only one can be selected at any time.

The following task demonstrates how to create a button with a toggle functionality using a movie clip.

To create a button with a toggle functionality:

1. Create a movie clip symbol.

2. Go to symbol-editing mode for the movie clip.

3. In the first keyframe, add a **stop()** action.

4. Insert another keyframe, and in this second keyframe, add another **stop()** action.

   The **stop()** action in both keyframes will prevent this movie clip from playing automatically and will stop the playhead on each keyframe .

5. Insert a new layer.

6. Create graphics that correspond to the off state in the first keyframe and graphics that correspond to the on state in the second keyframe .

7. Exit symbol-editing mode, and return to the main Stage.

8. Place an instance of your movie clip on the Stage, and give it an instance name in the Properties inspector.

9. Create a new layer, select the keyframe on frame 1 of this layer, and open the Actions panel. Make sure you are on the main Timeline.

10. Create an event handler for your movie clip instance as described in Chapter 4 to detect a mouse click. Inside the curly braces of the event-handler function, enter the target path for your movie clip, then a period, and then the method `play()` .

11. Test your movie (Test > Control Movie > in Flash Professional).

    When you click the movie clip, Flash targets the movie clip and moves the playhead to the next keyframe and stops. Each click toggles between two different states **F**.

stop() actions

C The toggle-button movie clip contains a **stop()** action in both keyframes.

D The first keyframe contains graphics representing the button's off state, and the second keyframe contains graphics representing the button's on, or depressed, state.

```
toggleButton_mc.addEventListener(MouseEvent.CLICK, doToggle);
function doToggle(myevent:MouseEvent):void {
    toggleButton_mc.play();
}
```

E The full script on the main Timeline listens for a mouse click and responds by playing the timeline of the movie clip.

F When the movie clip plays, the playhead moves from the first keyframe (left) to the second keyframe (right). From the second keyframe, the playhead loops back to the first keyframe (the default movie clip behavior when it reaches the end of its timeline).

Second keyframe contains content
Empty keyframe

G A movie clip with an empty first keyframe is invisible on the Stage. The second keyframe contains hidden content.

Creating a movie clip with hidden content

You can do the same thing to a movie clip that you do to a button to make it invisible—that is, leave the first keyframe blank so that the instance is invisible on the Stage initially. If the first keyframe of a movie clip is blank and contains a **stop()** action to keep it there, you can control when to expose the other frames inside that movie clip timeline. You could create a movie clip with an embedded video but keep the first keyframe blank. Then you could place this movie clip on the Stage and, at the appropriate time, advance to the next frame to reveal the video to the user.

Note that you have other ways of using ActionScript to hide or reveal the contents of a movie clip or to place content on the Stage dynamically; you'll learn about these possibilities in upcoming chapters. But being aware of both the simple (frame-based, as described here) and sophisticated (purely ActionScript-based) approaches will help you tackle a broader range of animation and interactivity challenges.

To create an "invisible" movie clip:

1. Create a movie clip symbol.

2. Go to symbol-editing mode for the movie clip, and insert a new keyframe on frame 2 of its timeline.

3. Leave the first keyframe of this layer empty, and begin placing graphics and animations in the second keyframe **G**.

4. Add a new layer to hold ActionScript. Select the keyframe on frame 1 of this layer, and open the Actions panel.

Continues on next page

5. Add a **stop()** action .

6. Exit symbol-editing mode, and return to the main Timeline.

7. Drag an instance of the movie clip from the Library to the Stage.

   The instance appears on the Stage as an empty circle . The empty circle represents the registration point of the instance, allowing you to place the instance exactly where you want it.

stop() action

H This movie clip has a **stop()** action in its first frame.

Movie clip symbol in the Library

Movie clip instance placed on the Stage

I An instance of a movie clip with an empty first frame appears as an empty circle.

Frame label

A This timeline (left) has a frame label on its first keyframe. Frame labels are added in the Properties inspector (right).

Using Frame Labels

When you navigate different timelines, it's useful to use frame labels, which are names that you give specific keyframes on a timeline. Frame labels are created in the Properties inspector in the Frame Label field and appear as tiny flags on the timeline **A**. By using frame labels, you mark important spots in your animation without worrying about the exact frame numbers.

In ActionScript, you can retrieve the name of any frame label with **currentLabel**, a property of the **MovieClip** class. The **currentLabel** property holds the most recently encountered frame label name (a string). For example, you can construct a conditional statement to check on the location of the playhead, like so:

```
if (this.currentLabel == "SomeLabel") {
    // do something
}
```

Note that the frame label is in quotation marks because it is a string value. If the playhead isn't on a frame with a frame label, the property **currentLabel** returns the last frame label encountered. The useful counterpart to **currentLabel** is the property **currentFrame**, which is the frame number of the playhead.

You can also use ActionScript to retrieve all the frame labels in a timeline and their associated frame numbers. Each frame label that you create on a timeline is automatically represented in ActionScript as an object of the **FrameLabel** class.

Continues on next page

These objects have two properties: a **name** property, which is the name of the frame label, and a **frame** property, which is the number of the frame. You can access the properties of each **FrameLabel** object by using the **currentLabels** property of the **MovieClip** class (note the similarity of the **currentLabel** and **currentLabels** property, except for the plural). The **currentLabels** property returns an **Array** of all the **FrameLabel** objects in the timeline. (An **Array** is another type of object that holds data in an orderly manner, which you'll learn more about in Chapter 11, "Manipulating Information.") You access the data in an **Array** with the square brackets. So, you can find out the name of the first frame label in a timeline with the following statement:

`this.currentLabels[0].name;`

And you can find out the frame number of the first frame label with this statement:

`this.currentLabels[0].frame;`

The square brackets access the different **FrameLabel** objects, beginning with the number 0 **B**.

this.currentLabels[0].name is "intro"
this.currentLabels[0].frame is 1

this.currentLabels[1].name is "resume"
this.currentLabels[1].frame is 7

this.currentLabels[2].name is "photos"
this.currentLabels[2].frame is 14

this.currentLabels[3].name is "bio"
this.currentLabels[3].frame is 20

B Each frame label is an instance of the **FrameLabel** class. Each instance has a **name** property and a **frame** property. Access each instance from the **currentLabels** array.

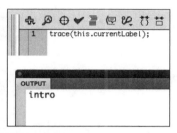

C The first keyframe of this timeline has the frame label called **intro**.

D The **trace** statement in the Actions panel (above) shows up in the Output panel (below).

To retrieve the current frame label on a timeline:

1. On the timeline, select a keyframe and in the Properties inspector, give it a frame label **C**.

2. Open the Actions panel, and in the Script pane, enter

   `trace(this.currentLabel);`

   The **trace** command lets you display expressions in the Output panel in Flash authoring mode for testing purposes. This statement displays the name of the current frame label **D**.

To retrieve any of the frame labels and numbers on a timeline:

1. On the timeline, create multiple keyframes, each with its own frame label .

2. Select the first keyframe and open the Actions panel. In the Script pane, first enter a **stop()** command:

```
stop();
```

The **stop()** command will prevent the playhead from moving.

3. On the next line, enter the following code:

```
for (var i:uint = 0; i <
→ this.currentLabels.length;
→ i++) {
   trace("frame " +
→ this. currentLabels[i].frame +
→ ": "+ this.currentLabels[i].name);
}
```

The **for** statement is a looping statement that repeats actions within its curly braces. This statement displays the frame label number and frame label name of each **FrameLabel** object, represented by **this.currentLabels[i]** **F**.

E Create a timeline with multiple keyframes.

```
stop();
for (var i:uint = 0; i < this.currentLabels.length; i++) {
    trace("frame " + this.currentLabels[i].frame + ": " + this.currentLabels[i].name);
}
```

```
OUTPUT
    frame 1: intro
    frame 7: resume
    frame 13: photos
    frame 19: bio
```

F The code in the Actions panel (above) contains a looping statement that displays all the frame label names and numbers in the Output panel (below).

Managing External Communication

Flash provides powerful tools to communicate with other applications, such as Web browsers, and with other files, such as images, videos, and other Flash movies. Flash can link to your favorite Web sites, trigger a JavaScript function, or even relay information to and from servers for data-driven applications. Although many of these functions that connect to databases are beyond the scope of this book, this chapter introduces you to some of the most popular ways Flash can communicate with HTML and JavaScript through the Web browser.

You'll learn to work with external images, video, and Flash movies. You can use one main Flash movie to load in external content to create modular projects that are easier to edit and have smaller file sizes. Your main Flash movie might serve simply as an interface that loads your portfolio of work when the viewer selects individual samples. You can manage the communication from the main Flash movie to its loaded movie to control its appearance and playback.

Finally, you'll learn to communicate with your movie's playback environment. You'll learn how to detect the amount of data that has downloaded to users' computers so you can tell users how much longer they have to wait before your movie begins. Keeping track of these external factors will help you provide a friendly and customized user experience.

Communicating with the Web Browser

Flash connects to the Web browser through the method **navigateToURL()**. This method takes one parameter, which is a **URLRequest** object that contains all the information needed to make the connection, such as the address to the Web site. The *URL* is the address that points to a specific file, whether on the Internet or on your local hard drive. Use an *absolute URL* (a complete address to a specific file) to link to any Web site, or use a *relative URL* (a path to a file that's described in relation to the current directory) to link to pages in the same Web site or local files contained on your hard drive or a CD or DVD. The **navigateToURL()** method also provides ways to target different browser windows, if you want to control where the new link appears.

Connecting to the Web

Connecting to the Web requires several steps. You must first instantiate the **URLRequest** object and define the URL as a property of the object, like so:

```
var myURL:URLRequest = new
→ URLRequest();
myURL.url="http://www.adobe.com";
```

Or, you can combine the two statements and define the **url** property at the same time you instantiate the object, like so:

```
var myURL:URLRequest = new
→ URLRequest("http://www.adobe.com");
```

Note that the **url** property is a string, so it must be enclosed within quotation marks. Next, use **navigateToURL()** with the **URLRequest** object as its parameter, as in the following:

```
navigateToURL(myURL);
```

If you test your Flash movie by choosing Control > Test Movie > in Flash Professional or play it in Flash Player, the method **navigateToURL()** automatically launches the default browser and loads the specified Web address in a new window.

To link to a Web site:

1. Create a button symbol, drag an instance from the Library to the Stage, and give it a name in the Properties inspector.

    You'll assign the **navigateToURL()** method to a mouse click on this button.

2. Select the first frame of the main Timeline, and open the Actions panel.

3. Instantiate a new object from the **URLRequest** class with the Web address as its parameter:

    ```
    var myURL:URLRequest = new
    → URLRequest("http://www.adobe.com");
    ```

    In this example, the new object called **myURL** is created and the Adobe Web site is assigned to its **url** property.

```
var myURL:URLRequest = new URLRequest("http://www.adobe.com");
mybutton_btn.addEventListener(MouseEvent.CLICK, clickButton);
function clickButton(myevent:MouseEvent):void {
    navigateToURL(myURL);
}
```

Ⓐ The **navigateToURL()** method requires a **URLRequest** object as a parameter. The **URLRequest** object (called **myURL** here) points to the Web site address (http://www.adobe.com).

Ⓑ In the Publish Settings dialog box, set your SWF file to allow remote (network only) access.

4. Create an event handler that detects a mouse click on your button (see Chapter 4, "Advanced Buttons and Event Handling," to learn more about event handling), and in the function of your event handler, add the **navigateToURL()** method, as in the following statements:

mybutton_btn.addEventListener
→ (MouseEvent.CLICK, clickButton);
function clickButton(
→ myevent:MouseEvent):void {
   navigateToURL(myURL);
}

In this example, when the mouse is clicked on **mybutton_btn**, Flash uses the **myURL** object to link to the Web Ⓐ.

5. Choose File > Publish Settings.

The Publish Settings dialog box opens.

6. On the Flash tab, under the "Local playback security" option, choose "Access network only" Ⓑ. Click OK.

This will prevent you from getting a security error message when you test your SWF file and the file, which will play locally from your hard drive, tries to access a Web site on the Internet.

Continues on next page

7. Publish your Flash movie, and play it in either the Flash Player or a browser.

When you click the button you created, the Web site loads in a new window . Click the Close button in your browser to close the window and return to your Flash movie.

> **TIP** If you skip steps 5–6 (changing the Publish Settings) and then test the movie in a browser from your hard drive, you may see a security warning when you click the button that calls the `navigateToURL()` method. For more about working around this issue, see the sidebar "Flash Player Security: Mixing Local and Remote Content," later in this chapter. However, testing the movie in Flash or over the Internet in a Web browser won't cause the security warning to appear.

C The Flash movie (top) links to the Adobe site in a new browser window (bottom).

Hyperlinks in Text

You can also link to the Web from text. With the Text tool, select either Classic Text > Static, or TLF Text > Read Only or Selectable. Create your text and select the characters you want to be hyperlinked. In the Properties inspector, enter the address of the Web site in the Link field and choose where you want the Web site to load in the Target field **D**. Your text will display with an underline to show that it's linked to a URL. When your viewers click the text, the Web site will load in the browser window indicated by the Target field. You can also create hyperlinks with Classic Text > Dynamic, but the entire field becomes clickable.

Text field on the Stage

D A Web address in the Link field of the Properties inspector creates a hyperlink in the selected text of a text field. The Target field in the Properties inspector determines where the link will open. In this figure, `_blank` is selected, so the link will open in a new browser window.

```
var myURL:URLRequest = new URLRequest("mailto: yourname@domain.com");
mybutton_btn.addEventListener(MouseEvent.CLICK, clickButton);
function clickButton(myevent:MouseEvent):void {
    navigateToURL(myURL, "_self");
}
```

E Enter e-mail recipients after **mailto:** for the **URLRequest** object. When the **URLRequest** object is passed to the **navigateToURL()** method, the browser will open the default mail application and preaddress an e-mail message.

F A new e-mail message appears in your default mail program.

Contact: yourname@yourdomain.com

G This e-mail address is also a button that connects to the browser via **mailto:**.

To preaddress an e-mail:

1. Instantiate a new object from the **URLRequest** class with **"mailto:"** followed by the e-mail address of the person who should receive the e-mail enclosed in quotation marks as its parameter:

```
var myURL:URLRequest = new
→ URLRequest("mailto:yourname@
→ domain.com");
```

In this example, the new object is called **myURL** and its **url** property is a different scheme for sending e-mail.

2. Make a call to the **navigateToURL()** method, like so:

```
navigateToURL(myURL, "_self");
```

The second parameter, **_self**, enclosed in quotation marks, is intended to prevent a new window from opening **E**.

When the code executes, the user's default e-mail application opens with a new preaddressed e-mail message **F**. The viewer then types a message and clicks Send. Use this method to preaddress e-mail that viewers can use to contact you about your Web site or to request more information.

TIP It's a good idea to spell out the e-mail address of the **mailto:** recipient in your Flash movie **G**. If a person's browser isn't configured to send e-mail, an error message appears instead of an e-mail form. By spelling out the address, you allow users to enter it in their e-mail applications.

Linking with a relative path

You can use relative paths rather than absolute URLs to specify local files instead of files on the Web. This method lets you distribute your Flash movie on portable media such as a DVD without requiring an Internet connection. Instead of using the complete URL http://www.myServer.com/images/photo.jpg, for example, you can specify just images/photo.jpg, and Flash will look inside the folder called images to find the file called photo.jpg.

To link to a file using a relative path:

When specifying the URL in the **URLRequest** object, use a slash (/) to separate directories and two periods (..) to move up one directory **H**.

Be sure to place your published SWF and your linked file in the correct level in the folder hierarchy **I**.

Flash looks for the file using the relative path and loads it into a new browser window **J**.

Working with browser windows

When you play your Flash movie in a browser window, the **navigateToURL()** method loads the new Web address in a new, blank window if you provide the **URLRequest** object as its only parameter. To make the Web address load into the same window or a named window, enter **"_self"** or another name as the second parameter in the **navigateToURL()** method for the window.

```
var myURL:URLRequest = new URLRequest("../images/photo.jpg");
mybutton_btn.addEventListener(MouseEvent.CLICK, clickButton);
function clickButton(myevent:MouseEvent):void {
    navigateToURL(myURL);
}
```

H This relative URL defined in the **URLRequest** object goes up one directory level and looks for a folder called images, which contains a file called photo.jpg.

I Your Flash movie (SWF) and its accompanying HTML file are in a directory that's at the same level as the directory that contains the file photo.jpg.

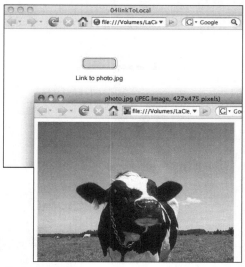

J The Flash movie (top) links to the local file in a new browser window (bottom).

To open a Web site in the same window:

Specify **_self**, enclosed in quotation marks, as the second parameter in the `navigateToURL()` method, like so:

`navigateToURL(myURL, "_self");`

When you test your movie in a browser, the new Web address loads in the same window as the Flash movie, replacing it. Use the back button to return to your Flash movie.

TIP Security restrictions prevent a Flash movie from linking to a Web site with a window name of _self, _parent, or _top if the SWF is located in a different domain (different Web site address) than its HTML page. This issue is discussed in the sidebar "Flash Player Security: Loading Across Domains," below.

Flash Player Security: Mixing Local and Remote Content

This chapter is all about how a Flash movie communicates with its external environment to access other scripts, files, and data. However, there are security features that restrict Flash movies from communicating with and loading other files and data from locations other than its own. This protects users from the possibility of a Flash movie secretly loading a file from the user's hard drive and sending it over the Internet, for example.

You'll come across this security issue when you mix local content (when you test Flash files on your computer) with remote content (when you link to a Web site). You will see a security warning message when the locally running SWF file tries to access any network resource ⓚ. This includes the `navigateToURL()` method and many of the other actions I'll discuss in this chapter.

One way to prevent the warning is to change the "Local playback security" setting in the Publish Settings dialog box from "Access local files only" to "Access network only," as explained in the task "To link to a Web site." However, you'll have to remember to change this setting for each Flash document you test locally that accesses a remote resource.

You can make a single change to resolve this issue for all your Flash documents. The simplest way is to specify a *trusted* location on your computer—a folder within which any Flash movies are trusted by the Flash Player and don't cause this security warning. The next task, "To designate a trusted location on your computer," shows you how.

ⓚ The Flash Player Security dialog indicates that a SWF has tried to access the network and isn't allowed to. Click the Settings button to create a trusted location on your computer, which prevents this warning.

To designate a trusted location on your computer:

1. Go to the Adobe Flash Player Global Security Settings panel on any browser (http://www.macromedia.com/support/ documentation/en/flashplayer/help/ settings_manager04.html).

2. In the Settings Manager, click the Edit locations menu and choose Add location ⬤.

3. In the dialog box that appears, click the "Browse for folder" button ⓜ; another dialog box will allow you to choose a folder whose contents will always be trusted by the Flash Player.

   In general, you should choose a folder that contains your Flash projects (sub-folders of this folder are trusted as well). You also need to be careful to never place in that folder any SWF files that you don't completely trust.

4. Click the Confirm button. The dialog box closes, and you return to the Set-tings Manager.

   Your newly added location appears in the bottom field ⓝ. With this setting, the Flash Player will no longer trig-ger the error message when you test local SWF files that are in the trusted location.

5. Restart the browser.

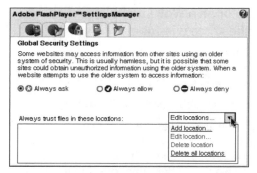

⬤ You can specify a location on your computer whose contents are trusted by the Flash Player.

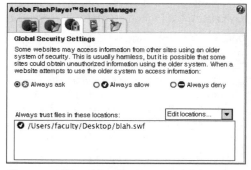

ⓜ Choose a single SWF file or a folder to designate as trusted.

ⓝ The newly designated folder appears in the bottom field and is set to be a trusted location.

Using JavaScript to control new window parameters

When Flash opens new browser windows to load a URL, the appearance and location of these new windows are set by the browser's preferences. If you play a Flash movie in a browser that shows the location bar and the toolbar, for example, and you open a new window, the new window also has a location bar and a toolbar. You can't control these window parameters directly with Flash, but you can control them indirectly with JavaScript.

JavaScript is the scripting language for your Web browser. Most of the time, your Flash movie will play in an HTML file in a Web browser. You can use the ActionScript class **ExternalInterface** to communicate with the JavaScript that is written in the HTML file. Use the **call()** method from the Flash movie, like so:

```
ExternalInterface.call(
⟶ "somefunction");
```

This statement triggers the JavaScript function called **somefunction** in the HTML page that plays your Flash movie. JavaScript is in the head of an HTML file and would look something like this:

```
<script language="javascript">
function somefunction() {
    alert ("hello");}
</script>
```

The **call()** method can also pass parameters (**Boolean**, **Number**, or **String** data types) to the JavaScript function. Simply add additional parameters to the **call()** method, like so:

```
ExternalInterface.call(
⟶ "somefunction", param1, param2);
```

The parameters called **param1** and **param2** will now be passed to the JavaScript function.

Continues on next page

TABLE 6.1 JavaScript Window Properties

Property	Description
height	Vertical dimension, in pixels
width	Horizontal dimension, in pixels
left	X-coordinate of left edge
top	Y-coordinate of top edge
resizable	Resizable area in the bottom-right corner that allows the window to change dimensions (**yes**/**no** or **1**/**0**)
scrollbars	Vertical and horizontal scroll bars (**yes**/**no** or **1**/**0**)
directories	Also called links, where certain bookmarks are accessible (**yes**/**no** or **1**/**0**)
location	Location bar, containing URL area (**yes**/**no** or **1**/**0**)
menubar	Menu bar, containing drop-down menus such as File and Edit; works only in the Windows operating system (**yes**/**no** or **1**/**0**)
status	Status bar in the bottom-left corner, containing browser status and security (**yes**/**no** or **1**/**0**)
toolbar	Toolbar, containing the back and forward buttons and other navigation aides (**yes**/**no** or **1**/**0**)

You can use the JavaScript function **window.open()** to open a new window and control several window properties. The JavaScript function takes three parameters: the URL, the new window name, and the window properties. These properties specify the way the window looks, how it works, and where it's located on the screen **❶**. When you define these window properties, use **yes (1)**, **no (0)**, or a number specifying pixel dimensions or coordinates. **Table 6.1** lists the most common window properties that are compatible with all major Web browsers.

❶ You can set the properties of a browser window with JavaScript.

To open a custom window with JavaScript:

1. Create a button symbol and place an instance of it on the Stage. In the Properties inspector, give it a name.

   You will assign an event handler for a button click on this button that opens a new custom browser window using JavaScript.

2. Select the first frame of the Timeline, and open the Actions panel.

3. Add an event listener to detect a mouse click over your button.

4. Create the event-handler function. Between the curly braces of the function, declare and initialize three variables for your URL, your new window name, and your window properties, like so:

```
var myurl:String =
→"http://www.adobe.com";
var mywindow:String = "newwindow";
var myfeatures:String =
→"width=200, height=250, left=80,
→right=180, toolbar=0,
→location=0, directories=0
```

These variables will be used as parameters for your JavaScript function.

5. On the next line, still within the event-handler function, write the `call()` method of the `ExternalInterface` class with the name of the JavaScript function and then the three variables as parameters separated by commas, as in the following ℗:

```
ExternalInterface.call(
→"openwindow", myurl, mywindow,
→myfeatures);
```

Flash makes the browser execute the JavaScript function called `openwindow` and passes three parameters.

6. Publish your Flash movie. Open the HTML file that gets created in the publishing process in an HTML editing application like Dreamweaver. In the head of the HTML file, add the following JavaScript code ℗:

```
<script language="javascript">
function openwindow (URL,
→windowname, windowfeatures){
window.open(URL, windowname,
→windowfeatures);
}
</script>
```

Continues on next page

```
mybutton_btn.addEventListener(MouseEvent.CLICK, clickButton);
function clickButton(myevent:MouseEvent):void {
    var myurl:String = "http://www.peachpit.com";
    var mywindow:String = "newwindow";
    var myfeatures:String = "width=200, height=250, left=80, top=180, toolbar=0, location=0, directories=0";
    ExternalInterface.call("openwindow", myurl, mywindow, myfeatures);
}
```

℗ The three variables **myurl**, **mywindow**, and **myfeatures** are strings that provide information to pass to the JavaScript function in the HTML page. The **call()** method triggers the function called **openwindow** and passes the three parameters to it.

```
<head>
<meta http-equiv="Content-Type" content="text/html; charset=iso-8859-1" />
<title>OpenNewWindow</title>
<body bgcolor="#ffffff">

<script language="javascript">
    function openwindow (URL, windowname, windowfeatures){
    window.open(URL, windowname, windowfeatures);
    }
</script>

</head>
```

℗ You must add the JavaScript function (highlighted in gray) in the head of the HTML page that plays your Flash movie.

The **openwindow** function has three parameters: **URL**, **windowname**, and **windowfeatures**. When this function is called, three parameters are passed from Flash and used in this function.

7. Save the modified HTML page and upload the HTML file and the SWF file to your server to test it on the Web.

When you click the button that you created, Flash passes the three parameters containing the Web address, the window name, and the window features to the JavaScript function in the HTML page called **openwindow**. Then a new window with those features opens **R**.

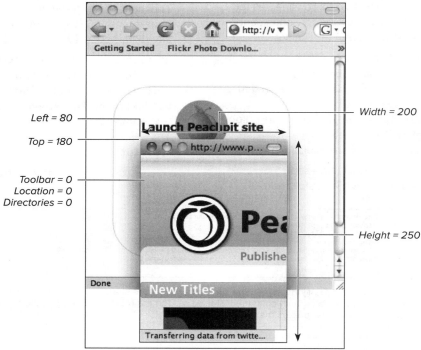

R The new window created by the JavaScript function is a customized window without most features.

TIP It's important that you test the `ExternalInterface.call()` method over the Internet, not locally on your hard drive. Security restrictions won't allow you to open a new window to a Web site from your local hard drive.

TIP Some browsers and browser configurations may block pop-up windows at any time, so testing the functionality for your particular target environment is important. Also, make sure that the `ExternalInterface.call()` method happens as a result of a direct user action (clicking a button), and something that happens automatically.

TIP The `ExternalInterface` class is supported in these environments: Internet Explorer 5.0 and later for Windows, Firefox 1.0 and later, Mozilla 1.7.5 and later, Netscape 8.0 and later, or Safari 1.3 and later for the Mac. The `ExternalInterface` class is not supported in a stand-alone player.

TIP You can use the `ExternalInterface.call()` method to call other JavaScript functions defined in your HTML page, not just to open custom browser windows.

TIP Make sure you don't overwrite your HTML file that contains the added JavaScript function when you republish your Flash movie. If you make changes to your Flash movie, change the Publish Settings so you just publish a SWF file.

TIP More JavaScript window properties are available, but many of them work in only one or some of the most popular browsers. The properties `innerHeight` and `innerWidth`, for example, define the dimensions of the window content area, but these properties are unique to Mozilla-based browsers such as Netscape Navigator and Firefox. You're safe if you stick to the properties listed in Table 6.1.

TIP Security restrictions only allow a Flash movie to communicate with JavaScript on an HTML page that is in the same sandbox (see the Flash Player Security sidebars "Mixing Local and Remote Content" and "Loading Across Domains"). You can allow access by changing the `AllowScriptAccess` parameter to `always` (for both the embed and object tags) in the HTML page and adding the following statement in Flash:

```
flash.system.Security.allowDomain(
→ "domainName").
```

Loading External Flash Movies

Another way to communicate with external content is to load other Flash movies into your first Flash movie. You use the **Loader** class to do this. The **Loader** class provides the **load()** method to combine many kinds of external content into a Flash movie. The original, container Flash movie establishes the frame rate, the Stage size, and the background color, but you can layer multiple external SWF files and even navigate within their timelines.

Loading external Flash movies has many benefits. It keeps your Flash project small and lets you maintain quick download times. It also lets you edit the external Flash movies separately for a more modular way of working. For example, if you build a Web site to showcase your Flash animation work, you can keep all your individual animations as separate SWF files. Build the main interface so that your potential clients can load each animation as they request it. That way, your viewers download only the content that's needed, as it's needed. The main interface doesn't become bloated with the inclusion of every one of your Flash animations **A**.

After you've loaded an external SWF file into Flash with the **Loader** class, you must add it to the display list, which makes it visible to the viewer. You'll learn more about the display list in the next chapter, "Controlling and Displaying Graphics." You add objects to the display list with the method **addChild()**.

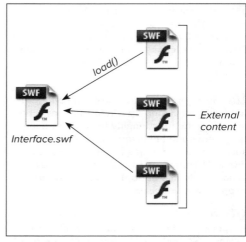

A You can keep data-heavy content separate by maintaining external SWF files. Here, the interface.swf movie loads the animation files one by one as they're requested.

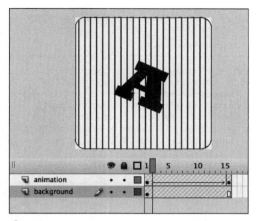

B An animation of the letter A spins on a vertical grid.

To load an external Flash movie:

1. Create the external Flash movie you want to load.

   For this example, keep the animation at a relatively small Stage size **B**.

2. Publish your external movie as a SWF file.

3. Open a new Flash document to create the main, container movie that will load your external Flash movie.

4. Select the first frame of the main Timeline, and select the Actions panel.

5. Create a new **URLRequest** object with the name of the external SWF file as the **url** property, as in the following:

   ```
   var myrequest:URLRequest = new
   → URLRequest("letterA.swf");
   ```

   In this example, the external SWF that you want to load is called letterA.swf, and it lies in the same folder as the main Flash movie. If your external movie will be in a different directory, you can specify the path by using the slash (/) to drill down a directory or double periods (..) to move up a directory. If your SWF file resides on a Web site, you can enter an absolute path to the file.

6. On the next line, create a new **Loader** object with the following code:

   ```
   var myloader:Loader =
   → new Loader();
   ```

7. On the next line, call the **load()** method for your new **Loader** object and use the **URLRequest** object as the parameter:

   ```
   myloader.load(myrequest);
   ```

8. On the last line, call the **addChild()** method to add the **Loader** object to the Stage to display it **C**:

stage.addChild(myloader);

The Stage is the top-level display object. You can also add the **Loader** object to other **DisplayObjectContainer** objects on the Stage, if you desire.

9. Publish your movie.

10. Place the SWF file, its HTML file, and the external SWF file in the same directory.

11. Play the main movie in Flash Player or a browser.

Flash loads the external movie, which sits on top of your original movie and begins playing **D**.

TIP Be careful when mixing Flash movies authored in ActionScript 3 and others authored in previous versions, especially when loading movies. ActionScript 2 movies can't load ActionScript 3 movies. ActionScript 3 movies can load ActionScript 2 movies and earlier, but there are limitations, such as not being able to access the loaded movie's variables or functions. In general, it's best to migrate all movies written in ActionScript 2 or earlier to ActionScript 3 to keep all externally loaded Flash content consistent.

```
var myrequest:URLRequest = new URLRequest("letterA.swf");
var myloader:Loader = new Loader();
myloader.load(myrequest);
stage.addChild(myloader);
```

C The full code to load an external SWF file called letterA.swf into your Flash movie. The **URLRequest** object holds the information on what file to get and where to get it, and the **load()** method loads it into the **Loader** object. Do not forget to display the **Loader** object on the Stage with the **addChild()** method.

letterA.swf movie   *Main Flash movie*

D The external movie of the spinning letter loads into the bigger main Flash movie.

To unload a movie:

- Use the **unload()** method on the **Loader** object, like so:

  myloader.unload();

  This statement unloads the Flash movie that was loaded into **myloader** from the previous task.

or

- Use the **unloadAndStop()** method, like so:

  myloader.unloadAndStop();

  This statement unloads the Flash movie that was loaded into **myloader** and shuts down any video or sounds that may continue to play.

Flash Player Security: Loading Across Domains

Loading external SWFs and other content and data introduces data security issues and some restrictions you should be aware of. Because SWFs published on the Internet can be loaded into any Flash movie, the potential exists for private information and sensitive data held in variables in the SWF to be accessed. To prevent this abuse, Flash movies operate in their own secure space, called a *sandbox*. Only movies playing in the same sandbox can access and/or control each other's variables and other Flash elements. The sandbox is defined by the domain in which the Flash movie resides. So, a movie on www.adobe.com can access other movies on www.adobe.com without restriction, because they're in the same domain.

If you need to load content or data that reside in different domains, you can call the ActionScript method **Security.allowDomain("domainName")** within those SWFs, and movies from the specified domain can access their variables. For more specific information and details about domain-based authentication and granting access, see the Flash Help topic (www.adobe.com/products/flashplayer/security/). Current information is also available as a white paper on the Adobe Web site.

To replace a loaded movie:

Use the **load()** method with a different **URLRequest** object. If you instantiate a second **URLRequest** object with a second SWF as its **url** property, you can load it into the original **Loader** object. Continuing with the previous task, add the following code when you want to replace the loaded movie:

```
var myrequest2:URLRequest =
→ new URLRequest("letterB.swf");
myloader.load(myrequest2);
```

This statement creates a new **URLRequest** object and loads the second external movie in the same loader, replacing the first movie **E**.

TIP You can change the location of the loaded movie by assigning different values to the X and Y properties of the Loader object. For example, **myloader.x = 40** positions the Loader object 40 pixels from the left edge of the Stage. Learn more about the different properties of the **Loader** object in the next chapter, which deals with manipulating graphics.

myrequest in myloader

```
var myrequest:URLRequest = new URLRequest("letterA.swf");
var myloader:Loader = new Loader();
myloader.load(myrequest);
stage.addChild(myloader);

mybutton_btn.addEventListener(MouseEvent.CLICK, clickbutton);
function clickbutton(myevent:MouseEvent) {
    var myrequest2:URLRequest = new URLRequest("letterB.swf");
    myloader.load(myrequest2);
}
```

Replace loaded movie with another

Replace loaded movie with another

myrequest2 in myloader

E In the ActionScript code (top), the first external SWF movie (letterA.swf) loads in automatically. Then, when the user clicks the button on the Stage, a second **URLRequest** object is created for another external SWF movie (letterB.swf). When it is loaded into the same **Loader** object, the first movie is replaced.

Characteristics of Loaded Flash Movies

The following is a list of things to keep in mind when you're loading external Flash movies:

- Loaded movies have transparent Stages. To have an opaque Stage, create a filled rectangle in the bottom layer of your loaded movie **F**.

- Loaded movies are aligned with the registration point of the object that they are loaded into. That means the loaded movies are aligned to the top-left corner of the Stage (x = 0 and y = 0 for both the loaded movie and the Stage). So, loaded movies with smaller Stage sizes still show objects that are off their Stage **G**. Create a mask to block objects that may go beyond the Stage and that you don't want your audience to see. Likewise, loaded movies with larger Stage sizes are cropped at the bottom and right boundaries **H**.

- **Loader** objects can have only one loaded movie, so new calls to **load()** will bump out the existing loaded movie and replace it with the new loaded movie.

- You can have multiple loaded Flash movies as long as you have a unique **Loader** object for each loaded movie. Each time you use the **addChild()** method to display the loaded movie, it will be placed on top of the previously loaded movies. See the next section and Chapter 7, "Controlling and Displaying Graphics," for more information about managing depth levels of objects on the display list.

F The Stage of an external SWF is transparent when the SWF is loaded into the main Flash movie.

G Smaller external SWFs are aligned at the top-left corner and display the work area off their Stages. Consider using masks or external SWFs with the same Stage dimensions.

H Larger external SWFs get cropped when they're loaded in a smaller main Flash movie.

Controlling Loaded Flash Movies

When you load an external Flash movie, you'll likely want to control its timeline or find out some information about the movie. For example, to better fit your design, you need to know the loaded movie's width and height so you can move it to an appropriate location on the Stage. Or, you can stop or play the loaded movie, or navigate to different spots on its timeline.

Before you can control the loaded Flash movie or get information about its properties, however, you have to wait until the entire external SWF has loaded. You can detect when the loading process is complete by accessing the **LoaderInfo** object of your loaded object. The **LoaderInfo** object provides events such as **Event.COMPLETE** or **Event.OPEN** that tells you the status of the load progress. The **LoaderInfo** object also provides information such as the amount of data that has loaded, the total amount of data of the loaded object, the loaded movie's SWF version, its frame rate, the URL from where it is being loaded, and other useful properties.

LoaderInfo and contentLoaderInfo

To access the **LoaderInfo** object, you use the **contentLoaderInfo** property of your **Loader** object. For example, consider the following statements that create a **URLRequest** and a **Loader**, and then load an external SWF file:

```
var myrequest:URLRequest =
→ new URLRequest("letterA.swf");
var myloader:Loader = new Loader();
myloader.load(myrequest);
```

After the **load()** call is made, you can access the **LoaderInfo** and its properties with the **contentLoaderInfo** property, like so:

```
myloader.contentLoaderInfo.bytesLoaded
```

This statement returns the amount of data that has loaded into the **myloader** object. The next statement,

myloader.contentLoaderInfo.content

returns the object (in this case, the external SWF) that is loaded into **myloader**. Table 6.2 lists a few of the useful properties and events of the **LoaderInfo** object.

Detecting a successful load

Only after a load is successful is it safe to control the loaded movie or access its properties (like width or height). Create an event handler that detects the **Event.COMPLETE** event of the **LoaderInfo** class as follows:

```
myloader.contentLoaderInfo.
→ addEventListener(Event.COMPLETE,
→ swfLoaded);
function swfLoaded(
→ myevent:Event):void {
var mycontent:MovieClip =
→ myevent.target.content;
    // do something with mycontent
}
```

In this example, when Flash detects the completion of a load process into the **myloader** object, it calls the **swfLoaded** function. The content of the event target (the loaded SWF) is assigned to a movie clip variable called **mycontent** for ease of manipulation and control.

TABLE 6.2 LoaderInfo Properties and Events

Property	Description
actionScriptVersion	ActionScript version of the loaded SWF
bytesLoaded	Amount of data that is loaded
bytesTotal	Total amount of data in the file
content	The loaded object associated with the **LoaderInfo** object
loader	The **Loader** object associated with the **LoaderInfo** object
frameRate	Frame rate of the loaded file
height	Vertical dimension, in pixels
width	Horizontal dimension, in pixels
loaderURL	URL of the Flash movie that initiated the load
url	URL of the file being loaded
swfVersion	Player version of the loaded SWF
Event.COMPLETE	Dispatches when the file is completely downloaded
Event.OPEN	Dispatches when the file begins to load
ProgressEvent.PROGRESS	Dispatches when the file is loading
Event.UNLOAD	Dispatches when the loaded file is removed or replaced
IOErrorEvent.IO_ERROR	Dispatches when an error in the loading happens

To target and control a loaded Flash movie:

1. As in the preceding tasks, create an animation to serve as an external Flash movie, and export it as a SWF file.

2. Open a new Flash document, select the first frame of the Timeline, and open the Actions panel.

3. Instantiate a **URLRequest** object and a **Loader** object and make a call to the **load()** method to start loading the external SWF, as in the following code:

```
var myrequest:URLRequest =
→ new URLRequest("letterA.swf");
var myloader:Loader =
→ new Loader();
myloader.load(myrequest);
```

4. On the next available line, display the Loader object with the **addChild()** method, as follows:

```
stage.addChild(myloader);
```

The code so far should appear like the code in **A**.

5. Add an event listener to the **myloader.contentLoaderInfo** object (which references the **LoaderInfo** object) and listen for the **Event.COMPLETE** event, as in the following **B**:

```
myloader.contentLoaderInfo.
→ addEventListener(
→ Event.COMPLETE, swfLoaded);
```

```
var myrequest:URLRequest = new URLRequest("letterA.swf");
var myloader:Loader = new Loader();
myloader.load(myrequest);
stage.addChild(myloader);
```

A The external SWF called letterA.swf loads into the **Loader** object called **myloader** and is displayed on the Stage.

```
var myrequest:URLRequest = new URLRequest("letterA.swf");
var myloader:Loader = new Loader();
myloader.load(myrequest);
stage.addChild(myloader);

myloader.contentLoaderInfo.addEventListener(Event.COMPLETE, swfLoaded);
```

B When the listener detects the completion of the loading, it triggers the function called **swfLoaded**.

6. On the next available line, create a function with an **Event** type as the parameter. In the body of the function, assign the **target.content** property of the event object to a new movie clip, like so:

```
function swfLoaded(
→ myevent:Event):void {

var mycontent:MovieClip =
→ myevent.target.content;
}
```

This event handler, when executed, puts the content of the event target in a variable typed to a movie clip. The content of the event target is the loaded object, or the external SWF, which you know belongs to the **MovieClip** class. This helps you reference the external SWF, change its properties, and navigate its timeline.

7. Within the body of the event-handler function, add additional statements that navigate the timeline of the external SWF or reference its properties. For example, consider the following statement:

mycontent.gotoAndStop(5);

This statement moves the playhead of the loaded SWF to frame 5 and stops there **C**.

8. Publish your movie, and place the SWF and its HTML in the same directory as the external SWF file.

9. Play the movie in Flash Player or a browser.

Flash loads the external SWF. When it detects the completion of the load, Flash goes to a different spot on its timeline **D**.

```
var myrequest:URLRequest = new URLRequest("letterA.swf");
var myloader:Loader = new Loader();
myloader.load(myrequest);
stage.addChild(myloader);

myloader.contentLoaderInfo.addEventListener(Event.COMPLETE, swfLoaded);
function swfLoaded(myevent:Event):void {
    var mycontent:MovieClip = myevent.target.content;
    mycontent.gotoAndStop(5);

}
```

C When the function called **swfLoaded** is triggered, the external SWF is assigned to the **MovieClip** variable **mycontent**. The highlighted portions of the code control the playhead of the loaded external SWF.

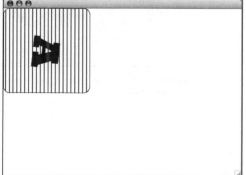

D The playhead on the Timeline of the loaded external SWF stops at frame 5 (so this animated letter "A" stops spinning).

Managing multiple Flash movies

When you load an external Flash movie and use **addChild()** to display it on the Stage, Flash adds the object to a display list, which is a list that Flash uses to keep track of the stacking order of objects. You'll learn much more about the display list in Chapter 7, because it is used to display all sorts of objects on the Stage—movie clips, bitmaps, graphics, as well as loaded movies.

Think of the display list as a stack of items, and each time you add an object to the Stage with **addChild()**, you add to the top of the stack. So the most recent **addChild()** statement will be the topmost object that overlaps all the other objects. If you want to bring an object that's lower in the stack to the top, simply call **addChild()** for that object, and Flash will pull it out of the list and put it on the top. If you want to remove an object from the stack entirely, use **removeChild()** ⒠.

To put a loaded movie on top of others:

Make a call to the **addChild()** method, like so:

```
stage.addChild(myloader);
```

This statement adds the Flash movie loaded into **myloader** to the top of the Stage, overlapping other objects that may already be present on the Stage ⒡.

⒠ The **addChild()** method puts the **Loader** object on display on the Stage. The most recent **addChild()** method will be on top.

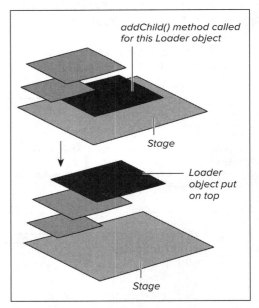

⒡ When you call an **addChild()** method for a **Loader** object already displayed, it pulls it from the display list and puts it on the top.

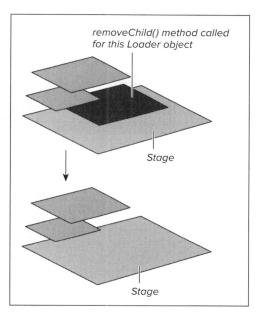

removeChild() method called
for this Loader object

Stage

Stage

G When you call a `removeChild()` method for a **Loader** object already displayed, it pulls it from the display list so it is no longer visible.

To remove a loaded movie from the Stage:

Make a call to the `removeChild()` method, like so:

`stage.removeChild(myloader);`

This statement removes the `myloader` object from the Stage so it is no longer visible. The `myloader` object, however, still exists. It can be added to the Stage at a later point in time or deleted entirely if it is no longer needed **G**.

Loaded Movies and root

If you've worked with previous versions of ActionScript, you know that the **_root** property always referred to the main Timeline, even when an external SWF was loaded into another Flash movie. That made loaded Flash movies a little tricky if ActionScript from their timeline made reference to **_root**. In ActionScript 3, the new **root** property behaves a little differently. The **root** property within the loaded SWF represents the instance of the main class of that SWF (the main Timeline of that SWF, equivalent to the **Loader** object's **content** property). Hence, there can be multiple **root** instances in a Flash movie if external content is loaded into the player with the **Loader** class.

Loading External Images

Using the same method that loads external Flash files into your movie dynamically, you can load images dynamically, including JPEG, progressive JPEG, GIF, and PNG images. The process is similar: create a **URLRequest** object to define the URL or path to your image file, create a **Loader** object, and then use the **load()** method to pull images into your **Loader** object. Finally, display the loaded images by adding the **Loader** object to the display list with **addChild()**. As is the case with external SWFs, keeping images separate from your Flash movie reduces the size of your Flash movie, saves download time, and makes revisions quicker and easier because you can edit the images without needing to open the actual Flash file.

Loaded images follow many of the same rules that loaded movies do, and those rules are worth repeating here:

- Loaded images are aligned at the registration point of the object that they are loaded into. That means images loaded on the Stage are aligned at their top-left corners (x = 0 and y = 0 for both the loaded movie and the Stage).

- **Loader** objects can have only one loaded image, so new calls to **load()** will bump out the existing loaded image and replace it with the new loaded image.

- You can have multiple loaded images as long as you have a unique **Loader** object for each loaded image. Each time you use the **addChild()** method to display the loaded image, it will be placed on top of the previously loaded image.

```
var myrequest:URLRequest = new URLRequest("someimage.jpg");
var myloader:Loader = new Loader();
myloader.load(myrequest);
stage.addChild(myloader);
```

A This ActionScript code loads an image called someimage.jpg and displays it on the Stage.

Same directory

SWF   JPG   HTML

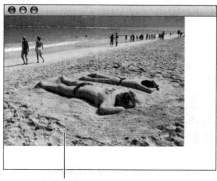

External image loaded into SWF

B The image file, someimage.jpg, is in the same directory as the SWF and HTML (top). When the Flash movie plays, the external image loads (bottom).

To load an external image:

1. Select the first frame of the main Timeline, and select the Actions panel.

2. Create a new **URLRequest** object with the name of the external image file as the **url** property, as in the following:

   var myrequest:URLRequest =
   → new URLRequest("someimage.jpg");

   In this example, the external image that you want to load is called someimage. jpg, and it is in the same folder as the main Flash movie. If your external image will be in a different directory, you can specify the path by changing directories using the slash (/) or double periods (..). If your image file resides on a Web site, you can enter an absolute path to the file.

3. On the next line, create a new **Loader** object with the following code:

   var myloader:Loader =
   → new Loader();

4. On the next line, call the **load()** method for your new **Loader** object, and use the **URLRequest** object as the parameter:

   myloader.load(myrequest);

5. On the last line, call the **addChild()** method to add the **Loader** object to the Stage to display it **A**:

   stage.addChild(myloader);

   The Stage is the top-level display object. You can also add the **Loader** object to other **DisplayObjectContainer** objects on the Stage, if you desire.

6. Publish your movie, and place your image in the correct directory so your Flash movie can find it.

   Flash loads the external image, which sits on top of your original movie. The top-left corner of the JPEG aligns with the top-left corner of the Stage **B**.

To remove or replace a loaded image:

- To unload an image, make a call to the **unload()** method of the **Loader** object. To remove the image from the display, make a call to the **removeChild()** method of the Stage.

- To replace an image, use the **load()** method, and load another **URLRequest** object into the same **Loader** object. The new image will replace the old one.

To change the properties of a loaded image:

Assign new values to the **Loader** object properties to change the appearance of the loaded image. For example, **myloader.x = 100** moves the horizontal position of the **myloader** object and its loaded image 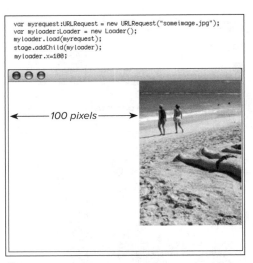.

To put a loaded image on top of others:

Make a call to the **addChild()** method for the **Loader** object, like so:

```
stage.addChild(myloader);
```

This statement puts the image loaded into **myloader** to the top of the Stage, overlapping other objects that may already be present on the Stage.

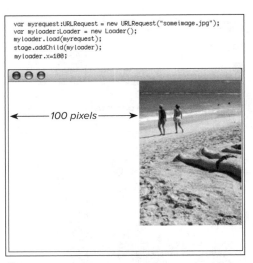

```
var myrequest:URLRequest = new URLRequest("someimage.jpg");
var myloader:Loader = new Loader();
myloader.load(myrequest);
stage.addChild(myloader);
myloader.x=100;
```

← 100 pixels →

C Assigning values for the X and Y properties of the **Loader** object puts it in a different position on the Stage.

Accessing the Loaded Content's Properties

Often, when you load external content (a SWF or an image file), you'll want to find out its dimensions (height and width) so you can place it in the correct location on the Stage or scale it appropriately. However, it's important that you use an event listener to listen for the **Event.COMPLETE** of the load (the Loader's **contentLoaderInfo**) before you attempt to access the properties of the external SWF or image. For example, if you try to get the width or height of the loaded image before it's completely loaded, the information you receive will not be correct.

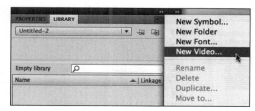

A Choose New Video from the Library panel's Options menu.

Communicating with External Video

In Chapter 2, "Working with Video," you learned how to embed video in a SWF file and also how to create an external Flash Video (FLV/F4V) file that loads into a player skin in a SWF file. However, you don't have to rely on the preset skins that are provided to you. Using ActionScript, you can control the loading and playback of external video to build your own playback features and use video in a less conventional way.

Once you have an FLV/F4V file, use a **NetConnection** object and a **NetStream** object to load the video stream into Flash. The **NetConnection** object provides the means to play back an FLV file from your local drive or Web address, whereas the **NetStream** object makes the actual connection and tells Flash to play the video. To receive the streaming video, you must also have a video object on the Stage. You can do this in one of two ways: create a video symbol in your Library and place an instance on the Stage where you want the video to appear, or create a video symbol and attach it to the Stage purely with ActionScript using the **Video** class.

To dynamically load external video with a video symbol placed on the Stage:

1. Convert your video file to an FLV or F4V file, as described in Chapter 2.

2. Open a new Flash document with its Stage size large enough to accommodate the video file.

3. Open the Library. From the Library panel's Options menu, choose New Video **A**.

   The Video Properties dialog box appears.

   Continues on next page

4. Give your symbol a name in the Symbol field; in the Type field, choose Video (ActionScript-controlled) 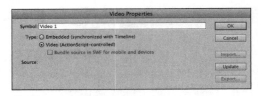.

A new video symbol appears in the Library.

5. Place an instance of the video symbol on the Stage.

6. Modify its width and height to match the external video file that will be loaded in, and give it an instance name in the Properties inspector. In this example, the instance name is **videoHolder** .

Your external video will play inside this video instance.

7. Select the first frame of the main Timeline, and in the Actions panel, create a new instance from the **NetConnection** class as follows:

```
var myVideo:NetConnection =
→ new NetConnection();
```

A new **NetConnection** object is instantiated.

8. On the next line, enter the name of the **NetConnection** object you just created followed by a period, and then enter the **connect()** method with **null** as its parameter:

```
myVideo.connect(null);
```

The **null** parameter tells Flash that it isn't connecting through the Flash Communication Server but instead to expect a download from the local hard drive or a Web address.

9. On the next line, declare and instantiate a new **NetStream** object with the **NetConnection** object as its parameter:

```
var newStream:NetStream =
→ new NetStream(myVideo);
```

A new **NetStream** object is instantiated.

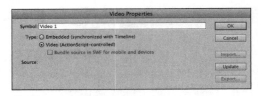

B The Video Properties of your new video symbol.

C A video symbol placeholder named **videoHolder** is placed on the Stage. The instance looks like a square with an x inside it.

```
var myVideo:NetConnection = new NetConnection();
myVideo.connect(null);
var newStream:NetStream = new NetStream(myVideo);
videoHolder.attachNetStream(newStream);
newStream.play("kayak.flv");
```

D A **NetConnection** object and a **NetStream**
object are used to load and play an external FLV.

```
var myVideo:NetConnection = new NetConnection();
myVideo.connect(null);
var newStream:NetStream = new NetStream(myVideo);
videoHolder.attachNetStream(newStream);
newStream.play("kayak.flv");

newStream.addEventListener(AsyncErrorEvent.ASYNC_ERROR, errorhandler);
function errorhandler(myevent:AsyncErrorEvent) {
    //ignore error
}
```

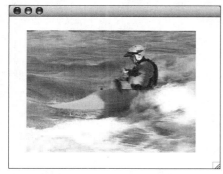

E The ActionScript code (top) loads the external
FLV file named kayak.flv into the **videoHolder**
instance on the Stage and plays.

10. Enter the instance name of the video
symbol instance you placed on the
Stage followed by a period. Enter the
attachNetStream() method with the
video source parameter:

videoHolder.attachNetStream(
→ **newStream);**

In this example, the name of the new
NetStream object is the video source
parameter.

11. On the next line, enter the name of the
NetStream object followed by a period
and then the method, **play()**. As the
parameter for the **play()** method, enter
the name of the external FLV or F4V file
that you want to play on the Stage **D**.

newStream.play("kayak.flv");

As in this example, make sure the filename is enclosed by quotation marks.

12. On the next line, enter the following
event listener to detect asynchronous
error events and ignore them. See the
sidebar "Asynchronous Error Events" for
details regarding this error event.

newStream.addEventListener (
→ **AsyncErrorEvent.ASYNC_ERROR,**
→ **asyncErrorHandler);**
function asyncErrorHandler (
→ **myevent:AsyncErrorEvent):void**
{
    // ignore error
}

13. Publish your movie, and place the SWF
file in the same directory as the video
file whose name you entered.

Flash attaches your external video file
to the instance of the video symbol on
the Stage and begins to stream the
video **E**.

To dynamically load external video with a video object:

1. Modify the file created in the previous task by deleting the video instance on the Stage.

2. Instead of creating a video symbol in the Library beforehand (steps 3–6 of the previous task), create a **Video** object with ActionScript, like so:

```
var videoHolder:Video =
→ new Video(320, 240);
```

This statement creates a new object called **videoHolder** from the **Video** class, which is 320 pixels wide by 240 pixels high.

3. Add the new **Video** object to the Stage with the **addChild()** method:

```
stage.addChild(videoHolder);
```

4. Publish your movie, and place the SWF file in the same directory as the video file whose name you entered.

The full ActionScript code **F** is similar to the one in the previous task, but Flash creates the **Video** object dynamically.

TIP Move the **Video** object, whether dynamically generated or placed on the Stage manually, by assigning new values to its **X** and **Y** properties. You'll learn more about changing graphics displayed on the Stage in the next chapter.

TIP When working with FLV or F4V files for playback, you may need to configure your server to handle the file type (by telling the server its **MIME** type and file extension). Check with your hosting service to make sure the server can handle FLV and F4V files.

```
var myVideo:NetConnection = new NetConnection();
myVideo.connect(null);
var newStream:NetStream = new NetStream(myVideo);

var videoHolder:Video = new Video(320, 240);
stage.addChild(videoHolder);
videoHolder.attachNetStream(newStream);

newStream.play("kayak.flv");

newStream.addEventListener(AsyncErrorEvent.ASYNC_ERROR, errorhandler)
function errorhandler(myevent:AsyncErrorEvent){//ignore error
}
```

F The ActionScript code (top) loads the external FLV file named kayak.flv into the dynamically created **Video** object and plays. The **Video** object is aligned at the top-left corner of the Stage, but you can change its X and Y properties to move it anywhere you want.

TABLE 6.3 Playback Methods of the NetStream Object

Method	Description
pause()	Pauses the video
resume()	Begins playing at the point where the video is paused
seek()	Seeks to any point in the stream provided by the parameter, in seconds
togglePause()	Alternates between pausing or resuming playback of the video

Controlling playback of externally loaded video

There are several methods that you can call to control the playback of the video stream. See **Table 6.3** for a description of the various commands. All of these methods are called from the **NetStream** object. The following task creates buttons for the four methods to control the playback of the video.

Asynchronous Error Events

Cue points are information embedded in FLV and F4V files that you can create when you originally encode your video, or in the Properties inspector. They provide a way for ActionScript to detect the specific spots along the video stream with the **MetaDataEvent** event handler (see Chapter 2 for more information on creating and detecting cue points).

If your video has cue points, Flash requires that you write event handlers for them; otherwise, errors may be generated. However, if you are not interested in cue points or metadata and simply want to play the video, you must add the following bit of code to tell Flash to ignore any asynchronous errors:

```
newStream.addEventListener(AsyncErrorEvent.ASYNC_ERROR, asyncErrorHandler);
function asyncErrorHandler(myevent:AsyncErrorEvent):void
{
    // ignore error
}
```

The sample code adds a listener on the **NetStream** object called **newStream** for the asynchronous error event, which happens when no event handler exists to deal with cue points and metadata from an FLV/F4V.

To control playback of externally loaded video:

1. Continue with the file created in the previous task in which you load and play an external video.

2. Create a button symbol, and place four instances of the button symbol on the Stage.

3. In the Properties inspector, give unique names to the four instances and add text to describe their function. In this example, name the four instances **pause_btn**, **resume_btn**, **toggle_btn**, and **seek_btn** .

4. Select the first frame of the Timeline and open the Actions panel.

5. On the next available line in the Script pane, create an event handler for each of the four buttons to detect a mouse click.

6. In the function of each event handler, make a call to a method of the **NetStream** object 🄗.

7. Publish your movie, and place the SWF file in the same directory as the video file that you want to load.

   The full ActionScript code 🄘 creates the necessary objects to load the video file and provides event handlers to control its playback.

🄖 Four button instances placed on the Stage.

```
pause_btn.addEventListener(MouseEvent.CLICK, pausefunction);
function pausefunction(myevent:MouseEvent):void {
    newStream.pause();
}

resume_btn.addEventListener(MouseEvent.CLICK, resumefunction);
function resumefunction(myevent:MouseEvent):void {
    newStream.resume();
}

toggle_btn.addEventListener(MouseEvent.CLICK, togglefunction);
function togglefunction(myevent:MouseEvent):void {
    newStream.togglePause();
}

seek_btn.addEventListener(MouseEvent.CLICK, seekfunction);
function seekfunction(myevent:MouseEvent):void {
    newStream.seek(1);
}
```

🄗 The mouse click event handlers for the four buttons on the Stage. Each button calls a different method of the **NetStream** object called **newStream**.

```
var myVideo:NetConnection = new NetConnection();
myVideo.connect(null);
var newStream:NetStream = new NetStream(myVideo);
var videoHolder:Video = new Video(320, 240);
stage.addChild(videoHolder);
videoHolder.attachNetStream(newStream);

newStream.play("kayak.flv");

pause_btn.addEventListener(MouseEvent.CLICK, pausefunction);
function pausefunction(myevent:MouseEvent):void {
    newStream.pause();
}

resume_btn.addEventListener(MouseEvent.CLICK, resumefunction);
function resumefunction(myevent:MouseEvent):void {
    newStream.resume();
}

toggle_btn.addEventListener(MouseEvent.CLICK, togglefunction);
function togglefunction(myevent:MouseEvent):void {
    newStream.togglePause();
}

seek_btn.addEventListener(MouseEvent.CLICK, seekfunction);
function seekfunction(myevent:MouseEvent):void {
    newStream.seek(1);
}

newStream.addEventListener(AsyncErrorEvent.ASYNC_ERROR, errorhandler)
function errorhandler(myevent:AsyncErrorEvent){//ignore error
}
```

🄘 The ActionScript code (top) loads the external FLV. The buttons (bottom) control its playback. Create your own playback skin using these methods.

Detecting the status of the video stream

The **NetStream** object dispatches events (**NetStatusEvent**) at various points during the data stream. The different **NetStatusEvent** conditions are captured in its property **info.code** as a string. For example, if the **play()** method can't find the correct video file, the **info.code** property returns a value of **NetStream.Play.StreamNotFound**.

Two important string values, **"NetStream. Play.Start"** and **"NetStream.Play.Stop"**, can help you detect the start and end of a loaded video to better manage the video streams. For example, you could create an event handler to listen for the end of a loaded video. When the video finishes playing, you automatically load the next video in the queue.

To detect the end of externally loaded video:

1. Continue with the file created in the previous task in which you loaded and played an external video.

2. Select the first frame on the Timeline and open the Actions panel.

3. On the next available line, add an event listener on your **NetStream** object to detect the **NetStatusEvent.NET_STATUS** event as follows:

```
newStream.addEventListener(
→ NetStatusEvent.NET_STATUS,
→ statusHandler);
```

4. On the next line, create the function with the **NetStatusEvent** as a parameter, like so:

```
function statusHandler(
→ myevent:NetStatusEvent):void {
    // do something
}
```

When there is a change in the condition of the video stream, the function called **statusHandler** will be triggered.

5. Between the curly braces of the function, add a conditional statement that checks whether the **info.code** property of the event matches a string that indicates the video has finished:

```
if (myevent.info.code ==
→ "NetStream.Play.Stop") {
    // video has stopped
}
```

6. Add additional statements to be carried out when the video finishes **❶**. Publish your movie, and place the SWF file in the same directory as the video file that you want to load.

When Flash detects the end of the video, **myevent.info.code** matches the string **"NetStream.Play.Stop"** and additional instructions can be given.

```
newStream.addEventListener(NetStatusEvent.NET_STATUS, statusHandler);
function statusHandler(myevent:NetStatusEvent):void {
    if (myevent.info.code == "NetStream.Play.Stop") {
        newStream.play("video2.flv");
    }
}
```

❶ When Flash detects the end of the first video stream, it automatically plays another video, called video2.flv.

Detecting Download Progress: Preloaders

All the hard work you put into creating complex interactivity in your movie will be wasted if your viewers have to wait too long to download the movie over the Web and leave. You can avoid losing viewers by creating short animations that entertain them while the rest of your movie downloads. These diversions, or *preloaders*, tell your viewers how much of the movie has downloaded and how much longer they have to wait. When enough data has been delivered over the Web to the viewers' computers, you can trigger your movie to start. In effect, you hold back the playhead until you know that all the frames are available to play. Only then do you send the playhead to the starting frame of your movie.

Preloaders must be small because you want them to load almost immediately, and they should be informative, letting your viewers know what they're waiting for.

Flash provides many ways to monitor the state of the download progress. You can test for the number of frames that have downloaded with the **MovieClip** class properties **framesLoaded** and **totalFrames**. But the frames of your movie most likely contain data that aren't evenly spread, so testing the amount of data (measured in bytes) is a more accurate gauge of download progress.

As you learned earlier in the section "Controlling Loaded Flash Movies," you can access information about the status of any load with the **LoaderInfo** object. Earlier you used it to determine when an external SWF had completely loaded. But you can also use it to determine when the main SWF (or any loading file) has completely loaded, or check on its download progress. Use the **ProgressEvent** event with the properties **bytesLoaded** and **bytesTotal** to help you monitor the download progress.

The concept of a preloader is simple. You tell Flash to compare the amount of data loaded with the total data in the movie. As this ratio changes, you can display the percentage numerically with a dynamic text field or represent the changing ratio graphically, such as with a growing, horizontal progress bar. Because they often show the progress of the download, these preloaders are sometimes known as *progressive preloaders*.

Registration point

A A rectangular movie clip with its registration point on the far-left edge can be used as a graphical representation of download progress.

stop action

B The **stop()** method is put on the very first frame on the Timeline to pause your movie until all the data has downloaded.

To create a preloader that graphically shows download progress:

1. Create a long rectangular movie clip symbol.

   Make sure its registration point is at its far-left edge **A**.

2. Place an instance of the symbol on the Stage, and give it an instance name (this example uses **bar_mc**).

   Your preloader is a rectangle that grows longer according to the percentage of downloaded frames. Flash will dynamically change the properties of the rectangular movie clip to stretch it out. Because the bar should grow from left to right, the registration point is placed on the left edge.

3. Select the first frame of the main Timeline, and open the Actions panel.

4. Enter **stop()**.

   The **stop()** method prevents your movie from playing until it has downloaded completely **B**.

5. On the next line, add an event listener on the main Timeline's **loaderInfo** property. Listen for the **ProgressEvent.PROGRESS** event, like so:

   ```
   root.loaderInfo.addEventListener (
   → ProgressEvent.PROGRESS,
   → progressHandler);
   ```

   The loading of your main Flash movie is happening on the root Timeline, so you can use **loaderInfo** to access its load properties. Whenever download progress is detected, the function called **progressHandler** is called.

Continues on next page

6. On the next line, create the function called **progressHandler** with a **ProgressEvent** event as its parameter:

```
function progressHandler(
→ myevent:ProgressEvent):void {
    // show progress
}
```

7. Between the curly braces of the function, declare a variable and assign the ratio of bytes downloaded to total bytes with the following:

```
var myprogress:Number =
→ myevent.bytesLoaded /
→ myevent.bytesTotal;
```

The amount of data loaded is defined in the **ProgressEvent**'s **bytesLoaded** property. The total data is defined in the **ProgressEvent**'s **bytesTotal** property. Dividing the first over the second provides a ratio of the overall progress.

8. On the next line (but still within the function), add the following:

```
bar_mc.scaleX = myprogress;
```

The bar on the Stage is scaled horizontally according to the download ratio **C**.

9. On a new line outside the event handler, create a new listener on the root Timeline's **loaderInfo** property to detect the **Event.COMPLETE** event:

```
root.loaderInfo.addEventListener(
→ Event.COMPLETE, finished);
```

This second listener listens for the completion of the download and will call the function called **finished**.

10. On the next line, create the function called **finished** with an **Event** event as its parameter:

```
function finished(
→ myevent:Event):void {
    play();
}
```

In this example, when the function is called, the Flash movie begins playing **D**.

```
stop();
root.loaderInfo.addEventListener(ProgressEvent.PROGRESS, progressHandler);
function progressHandler(myevent:ProgressEvent):void {
    var myprogress:Number = myevent.bytesLoaded/myevent.bytesTotal;
    bar_mc.scaleX = myprogress
}
```

C As the movie downloads, its progress is captured in the variable **myprogress**, which measures the ratio of **bytesLoaded** to **bytesTotal** of the loading movie. This ratio is used to scale the rectangle on the Stage.

```
stop();
root.loaderInfo.addEventListener(ProgressEvent.PROGRESS, progressHandler);
function progressHandler(myevent:ProgressEvent):void {
    var myprogress:Number = myevent.bytesLoaded/myevent.bytesTotal;
    bar_mc.scaleX = myprogress
}

root.loaderInfo.addEventListener(Event.COMPLETE, finished);
function finished(myevent:Event):void {
    play();
}
```

D When the loading process is complete, the function called **finished** is triggered. Flash begins playing the main Timeline.

Rectangular movie clip
removed at keyframe 2

Movie begins from
this point forward

E The real movie begins at keyframe 2 after the
rectangular movie clip is removed.

Current location of playhead

Data transfer rate   Progress of download

Causes delay during playback

F The Bandwidth Profiler shows the individual
frames that cause pauses during playback
because the amount of data exceeds the data
transfer rate. The alternating light and dark
bars represent different frames. Notice how
the progress of the download (about 8 out of
10 frames have loaded completely) affects the
proportion of the movie clip (about 80 percent).

11. Begin the actual content of your
Flash document from the second
keyframe **E**.

12. Test your movie (Control > Test Movie >
in Flash Professional).

13. Choose View > Bandwidth Profiler
(Ctrl-B for Windows, Cmd-B for Mac)
and choose View > Simulate Download.

The Bandwidth Profiler is an information window above your movie in Test
Movie mode; it displays the number of
frames and the amount of data in each
frame as vertical bars. If the vertical
bars extend over the bottom of the red
horizontal line, there is too much data
to be downloaded at the bandwidth
setting without causing a stutter during playback. The Simulate Download
option simulates actual download
performance **F**. The green bar at the
top shows the download progress. The
triangle marks the current location of
the playhead. The playhead remains
in frame 1 until the green progress bar
reaches the end of the timeline. Only
then does the playhead begin moving.

TIP You won't see your preloader working
unless you build an animation with many
frames containing fairly large graphics that
require lengthy download times. If your animation is small, you'll see your preloader whiz by
because all the data will download quickly and
begin playing almost immediately.

TIP Explore other graphical treatments of
the download progress. Stretching the length
of a movie clip is just one way to animate the
download process. With subtle changes to
your ActionScript, you can apply a variety of
animated effects to your preloader.

Showing numeric download progress

Often, a preloader has an accompanying display of the percentage of download progress. This display is accomplished with a text field placed on the Stage. You'll learn more about text in Chapter 10, "Controlling Text," but you can use the steps in the following task now to add a simple numeric display.

The Bandwidth Profiler

The Bandwidth Profiler is a handy option to see how data is distributed throughout your Flash movie and how quickly (or slowly) it will download over the Web. In Test Movie mode (after choosing Control > Test Movie > in Flash Professional), choose View > Bandwidth Profiler (Ctrl-B for Windows, Cmd-B for Mac) to see this information.

The left side of the Bandwidth Profiler shows movie information, such as Stage dimensions, frame rate, file size, total duration, and preload time in frames and seconds. It also shows the Bandwidth setting, which simulates actual download performance at a specified rate. You can change that rate in the View > Download Settings menu and choose the Internet connection speed that your viewers are likely to have. Flash gives you options for DSL and T1 lines, for example.

The bar graph on the right side of the Bandwidth Profiler shows the amount of data in each frame of your movie. You can view the graph as a streaming graph (choose View > Streaming Graph) or as a frame-by-frame graph (choose View > Frame by Frame Graph). The streaming graph indicates how the movie downloads over the Web by showing you how data streams from each frame, whereas the frame-by-frame graph indicates the amount of data in each frame. In Streaming Graph mode, you can tell which frames will cause hang-ups during playback by noting which bar exceeds the given Bandwidth setting.

To watch the actual download performance of your movie, choose View > Simulate Download. Flash simulates playback over the Web at the given Bandwidth setting. A green horizontal bar at the top of the window indicates which frames have been downloaded, and the triangular playhead marks the current frame.

G This TLF text field is called `myTextField_txt`.

Text field

H The text field displays the percentage of the download progress along with the graphical representation.

I In this figure, you can see the relationship between the **Loader** object, the external file that it loads, and the associated **LoaderInfo** object that provides information about the content and the loading process (see Table 6.2). The **contentLoaderInfo** property of the **Loader** object references the **LoaderInfo** object. The **loaderInfo** property of the content also references the **LoaderInfo** object. So for loading external content, use the **contentLoaderInfo** property of the **Loader** object. For the main SWF, use the **loaderInfo** property of **root**.

To add a numeric display to the preloader:

1. Continuing with the file from the preceding task, select the Text tool and choose TLF Text > Read Only (or Classic Text > Dynamic), and drag out a text field on the Stage.

2. In the Properties inspector, give the text field an instance name **G**.

• As with buttons and movie clip symbols, the instance name of the text field lets you target the text field and control it using ActionScript.

3. Select the first frame of the main Timeline, and open the Actions panel.

4. Within the curly braces of the function called **progressHandler**, enter the following:

```
myTextField_txt.text = Math.round(
→ myprogress * 100) + "%";
```

The percentage of download progress is rounded to a whole number by the **Math.round()** method. The percent (%) character is appended to the end, and the result is assigned to the **text** property of your text field, displaying it on the Stage **H**.

Detecting download progress of external images and movies

Monitoring the download progress of external images and movies is very similar to monitoring the download progress of the main Flash movie. You can use the identical code, but instead of adding your listener to **root.loaderInfo**, you'll add your listener to **myloader.contentLoaderInfo** (provided that your **Loader** object is named **myloader**). Recall that your **Loader**'s **contentLoaderInfo** refers to the **LoaderInfo** object of the loaded content. You can visualize the relationship in **I**.

To create a preloader for external images or movies:

1. Create a small rectangular movie clip symbol.

   Make sure its registration point is at the far-left edge.

2. Place an instance of the symbol on the Stage, and give it a name in the Properties inspector .

   The properties of the rectangle will change in proportion to the number of bytes that are downloaded. This will act as a visual indicator to the audience that the movie is loading.

J A new rectangular movie clip is given an instance name of **bar_mc**.

K A TLF text field is given an instance name of **myTextField_txt**.

3. Select the Text tool and drag out a text field on the Stage. In the Properties inspector, select TLF Text and Read Only from the drop-down lists (or Classic Text and Dynamic) and give the field an instance name **K**.

   The text field will display the percentage of download progress.

4. Select the first frame of the main Timeline, and open the Actions panel.

5. Create a new **URLRequest** object with the name of the external file as the **url** property as in the following:

```
var myrequest:URLRequest =
→ new URLRequest("someimage.jpg");
```

   In this example, the external file is a JPEG that you want to load, and it lies in the same folder as the main Flash movie. You can use an absolute URL to an image or SWF on the Internet as well.

6. On the next line, create a new **Loader** object with the following code:

```
var myloader:Loader =
→ new Loader();
```

7. On the next line, call the **load()** method for your new **Loader** object and use the **URLRequest** object as the parameter. Add the Loader object to the Stage **L**:

```
myloader.load(myrequest);
stage.addChild(myloader);
```

The code so far should be familiar if you've read the previous section in this chapter.

8. On the next line, add an event listener to the **Loader** object's **contentLoaderInfo** property and listen for the **ProgressEvent.PROGRESS** event as in the following code:

```
myloader.contentLoaderInfo.
→ addEventListener(ProgressEvent.
→ PROGRESS, progresshandler);
```

9. On the next line, enter the event-handler function as you did for the previous task. The full code so far is shown in **M**.

10. Next, add a second event listener to the **Loader** object's **contentLoaderInfo** property and listen for the **Event.COMPLETE** event as in the following code:

```
myloader.contentLoaderInfo.
→ addEventListener(Event.COMPLETE,
→ alldone);
```

As soon as the **Event.COMPLETE** event has dispatched from the loading process, the function called **alldone** will be called.

Continues on next page

```
var myrequest:URLRequest = new URLRequest("someimage.jpg");
var myloader:Loader = new Loader();
myloader.load(myrequest);
stage.addChild(myloader);
```

L An external file called someimage.jpg loads into the **Loader** object called **myloader**.

```
var myrequest:URLRequest = new URLRequest("someimage.jpg");
var myloader:Loader = new Loader();
myloader.load(myrequest);
stage.addChild(myloader);

myloader.contentLoaderInfo.addEventListener(ProgressEvent.PROGRESS, progresshandler);
function progresshandler(myevent:ProgressEvent):void {
    var myprogress:Number=myevent.bytesLoaded / myevent.bytesTotal;
    bar_mc.scaleX=myprogress;
    myTextField_txt.text = Math.round(myprogress * 100) + "%";
}
```

M When the external file begins to load, the **Loader** object's **contentLoaderInfo** property can be used to access the **LoaderInfo** object. The **ProgressEvent.PROGRESS** event is dispatched as the load happens, and the ratio of downloaded data to total data is displayed graphically with the movie clip and in a dynamic text field.

11. On a new line, enter the function called **alldone** as follows:

```
function
alldone(myevent:Event):void {
    removeChild(myTextField_txt);
    removeChild(bar_mc);
}
```

When the load is complete, the text field and movie clip are removed 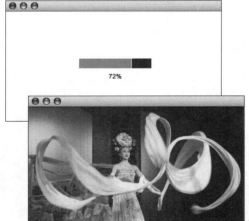.

12. Test your movie.

As your external movie or image loads into your **Loader** object, the text field displays the percentage of total bytes downloaded, and the rectangular movie clip grows longer. When the entire movie or image has loaded, the text field and elongated rectangular movie clip disappear 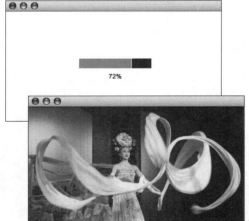.

```
var myrequest:URLRequest = new URLRequest("someimage.jpg");
var myloader:Loader = new Loader();
myloader.load(myrequest);
stage.addChild(myloader);

myloader.contentLoaderInfo.addEventListener(ProgressEvent.PROGRESS, progresshandler);
function progresshandler(myevent:ProgressEvent):void {
    var myprogress:Number=myevent.bytesLoaded / myevent.bytesTotal;
    bar_mc.scaleX=myprogress;
    myTextField_txt.text = Math.round(myprogress * 100) + "%";
}

myloader.contentLoaderInfo.addEventListener(Event.COMPLETE, alldone);
function alldone(myevent:Event):void {
    removeChild(myTextField_txt);
    removeChild(bar_mc);
}
```

N The complete code for a preloader for external content. The last event handler detects when the load is complete. When the load is complete, the preloader (movie clip and dynamic text field) are removed from the Stage.

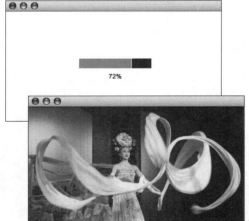

O During the loading progress, Flash updates the contents of the text field called **myTextField_txt** and stretches the rectangular movie clip called **bar_mc** in proportion to the percentage of downloaded bytes (top). When loading is finished, the image called someimage.jpg appears in the Loader and the text field and rectangular movie clip disappears (bottom).

Controlling and Displaying Graphics

ActionScript's ability to create, control, and display graphical elements on the fly and in response to events is what makes Flash truly powerful. You can create and manipulate many objects such as movie clips, buttons, images, and even shapes and masks. Properties that control how these objects appear, such as position, scale, rotation, transparency, color, and blending effects, can all be changed with ActionScript. You can even have control over motion tweens that you create purely with ActionScript, or control the individual pixels in bitmap images.

Flash also gives you many methods to control an object's behavior. You can make objects draggable so that viewers can pick up puzzle pieces and put them in their correct places, or you can develop a more immersive online shopping experience in which viewers can grab merchandise and drop it into their shopping carts. In this chapter, you'll learn how to control collisions and overlaps with other objects, and you'll learn how to generate different objects dynamically so that new instances appear on the Stage during playback.

In This Chapter

Understanding the Display List

The key to successfully manipulating graphics on the Stage is to understand what is known as the *display list*. The display list is the hierarchy of visible objects on the Stage. The display list lets Flash (and you) keep track of what the user sees, the visual relationships between objects, and the stacking order (or overlapping) of the objects.

Conceptually, it's much like the folder structure on your computer desktop and can be represented as a tree structure **A**. The top-level element is the Stage. Each time you play a Flash movie in a Web browser, the Flash Player opens your SWF and places it on the Stage. So the Stage is the container that holds your main SWF. Inside your main SWF you can place other elements, such as buttons, text, video, bitmaps, and other objects—all of which are instances of a big class known as **DisplayObject**. You'll be using many of the properties of the **DisplayObject** class to control the

objects' appearances. You can also have elements on your main SWF that contain **DisplayObject** objects. These are known as **DisplayObjectContainer** objects and include objects like a **Sprite** object, a **Loader** object, a **MovieClip** object, and the Stage itself. So you can think of the main SWF on the Stage as your desktop, the **DisplayObject**s as individual files, and the **DisplayObjectContainer**s as folders that can contain additional folders or files.

One of the most important methods of the **DisplayObjectContainer** class is one that you've already used in previous chapters—**addChild()**. This method adds an element (either another **DisplayObjectContainer** or a **DisplayObject**) to the display list and makes it visible. As you add more **DisplayObject**s and **DisplayObjectContainer**s to your display list, you need to keep track of how they overlap. Flash keeps track of each object with a number, known as an index, that begins at 0 and increases in whole numbers. Objects with higher display list index numbers overlap those with lower numbers.

A The display list can be represented hierarchically like a tree (top) where the Stage is the top-level **DisplayObjectContainer**. You can also think of the display list like your computer desktop, where the Stage is at the bottom and the objects you add to it are folders (**DisplayObjectContainer**s) or files (**DisplayObject**s). The folders can contain other folders or files.

Changing Visual Properties

Many **DisplayObject** properties—**alpha**, **rotatation**, **scaleX**, **scaleY**—define how the object looks. By using dot syntax, you can target any object of the class and change any of those characteristics during playback. **Table 7.1** summarizes many properties that are available to all the objects

in the **DisplayObject** class, which include movie clips, text fields, videos, bitmaps, buttons, dynamically drawn shapes, loaders, sprites, and the Stage. You've already learned about some of these objects in previous chapters, and you'll learn about the others in this and upcoming chapters.

The following tasks demonstrate how to change a few of the common properties of an object.

TABLE 7.1 DisplayObject Properties

Property	Value	Description
alpha	Number (0 to 1)	Transparency, where 0 is totally transparent and 1 is opaque.
visible	**true** or **false**	Whether an object can be seen.
name	String	Instance name of the object.
rotation	Number	Degree of rotation in a clockwise direction from the registration point.
rotationX	Number	Degree of rotation around the x-axis from its original orientation.
rotationY	Number	Degree of rotation around the y-axis from its original orientation.
rotationZ	Number	Degree of rotation around the z-axis from its original orientation.
width	Number in pixels	Horizontal dimension.
height	Number in pixels	Vertical dimension.
x	Number in pixels	Horizontal position of the object's registration point.
y	Number in pixels	Vertical position of the object's registration point.
z	Number in pixels	Depth position of the object's registration point.
scaleX	Number (0 to 1)	Percentage of the original object's horizontal dimension.
scaleY	Number (0 to 1)	Percentage of the original object's vertical dimension.
scaleZ	Number (0 to 1)	Percentage of the original object's depth dimension.
blendMode	String	Which blend mode to use to visually combine colors.
cacheAsBitmap	**true** or **false**	Whether to redraw the contents of the object every frame (**false**) or use a static bitmap of the object's contents (**true**).
opaqueBackground	Numeric color value	Nontransparent background color for the instance.
scrollRect	**Rectangle** object	Window of visible content of the object, which can be changed to efficiently simulate scrolling.
loaderInfo	**LoaderInfo** object	Returns a **LoaderInfo** object containing information about the loading process.
mask	**DisplayObject**	Sets the mask area (visible area) of the object.
filters	**Array** of filter objects	Set of graphical filters to apply to this object.
scale9Grid	**Rectangle** object	Nine regions that control how the movie clip distorts when scaling.
transform	**Transform** object	Values representing color, size, and position changes applied to the instance.

To change the position of an object:

1. For this example, create a movie clip and place an instance of it on the Stage. In the Properties inspector, give it a name **B**.

2. Select the first frame of the Timeline, and open the Actions panel.

3. Enter the instance name, then a dot, followed by the property **x**. Enter an equals sign followed by a number in pixels, like so:

   `myMovieClip_mc.x = 100;`

   This statement positions the movie clip called **myMovieClip_mc** 100 pixels from the left edge of the Stage.

4. On a new line, enter the instance name, then a dot, followed by the property **y**. Enter an equals sign followed by a number in pixels, like so:

   `myMovieClip_mc.y = 50;`

   This statement positions the movie clip called **myMovieClip_mc** 50 pixels from the top edge of the Stage.

5. Test your movie (Control > Test Movie > in Flash Professional).

   Both statements change the original horizontal and vertical position of the movie clip called **myMovieClip_mc** on the Stage **C**.

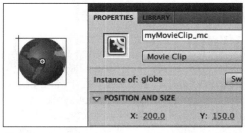

B This movie clip instance on the Stage is called `myMovieClip_mc`.

C The instance moves position.

D The coordinate space for the Stage (top). The x position increases from the left and the y position increases from the top. The coordinate space for a movie clip (bottom) can go into negative values.

E The original instance (top) rotates clockwise as a result of the new value assigned to the **rotation** property.

TIP The x- and y-coordinate space for the main Timeline is different from movie clip time-lines. In the main Timeline, the x-axis begins at the left edge and increases to the right; the y-axis begins at the top edge and increases to the bottom. Thus, x = 0, y = 0 corresponds to the top-left corner of the Stage. For movie clips, the coordinates x = 0, y = 0 correspond to the registration point (the crosshair). The value of x increases to the right of the registration point and decreases into negative values to the left of the registration point. The value of y increases to the bottom and decreases into negative values to the top **D**.

To change the rotation of an object:

In the Actions panel, assign a number to the property **rotation** of an instance, like so:

```
myMovieClip_mc.rotation = 45;
```

This statement rotates the movie clip called **myMovieClip_mc** 45 degrees clockwise from its registration point **E**.

To change the 3D rotation of an object:

In the Actions panel, assign a number to the property **rotationX**, **rotationY**, or **rotationZ** of an instance, like so:

`myMovieClip_mc.rotationY = 45;`

This statement rotates the movie clip called **myMovieClip_mc** in 3D space around the y-axis .

To change the size of an object:

- In the Actions panel, assign a decimal to the property **scaleX** or **scaleY** of an instance, like so:

  `myMovieClip_mc.scaleX = .5;`

  This statement makes the movie clip called **myMovieClip_mc** scale down in the horizontal direction 50 percent of its original size .

Or

- In the Actions panel, assign a number to the property width and height of an instance, like so:

  `myMovieClip_mc.width = 250;`

  This statement makes the movie clip called **myMovieClip_mc** change its horizontal dimension to 250 pixels .

TIP The **scaleX** and **scaleY** properties control the percentage of the *original* object, which is different from what may be on the Stage. For example, if you place an instance of a movie clip on the Stage and manually shrink it **50 percent with the Free Transform tool, and then you assign 1 to scaleX and assign 1 to scaleY during playback, your movie clip will double in appearance.**

`myMovieClip_mc.rotationY = 45;`

F The original instance (top) rotates along the y-axis in 3D (like a door swinging along its vertical hinge) as a result of the new value assigned to the **rotationY** property.

`myMovieClip_mc.scaleX = .5;`

G The original instance (top) squishes horizontally as a result of the new value assigned to the **scaleX** property.

`myMovieClip_mc.width = 250;`

← 250 pixels →

H The instance can squish or stretch to the specified pixel dimension as a result of the new value assigned to the **width** property.

`myMovieClip_mc.alpha = .2;`

The original instance (top) becomes more transparent as a result of the new value assigned to the **alpha** property.

To change the transparency of an object:

In the Actions panel, assign a decimal to the property **alpha** of an instance, like so:

`myMovieClip_mc.alpha = .2;`

This statement changes the transparency of the movie clip called **myMovieClip_mc** so it is 20 percent opaque **I**.

TIP There is a difference between an `alpha` of 0 and a `visible` of `false`, although the result may look the same. When the `visible` property is `false`, the object literally can't be seen. Buttons and other interactive objects don't respond. When `alpha` is 0, on the other hand, buttons and other interactive objects are transparent, but can still respond.

Assigning values that are relative

In the previous examples, you learned to assign a fixed value to change various properties of objects. However, often you'll want to change an object's property relative to its current value or relative to another object's property. You may want to rotate a cannon 10 degrees each time your viewer clicks a button, for example. Or you may want to move an image to align its left edge with another image. To change the property of one object based on the property of another object, simply reference the second object on the right side of the equals sign in an expression, like so:

J The top square (**myimage**) moves relative to where the bottom square (**myimage2**) is located.

```
myimage.x = myimage2.x +
→ myimage2.width;
```

The statement on the right side of the equals sign is resolved and the result is assigned to the property on the left side of the equals sign. In this example, the object called **myimage** moves so that its left edge is aligned with the right edge of **myimage2** **J**.

To change an object's property based on its own current value, you can write the expression:

```
myimage.rotation = myimage.rotation
→ + 10;
```

This expression adds 10 degrees to the current angle of the object named **myimage**. A shortcut way of writing this statement is as follows:

```
myimage.rotation += 10;
```

```
clockhand_mc.addEventListener(MouseEvent.CLICK, rotate);
function rotate(myevent:MouseEvent):void {
    clockhand_mc.rotation += 30;
}
```

K At each mouse click, 30 degrees is added to the current value of **rotation**.

L The instance called **clockhand_mc** rotates 30 degrees at each mouse click.

TIP You can use shortcuts like the addition assignment operator in this task to add and subtract values by using combinations of the arithmetic operators. You'll learn about these combinations in Chapter 9, "Controlling Information Flow."

To assign a property that is relative to its current value:

1. Create a movie clip, place an instance on the Stage, and give it an instance name in the Properties inspector.

   In this task, you'll assign a new value to the **rotation** property based on the object's current value of **rotation**. Each time you click the object, it will add 30 degrees.

2. Select the first frame of the main Timeline, and open the Actions panel.

3. Create an event handler by adding a listener to the movie clip to detect a mouse click, like so:

   clockhand_mc.addEventListener(
   ↪ MouseEvent.CLICK, rotate);

   In this example, Flash listens for a mouse click over the movie clip called **clockhand_mc** and triggers a function called **rotate** in response.

4. On the next available line, add the event-handler function as follows:

   function
   rotate(myevent:MouseEvent):void {
   **   clockhand_mc.rotation += 30;**
   }

   The addition assignment operator is the plus and equals signs together. It will read the value of the **rotation** property, add to it the amount written to the right of the operator, and store the result back in the property's value **K**.

5. Test your movie (Control > Test Movie > in Flash Professional).

   Each time the movie clip is clicked, Flash will get the current value of **clockhand_mc** and add 30 degrees to its clockwise rotation **L**.

Modifying the Color

To modify the color of a **DisplayObject** object, you can use the **ColorTransform** class, which provides properties to which you assign new colors or new values for the red, blue, green, and alpha channels.

Every **DisplayObject** has a **transform** property, which is an instance of the **Transform** class. The **Transform** object contains a snapshot of all the transformations that have been applied to the object, including color changes, scaling, rotation, and more. The color changes are specifically defined in another property called **colorTransform**, which is an instance of the **ColorTransform** class. This means you can retrieve or assign color transformations by referencing the target path **myimage.transform.colorTransform**, where **myimage** would be the name of the object you want to modify.

The first step in modifying an object's color is instantiating a new **ColorTransform**

object. Then you define color changes as a new value of the **color** property of your new **ColorTransform** object. Your code would look similar to this:

```
var mynewcolor:ColorTransform = new
→ ColorTransform();
mynewcolor.color = 0x0D69F2;
```

In this example, **mynewcolor** is the name of your new **ColorTransform** object. The new value of the **color** property is in the form 0xRRGGBB (hexadecimal equivalents for the red, green, and blue components of a color). You can find the code for any color in the Color Mixer panel. Choose a color in the color spectrum, and the hexadecimal value for that color appears in the display underneath **A**.

Finally, once you've defined a new color in the **color** property of your **ColorTransform** instance, you assign it to your object like this:

```
myimage.transform.colorTransform =
→ mynewcolor;
```

Hex code

A The Color Mixer panel has a display window to show the selected RGB code in hexadecimal code.

```
var mycolorchange:ColorTransform = new ColorTransform();
```

B The new **ColorTransform** object is called **mycolorchange**.

```
var mycolorchange:ColorTransform = new ColorTransform();
mycolorchange.color = 0x0D69F2;
```

C A new color is assigned to the **color** property of your **ColorTransform** object.

```
var mycolorchange:ColorTransform = new ColorTransform();
mycolorchange.color = 0x0D69F2;
stage.addEventListener(MouseEvent.CLICK, changecolor);
function changecolor(myevent:MouseEvent):void {
    image_mc.transform.colorTransform = mycolorchange;
}
```

D A mouse click will assign the new color to the **transform.colorTransform** property of the instance called **image_mc**, changing its color.

E The original instance (top) changes color (bottom) when it is clicked. Notice that the entire object changes color.

To set the color of an object:

1. Create a movie clip symbol whose color you want to modify, place an instance of it on the Stage, and name it in the Properties inspector. This example uses a movie clip, but you can change the color of any **DisplayObject** or **DisplayObjectContainer**.

2. Select the first frame of the main Timeline, and open the Actions panel.

3. Create a new instance from the **ColorTransform** class **B**.

4. On the next line, enter the instance name of your new **ColorTransform** object, then a dot, the **color** property, and equals sign, and then the six-digit hexadecimal code for your new color **C**.

5. Assign an event handler to detect a mouse click. When you click on the Stage, you will change the color of your movie clip.

6. Within the body of the event-handler function, enter a statement that assigns your new **ColorTransform** object to the movie clip's **transform.colorTransform** property. The full code, including the event handler, is shown in **D**.

7. Test your movie (Control > Test Movie > in Flash Professional).

   In the first frame, a **ColorTransform** object is instantiated and a new value is assigned to its **color** property. When you click the Stage, your **ColorTransform** object is assigned to your movie clip, changing its color **E**.

Making advanced color transformations

The property **color** lets you change only an object's color. To change its brightness or its transparency, or change each red, green, or blue component separately, you must specify multiplier and offset properties. There is one property to define a multiplier and one to specify an offset value for each of the RGB components as well as the alpha (transparency). These properties are the same as those in the Advanced Effect dialog box that appears when you apply an advanced color effect to an instance 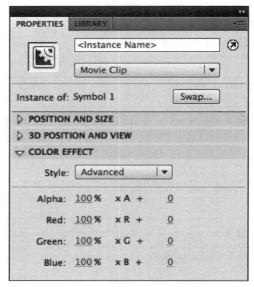. The only difference is that in the dialog box you specify the multiplier as a percentage (0–100), but in ActionScript, the multiplier properties are set as decimal numbers. A multiplier is usually in the range 0–1, which corresponds to 0–100% (for example, 25% is specified as **.25**). However, the multiplier can be any decimal number (such as **2** to double the value, for instance).

You can specify multiplier and offset properties in two ways. The **ColorTransform** class has individual multiplier and offset properties for each color channel, described in **Table 7.2**. To change just one of these properties, assign a new value to the appropriate property.

You may want to set several of the multiplier or offset properties for a **ColorTransform** instance, which is cumbersome to do one property at a time. As an alternative, you can specify the multiplier and offset values as parameters when you call the constructor function to create your **ColorTransform** instance. To set the properties as parameters in the constructor function, you must specify all eight in the following order: red multiplier, green multiplier, blue multiplier, alpha multiplier,

F The options for advanced effects in the Properties inspector control the RGB and alpha percentages and offset values for any instance.

TABLE 7.2 ColorTransform Properties

Property	Value
redMultiplier	Decimal number to multiply by the red component.
redOffset	Offset (−255 to 255) of the red component.
greenMultipler	Decimal number to multiply by the green component.
greenOffset	Offset (−255 to 255) of the green component.
blueMultiplier	Decimal number to multiply by the blue component.
blueOffset	Offset (−255 to 255) of the blue component.
alphaModifier	Decimal number to multiply by the alpha (transparency).
alphaOffset	Offset (−255 to 255) of the alpha (transparency).
color	Hex color (0xRRGGBB) Setting this property sets the offset and multiplier properties accordingly.

red offset, green offset, blue offset, alpha offset. Here's an example:

```
var mynewcolor:ColorTransform = new
→ ColorTransform (1, .3, .2, 1, 0, 0,
→ 0, 0);
```

When you call the **ColorTransform** constructor without parameters as you did previously, the **ColorTransform** object is created with the default parameters that maintain the movie clip's color—1 for each multiplier and 0 for each offset.

To transform the color and alpha of an object:

1. Create a movie clip symbol whose color you want to modify, place an instance of it on the Stage, and name it in the Properties inspector. This example uses a movie clip, but you can change the color of any **DisplayObject** or **DisplayObjectContainer**.

2. Select the first frame of the main Timeline, and open the Actions panel.

3. Create a new instance from the **ColorTransform** class. Provide eight parameters in the constructor function for the RGB and alpha multipliers and the RGB and alpha offset values **G**.

   The properties for the color transformation are defined in the parameters of your **ColorTransform** constructor call.

4. Assign an event handler to detect a mouse click. When you click on the Stage, you will change the color of your movie clip.

5. Within the body of the event-handler function, enter a statement that assigns your new **ColorTransform** object to the movie clip's **transform.colorTransform** property. The full code, including the event handler, is shown in **H**.

Continues on next page

```
var mycolorchange:ColorTransform = new ColorTransform(1, .3, .2, 1, 0, 0, 0, 0);
```

G A new **ColorTransform** object is created with red, green, blue, and alpha multiplier and offset values assigned as properties at the same time.

```
var mycolorchange:ColorTransform = new ColorTransform(1, .3, .2, 1, 0, 0, 0, 0);
stage.addEventListener(MouseEvent.CLICK, changecolor);
function changecolor(myevent:MouseEvent):void {
    image_mc.transform.colorTransform = mycolorchange;
}
```

H A mouse click will assign the color changes to the **transform.colorTransform** property of the instance called **image_mc**, changing its color and/or alpha.

6. Test your movie (Control > Test Movie > in Flash Professional).

In the first frame, a **ColorTransform** object is instantiated and the new color properties are defined. When you click your movie clip, your **ColorTransform** object is assigned to your movie clip, changing its color and transparency .

TIP If you don't want to define the color transformation values when you instantiate your new **ColorTransform** instance, you can do so by specifying a value for each property, like so:

```
var mynewcolor:ColorTransform=new
→ ColorTransform();
mynewcolor.redMultiplier=.3;
mynewcolor.greenMultiplier=.2;
mynewcolor.blueMultiplier=1;
mynewcolor.alphaMultiplier=1;
mynewcolor.redOffset=0;
mynewcolor.greenOffset=0;
mynewcolor.blueOffset=0;
mynewcolor.alphaOffset=0;
image_mc.transform.colorTransform =
→ mynewcolor;
```

In this example, the transparency doesn't change, but the colors shift to a bluer hue.

I The original image (top) is assigned new color values for its RGB and alpha channels, and as a result, shifts colors (bottom).

To change the brightness of a movie clip:

Increase the offset parameters for the red, green, and blue components equally, but leave the other parameters unchanged.

If your **ColorTransform** object is called **mynewcolor**, for example, set its properties individually as follows to increase the brightness about 50 percent:

```
mynewcolor.redMultiplier = 1;
mynewcolor.greenMultiplier = 1;
mynewcolor.blueMultiplier = 1;
mynewcolor.alphaMultiplier = 1;
mynewcolor.redOffset = 125;
mynewcolor.greenOffset = 125;
mynewcolor.blueOffset = 125;
mynewcolor.alphaOffset = 0;
```

Or, instantiate your **ColorTransform** object with these parameters:

```
var mynewcolor:ColorTransform= new
→ ColorTransform(1, 1, 1, 1, 125, 125,
→ 125, 0);
```

If you want to increase the brightness completely so your object turns white, you can set the offset parameters of red, green, and blue to their maximum (255), as follows:

```
mynewcolor.redMultiplier = 1;
mynewcolor.greenMultiplier = 1;
mynewcolor.blueMultiplier = 1;
mynewcolor.alphaMultiplier = 1;
mynewcolor.redOffset = 255;
mynewcolor.greenOffset = 255;
mynewcolor.blueOffset = 255;
mynewcolor.alphaOffset = 0;
```

To change the transparency of a movie clip:

Decrease either the offset or the percentage parameter for the alpha component and leave the other parameters unchanged.

Decrease **alphaMultiplier** to 0 or decrease **alphaOffset** to −255 for total transparency.

Blending Colors

If you've used a graphics manipulation program such as Photoshop or Fireworks, you've likely seen a *blend mode* option, which is a way to control how the colors of overlapping objects interact. Normally, when one object overlaps another, the object is opaque and completely blocks the object below from view. By applying a blend mode to the top object, you can change this behavior and show a mix of the colors of the two objects rather than just the color of the top object.

You can manually apply a blend mode to a movie clip or a button from within the authoring tool by selecting an instance on the Stage and choosing the desired mode from the Blending menu in the Display section of the Properties inspector **Ⓐ**. You can also apply a blend mode using ActionScript by setting a value for a **DisplayObject**'s **blendMode** property.

Each of the blend modes works by examining the overlapping portions of graphical objects. The color value of each pixel from the top (or *blend*) object is taken together with the color of the pixel directly below it in the bottom (or *base*) object. The two color values are then plugged into a mathematical formula to determine the resulting color displayed in that pixel location on the screen. The blend mode you choose determines the mathematical formula that's used (and hence the output color). **Table 7.3** describes the blend modes available in Flash.

To designate a blend mode for an instance, set the **blendMode** property to the appropriate string, or use the properties from the **BlendMode** class. The following two statements are identical:

```
myMovieClip.blendMode = "darken";
myMovieClip.blendMode =
→ BlendMode.DARKEN;
```

Note that the **blendMode** property of the **DisplayObject** starts with a lowercase letter, but the **BlendMode** class that you reference to assign different blend modes starts with an uppercase letter.

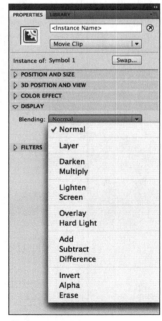

Ⓐ The Blend mode menu in the Properties inspector.

TABLE 7.3 Blend Mode Properties

Blend Mode	ActionScript Value	Description
Darken	BlendMode.DARKEN or "darken"	Color values are compared and the darker of the two is displayed, resulting in a darker image overall. Often used to create a background for (light) text.
Lighten	BlendMode.LIGHTEN or "lighten"	Lighter of the two color values is displayed, leading to a lighter image overall. Often used to create a background for (dark) text.
Multiply	BlendMode.MULTIPLY or "multiply"	Color values are multiplied to get the result, which is usually darker than either value.
Screen	BlendMode.SCREEN or "screen"	Opposite of Multiply; the result is lighter than either original color. Typically used for highlighting or flare effects.
Overlay	BlendMode.OVERLAY or "overlay"	Uses Multiply if the base color is darker than middle gray or Screen if it's lighter.
Hard Light	BlendMode.HARDLIGHT or "hardlight"	Opposite of Overlay; uses Screen if the base color is darker than middle gray or Multiply if it's lighter.
Add	BlendMode.ADD or "add"	Adds the two colors together, making a lighter result. Often used for a transition between images.
Subtract	BlendMode.SUBTRACT or "subtract"	Subtracts the blend color from the base color, making the resulting color darker. Often used as a transition effect.
Difference	BlendMode.DIFFERENCE or "difference"	Darker color is subtracted from the lighter one, resulting in a brighter image, often with unnatural results.
Invert	BlendMode.INVERT or "invert"	Displays the inverse of the base color anywhere the blend clip overlaps.
Alpha	BlendMode.ALPHA or "alpha"	Creates an alpha mask. The blend clip doesn't show, but any alpha values of the blend clip are applied to the base clip, making those areas transparent. The clips must be inside another clip with Layer mode applied.
Erase	BlendMode.ERASE or "erase"	Inverse of Alpha mode. The blend clip doesn't show. Under opaque areas on the blend clip, the base clip becomes transparent; beneath transparent areas on the blend image, the base clip is visible, creating a stencil or cookie-cutter effect. The clips must be inside a Layer mode clip.
Layer	BlendMode.LAYER or "layer"	Special container blend mode in Flash. Any blends inside a display object set to Layer don't affect images outside the layer clip.
Normal	BlendMode.NORMAL or "normal"	Blend image is opaque (no blending takes place).
Shader	BlendMode.SHADER or "shader"	Used to specify a custom blending effect created with Pixel Bender (see the sidebar "What Is Pixel Bender?").

To change color blending between two objects:

1. Create two movie clip symbols whose colors will be blended.

2. Put one instance of each symbol on the Stage, overlapping as desired. Give the top (blend) movie clip an instance name in the Properties inspector **B**.

3. Select the first keyframe, and open the Actions panel.

4. Enter the target path of your blend movie clip, a dot, the property **blendMode**, and then an equals sign.

5. Continuing on the same line, enter a string value for the desired blend mode, or use the equivalent property from the **BlendMode** class **C**.

   The blend mode is applied to the blend movie clip, altering the color interaction between the two movie clips.

B The top image is a movie clip called **cow_mc**.

```
cow_mc.blendMode = BlendMode.MULTIPLY;
```

C Assign the value **BlendMode.MULTIPLY** to the **blendMode** property of your instance. **BlendMode. MULTIPLY** is a constant of the **BlendMode** class that makes it easier for you to assign values.

What Is Pixel Bender?

You've seen how you can create special visual effects (such as blurs and drop shadows) with the filter classes and apply them to images. If you want to create your own filters, you can use a technology from Adobe called Pixel Bender. Pixel Bender is a separate development platform and a separate language that is more specialized than ActionScript.

Essentially, with Pixel Bender you can write code for your own custom filter and save it as a .pbj file. In Flash, you load the .pbj filter and use two new classes, the **Shader** class and the **ShaderFilter** class, to apply the new filter to an image.

Pixel Bender is an exciting tool that opens new visual possibilities that can unleash the creativity of the Flash community.

D The top image interacts with the bottom image in more complex ways with color blending.

6. Test your movie.

The colors of the movie clips on the Stage blend together according to the blend mode selected **D**.

TIP Blend modes can only be applied to movie clips, buttons, or TLF text in the authoring environment of Flash, but can be applied to all objects of the `DisplayObject` or `DisplayObjectContainer` class with ActionScript.

TIP It's helpful to use the Flash authoring environment to experiment with different blend modes using the images you want to combine, even if you ultimately plan to apply the effect using ActionScript.

TIP The `blendMode` properties `erase` and `alpha` (`BlendMode.ERASE` and `BlendMode.ALPHA`) work a little differently in that you need to assign `BlendMode.LAYER` or the value `layer` to the `blendMode` property of the parent. If you have your two movie clips on the main Stage, you can set `MovieClip(root).blendMode = BlendMode.LAYER`.

Applying Special Effects with Filters

Flash graphics can look nice, but it's the little finishing touches that turn a good graphic into a great one. These finishing touches are usually subtle—the soft glow of light emanating from a mysterious orb or the drop shadow behind an object that creates a sense of depth. As mentioned in Chapter 1, "Building Complexity," Flash includes a number of filter effects that can be used to create these finishing touches and to manipulate complex graphics. These filter effects are built into Flash Player, so using them adds nothing to the download size of your SWF file. For advanced users, you can add these effects not only within the authoring environment but also dynamically using ActionScript. In fact, in addition to the filters available with the drawing tools, four filters—the

Convolution, Color Matrix, Displacement Map, and Shader filters—can only be applied using ActionScript.

Each filter is represented as a class in ActionScript (**Table 7.4**). To apply a filter effect to an object, you first create an instance of the filter you want. Each filter can be customized with several values, which are usually set as parameters of the constructor function that is called to create the filter object, like this:

```
var myBlur:BlurFilter = new
→ BlurFilter(3, 0, 1);
```

Once you have defined one or more filter objects, you apply them to a **DisplayObject** instance to take effect. Objects of the **DisplayObject** class have a **filters** property that takes an **Array** (an object that is a set of objects or values) containing one or more filter objects. (You'll learn more about the **Array** class in Chapter 11, "Manipulating Information.")

TABLE 7.4 Filter Classes

Filter Class Name	Description
BevelFilter	Adds a beveled edge to an object, making it look three-dimensional.
BlurFilter	Makes an object looked blurred.
ColorMatrixFilter	Performs complex color transformations on an object.
ConvolutionFilter	A highly customizable filter that can be used to create unique filter effects beyond those included with Flash by combining pixels with neighboring pixels in various ways.
DisplacementMapFilter	Shifts pixel values according to values in a map image to create a textured or distorted effect.
DropShadowFilter	Adds a drop shadow to an object.
GlowFilter	Adds a colored halo around an object.
GradientBevelFilter	Like the Bevel filter, with the additional ability to specify a gradient color for the bevel.
GradientGlowFilter	Like the Glow filter, with the additional ability to specify a gradient color for the glow.
ShaderFilter	Applies a custom filter made with Pixel Bender (see the sidebar "What Is Pixel Bender?").

This allows a single **DisplayObject** to be affected by multiple filters—for example, an object can have a beveled edge and also cast a drop shadow. Most often, you can create the **Array** instance and assign it to the **filters** property in a single statement. Pass your filter object or objects as parameters of the new **Array** constructor function, like this:

```
myimage_mc.filters = new
→ Array(myBlur);
```

When you pass objects as parameters to the **Array** constructor, those objects are automatically added into the **Array** object; in this example, the **new Array()** constructor function creates a new **Array** object, and the object passed as a parameter (the filter object) is added into the array. The **Array** instance is then stored in the object's **filters** property, causing any filter objects it contains (just one, in this case) to be applied to the target object.

In the next task, you'll see how to apply a drop-shadow filter to a movie clip. The procedure for applying any other filter to a **DisplayObject** is the same; the only difference is that with each one, you use the specific parameters for that filter when calling the constructor function to create the filter object.

To dynamically add a drop-shadow filter effect:

1. For this example, create a movie clip symbol; place an instance on the Stage, and give it an instance name in the Properties inspector.

2. Select the first keyframe, and open the Actions panel.

3. Instantiate a **DropShadowFilter**, like so:

   ```
   var dropshadow:DropShadowFilter=
   → new DropShadowFilter();
   ```

   The filter's constructor function is added without parameters. (You'll add them next.)

4. Between the parentheses, enter values separated by commas as parameters for the constructor function **A**.

   The **DropShadowFilter** constructor takes up to 11 parameters, which match different options. However, they're all optional, and you can specify just some of them if you wish. To get you started, the first six are the offset distance (a number of pixels), the shadow angle (a number of degrees), the shadow color (a hexadecimal numeric color value), alpha (a number from 0 to 1), and **blurX** and **blurY** (both numbers).

Continues on next page

```
var dropshadow:DropShadowFilter = new DropShadowFilter(25, 45, 0x000000, .7, 20, 20);
```

A Create a new filter. Each filter has its own set of properties that you define when you create a new instance. This **DropShadowFilter** object makes a shadow at 25 pixels distance, 45 degrees, with a black color, at 70% alpha, and with a horizontal and vertical blur of 20.

5. On the next line, enter your target object's name, a dot, and then the property **filters**.

6. On the same line, enter an equals sign and the constructor **new Array()**.

This creates a new **Array** object.

7. Between the parentheses of the **Array** constructor, enter the name of your filter object 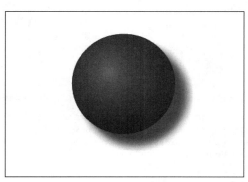**B**.

Your filter object is added into the new **Array** as it's created. The **Array** is assigned to the **filters** property of your movie clip and the filter takes effect.

8. Test your movie.

Your movie clip instance on the Stage has a drop shadow applied with the properties you specified **C**.

To dynamically remove a filter effect:

1. Enter the target path for your object, a dot, and then the property **filters**.

2. On the same line, enter an equals sign and the constructor **new Array()**.

You assign a new array with no filters, effectively removing any existing filters on your object.

TIP Because the **filters** property accepts an **Array**, you can apply multiple filters to an object. To add multiple filters to an object, instantiate all the filter objects first, and then add them all as parameters to the new **Array()** constructor that is assigned to the **filters** property (step 7). For instance, if you create two filter objects named **filter1** and **filter2**, this line of code applies both filters to a movie clip named **myimage_mc**:

```
myimage_mc.filters = new
→ Array(filter1, filter2);
```

```
var dropshadow:DropShadowFilter = new DropShadowFilter(25, 45, 0x000000, .7, 20, 20);
myimage_mc.filters = new Array(dropshadow);
```

B The new filter object is put in the **filters** array of your movie clip.

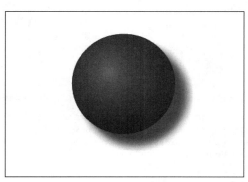

C This image of a ball has a drop shadow automatically generated from the **DropShadowFilter**.

Creating Drag-and-Drop Interactivity

Drag-and-drop behavior gives the viewer one of the most direct interactions with the Flash movie. Nothing is more satisfying than grabbing a graphic on the screen, moving it around, and dropping it somewhere else. It's a natural way of interacting with objects, and you can easily give your viewers this experience. Creating drag-and-drop behavior in Flash involves two basic steps: assigning an event handler that triggers the drag action on an object, and assigning an event handler that triggers the drop action.

Usually during drag-and-drop interactivity, the dragging begins when the viewer presses the mouse button with the pointer over the graphic. When the mouse button is released, the dragging stops. Hence,

the action to start dragging is tied to a **MouseEvent.MOUSE_DOWN** event, and the action to stop dragging is tied to a **MouseEvent.MOUSE_UP** event.

In many cases, you may want the draggable graphic to snap to the center of the user's pointer as it's being dragged rather than wherever the user happens to click, described in the task "To center the draggable object," or you may want to limit the area where viewers can drag graphics, as described in the task "To constrain the draggable object."

The methods **startDrag()** and **stopDrag()** are methods of the **Sprite** class, which is a general **DisplayObjectContainer** class for handling graphics. It is similar to the **MovieClip** class, but it does not contain a timeline. Movie clip objects are a subclass of the **Sprite** class. In these examples, you'll use movie clips as the draggable graphics.

To start dragging an object:

1. Create a movie clip symbol, place an instance of it on the Stage, and name it in the Properties inspector **A**.

2. Select the first frame of the main Timeline, and open the Actions panel.

3. Enter the name of your movie clip, a dot, and then the method **addEventListener()**. Between the parentheses of the method, enter **MouseEvent.MOUSE_DOWN** and a name for a function, as follows:

```
eyes_mc.addEventListener(
→ MouseEvent.MOUSE_DOWN,
→ startDragging);
```

The completed statement listens for a **MOUSE_DOWN** event and triggers the function called **startDragging** if it detects that event.

4. On the next line, create the function called **startDragging** with a **MouseEvent** parameter. Between the curly braces of the function, enter the name of your movie clip followed by the method **startDrag()**, like so:

```
function startDragging(
→ myevent:MouseEvent):void {
    eyes_mc.startDrag();
}
```

The movie clip called **eyes_mc** will be dragged when this function is called **B**.

5. Test your movie.

When your pointer is over the movie clip and you press your mouse button, you can drag the clip around.

A This movie clip instance on the Stage is called **eyes_mc**.

```
eyes_mc.addEventListener(MouseEvent.MOUSE_DOWN, startDragging);
function startDragging(myevent:MouseEvent):void {
    eyes_mc.startDrag();
}
```

B The **MouseEvent.MOUSE_DOWN** event handler that makes the movie clip instance start dragging.

To stop dragging an object:

1. Using the file you created in the preceding task, select the first frame of the Timeline and open the Actions panel.

2. On a new line, enter the name of your movie clip, a dot, and then the method **addEventListener()**. Between the parentheses of the method, enter **MouseEvent.MOUSE_UP** and a name for a function, as follows:

```
eyes_mc.addEventListener(
→ MouseEvent.MOUSE_UP,
→ stopDragging);
```

The completed statement listens for a **MOUSE_UP** event and triggers the function called **stopDragging** if it detects that event.

3. On the next line, create the function called **stopDragging** with a **MouseEvent** parameter. Between the curly braces of the function, enter the name of your movie clip followed by the method **stopDrag()**, like so:

```
function stopDragging(
→ myevent:MouseEvent):void {
   eyes_mc.stopDrag();
}
```

The movie clip called **eyes_mc** will stop being dragged when this function is called **C**.

4. Test your movie.

When your pointer is over the movie clip and you press your mouse button, you can drag it. When you release your mouse button, the dragging stops **D**.

TIP Only one movie clip or sprite can be dragged at a time using this method.

TIP If you have multiple objects that you want the user to drag and drop, you can make your function more generic and refer to the target of the mouse click. Use the **target** property of the MouseEvent object to call the **startDrag()** and **stopDrag()** methods, like so:

```
function startDragging(
→ myevent:MouseEvent):void {
   myevent.target.startDrag();
}
function stopDragging(
→ myevent:MouseEvent):void {
   myevent.target.stopDrag();
}
```

```
eyes_mc.addEventListener(MouseEvent.MOUSE_UP, stopDragging);
function stopDragging(myevent:MouseEvent):void {
   eyes_mc.stopDrag();
}
```

C The **MouseEvent.MOUSE_UP** event handler that makes the movie clip instance stop dragging.

D The movie clip instances of the eyes dragged and dropped around the Stage.

To center the draggable object:

Place your pointer inside the parentheses for the **startDrag()** method, and enter the Boolean value **true**, as in **startDrag(true)**.

The **startDrag()** method's first parameter, **lockCenter**, is set to **true**. After you press the mouse button when your pointer is over the movie clip to begin dragging, the registration point of your movie clip snaps to the mouse pointer.

TIP If you set the **lockCenter** parameter to **true**, make sure the area of your object covers its registration point. If it doesn't, then after the object snaps to your mouse pointer, your pointer will no longer be over any graphic area and Flash won't be able to detect when to stop the drag action **E**.

To constrain the draggable object:

1. Insert a new line in the Actions panel and create a new object of the **Rectangle** class with four parameters— x-position, y-position, width, and height—like so **F**:

   ```
   var myBoundaries:Rectangle = new
   → Rectangle(20, 30, 100, 50);
   ```

   The **Rectangle** object is used to define the boundaries of the draggable motion. The **Rectangle** object isn't an actual visible graphic, but just an abstract object to help do geometric manipulations.

E If this movie clip (which has an empty space in the middle) were to be dragged and the **lockCenter** parameter set to **true**, the mouse pointer would hover over the middle and not be able to stop the dragging motion.

```
var myBoundaries:Rectangle = new Rectangle(20,30,100,50);
```

F The boundaries of a dragging motion can be restricted by first creating a **Rectangle** object to act as the boundaries.

2. Place your pointer inside the parentheses for the **startDrag()** method, and enter **true** or **false** for its first parameter (the **lockCenter** parameter), then a comma, and then the name of your **Rectangle** object **G**.

The pixel coordinates of your **Rectangle** object are relative to the container object in which the movie clip resides. If the draggable movie clip sits on the Stage, the pixel coordinates correspond to the Stage. If the draggable movie clip is within another object, the coordinates refer to the registration point of the parent **H**.

TIP You can use the dimensions of the Rectangle object to force a dragging motion along a horizontal or a vertical track, as in a scroll bar. Set the width of your Rectangle object to 1 pixel to restrict the motion to up and down, or set the height of your Rectangle object to 1 pixel to restrict the motion to left and right.

TIP To define the Rectangle object as the second parameter to constrain the draggable motion, you must also set the startDrag() method's first parameter (lockCenter) to true or false.

TIP A shortcut to coding the Rectangle boundary is to create the new Rectangle object within the startDrag() method. The following statement is also valid:

```
eyes_mc.startDrag(false, new
⟶ Rectangle(0, 0, 100, 20));
```

```
var myBoundaries:Rectangle = new Rectangle(20,30,100,50);
eyes_mc.startDrag(true, myBoundaries);
```

G Use the **Rectangle** object as the second parameter in the **startDrag()** method to constrain the drag motion.

H The x- and y-coordinates of the **eyes_mc** object are constrained by the bounds of the **Rectangle** object.

Detecting Collisions

Now that you can make an object that can be dragged around the Stage, you'll likely want to check whether that object intersects another object. The game of Pong, for example, detects collisions between draggable paddles and a ball.

To detect collisions between objects, use one of two methods of the **DisplayObject** class: **hitTestObject()** or **hitTestPoint()**. The first method lets you check whether the bounding boxes of any objects intersect. The *bounding box* of an object is the minimum rectangular area that contains the graphics. This method is ideal for graphics colliding with other graphics, such as a ball with a paddle, a ship with an asteroid, or a puzzle piece with its correct resting spot. In the following example, if the object **ball** intersects with the object called **paddle**, the method returns a value of **true**:

```
ball.hitTestObject(paddle);
```

The second method checks whether a certain x-y coordinate intersects with an object. This method is point specific, which makes it ideal for checking whether only the registration point of a graphic or the mouse pointer intersects with an object. In this case, the **hitTestPoint()** method is used, and you provide an x value, a y value, and the **shapeflag** parameter (which is **true** or **false**). The **shapeflag** parameter indicates whether Flash should use the bounding box of an object (**false**) or the shape of the graphics it contains (**true**) in deciding if the point is in contact with the object **A**.

The **hitTestObject()** and **hitTestPoint()** methods work for all objects in the **DisplayObject** class, but in the following examples, you'll just use movie clip objects.

Bounding box

A When the **shapeFlag** is **true** (top), then according to Flash, the two objects aren't intersecting; only the shapes are considered. When the **shapeFlag** parameter is **false** (bottom), the two objects are intersecting because the bounding box is considered.

To detect an intersection between two objects:

1. Create a movie clip, place an instance of it on the Stage, and name it in the Properties inspector.

2. Create another movie clip, place an instance of it on the Stage, and name it in the Properties inspector.

3. Select the first frame of the main Timeline and open the Actions panel; assign actions to make the second movie clip instance draggable.

4. Create a new line in the Script pane at the end of the current script, and add an event listener to detect the **Event.ENTER_FRAME** event **B**.

   The **Event.ENTER_FRAME** event occurs at the frame rate of the movie, which makes it ideal for checking the **hitTestObject()** method continuously.

5. On the next line, create the function that gets triggered for the **ENTER_FRAME** event. Between the curly braces of the function, enter the word **if**, then a set of parentheses.

6. For the condition (between the parentheses), enter the name of the draggable movie clip followed by a period, and then enter **hitTestObject()**.

7. Within the parentheses of the **hitTestObject()** method, enter the name of the stationary movie clip.

8. Immediately after the **hitTestObject()** method, enter two equals signs followed by the Boolean value **true**.

9. Enter a set of curly braces to complete the **if** statement. Between those curly braces, choose an action to be performed when this condition is met.

   The final script should look like **C**.

10. Test your movie **D**.

Continues on next page

```
spaceship_mc.startDrag(true);
stage.addEventListener(Event.ENTER_FRAME, detectCollision);
```

B The **Event.ENTER_FRAME** event happens continuously at the frame rate of your Flash movie.

```
spaceship_mc.startDrag(true);
stage.addEventListener(Event.ENTER_FRAME, detectCollision);

function detectCollision(myevent:Event):void {
    if (spaceship_mc.hitTestObject(asteroid_mc) == true) {
        spaceship_mc.nextFrame();
    }
}
```

C Flash monitors the intersection between the two objects **spaceship_mc** and **asteroid_mc**. If there is a collision, the **spaceship_mc** movie clip advances to the next frame.

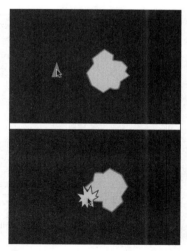

D Dragging the **spaceship_mc** movie clip into the bounding box of the **asteroid_mc** movie clip advances the spaceship movie clip to the next frame, which displays an explosion.

TIP If you're only checking if something is true (known as *Boolean value*) in an if statement as you do in this task, you can leave out the last part, `== true`. Flash returns `true` or `false` when you call the `hitTestObject()` method, and the `if` statement tests `true` and `false` values. You'll learn more about conditional statements later in the book.

TIP It doesn't matter whether you test the moving movie clip to the target or the target to the moving movie clip. The following two statements detect the same collision:

```
spaceship.hitTestObject(asteroid);
asteroid.hitTestObject(spaceship);
```

To detect an intersection between a point and an object:

1. Continuing with the same file you created in the preceding task, select the first frame of the main Timeline and open the Actions panel.

2. Place your pointer within the parentheses of the `if` statement.

3. Change the condition so it reads as follows:

   ```
   asteroid_mc.hitTestPoint(
   → spaceship_mc.x, spaceship_mc.y,
   → true)
   ```

   The **hitTestPoint()** method now checks whether the x and y positions of the draggable movie clip **spaceship_mc** intersect with the shape of the movie clip **asteroid_mc** **E**.

4. Test your movie.

TIP The properties mouseX and mouseY are values of the current x and y positions of the pointer on the screen. You can use these properties in the parameters of the **hitTestPoint()** method to check whether the pointer intersects a movie clip. This expression returns `true` if the pointer intersects the movie clip **asteroid_mc**:

```
asteroid_mc.hitTestPoint(mouseX,
→ mouseY, true)
```

```
spaceship_mc.startDrag(true);
stage.addEventListener(Event.ENTER_FRAME, detectCollision);

function detectCollision(myevent:Event):void {
    if (asteroid_mc.hitTestPoint(spaceship_mc.x, spaceship_mc.y, true) == true) {
        spaceship_mc.nextFrame();
    }
}
```

E The ActionScript (above) tests whether the registration point of the **spaceship_mc** movie clip intersects with any shape in the **asteroid_mc** movie clip. Notice that the spaceship is safe from collision because its registration point is within the crevice and clear of the asteroid.

Generating Graphics Dynamically

Creating graphics on the fly—that is, during playback—opens a new world of exciting interactive possibilities. Imagine a game of Asteroids in which enemy spaceships appear as the game progresses. You can store those enemy spaceships as movie clip symbols in your Library and create instances on the Stage with ActionScript as you need them. Or, if you want an infinite supply of a certain draggable item (such as merchandise) to be pulled off the shelf of an online store, you can make a duplicate of the object each time the viewer drags it away from its original spot. Or you can create entirely new graphics by drawing lines, shapes, and curves with solid color or gradients. All the while, you maintain the power to modify properties and control color, blending, and filters for those objects.

Flash provides many ways to dynamically generate graphics, and in the previous chapter, you learned about one of them (by loading external images). All the processes begin with creating a new `DisplayObject` or `DisplayObjectContainer` with the constructor function, `new`. To create a new `Sprite` object, for example, you can use `var myNewSprite:Sprite = new Sprite()`. The next step would be to do something with the new object (which depends on what kind of object you decided to create), and then display the object by putting it on the display list with `addChild()`. The challenge is knowing which object of the `DisplayObject`

or `DisplayObjectContainer` class to choose from. Among the considerations:

- Create a new **Loader** object to load in an external image or SWF (discussed in the previous chapter).

- Create a new **Sprite** object or **MovieClip** object for interactivity like drag-and-drops, for dynamic drawing, and for attaching other `DisplayObject` or `DisplayObjectContainer` objects with `addChild()`. The **MovieClip** object differs from the **Sprite** object in that it has a timeline.

- Create a new **Shape** object if you just want to use ActionScript to draw lines, curves, and shapes.

- Create a new **BitMap** object to display bitmap images and manipulate the data at a pixel level.

Creating new movie clips

You can dynamically create new instances of existing movie clip symbols in your Library.

You must first identify the movie clip symbol in your Library so you can reference it in ActionScript and make new instances. You do so by setting the Linkage properties in the Symbol Properties dialog box. In this panel, you indicate the class name for your movie clip and the preexisting class that you want Flash to extend to it. In essence, you are creating your own custom class for your movie clip symbol and extending a preexisting class to share its methods and properties.

To create a movie clip instance from a Library symbol:

1. Create a movie clip symbol.

   The movie clip symbol is stored in your Library.

2. From the Library Options menu, choose Properties .

   The Symbol Properties dialog box appears.

3. Click the Advanced button to expand the dialog box. In the Linkage section, select the Export for ActionScript check box. Leave "Export in frame 1" selected.

4. In the Class field, enter a name to identify your movie clip. Leave the Base class as flash.display.MovieClip and click OK ⓑ.

   A dialog box may appear that warns you that your class could not be found and one will automatically be generated for you ⓒ. Click OK. In this example, the class name for your Library symbol is **BaldMan**. This new class inherits from the **MovieClip** class, which means it has all the same methods and properties of the **MovieClip** class. Your class name will be used to create new instances of your movie clip. Make sure that your class name doesn't contain any periods.

5. Select the first frame of the main Timeline, and open the Actions panel.

6. On the first line, create a new instance of your movie clip symbol, referencing its class name (created in step 4), like so:

   ```
   var Larry:BaldMan = new BaldMan();
   ```

   A new instance of a movie clip, specifically the movie clip in your Library, is created.

ⓐ Choose Properties from the Options menu in the Library.

ⓑ The new class name for your Library symbol here is **BaldMan**, and it has all the same methods and properties of the **MovieClip** class.

ⓒ The warning dialog box, which you can ignore.

```
var Larry:BaldMan = new BaldMan();
stage.addChild(Larry);
```

D Create a new instance of your Library symbol and add it to the display list.

E When the new instance is put on the display list, its registration point is aligned with the registration point of the `DisplayObjectContainer`. Since this instance was added to the Stage, its center point is at the top-left corner of the Stage.

7. On the next line, enter **stage**, a period, and then the method **addChild()**. Within the parentheses, put your new movie clip instance **D**.

   The **addChild()** method is required to add your new instance to the display list to see it. The new instance called **Larry** is put on the Stage.

8. Test the movie **E**.

   The default position of your new instance is at the registration point of its parent (the **DisplayObjectContainer**). So, in this example, the registration point of the new movie clip instance is at the top-left corner of the Stage. Use the properties **x** and **y** to move the new instance to your desired position.

TIP When you add objects to the display list, they are affected by the properties of the `DisplayObjectContainer` that you add them to. For example, suppose you create a new `Sprite` object, add it to the Stage, and change its transparency to 50 percent, like so:

```
var mySprite:Sprite = new Sprite();
stage.addChild(mySprite);
mySprite.alpha = .5;
```

Now, if you created your new `BaldMan` instance and attached it to the `Sprite` object, the `BaldMan` instance would be 50 percent transparent:

```
var Larry:BaldMan = new BaldMan();
mySprite.addChild(Larry);
```

TIP Objects are also affected by ActionScript that may be assigned to the `DisplayObjectContainer`. If the `DisplayObjectContainer` is draggable, for example, the added object is also draggable.

Controlling Stacking Order

When you generate multiple **DisplayObjects** and put them on the display list, you need a way to control how each one overlaps the other. If you have multiple draggable objects, you'll notice that the objects maintain their depth level even while they're being dragged, which can seem a little odd. In a drag-and-drop interaction, you expect that the item you pick up will come to the top, which requires that you control the stacking order.

Controlling the stacking order is a simple matter of reordering the objects on the display list. Recall that Flash maintains a tree-like hierarchy of the objects on the display list, giving each object an index number that determines which object is overlapping others **A**.

The methods of the **DisplayObjectContainer** class provide several ways to access the objects on the Stage and to move them to different levels, add new objects, or remove them completely. These methods work for both dynamically generated objects as well as objects you create on the Stage manually. See **Table 7.5** for a description of the various methods.

A Controlling the stacking order or overlapping of objects on the display list depends on each object's index number.

circle

Before   *After*

B The result of the statement **addChild(circle)**.

square

Before   *After*

C The result of the statement
setChildindex(square, 0).

To move an object to the front:

Call the **addChild()** method, as in:

addChild(circle);

The **circle** object is added to the top of the display list. If the object is already present on the display list, it is pulled from its current position and added to the top, and all the objects are shuffled downward and reassigned the appropriate index numbers automatically **B**.

To move an object to the back:

Call the **setChildIndex()** method and use the object name and the index number 0 as its parameters, as in:

setChildindex(square, 0);

The **square** object is placed at the bottom of the display list. The object must already be present on the display list **C**.

Continues on next page

TABLE 7.5 DisplayObjectContainer Methods

Method	Description
addChild(child)	Adds a child object.
addChildAt(child, index)	Adds a child object at the specified index.
getChildAt(index)	Retrieves the child object at the specified index.
getChildByName(name)	Retrieves the child object at the specified name (a string).
getChildIndex(child)	Retrieves the index position of the child object.
getObjectsUnderPoint(point)	Returns an array of objects that lie under the specified point (a **Point** object).
removeChild(child)	Removes a child object.
removeChildAt(index)	Removes a child object at the specified index level.
setChildIndex(child, index)	Changes the position of an existing child to the specified index.
swapChildren(child1, child2)	Swaps the stacking order of the two specified child objects.
swapChildrenAt(index1, index2)	Swaps the stacking order of two child objects at the specified index numbers.

Or

Call the **addChildAt()** method and use the name of the object and the index number 0 as its parameters, as in:

addChildAt(square, 0);

The **square** object is placed at the bottom of the display list. If the object is already present on the display list, it is pulled from its current position and placed at the bottom, and all the objects are shuffled and reassigned the appropriate index numbers automatically.

To swap two objects:

Call the **swapChildren()** method and use the two objects as its parameters, as in:

swapChildren(circle, square);

The **circle** and the **square** objects switch places in the stacking order **D**.

To remove an object:

Call the **removeChild()** method and use the object as its parameter, as in:

removeChild(triangle);

The **triangle** object is removed from the display list and disappears from the Stage **E**.

Or

If you don't know the name of the object but know its index (for example, it is at the very bottom with an index of 0), use the **removeChildAt()** method and use the index number 0 as its parameter, as in:

removeChildAt(0);

The object at the very bottom of the display list (index 0) is removed and disappears **F**.

square   circle

Before · *After*

D The result of the statement **swapChildren(circle, square)**.

triangle

Before · *After*

E The result of the statement **removeChild(triangle)**.

Before · *After*

F The result of the statement **removeChildAt(0)**.

Creating Vector Shapes Dynamically

Drawing vector lines, curves, and shapes, and using colors or gradients to fill those shapes, is a process that you can do with Flash's drawing tools or purely with Action-Script using the **graphics** property of the **Shape**, **Sprite**, or **MovieClip** objects. You can use the drawing methods to create your own simple paint and coloring application, or you can draw bar graphs or pie charts or connect data points to visualize numerical data that your viewer inputs.

To use the drawing methods, you must start with a new object, and the simplest is the **Shape** object. You create a new **Shape** object like any other object, with a statement such as **var myShape:Shape = new Shape()**. You can also use a **Sprite** object or a **MovieClip** object if you plan to have your object contain other objects within it (the **Shape** class is a subclass of the **DisplayObject** class, whereas the **Sprite** and **MovieClip** classes are subclasses of the **DisplayObjectContainer** class), or if you want additional functionality that the **Shape** class doesn't provide (such as drag and drop). Your new object acts as the canvas that holds the drawing you create. It also acts as the point of reference for all your drawing coordinates. If you place your object at the top-left corner of the Stage (at x = 0, y = 0), all the drawing coordinates are relative to that registration point.

The **Shape**, **Sprite**, and **MovieClip** classes have a property called **graphics**. This property is an instance of the **Graphics** class, which provides many methods that enable you to create vector graphics. The process is straightforward: You define the styles of your graphics (colors, line weights, etc.), give Flash coordinates as to where to begin the drawing, and then draw your lines, curves, or shapes. See **Table 7.6** (on the next page) for a description of the **Graphics** class drawing methods.

Creating lines and curves

The **lineStyle()** method sets the characteristics of your stroke, such as its point size, color, and transparency. The **moveTo()** method sets the beginning point of your line or curve, like placing a pen on paper. The **lineTo()** and **curveTo()** methods draw lines and curves by setting the end points and, in the case of curves, determine its curvature. The **clear()** method erases all the drawing on an object.

Color, line width, and transparency are just the beginning of the ways you can style lines you draw in ActionScript. Flash provides additional line-style properties to control how lines scale and the style of the corners (*joints*) and ends (*caps*) of the lines you draw. You can also create lines that use a gradient rather than a solid color. All these techniques are demonstrated in the next several tasks.

To create straight lines:

1. Select the first frame of the main Time-line, and open the Actions panel.

2. Declare a variable with the data type **Shape**, enter an equals sign, and then enter **new Shape()** to create a new **Shape** instance.

   An empty **Shape** object is created.

3. On the next line, enter the name of your **Shape** object, followed by a period, fol-lowed by the property **graphics**; then call the **lineStyle()** method.

TABLE 7.6 Graphics Methods

Method	Description
`beginBitmapFill(bitmap, matrix, repeat, smooth)`	Fills a drawing area with a bitmap image.
`beginFill(color, alpha)`	Specifies the fill color as a hex code and transparency.
`beginGradientFill(type, colors, alphas, ratios, matrix, spread, interpolation, focalpoint)`	Specifies the gradient fill.
`clear()`	Clears the drawing and resets the fill and line style settings.
`curveTo(controlx, controly, x, y)`	Draws a curve to the x, y point with the control points **controlx** and **controly** that determine curvature.
`drawCircle(x, y, radius)`	Draws a circle at location x, y with a specified radius.
`drawEllipse(x, y, width, height)`	Draws an ellipse at location x, y with a specified width and height.
`drawRect(x, y, width, height)`	Draws a rectangle at location x, y with a specified width and height.
`drawRoundRect(x, y, width, height, ellipsewidth, ellipseheight)`	Draws a rectangle at location x, y with a specified width and height and rounded corners.
`endFill()`	Applies a fill.
`lineGradientStyle(type, colors, alphas, ratios, matrix, spread, interpolation, focalpoint)`	Specifies a gradient for the line style.
`lineStyle(thickness, color, alpha, pixelhinting, scalemode, caps, joints, miter)`	Specifies a line style.
`lineTo(x, y)`	Draws a line to the specified x, y location.
`moveTo(x, y)`	Moves the drawing position to the specified x, y location.

```
var myShape:Shape = new Shape();
myShape.graphics.lineStyle(4, 0x000000, 1);
```

A Define the line style (stroke thickness, color, and transparency) before you begin drawing.

```
var myShape:Shape = new Shape();
myShape.graphics.lineStyle(4, 0x000000, 1);
myShape.graphics.moveTo(0, 100);
```

B The beginning of this line is at x = 0, y = 100.

```
var myShape:Shape = new Shape();
myShape.graphics.lineStyle(4, 0x000000, 1);
myShape.graphics.moveTo(0, 100);
myShape.graphics.lineTo(400, 100);
```

C This straight line is drawn with a 4-point black stroke. The virtual pen tip is now positioned at x = 400, y = 100 and ready for a new **lineTo()** method.

4. For the parameters of the **lineStyle()** method, enter a number for thickness, a hex number for the color (in the form 0xRRGGBB), and a number for the transparency **A**.

   The thickness is a number from 0 to 255; 0 is hairline thickness (which maintains its hairline thickness even when scaled), and 255 is the maximum point thickness.

   The RGB parameter is the hex code referring to the color of the line. You can find the hex code for any color in the Color Mixer panel below the color picker. Red, for example, is **0xFF0000**.

   The transparency is a number from 0 to 1 for the line's alpha value; 0 is completely transparent, and 1 is completely opaque.

   The **lineStyle()** method can take up to 8 parameters, but only the first (thickness) is required.

5. On the next line, enter your **Shape** object's name followed by a period and the property **graphics**, and then call the **moveTo()** method.

6. With your pointer between the parentheses, enter the x- and y-coordinates where you want your line to start, separating the parameters with a comma **B**.

7. On the next line, enter your **Shape** object's name followed by a period and the property **graphics**, and then call the **lineTo()** method.

8. With your pointer between the parentheses, enter the x- and y-coordinates of the end point of your line, separating the parameters with a comma **C**.

   The end point of your line segment automatically becomes the beginning point for the next, so you don't need to use the **moveTo()** method to move the coordinates.

Continues on next page

9. If you wish, continue adding more `lineTo()` methods to draw more line segments.

10. On the last line, enter **stage**, a period, and the method **addChild()** with the name of your **Shape** object within the parentheses .

The lines that you drew won't be visible unless you add them to the display list.

11. Test your movie.

TIP You can change the line style at any time, so multiple line segments can have different thicknesses, colors, transparencies, and so forth. Add a `lineStyle()` method before the `lineTo()` method whose line you want to modify.

TIP After you finish your drawing, you can modify its properties by modifying the properties of the **Shape** object—for example, by rotating or scaling the entire object. Or you can affect the behavior of your drawing by calling a method. For example, if you used a **Sprite** or **MovieClip** object instead of a **Shape**, you could make your drawing draggable by calling its **startDrag()** method!

To create paths with square corners and ends:

Add additional parameters to the `lineStyle()` call for pixel hinting, scale mode, cap style, joint style, and miter limit:

Pixel hinting takes a **true**/**false** value. With pixel hinting on, Flash draws anchor and curve points on exact pixels rather than fractions of pixels, leading to smoother curves.

Scale mode determines what happens to the line when the object's size is scaled up or down. It can be one of four values: **LineScaleMode.NORMAL** means lines scale normally; **LineScaleMode.NONE** means line thickness doesn't scale; **LineScaleMode.VERTICAL** means line thickness doesn't scale in the vertical direction; and **LineScaleMode.HORIZONTAL** means line thickness doesn't scale horizontally.

The remaining three parameters, cap style, joint style, and miter limit, are described in the sidebar "Cap and Joint Styles."

```
var myShape:Shape = new Shape();
myShape.graphics.lineStyle(4, 0x000000, 1);
myShape.graphics.moveTo(0, 100);
myShape.graphics.lineTo(400, 100);
stage.addChild(myShape);
```

D The code (top) draws and displays the **Shape** object on the Stage when you test the movie (below).

Cap and Joint Styles

When line thickness becomes large, the corners and ends are rounded off unless you control the cap and joint styles. Three parameters of the `lineStyle()` method allow greater control over this aspect of line styling.

The **cap style** parameter controls what the start and end of the lines will look like. The three options are **E** as follows:

- **No cap (`CapStyle.NONE`):** The end falls exactly at the end coordinate, resulting in a squared-off end.

- **Round (`CapStyle.ROUND`):** The end is rounded and extends slightly beyond the end x, y coordinate to add thickness to the end.

- **Square (`CapStyle.SQUARE`):** The end is squared off and extends slightly beyond the end x, y coordinate to add thickness to the end.

The **joint style** parameter determines the appearance of corners where two line segments are joined. These are the three options **F**:

- **Bevel (`JointStyle.BEVEL`):** The corner is flattened off perpendicular to the center of the angle and extends only slightly beyond the corner x, y coordinate.

- **Round (`JointStyle.ROUND`):** The corner is rounded off and extends beyond the corner x, y coordinate.

- **Miter (`JointStyle.MITER`):** The lines continue to a point beyond the corner coordinate. The point may be chopped short depending on the miter limit setting.

E The three cap styles are (left to right) no caps, round, and square, drawn here with a thick line. The overlaid thin line shows the actual end point.

F The three joint styles, bevel (left), round (middle), and miter (right).

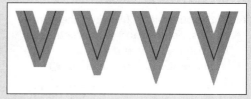

G This small angle is chopped off with miter limits of 1, 2, and 3 but extends fully with a limit of 4 or greater.

The **miter limit**, which is used only when the joint style is set to `JointStyle.MITER`, determines how far an angle extends beyond the true corner point before it's chopped short. For small angles without some sort of limit, the miter joint could extend across the width of the Stage or farther; the miter limit sets constraints on the joint.

The value you set is a number between 1 and 255. How this value translates into the actual distance that the angle extends before being cut short depends on the angle of the corner and the line thickness. In general, with small angles (smaller than 45 degrees), the default limit of 3 causes some trimming. It's a good idea to experiment with the specific line thickness and angle before using miter limits in a Flash movie. **G** shows some examples of different miter limits.

To create curved lines:

1. As you did in the previous task, create a new **Shape** object to serve as the drawing space.

2. On the next line, call the **lineStyle()** method of the **graphics** property of your **Shape** object, and enter the line thickness parameter and other optional parameters between the parentheses.

3. On the next line, enter your **Shape** object's name followed by a period and the property **graphics**, and then call the **moveTo()** method.

4. With your pointer between the parentheses, enter the x- and y-coordinates where you want your line to start, separating the parameters with a comma.

5. On the next line, enter your **Shape** object's name followed by a period and the property **graphics**, and then call the **curveTo()** method.

6. With your pointer between the parentheses, enter x- and y-coordinates for the control point and x- and y-coordinates for the end of the curve **H**.

   The *control point* is a point that determines the amount of curvature. If you were to extend a straight line from the control point to the end point of the curve, you would see that it functions much like the handle of a curve **I**.

7. On the last line, enter the **addChild()** method to add the **Shape** object to the display list.

8. Test your movie **J**.

```
var myShape:Shape = new Shape()
myShape.graphics.lineStyle(2, 0xFF0000, 1);
myShape.graphics.moveTo(200, 200);
myShape.graphics.curveTo(300, 100, 400, 200);
```

H The **curveTo()** method requires x- and y-coordinates for its control point and for its end point. This curve starts at (200,200) and ends at (400,200), with the control point at (300,100) (see **I**).

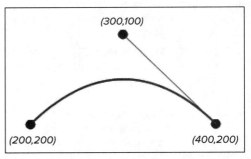

I By drawing a straight line from the control point to the end point, you can visualize the curve's Bézier handle. The dots have been added to show the two anchor points and the control point.

```
var myShape:Shape = new Shape()
myShape.graphics.lineStyle(2, 0xFF0000, 1);
myShape.graphics.moveTo(200, 200);
myShape.graphics.curveTo(300, 100, 400, 200);
addChild(myShape);
```

J The complete script draws and displays the curved line on the Stage.

TIP To reduce the repetition of writing the graphics property of the Shape object, use a with statement to change the scope temporarily. For example, note the savings in having not to repeat the target path:

```
with (myShape.graphics) {
lineStyle(5, 0xff0000, 100);
moveTo(200, 100);
curveTo(300, 100, 300, 200);
curveTo(300, 300, 200, 300);
curveTo(100, 300, 100, 200);
curveTo(100, 100, 200, 100);
}
```

Updating a drawing

The **clear()** method erases the drawings made with the **Graphics** drawing methods. In conjunction with an **Event.ENTER_FRAME** event or a **Timer** object, you can make Flash continually erase a drawing and redraw itself. This is how you can create curves and lines that aren't static but change.

The following task shows the dynamic updates you can make in a drawing by continuously redrawing lines.

```
var myShape:Shape = new Shape();
var counter:int = 0;
stage.addEventListener(Event.ENTER_FRAME, updateDrawing);
```

K The **Event.ENTER_FRAME** event will provide a way to continuously update a drawing.

```
var myShape:Shape = new Shape();
var counter:int = 0;
stage.addEventListener(Event.ENTER_FRAME, updateDrawing);
function updateDrawing(myevent:Event):void {
    myShape.graphics.clear();
    myShape.graphics.lineStyle(4);
    myShape.graphics.moveTo(100, 100);
    myShape.graphics.curveTo(150, 100 + counter, 200, 100);
    stage.addChild(myShape);
    counter++;
}
```

L Within the function, the drawing is cleared and a new curve is drawn with an increasing control point, which increases the curvature.

To update a drawing dynamically:

1. As you did in the previous task, create a new **Shape** object to serve as the drawing space.

2. On the next line, declare a variable called **counter** to hold an integer data type, and assign the number 0 to it.

3. On the next line, add an event listener to detect the **Event.ENTER_FRAME** event **K**.

4. On the next line, create the event-handler function. Between the curly braces of the function, add the following statements **L**:

```
myShape.graphics.clear();
myShape.graphics.lineStyle(4);
myShape.graphics.moveTo(100,100);
myShape.graphics.curveTo(150, 100
→ + counter, 200, 100);
stage.addChild(myShape);
counter++;
```

Each time the **ENTER_FRAME** event happens, Flash clears the current drawing in the **myShape** object and creates a new curve. Each curve is always a little different than the one before it, because the variable called **counter** adds a small amount to the curvature.

5. Test your movie **M**.

The line bends dynamically, creating a smile!

M The curve (top) is dynamically erased and redrawn to create an animation as it bends (bottom).

Creating fills and gradients

You can fill shapes with solid colors, transparent colors, or radial or linear gradients by using the methods **beginFill()**, **beginGradientFill()**, and **endFill()**. Begin the shape to be filled by calling either the **beginFill()** or the **beginGradientFill()** method, and mark the end of the shape with **endFill()**. If your path isn't closed (the end points don't match the beginning points), Flash automatically closes it when the **endFill()** method is applied.

Applying solid or transparent fills with **beginFill()** is fairly straightforward; specify a hex code for the color and a value from 0 to 1 for the transparency. Gradients are more complex. You control the gradient by adding up to eight parameters to the **beginGradientFill()** method call. These parameters are as follows:

Gradient type is either the value **GradientType.RADIAL** or **GradientType. LINEAR**. A radial gradient's colors are defined in rings from the inside to the outside. With a linear gradient, the colors are defined from left to right.

Colors takes an **Array** object of numeric color values. You must create an **Array** object and put the hex codes for the gradient colors into the array in the order in which you want them to appear. If you want blue on the left side of a linear gradient and red on the right side, for example, your array is created like this:

```
var colors:Array = new
Array(0x0000FF, 0xFF0000);
```

Alphas is also an **Array** object and contains the alpha values (0 through 1) corresponding to the colors in the order in which you want them to appear. If you want your blue on one side to be 50 percent transparent, you create an array like this:

```
var alphas:Array = new Array(.5, 1);
```

Ratios is an **Array** object containing values (0 through 255) that correspond to the colors, determining how they mix. The ratio value defines the point along the gradient where the color is at 100 percent. An array like **ratios = new Array(0, 127)** means that the blue is 100 percent at the left side and the red is 100 percent starting at the middle .

N Ratios determine the mixing of colors for your gradient. The entire width of your gradient (or radius, for a radial gradient) is represented on a range from 0 through 255. Ratio values of (0,255) represent the typical gradient where each color is at one of the far sides (top). Ratio values of (0,127) create a tighter mixing in the first half of the gradient (middle). Ratio values of (63,190) create a tighter mixing in the middle of the gradient (bottom).

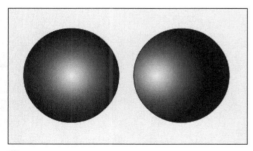

① Parameters for the matrix type. A radial gradient (left) and a linear gradient (right) are shown superimposed on a shape they would fill. Its width and height are indicated by w and h; r is the clockwise angle that it makes from the vertical; x and y are the position offset coordinates for the top-left corner of the gradient.

② The different spread methods are the same options in the Color panel Flow options.

③ The focal point of the gradient on the left is 0. The focal point of the gradient on the right is −0.5.

Matrix type is an object that represents size, position, scale, and rotation information. You can define properties that determine the size, position, and orientation of your gradient. You create a matrix and specify width and height properties (in pixels), an angle property (in radians), and x and y offset (position) coordinates **①**.

Spread method determines how the gradient behaves when the shape is larger than the gradient matrix. The parameter takes a string with one of three values: `SpreadMethod.PAD` fills out the shape with solid color, using the end color of the gradient; `SpreadMethod.REPEAT` causes the gradient pattern to repeat; and `SpreadMethod.REFLECT` causes the pattern to repeat in a mirror image of itself **②**.

Interpolation method instructs Flash how to calculate the blend between colors. The two values are `InterpolationMethod.RGB`, which blends colors more directly, resulting in a less spread-out appearance, and `InterpolationMethod.LINEAR_RGB`, which includes intermediate colors as part of blending colors, resulting in a more spread-out gradient.

Focal point ratio controls the *focal point* (center point) of a radial gradient and takes a number between −1 and 1. Normally, the focal point is the center of the gradient (0); a value between 0 and 1 (or −1) shifts the center toward one or the other edge by that percentage. For instance, a value of −0.5 shifts the focal point 50 percent between the center and the outer edge **③**.

To fill a shape with a solid color:

1. As you did in the previous task, create a new **Shape** object.

2. On the next line, call the **lineStyle()** method of the **graphics** property of your **Shape** object, and enter the line thickness parameter and other optional parameters between the parentheses.

3. On the next line, enter your **Shape** object's name followed by a period and the property **graphics**, and then call the **beginFill()** method.

4. With your pointer between the parentheses, enter the hex code for a color and a value for the alpha, separating your parameters with a comma **R**.

5. On a new line, enter your **Shape** object's name followed by a period and the property **graphics**, and then call the **moveTo()** method to identify the beginning of your drawing.

6. Use the **lineTo()** or **curveTo()** methods to draw a closed shape.

7. When the end point matches the beginning point of your shape, enter your **Shape** object's name followed by a period and the property **graphics**, and call the method **endFill()**.

   No parameters are required for the **endFill()** method. Flash fills the closed shape with the specified color.

8. On the last line, enter the **addChild()** method to add the **Shape** object to the display list.

9. Test your movie **S**.

```
var myShape:Shape = new Shape()
myShape.graphics.lineStyle(1, 0xFF0000, 1);
myShape.graphics.beginFill(0x7E6AE3, 1);
```

R This fill is light blue at 100 percent opacity.

```
var myShape:Shape = new Shape()
myShape.graphics.lineStyle(1, 0xFF0000, 1);
myShape.graphics.beginFill(0x7E6AE3, 1);
myShape.graphics.moveTo(100, 100);
myShape.graphics.lineTo(100, 200);
myShape.graphics.lineTo(200, 200);
myShape.graphics.lineTo(200, 100);
myShape.graphics.lineTo(100, 100);
myShape.graphics.endFill();
addChild(myShape);
```

(100,100)   (200,100)

(100,200)   (200,200)

S The end point of the last **lineTo()** method (100,100) matches the beginning point (100,100), creating a closed shape that can be filled. A blue box appears as a result of this code. The box was drawn counterclockwise from its top-left corner, but the order of line segments is irrelevant.

```
var myShape:Shape = new Shape();
var colors:Array = new Array(0xFF0000, 0x0000FF);
```

T The colors array is created with blue on one side and red on the other. If this gradient will be a linear gradient, blue (**0x0000FF**) will be on the left. If it will be a radial gradient, blue will be in the center.

```
var myShape:Shape = new Shape();
var colors:Array = new Array(0xFF0000, 0x0000FF);
var alphas:Array = new Array(1, 1);
```

U The **alphas** array is created with 100 percent opacity for both the blue and the red. The **ratios** array is created with blue on the far left side (or the center, in the case of a radial gradient) and with red on the far right side (or the edge of a radial gradient).

To fill a shape with a gradient:

1. As you did in the previous task, create a new **Shape** object.

2. On the next line, declare and instantiate a new **Array** object to hold your gradient's colors. In the parentheses of the constructor function, enter the numeric color values **T**.

   By adding parameters to the **new Array()** statement, you instantiate a new **Array** object and populate the array at the same time. The first color refers to the left side of a linear gradient or the center of a radial gradient.

3. Create another **Array** object, adding the alpha value corresponding to each color as a parameter.

   The constructor function call for this **Array** object should have the same number of parameters as the colors **Array** **U**.

4. Create a third **Array** object, entering ratio values defining the distribution of the colors in the gradient.

5. Declare and instantiate a new **Matrix** object. Don't enter any parameters in the constructor function call.

6. On the next line, enter the name of your **Matrix** object and call the **createGradientBox()** method.

   The **Matrix** class's **createGradientBox()** method is specially designed for creating **Matrix** objects to use when drawing gradients. The parameters you enter in this method call determine the size and position of the gradient.

   Continues on next page

7. Inside the parentheses of the **createGradientBox()** method call, enter parameters for width, height, rotation, x offset position, and y offset position **V**:

Width and **height** (numbers in pixels) determine the size of the gradient. Outside those dimensions, the colors will end or repeat according to the spread method you choose.

Rotation (number in radians) indicates how much to rotate the gradient—by default, linear gradients go from left to right, so if you want the gradient to go from top to bottom or at an angle, you must specify a rotation parameter. Otherwise, use 0.

X and y offset (numbers in pixels) indicate at what coordinate (relative to the movie clip's registration point) to begin the gradient.

8. On the next line, call the **lineStyle()** method of the **graphics** property of your **Shape** object, and enter the line thickness parameter between the parentheses.

9. On the following line, enter your **Shape** object's name and the property **graphics**, and call the **beginGradientFill()** method. In the parentheses, add the following parameters: the gradient type (**GradientType.LINEAR** or **GradientType.RADIAL**), your colors **Array**, your alphas **Array**, your ratios **Array**, and your **Matrix** object. Be sure to separate the parameters with commas.

All the information about your gradient that you defined in your arrays and **Matrix** object is fed into the parameters of the **beginGradientFill()** method **W**.

```
var myShape:Shape = new Shape();
var colors:Array = new Array(0xFF0000, 0x0000FF);
var alphas:Array = new Array(1, 1)
var ratios:Array = new Array(0, 255);
var matrix:Matrix = new Matrix();
matrix.createGradientBox(100, 100, 0, 100, 100);
```

V The width, height, rotation, and x, y coordinates of the gradient are defined as parameters of the **createGradientBox** method call.

```
var myShape:Shape = new Shape();
var colors:Array = new Array(0xFF0000, 0x0000FF);
var alphas:Array = new Array(1, 1);
var ratios:Array = new Array(0, 255);
var matrix:Matrix = new Matrix();
matrix.createGradientBox(100, 100, 0, 100, 100);
myShape.graphics.lineStyle(5, 0xFF0000, 1);
myShape.graphics.beginGradientFill(GradientType.LINEAR,
                    colors, alphas, ratios, matrix);
```

W The **beginGradientFill()** method takes several parameters that define how the gradient will be applied to the fill.

10. Still in the parentheses, if you wish to do so, enter a gradient spread method, interpolation method, and focal point ratio.

11. Add **moveTo()** and **lineTo()** method calls to draw a series of lines to create a closed shape.

12. On a new line, enter the name of your **Shape** object, a period, and the **graphics** property, and then call the **endFill()** method.

13. On the last line, enter the **addChild()** method to add the **Shape** object to the display list.

14. Test your movie.

Flash fills your shape with the gradient **X**.

TIP The **rotation** parameter of the **createGradientBox()** method takes radians, not degrees. Using radians is a way to measure angles using the mathematical constant pi. To convert degrees to radians, multiply by the number pi and then divide by 180. Using the **Math** class for pi (**Math.PI**), you can use this formula:

```
radians = degrees * (Math.PI / 180);
```

```
var myShape:Shape = new Shape();
var colors:Array = new Array(0xFF0000, 0x0000FF);
var alphas:Array = new Array(1, 1)
var ratios:Array = new Array(0, 255);
var matrix:Matrix = new Matrix();
matrix.createGradientBox(100, 100, 0, 100, 100);
myShape.graphics.lineStyle(5, 0xFF0000, 1);
myShape.graphics.beginGradientFill(GradientType.LINEAR,
                   colors, alphas, ratios, matrix);
myShape.graphics.moveTo(100, 100);
myShape.graphics.lineTo(100, 200);
myShape.graphics.lineTo(200, 200);
myShape.graphics.lineTo(200, 100);
myShape.graphics.lineTo(100, 100);
myShape.graphics.endFill();
addChild(myShape);
```

X The complete ActionScript code (top) creates a box with a linear gradient from blue to red (bottom).

Creating rectangles and circles

The **Graphics** class provides some methods to create common types of shapes—circles, rectangles, ellipses, and rectangles with rounded corners—saving you much time and effort. The following tasks lead you through creating a circle and rectangle, but the same process applies to ellipses and rounded rectangles with only different methods to consider. Refer to Table 7.6 earlier in this chapter for a description of all these methods.

When you use these methods, you still need to define the line style and the fill colors.

To create a circle:

1. Select the first frame of the main Timeline, and open the Actions panel.

2. As you did in the previous task, create a new **Shape** object.

3. On the next line, enter the name of your **Shape** object, a period, and the property **graphics**; then call the **lineStyle()** method. Enter parameters in between the parentheses to define the thickness, color, and/or transparency.

4. On the next line, enter your **Shape** object's name followed by a period and the property **graphics**, and then call the **beginFill()** method.

5. With your pointer between the parentheses, enter the hex code for a color and a value for the alpha, separating your parameters with a comma **Y**.

6. On a new line, enter your **Shape** object's name followed by a period and the property **graphics**, and then call the **drawCircle()** method.

7. With your pointer between the parentheses, enter a number for the x location, a number for the y location, and a number for the radius of the circle **Z**.

```
var myShape:Shape = new Shape();
myShape.graphics.lineStyle(1, 0xFF0000, 1);
myShape.graphics.beginFill(0x7E6AE3, 1);
```

Y Create a new **Shape** and define the line style and fill color.

```
var myShape:Shape = new Shape();
myShape.graphics.lineStyle(1, 0xFF0000, 1);
myShape.graphics.beginFill(0x7E6AE3, 1);
myShape.graphics.drawCircle(50, 60, 30);
```

Z The **drawCircle()** method is an easy way to create circles at any x and y position with a certain radius. This one is at x = 50, y = 60 with a 30-pixel radius.

```
var myShape:Shape = new Shape();
myShape.graphics.lineStyle(1, 0xFF0000, 1);
myShape.graphics.beginFill(0x7E6AE3, 1);
myShape.graphics.drawCircle(50, 60, 30);
addChild(myShape);
```

AA The full code (top) includes the `addChild()` method to display the shape.

8. On the last line, enter the **addChild()** method to add the **Shape** object to the display list.

9. Test your movie.

    Flash draws a circle positioned at the x and y location with the specified radius **AA**.

To create a rectangle:

Replace steps 6–7 in the previous task with the method **drawRect()**.

The four parameters of this method are the x and y positions of the top-left corner, and the width and height in pixels. The following statement creates a rectangle 200 pixels wide, 50 pixels tall, and snuggled in the top-left corner:

```
myShape.graphics.drawRect(0, 0, 200,
    50);
```

TIP The endFill() method is unnecessary when you use the methods that automatically draw circles and squares.

Advanced Drawing Methods

In addition to the drawing methods that you've learned here, Flash Player 10 supports some new advanced drawing methods that greatly expand the dynamic drawing capabilities.

In particular, **drawPath()** is a new method that consolidates the **moveTo()**, **lineTo()**, and **curveTo()** methods in a single call to make defining shapes less code heavy. The **drawPath()** method relies on a special kind of an array called a *vector* and represents the drawing methods as numeric identifiers. The method also keeps track of the direction of how a shape is drawn, which is called *winding*. You can draw a shape in either a clockwise direction or a counterclockwise direction, which has implications for intersecting shapes.

Another new method, **drawTriangles()**, can render triangles and map images to those triangles with the purpose of distorting images for 3D rendering.

These are two of several new important additions to the ActionScript drawing tools. Although they are substantially more complicated than the methods covered here, they can be powerful and greatly enhance what can be dynamically rendered. See the Adobe Help site for more information on the advanced methods of the **Graphics** class.

Using Dynamic Masks

You can turn any **DisplayObject** into a mask and specify another **DisplayObject** to be masked with **mask**, a property of the **DisplayObject** class. To do so, you simply assign one object as the **mask** property of the other. For example, in the statement **mypicture.mask = mywindow**, the object **mywindow** acts as a mask over the object **mypicture**. Recall that a mask is an area that defines the "hole" through which you can see content.

Because you can control all the properties of **DisplayObject**s, you can make your mask move or grow and shrink in response to viewer interaction. You can even combine a dynamic mask with the drawing methods you learned earlier in the chapter to create masks that change shape.

An effective combination assigns **startDrag()** and **stopDrag()** methods to a mask and creates a draggable mask. When you add **startDrag()** to a **MouseEvent.MOUSE_DOWN** handler and **stopDrag()** to a **MouseEvent.MOUSE_UP** handler, your viewer can control the position of the mask.

Traditional Masks

It seems counterintuitive that a mask is the area in which the masked object is visible. But if you think of a mask in terms of how a photographer or a painter uses one, it makes more sense. In traditional darkroom photography or in painting, a mask is something that protects the image and keeps it visible. A photographer would shield areas of light-sensitive paper from exposure to the light, and a painter would shield certain areas of the canvas from paint.

To set an object as a mask:

1. Create a **DisplayObject** for the object that will be masked. For this example, import a bitmap to the Stage and convert it to a movie clip symbol. In the Properties inspector, give it a name Ⓐ.

   This movie clip will be masked.

2. Create another **DisplayObject** for the object that will act as the mask. For this example, you will create a **Shape** object and dynamically draw a shape with the **Graphics** class methods.

   This **Shape** object will act as a mask.

3. Select the first frame of the main Timeline, and open the Actions panel.

4. Create a new **Shape** object.

5. On the next line, call the **beginFill()** method of the **Shape** object's **graphics** property to define the color of the fill.

   The actual color of the fill won't matter for the mask object, since it simply defines the area of the masked object that is visible. However, you still need to define a color.

6. On a new line, enter your **Shape** object's name followed by a period and the property **graphics**, and then call the **drawCircle()** method.

7. With your pointer between the parentheses, enter a number for the x location, a number for the y location, and a number for the radius of the circle Ⓑ.

A A movie clip containing a cityscape image will be the masked movie clip.

```
var myShape:Shape = new Shape();
myShape.graphics.beginFill(0x7E00E3, 1);
myShape.graphics.drawCircle(200, 200, 120);
```

B A dynamic circle is drawn with the **Sprite** object.

```
var myShape:Shape = new Shape();
myShape.graphics.beginFill(0x7E00E3, 1);
myShape.graphics.drawCircle(200, 200, 120);
addChild(myShape);
cityscape_mc.mask = myShape;
```

C The **mask** property makes the circle act as a mask over the **cityscape_mc** object.

8. On the next line, enter the **addChild()** method to add the **Shape** object to the display list.

   Flash draws a circle positioned at the x and y locations at the specified radius.

9. On the next line, enter the name of the object that will be masked (your movie clip on the Stage), a dot, the property **mask**, an equals sign, and then the object that will be the mask (the **Shape** object).

   Flash assigns the **Shape** object as the mask of the movie clip on the Stage.

10. Test your movie.

   The circle of the **Shape** reveals portions of the masked movie clip **C**.

To remove a mask:

To remove a **mask**, assign the **null** keyword to the masked object's mask property, as follows:

myImage.mask = null;

The object called **myImage** will no longer be masked.

> **TIP** You can specify the main Timeline as the object to be masked, and all the graphics on the main Timeline will be masked. To do so, enter `MovieClip(root)` as the target path for the **mask** property.

> **TIP** The stacking order of the mask object and the masked object doesn't matter when you use ActionScript to create a mask. Either of them can be in front or in back of the other, although it is more intuitive to always keep the mask in front of the masked object.

> **TIP** If the mask object is dynamically created, it doesn't necessarily have to be added to the display list. However, if you want to change the Stage (and the objects contained in it) or if you want the user to interact with the mask, you must put it on the display list before assigning the **mask** property.

Transparent masks

Different levels of transparency in the mask aren't recognized and don't normally affect the mask. To make the mask function with alpha levels, you must set both masked and mask **DisplayObject**s to use runtime bitmap caching, either by selecting the "Use runtime bitmap caching" check box in the Properties inspector (for objects on the Stage) or by setting the **cacheAsBitmap** property to **true** in ActionScript. Bitmap caching is a mode in which Flash treats the images as bitmaps, storing them in memory so it does not have to continuously redraw them.

Transparent masks will reveal the masked object in gradations, depending on the alpha value of the mask. This allows you to create masks with soft, feathered edges and vignette images.

To make a mask with transparencies:

Set the **cacheAsBitmap** property of the mask and the masked object to true before you assign the **mask** property, like so:

```
myImage.cacheAsBitmap = true;
myShape.cacheAsBitmap = true;
myImage.mask = myShape;
```

The object called **myShape** will reveal portions of the object called **myImage**, according to its transparent gradient **D**.

TIP Transparent masks only work in Action-Script. Masks created on the Timeline by defining the Layer properties (described in Chapter 1) don't support alpha transparencies even when "Use runtime bitmap caching" is turned on in the Properties inspector.

D An object with alpha transparency (above) can create a softer, more graduated mask (below) if **cacheAsBitmap** is set to **true**.

You'll create a draggable mask to uncover this movie clip of New York City called map_mc.

```
var mySprite:Sprite = new Sprite();
mySprite.graphics.beginFill(0x7E00E3, 1);
mySprite.graphics.drawCircle(200, 200, 100);
addChild(mySprite);
```

F A simple circle created dynamically will act as the mask. Use the **Sprite** object to create the circle because the **Sprite** class includes the **startDrag()** and **stopDrag()** methods, and the **Shape** object does not.

To create a draggable mask:

1. Create a **DisplayObject** for the object that will be masked. For this example, import a bitmap to the Stage and convert it to a movie clip symbol. In the Properties inspector, give it a name **E**.

    This movie clip will be masked.

2. Create another **DisplayObject** for the object that will act as the mask. For this example, you will create a **Sprite** object and dynamically draw a shape with the **Graphics** class methods.

    This **Sprite** object will act as a draggable mask. (You can't use a **Shape** object in this example because it is too simple of an object, and it doesn't support drag-and-drop methods).

3. Select the first frame of the main Timeline, and open the Actions panel.

4. Create a new **Sprite** object.

5. On the next line, call the **beginFill()** method of the **Sprite** object's **graphics** property to define the color of the fill.

6. On a new line, enter your **Sprite** object's name followed by a period and the property **graphics**, and then call the **drawCircle()** method.

7. With your pointer between the parentheses, enter a number for the x location, a number for the y location, and a number for the radius of the circle.

8. On the next line, enter the **addChild()** method to add the **Sprite** object to the display list.

    Flash draws a circle positioned at the x and y locations at the specified radius **F**.

Continues on next page

9. On the next line, set the **buttonMode** property of the **Sprite** object to **true**.

   This allows the **Sprite** object to receive **MouseEvent** events, like the **MOUSE_DOWN** event that will be needed for a drag action.

10. On the next line, enter the name of the object that will be masked (your movie clip on the Stage), a dot, the property **mask**, an equals sign, and then the object that will be the mask (the **Sprite** object) **G**.

    Flash assigns the **Sprite** object as the mask of the movie clip on the Stage.

```
var mySprite:Sprite = new Sprite();
mySprite.graphics.beginFill(0x7E00E3, 1);
mySprite.graphics.drawCircle(200, 200, 100);
addChild(mySprite);

mySprite.buttonMode = true;
map_mc.mask = mySprite;
```

G Make sure that the **buttonMode** property for your Sprite object is set to **true**.

```
var mySprite:Sprite = new Sprite();
mySprite.graphics.beginFill(0x7E00E3, 1);
mySprite.graphics.drawCircle(200, 200, 100);
addChild(mySprite);

mySprite.buttonMode = true;
map_mc.mask = mySprite;

mySprite.addEventListener(MouseEvent.MOUSE_DOWN, startdragging);
function startdragging(myevent:MouseEvent):void {
    mySprite.startDrag();
}
mySprite.addEventListener(MouseEvent.MOUSE_UP, stopdragging);
function stopdragging(myevent:MouseEvent):void {
    mySprite.stopDrag();
}
```

H The event handlers for the **MouseEvent.MOUSE_DOWN** and **MouseEvent.MOUSE_UP** events trigger the dragging and dropping actions on the **Sprite** object.

① The circle becomes a draggable mask.

11. On the next lines, create the event handler to detect the **MouseEvent.MOUSE_DOWN** event that triggers a **startDrag()** method on the **Sprite** object as follows:

```
mySprite.
addEventListener(MouseEvent.
→ MOUSE_DOWN, startdragging);
function startdragging (
→ myevent:MouseEvent):void {
    mySprite.startDrag();
}
```

When the mouse button is pressed on the mask, it becomes draggable.

12. On the next lines, create the event handler to detect the **MouseEvent.MOUSE_UP** event that triggers a **stopDrag()** method on the **Sprite** object as follows:

```
mySprite.
addEventListener(MouseEvent.
→ MOUSE_UP, stopdragging);
function stopdragging (
→ myevent:MouseEvent):void {
    mySprite.stopDrag();
}
```

When the mouse is released on the mask, it stops being dragged **①**.

13. Test your movie.

The **Sprite** acts as a mask, and the **MOUSE_DOWN** and **MOUSE_UP** handlers provide the drag-and-drop interactivity **①**.

Generating Motion Tweens Dynamically

Motion tweens that are created dynamically are animations generated and controlled purely with ActionScript and are not created on the Timeline at authortime. You can use dynamic tweens to create more responsive interactivity because the animation can be based entirely on user behavior at runtime. Dynamic tweens also make editing easier since you can modify the animation by simply changing ActionScript parameters rather than items on the Stage.

Dynamic motion tweens are generated with the **Tween** class. The **Tween** class isn't normally included in the ActionScript code, so to use it, you have to explicitly include the code with the **import** statement. To generate a tween, you instantiate a new **Tween** object and provide seven parameters:

Object is the instance name of the target of the motion tween.

Property is the name of the property that you want to animate. The property needs to be enclosed in quotation marks. For example, **"x"** or **"alpha"** are valid property parameters.

Function determines the easing of the tween. Flash provides many preset easing classes that you can use; for example, **Strong.easeIn** makes your tween ease in. See **Table 7.7** for a list of common easing functions.

Begin is the starting value of your property.

Finish is the ending value of your property.

Duration determines how long your tween lasts.

UseSeconds is a Boolean value that determines whether the Duration parameter is in seconds (**true**) or in frames (**false**).

In addition to basic tweening, the **Tween** class has many events that you can use to detect critical points in the tween (when it has been completed, for example), and many methods to control the tweening. See **Table 7.8** for some of the events and methods of the **Tween** class.

TABLE 7.7 Common Tween Easing Functions

Function	Description
None.easeNone	No ease.
Regular.easeIn	A slow start.
Regular.easeOut	A slow end.
Regular.easeInOut	A slow start and a slow end.
Strong.easeIn	A dramatically slow start.
Strong.easeOut	A dramatically slow end.
Strong.easeInOut	A dramatically slow start and end.
Bounce.easeOut	A bouncing effect at the end, where the ending value approaches after several rebounds toward the beginning value.
Elastic.easeOut	A yo-yo effect at the end, where the ending value approaches in a decaying sine-wave manner.

```
import fl.transitions.Tween;
import fl.transitions.easing.*;
```

A The **import** statements are required to include the code to use the **Tween** classes and associated classes.

To create a dynamic tween:

1. Any object of the **DisplayObject** or **DisplayObjectContainer** class can be dynamically animated. For this example, create a movie clip, place an instance of it on the Stage, and name it in the Properties inspector.

2. Select the first frame of the main Timeline, and open the Actions panel.

3. Enter the following two **import** statements to include the code for the **Tween** class and associated classes as follows **A**:

   ```
   import fl.transitions.Tween;
   import fl.transitions.easing.*;
   ```

   The asterisk is a wildcard, meaning that all the classes in the **easing** package will be imported.

Continues on next page

TABLE 7.8 Some Tween Methods and Events

Method or Event	Description
stop()	Stops the tween.
start()	Starts the tween from its beginning.
resume()	Starts the tween at the point when it was stopped.
yoyo()	Plays the tween in reverse.
TweenEvent.MOTION_FINISH	Occurs when the tween finishes.
TweenEvent.MOTION_STOP	Occurs when the tween is stopped with the **stop()** method.
TweenEvent.MOTION_START	Occurs when the tween starts with the **start()** or **yoyo()** method, but will not occur when the tween is instantiated.
TweenEvent.MOTION_RESUME	Occurs when the tween starts with the **resume()** method.

4. On the next line, declare a variable for a Tween object.

5. On the next line, enter your Tween object, then an equals sign, followed by the constructor for a new **Tween**. Provide the seven required parameters (the target object, its property, an easing function, the beginning value, the ending value, duration, and whether or not the duration is measured in seconds) **B**:

```
mytween = new Tween(myimage, "x",
→ Strong.easeIn, 0, 100, 2, true);
```

As soon as the tween is instantiated, the motion tween proceeds.

6. Test your movie **C**.

Flash dynamically animates the object called **myimage** from x=0 to x=100 in 2 seconds.

To stop a dynamic tween:

Call the method **stop()** on your **Tween** object, like so:

```
mytween.stop();
```

The animation stops.

To resume a dynamic tween:

Call the method **resume()** on your **Tween** object, like so:

```
mytween.resume();
```

The animation plays from the point where it was stopped.

To replay a dynamic tween:

Call the method **start()** on your **Tween** object, like so:

```
mytween.start();
```

The animation plays from its beginning.

```
import fl.transitions.Tween;
import fl.transitions.easing.*;
var mytween:Tween;
mytween = new Tween(myimage, "x", Strong.easeIn, 0, 100, 2, true);
```

B The tween starts immediately when the new **Tween** is instantiated.

C As a result of the dynamic tween, this square (called **myimage**) moves from x=0 to x=100 across the Stage in 2 seconds.

To detect the end of a dynamic tween:

1. Continue with the earlier task, "To create a dynamic tween."

2. Select the first frame of the main Timeline, and open the Actions panel.

3. Enter an additional **import** statement to include the code for the **TweenEvent** class:

    `import fl.transitions.TweenEvent;`

4. On the next available line, enter an event listener for your **Tween** object that listens for the **TweenEvent.MOTION_FINISH** event. For example:

    ```
    mytween.addEventListener(
    → TweenEvent.MOTION_FINISH,
    → tweendone);
    ```

When the animation defined by **mytween** finishes, the function called **tweendone** will be triggered.

5. Enter a function that responds to the **TweenEvent** **D**:

    ```
    function tweendone(myevent:
    → TweenEvent):void {
        mytween.start();
    }
    ```

In this example, when the tween called **mytween** finishes, it repeats itself by playing from its beginning **E**.

```
import fl.transitions.Tween;
import fl.transitions.easing.*;
import fl.transitions.TweenEvent;

var mytween:Tween;
mytween = new Tween(myimage, "x", Strong.easeIn, 0, 100, 2, true);

mytween.addEventListener (TweenEvent.MOTION_FINISH, tweendone);
function tweendone(myevent:TweenEvent):void {
    mytween.start();
}
```

D The event handler listens for the end of the dynamic tween and replays the animation.

E When the tween finishes (reaches x=100) at left, the square goes back to x=0 and repeats the animation, right.

Customizing Your Pointer

When you understand how to control graphics on the display list, you can build your own custom mouse pointer. Think about all the different pointers you use in Flash. As you choose different tools in the Tools panel—the Paint Bucket, the Eyedropper, the Pencil—your pointer changes to help you understand and apply them. Similarly, you can tailor the pointer's form to match its function in your Flash projects.

Customizing the pointer involves first hiding the default mouse pointer. Then you must match the location of your new graphic to the location of the hidden (but still functional) pointer. To do this, continuously assign the **mouseX** and **mouseY** properties to the **x** and **y** properties of a **DisplayObject**.

To hide the mouse pointer:

1. Select the first frame of the main Timeline, and open the Actions panel.

2. Enter **Mouse.hide()**.

   When you test your movie, the mouse pointer becomes invisible.

To show the mouse pointer:

Use the statement **Mouse.show()**.

To create your own mouse pointer:

1. Create any **DisplayObject** for your pointer. For this example, create a movie clip, place an instance of it on the Stage, and name it in the Properties inspector.

   This movie clip will become your pointer.

2. Select the first frame of the root Timeline, and open the Actions panel.

3. Enter **Mouse.hide()**.

   When this movie begins, the mouse pointer disappears.

4. On the next line, add an event listener (like the following) to the Stage to detect the **MouseEvent.MOUSE_MOVE** event:

   ```
   stage.addEventListener(MouseEvent.
   MOUSE_MOVE, moveCursor);
   ```

   When the mouse pointer moves on the Stage, the function called **moveCursor** is triggered.

```
Mouse.hide();

stage.addEventListener(MouseEvent.MOUSE_MOVE, moveCursor);
function moveCursor(myevent:MouseEvent):void {
    cursor_mc.x = mouseX;
    cursor_mc.y = mouseY;
    myevent.updateAfterEvent();
}
```

Ⓐ The X and Y properties for the movie clip **cursor_mc** follow the mouse pointer's position. Add the **updateAfterEvent()** method to the event object to force Flash to refresh the display and create smoother motion.

5. On the next line, create the function called **moveCursor**, like so:

```
function moveCursor(myevent:
→ MouseEvent):void {
    cursor_mc.x = mouseX;
    cursor_mc.y = mouseY;
    myevent.updateAfterEvent();
}
```

The first two lines of the function assign the location of the mouse pointer to the position of the movie clip called **cursor_mc**. The third line adds the **updateAfterEvent()** method of the event object, which forces Flash to redraw the screen whenever the event happens, independently of the frame rate. This will create a smoother motion of your mouse pointer because your user may be moving the pointer faster than the screen refresh rate.

6. Test your movie.

When the mouse pointer moves on the Stage, the movie clip follows to act as the custom pointer **Ⓐ**.

TIP To reactivate the hand cursor when rolling over buttons or other interactive objects, you must create new event handlers that set the visibility of your custom cursor to `false` for each button. The statement `Mouse.show()` can then reactivate the hand cursor. Use a `MouseEvent.MOUSE_OUT` event handler to restore your original settings.

Putting It Together: Animating Graphics with ActionScript

One of the most important concepts in interactivity is the idea of mapping, or translating, the property of one object to the property of another. Nearly all interfaces are based on this principle: In scrollbars, the vertical position (Y property) of a slider maps directly to the vertical position (Y property) of a block of text. In video controls, the horizontal position (X property) of the scrubber maps directly to the time position of a video (the parameter in the **FLVPlayback.seek()** method). In volume controls, the rotation of a dial maps directly to the volume property of a sound.

In the following task, you'll see how the Y position of the mouse cursor can map to the horizontal and vertical scaling of an image. You can break the interactivity down to three parts:

Listen for the MouseEvent.MOUSE_MOVE or Event.ENTER_FRAME event. You want to provide an immediate visual translation based on your viewer's input. As your viewer moves their mouse over the controls, they should receive visual/auditory feedback. So, listen for the different changes in mouse position.

Keep track of the mouseX and mouseY properties. The **mouseX** and **mouseY** properties represents the horizontal and vertical position of the mouse cursor. As the user moves their mouse, you can track the changing values of **mouseX** and **mouseY**.

Translate the changing values of mouseX and mouseY to a range of values appropriate for another set of properties. Do some algebraic manipulation to map the **mouseX** and/or **mouseY** values to a range that's

acceptable to your target property. For example, if you want the **mouseX** or **mouseY** value to map to the transparency of an object, you'll want to generate a range of values from 0 (transparent) to 1 (opaque).

To translate mouse movements to visual changes:

1. Create a movie clip, put it on the Stage, and name it in the Properties inspector.

   This movie clip will visually change, depending on the position of your mouse cursor **Ⓐ**.

2. Create a second movie clip, put in on the Stage next to the first movie clip, and name it in the Properties inspector.

   The second movie clip will act as the interface element for the user **Ⓑ**.

3. Select the first frame of the main Timeline, and open the Actions panel.

4. Add an event listener to the interface element (like the following) to detect the **MouseEvent.MOUSE_MOVE** event:

   ```
   scale_mc.addEventListener(
   → MouseEvent.MOUSE_MOVE,
   → scaleface);
   ```

   The function called **scaleface** is triggered whenever the mouse cursor moves over the movie clip called **scale_mc**.

5. On the next line, create a function called **scaleface**, which changes the **scaleX** and **scaleY** properties of the first movie clip based on the **mouseY** property, like so:

   ```
   function scaleface(myevent:
   → MouseEvent):void {
       face_mc.scaleX = .5 + (mouseY -
   → scale_mc.y) / scale_mc.height;
       face_mc.scaleY = face_mc.scaleX;
   }
   ```

A The movie clip called **face_mc** is placed on the Stage.

B Another movie clip called **scale_mc** is placed next to the first movie clip.

```
scale_mc.addEventListener(MouseEvent.MOUSE_MOVE, scaleface);
function scaleface(myevent:MouseEvent):void {
    face_mc.scaleX = .5 + (mouseY - scale_mc.y) / scale_mc.height;
    face_mc.scaleY = face_mc.scaleX;
}
```

C The code listens for mouse movement over the movie clip called **scale_mc** and translates the mouse position to scale changes of the movie clip called **scale_mc.**

The final code can be seen in **C**. In this example, we subtract the position of the **scale_mc** movie clip from the position of the mouse cursor, so the resulting value ranges from 0 to the height of the **scale_mc** movie clip. Dividing by the height results in a range from 0 to 1. We add .5 to this so the face doesn't actually get so small that it disappears. So the final range is from .5 to 1.5, which is assigned to the **scaleX** and **scaleY** of the Face movie clip.

6. Test your movie.

   When you move your mouse cursor over the interface element, the Face movie clip scales up or down, from 50% to 150% of its original size **D**.

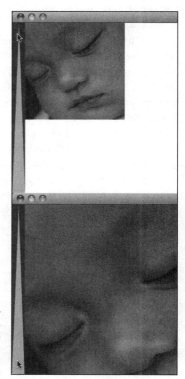

D An example of interactivity that maps user events to immediate visual changes. Moving the mouse in the upper portion of the **scale_mc** movie clip makes the image smaller (top), while moving the mouse in the lower portion of the **scale_mc** movie clip makes the image larger (bottom).

About Bitmap Images

One of the hallmark characteristics of Flash is that the images you create are vector images, whether you use the drawing tools in the authoring environment or the drawing methods of the **Graphics** class. For computer-based drawing, vectors are convenient because they allow you to deal with lines, shapes, text, and other objects as a single, resolution-independent unit rather than as a collection of pixels that must be controlled individually. However, as part of the process of displaying the Flash movie on a computer screen, the Flash Player has always converted those vectors to bitmap images behind the scenes.

ActionScript allows you to directly manipulate bitmap images. You've already seen some of the power of bitmap manipulation when you learned to apply filters. Filters are a bitmap manipulation technique, and inside the Flash Player a vector-based object is converted to a bitmap before any filter effect is applied to it. Controlling bitmap images requires that you use the **BitmapData** class. Using the properties and methods of the **BitmapData** class, you can create your own filters and graphical effects to enhance your Flash projects. You can add subtle touches, like converting an image to grayscale or fading two images together. Or add textures and distortions for more sophisticated visual displays.

Creating and Accessing Bitmap Data

A bitmap image consists of a series of rows and columns of colored dots known as *pixels*. Each pixel is assigned a single color value containing a mix of red, green, blue, and possibly alpha (transparency) values. When you use the **BitmapData** class to manipulate image information, all the changes are made to the individual pixel's color values.

The first step to manipulating a bitmap image is to create an instance of the **BitmapData** class. Sometimes you'll want to start with a new, blank image, and many times you'll want to manipulate an existing image, such as a digital photo.

As with most objects in ActionScript, to create a new **BitmapData** object you use the constructor function as in **var myBitmapData: BitmapData = new BitmapData(100, 200)**. This statement creates an object with a width of 100 pixels and a height of 200 pixels. The **BitmapData** constructor takes up to four parameters. You must use the first two parameters: a width and height for the image. You can optionally add two more parameters to specify whether the image will use transparency (alpha channel) information and what color to fill the image with initially.

Previously, you used hexadecimal numbers to specify color values in the form 0x*RRGGBB,* where *RR* is a two-digit value for the amount of red in the image, *GG* for the amount of green, and *BB* for the amount of blue. Several of the **BitmapData** methods require you to provide a numeric color parameter. For a **BitmapData** object with no alpha channel, the six-digit hexadecimal format is still used. If the **BitmapData** object has an alpha channel, however, use eight digits instead of six, like this: 0x*AARRGGBB*. In this case, you add two extra digits that represent the alpha value after the 0x prefix but before the two red digits. These two digits indicate the amount of transparency the color will have. As with the other color values, the possible alpha values range from 0 (00) to 255 (FF). Note that this is different from the **alpha** property of a **DisplayObject**, which uses a decimal from 0 to 1.

After you create a **BitmapData** object, you can use methods from the **BitmapData** class to manipulate its pixels and colors. The next step is to assign the **BitmapData** object as the **bitmapData** property of a **Bitmap** object. The **Bitmap** object is the **DisplayObject** that you must add to the display list to make your image visible.

To create new bitmap data:

1. Select the first frame of the Timeline and open the Actions panel.

2. Create a new instance of the **BitmapData** class, as in:

```
var myBitmapData:BitmapData =
→ new BitmapData(200, 100, false,
→ 0x33ee44);
```

The four parameters are width, height, alpha transparency, and color. Only the first two are required. This instance, called **myBitmapData**, is a 200-by-100-pixel rect-angle filled with a certain solid color.

If you set the alpha transparency param-eter to **false**, you should use a six-digit number; otherwise, use an eight-digit number to include the transparency information.

At this point, no image is visible. The **BitmapData** object is simply information about a collection of pixels that you can manipulate and then, at a later point, put into a **Bitmap** object to display on the Stage (explained later).

TIP If you leave off the fourth parameter for color in the **BitmapData** constructor func-tion, the **BitmapData** object is filled with solid white pixels by default.

Accessing images dynamically

In addition to creating an image filled with a single color, as in the previous task, you can create a **BitmapData** object with more interesting image information. You can create a new **BitmapData** object from a bitmap symbol in your Library. Or you can use the **load()** method of the **Loader** class to retrieve an image from an external image file, and then copy a snapshot of the **Loader** object into a **BitmapData** object. This transfer of image information from the **Loader** object to the **BitmapData** object requires the method **draw()**.

To create bitmap data from a Library symbol:

1. In your Flash document, add an image to the Library by choosing File > Import > Import to Library, browsing to your image file in the dialog box, and clicking OK.

Your image appears in the Library and is identified as a bitmap item.

2. Select the bitmap in the Library panel. In the Library panel's Options menu, choose Properties.

The Symbol Properties dialog box appears.

3. Click the Advanced button to reveal the Linkage section.

4. In the Linkage section, select the Export for ActionScript check box. Leave "Export in frame 1" selected.

5. In the Class field, enter a name to identify your bitmap. Leave the Base class as flash display.BitmapData and click OK **A**.

A dialog box appears, warning you that your class could not be found so one will automatically be generated. Click OK. In this example, the class name for your Library symbol is **Jumper**. This new class inherits from the **BitmapData** class, which means it has all the same methods and properties of the **BitmapData** class. Your class name will be used to create new instances of your **BitmapData**. Make sure that your class name doesn't contain any periods.

6. Select the first frame of the main Time-line, and open the Actions panel.

7. On the first line, create a new instance of your **BitmapData** object, referencing its class name (created in step 5), like so:

```
var myBitmapData:Jumper = new
→ Jumper(384, 256);
```

Include two parameters for its width and height. These parameters are required as they are for all **BitmapData** objects. A new instance of your **Jumper** class, which has all the characteristics of the **BitmapData** class, is created. The name of your new instance is **myBitmapData** B.

The bitmap image from the Library is now stored in a **BitmapData** object.

To create bitmap data from an externally loaded image:

1. As in the previous tasks covered in Chapter 6, create a **URLRequest** object; then create a **Loader** object and call the **load()** method to load an external image C.

2. Create the event handler to detect the completion of the loading process D.

Continues on next page

Ⓐ The Linkage section of the Symbol Properties dialog box. This Library symbol can be referenced with the class name **Jumper**. It will have all the same properties and methods of the **BitmapData** class.

```
var myBitmapData:Jumper = new Jumper(384,256);
```

Ⓑ Create a new **BitmapData** object with the class name that you defined in the Linkage section of the Symbol Properties dialog box. The first two parameters of the constructor specify the width and height of the bitmap, and are required.

```
var myrequest:URLRequest = new URLRequest("gymnast.jpg");
var myloader:Loader = new Loader();
myloader.load(myrequest);
```

Ⓒ Create a new **Loader** object and load an external file as described in the **URLRequest** object.

```
var myrequest:URLRequest = new URLRequest("gymnast.jpg");
var myloader:Loader = new Loader();
myloader.load(myrequest);

myloader.contentLoaderInfo.addEventListener(Event.COMPLETE, imgLoaded);
function imgLoaded(event:Event):void {

}
```

Ⓓ Create an event handler to detect when the loading is complete.

3. Between the curly braces of the event-handler function, create a new **BitmapData** object and reference your **Loader** object's width and height properties to specify its exact dimensions, like so:

```
var myBitmapData:BitmapData =
→ new BitmapData(myloader.width,
→ myloader.height);
```

4. On the next line, still within the curly braces of the function, enter the name of your **BitmapData** object, and then call the **draw()** method. Provide the **Loader** object as its parameter as in the following:

```
myBitmapData.draw(myloader);
```

This **draw()** method copies the image from the **Loader** object into the **BitmapData** object.

Your **BitmapData** object now contains the image information from the externally loaded file **E**.

TIP You can use the **draw()** method to copy image data from any **DisplayObject** source into your **BitmapData** object, not just a **Loader** object. For example, you can copy an image from a text field and put it into your **BitmapData** object and manipulate text at the pixel level.

TIP The **draw()** method has additional optional parameters so you can alter the image before putting it into your **BitmapData** object. The full parameters for the **draw()** method are as follows:

source: The **BitmapData** object from which to copy pixel information. This is the first, required parameter.

matrix: The **Matrix** object designating the transformations to the image.

colorTransform: The **ColorTransform** object designating the color changes to the image.

blendMode: The way in which the resulting bitmap will interact with colors below it. Use constants from the **BlendMode** class such as **BlendMode.MULTIPLY**.

clipRect: The **Rectangle** object designating the portion of the source bitmap to copy.

smoothing: A true or false value indicating whether the image will be smoothed when scaled or rotated.

You can pass **null** values for the parameters if you want to pass values for some but not all the parameters.

```
var myrequest:URLRequest = new URLRequest("gymnast.jpg");
var myloader:Loader = new Loader();
myloader.load(myrequest);

myloader.contentLoaderInfo.addEventListener(Event.COMPLETE, imgLoaded);
function imgLoaded(event:Event):void {
    var myBitmapData:BitmapData = new BitmapData(myloader.width, myloader.height);
    myBitmapData.draw(myloader);

}
```

E When the loading is complete, create a **BitmapData** object with dimensions that match the **Loader** object. Then copy the image data from the **Loader** into the **BitmapData** object.

To remove bitmap data from a BitmapData object:

In the Script pane, enter the name of your **BitmapData** object and a period; then call the method **dispose()**.

This frees up Flash's memory by setting the width and height of the **BitmapData** object to 0.

TIP Be careful not to try to manipulate or access a BitmapData object once you have called its dispose method; at that point, its width and height are set to 0, and its methods and properties won't work.

Displaying the bitmap data

So far, you've only learned to create bitmap data or load in bitmap data from another source—either from a Library symbol or an external file. To display your bitmap data, you must assign the data to the **bitmapData** property of a new object, the **Bitmap** object. The **Bitmap** object is a subclass of the **DisplayObject** class, which you add to the display list.

To display bitmap data:

1. Create an instance of the **Bitmap** class, like so:

   ```
   var myBitmap:Bitmap = new Bitmap();
   ```

   In this example, your new **Bitmap** object is called **myBitmap**.

2. Assign your **BitmapData** object to the **Bitmap** object's **bitmapData** property, like so:

   ```
   myBitmap.bitmapData = myBitmapData;
   ```

3. Call the **addChild()** method to add the Bitmap object to the display list:

   ```
   addChild(myBitmap);
   ```

   The bitmap data is now visible on the Stage 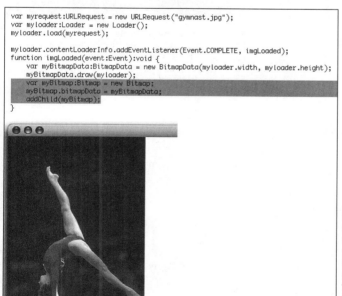.

Continues on next page

```
var myrequest:URLRequest = new URLRequest ("gymnast.jpg");
var myloader:Loader = new Loader();
myloader.load(myrequest);

myloader.contentLoaderInfo.addEventListener(Event.COMPLETE, imgLoaded);
function imgLoaded(event:Event):void {
    var myBitmapData:BitmapData = new BitmapData(myloader.width, myloader.height);
    myBitmapData.draw(myloader);
    var myBitmap:Bitmap = new Bitmap;
    myBitmap.bitmapData = myBitmapData;
    addChild(myBitmap);
}
```

F The highlighted code creates a new **Bitmap** object, puts the **BitmapData** object into it, and displays the image on the Stage (below). Although the image appears the same as if you added the **Loader** object to the Stage, the image is bitmap data and you can manipulate all the color and transparency information for each pixel.

TIP As a shortcut, you can pass the BitmapData object as a parameter when you create your Bitmap object, and it will be assigned as the bitmapData property, like so:

```
var myBitmap:Bitmap = new
→ Bitmap(myBitmapData);
```

TIP You can set the smoothing property of a Bitmap object to true to smooth out the image when it is scaled **G**.

```
myBitmap.smoothing = true;
```

G The **smoothing** property of the **Bitmap** object helps smooth out rough edges due to scaling and rotations. The top image has no smoothing, and the image appears pixilated. The bottom image has **smoothing** set to **true**.

Manipulating Bitmap Images

There is little use in creating a **BitmapData** object just to hold an image and display it through a **Bitmap** object. The real fun is in manipulating the image's pixels. The most basic way to do this is to draw color onto the bitmap.

You can change the color of a single pixel at a time using the **setPixel()** and **setPixel32()** methods. To cover a larger area, use the **fillRect()** method to set all the pixels in a rectangular portion of a **BitmapData** object to the same color; the **floodFill()** method lets you fill in a region of color with a different color, similar to the Paint Bucket tool in many graphics programs. Finally, using the **getPixel()** and **getPixel32()** methods you can identify the color of a pixel in a **BitmapData** object, much like the Eyedropper tool that is common in image-editing programs.

To draw single pixels:

1. Select the first keyframe on the Timeline, and open the Actions panel.

2. As you have done in the previous tasks, declare and instantiate a new BitmapData object with **width** and **height** parameters like the following:

   ```
   var myBitmapData:BitmapData = new
   → BitmapData(300, 300);
   ```

   This new **BitmapData** object is called **myBitmapData** and is 300 pixels by 300 pixels.

3. On a new line, enter the name of your **BitmapData** object and a period; then call the **setPixel()** method. For its parameters, specify an x-coordinate, a y-coordinate, and a color in hex code, like so:

   ```
   myBitmapData.setPixel(100, 100,
   → 0x993300);
   ```

   This method creates a single pixel at x = 100, y = 100 at a certain color specified by the hex code **Ⓐ**.

4. On the next line, create a new **Bitmap** object.

5. On the next line, assign the **BitmapData** object to the **bitmapData** property of your **Bitmap** object.

6. On the last line, add a call to the **addChild()** method to display the **Bitmap** object on the Stage **Ⓑ**.

   You may have to squint to find the lone pixel, but you'll see a single dot rendered on your **Bitmap** object on the Stage.

```
var myBitmapData:BitmapData = new BitmapData(300, 300);
myBitmapData.setPixel(100, 100, 0x993300);
```

Ⓐ A new **BitmapData** object called **myBitmapData** is created, which is 300 pixels square. The **setPixel()** method is called. The three parameters of the **setPixel()** method are the x- and y-coordinates and the color.

```
var myBitmapData:BitmapData = new BitmapData(300, 300);
myBitmapData.setPixel(100, 100, 0x993300);
var myBitmap:Bitmap = new Bitmap();
myBitmap.bitmapData = myBitmapData;
addChild(myBitmap);
```

Ⓑ The final code draws a red pixel at x = 100, y = 100. The bitmap information is put in a **Bitmap** object and displayed.

TIP The `setPixel()` method only accepts color values without an alpha channel; that is, color values specified as six-digit hexadecimal values. To change a pixel's color to a color that is partially transparent, use the `setPixel32()` method instead and specify an eight-digit hexadecimal code.

To fill a rectangle with a color:

1. Select the first keyframe on the Timeline, and open the Actions panel.

2. As you have done in the previous tasks, declare and instantiate a new **BitmapData** object with width and height parameters, and parameters for alpha and the color.

3. On the next line, create a **Rectangle** object with parameters for the x and y location, and the width and height **C**.

4. On a new line, enter the name of your **BitmapData** object and a period; then

call the `fillRect()` method with two parameters, like so:

myBitmapData.fillRect(myRectangle, 0x993300);

For the first parameter, enter the name of your **Rectangle** object, indicating the section of the **BitmapData** object that should be colored.

For the second parameter, enter a numeric color value indicating what color to set the pixels in the rectangle.

The `fillRect()` method fills a rectangular region with a solid color.

5. On the next line, create a new **Bitmap** object.

6. On the next line, assign the **BitmapData** object to the **bitmapData** property of your **Bitmap** object.

7. On the last line, add a call to the `addChild()` method to display the **Bitmap** object on the Stage **D**.

```
var myBitmapData:BitmapData = new BitmapData(500, 500, false, 0x33ee44);
var myRectangle:Rectangle = new Rectangle(0, 0, 100, 200);
```

C A new **Rectangle** object called **myRectangle** is created. This object represents a rectangular region at the coordinate (0, 0) that is 100 pixels wide and 200 pixels high.

```
var myBitmapData:BitmapData = new BitmapData(500, 500, false, 0x33ee44);
var myRectangle:Rectangle = new Rectangle(0, 0, 100, 200);

myBitmapData.fillRect(myRectangle, 0xAA3300);
var myBitmap:Bitmap = new Bitmap();
myBitmap.bitmapData = myBitmapData;
addChild(myBitmap);
```

D The `fillRect()` method fills the region defined by a **Rectangle** object with the color **0xAA3300**.

E A rectangular portion of the **BitmapData** object is filled with a color.

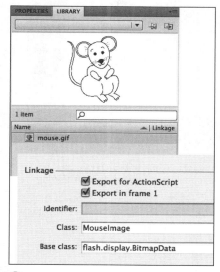

F This bitmap symbol is linked to the class called **MouseImage**, which inherits the methods and properties of the **BitmapData** class.

```
var myBitmapData:MouseImage = new MouseImage(422, 492);
```

G A new **BitmapData** object is created from your custom class (from the Library).

```
var myBitmapData:MouseImage = new MouseImage(422, 492);
myBitmapData.floodFill(10, 30, 0x55cc33);
```

H The **BitmapData** class's **floodFill()** method takes three parameters: the x and y location of the starting point of the fill and the fill color.

8. Test your movie.

   The **Bitmap** object is drawn on the Stage, and the rectangular region is filled in with the color you chose **E**.

To fill a region with a color:

1. As in the previous tasks, create a **BitmapData** object. For this example, import an image that has one or more regions of solid color into the Library. In the Linkage section of the Symbol Properties dialog box, identify the Library symbol with its own class name that extends the **BitmapData** class **F**.

2. In the Actions panel, create a new instance of your Library symbol, giving parameters for its width and height **G**.

   The new instance is a **BitmapData** object.

3. On a new line, enter the name of your **BitmapData** object and a period; then call the **floodFill()** method with three parameters **H**:

   x: The x-coordinate of the pixel to use as the starting point for the fill operation

   y: The y-coordinate of the starting pixel

   color: The numeric color to set as the color for the affected pixels

   When the **floodFill()** call is made, regions of similar color connected to the x- and y-coordinates are filled with the new color specified.

4. On the next line, create a new **Bitmap** object.

5. On the following line, assign your **BitmapData** object (the one from the Library) to the **bitmapData** property of your **Bitmap** object.

Continues on next page

6. On the last line, add a call to the
   addChild() method to display the
   Bitmap object on the Stage .

7. Test your movie.

   Flash first creates an instance of your
   Library symbol, which is a **BitmapData**
   object. Then, at the specified coordinate, the region of similar color is
   filled with a new color. Finally, the
   BitmapData is assigned to a **Bitmap**
   object and displayed on the Stage **J**.

TIP Unlike many image-editing programs,
which allow you to specify a tolerance level for
filling a region, the floodFill() method only
fills pixels whose color is exactly the same as
the starting pixel.

To get a color from an image:

Call the **getPixel()** method, as in:

myBitmapData.getPixel(100, 200);

The color information for the particular
pixel at x = 100, y = 200 for the **BitmapData**
object called **myBitmapData** is returned.
The returned value, however, is not in
the familiar hexadecimal code. To convert the returned value, use the method
toString(16).

TIP The color value provided by the
getPixel() method only includes the red,
green, and blue color information for the
chosen pixel. If you want to know the alpha
channel value as well, you must use the
getPixel32() method instead.

```
var myBitmapData:MouseImage = new MouseImage(422, 492);
myBitmapData.floodFill(10, 30, 0x55cc33);

var myBitmap:Bitmap = new Bitmap(myBitmapData);
addChild(myBitmap);
```

I The final code, which displays the manipulated
bitmap data in a **Bitmap** object.

J In this example, the **BitmapData** object is
filled with continuous regions of color starting
at x = 10, y = 30.

Copying, layering, and blending images

In addition to setting colors directly on an image, a common image-manipulation task is to incorporate part or all of one image into another image. Perhaps you want to duplicate an image in multiple places on the screen, or you want to copy several images onto one for a collage effect. The **BitmapData** class offers several ways to accomplish the task of copying image data.

You have already used the **draw()** method to copy a source image to a **BitmapData** object; that same method can be used to copy all or part of a **BitmapData** object onto another using the optional parameters of the **draw()** method to manipulate the image.

K This bitmap symbol is linked to the class called **Daisies**, which inherits the methods and properties of the **BitmapData** class.

In addition, you can make an exact copy of a **BitmapData** object with the **clone()** method, copy all the colors with the **copyPixels()** method (or just a single color channel using **copyChannel()**), and even combine the colors of two **BitmapData** objects with the **merge()** method. The following tasks demonstrate the use of these methods.

To make an exact copy of a bitmap:

Call the **clone()** method and assign the returned value to another **BitmapData** object, like so:

```
var myCopy:BitmapData =
→ myBitmapData.clone();
```

This statement creates an exact duplicate of the **myBitmapData** object and assigns it to the object called **myCopy**, another **BitmapData** object.

To copy part of an image onto another image:

1. As in the previous tasks, create a **BitmapData** object. For this particular example, import a bitmap image into the Library. In the Linkage section of the Symbol Properties dialog box, identify the Library symbol with its own class name that extends the **BitmapData** class **K**.

2. In the Actions panel, create a new instance of your Library symbol, giving parameters for its width and height.

   The new instance is a **BitmapData** object. Don't forget the width and height parameters, because they are required to create a new **BitmapData** object.

Continues on next page

3. On a new line, create another **BitmapData** object, specifying parameters for its width, height, alpha, and color. This **BitmapData** object will be the one that first image will be copied onto. This **BitmapData** object can contain an image, a solid color, or any other bitmap information.

   In this example, the second **BitmapData** object will simply have a solid background color **L**.

4. On the next line, create a **Rectangle** object with four parameters: the x, y, width, and height values corresponding to the rectangular portion of the source **BitmapData** object that you want to copy.

5. On the next line, create a **Point** object with two parameters, which are the x- and y-coordinates of the pixel in the destination **BitmapData** object where you want the top-left corner of the copied pixels to be placed **M**.

6. On a new line, enter the name of the second **BitmapData** object (the colored rectangle) and then a period. Then call the **copyPixels()** method with three parameters **N**:

   sourceBitmap: The **BitmapData** object from which to copy pixel information (in this example, the new instance of the Library symbol)

   sourceRect: The **Rectangle** object designating the portion of the source bitmap to copy

   destPoint: The **Point** object designating the x- and y-coordinates on the destination image where the top-left corner of the copied rectangle should be positioned

7. On the next line, create a new **Bitmap** object.

```
var srcBitmapData:Daisies = new Daisies(320, 212);
var destBitmapData:BitmapData = new BitmapData(290, 212, false, 0xff0000);
```

L The **BitmapData** object from the Library (the daisies picture) will be the source bitmap, and another **BitmapData** object that is 290 wide by 212 high filled with a red color will be the destination bitmap.

```
var srcBitmapData:Daisies = new Daisies (320,212);
var destBitmapData:BitmapData = new BitmapData(290, 212, false, 0xff0000);

var cropping:Rectangle = new Rectangle(75, 35, 103, 126);
var destBitmapDataPoint:Point = new Point(43, 43);
```

M The source cropping **Rectangle** and destination **Point** objects are created, with values entered in their constructor functions.

```
var srcBitmapData:Daisies = new Daisies (320,212);
var destBitmapData:BitmapData = new BitmapData(290, 212, false, 0xff0000);

var cropping:Rectangle = new Rectangle(75, 35, 103, 126);
var destBitmapDataPoint:Point = new Point(43, 43);

destBitmapData.copyPixels(srcBitmapData, cropping, destBitmapDataPoint);
```

N Using the source bitmap, cropping rectangle, and destination point parameters for the **copyPixels()** method gives you fine-tuned control over the copying and pasting of image data.

8. On the following line, assign your **BitmapData** object (the one that contains the copied pixels) to the **bitmapData** property of your **Bitmap** object.

9. On the last line, add a call to the **addChild()** to display the **Bitmap** object on the Stage.

10. Test your movie.

Flash copies the pixels from the first **BitmapData** object onto the second according to the boundaries indicated by the **Rectangle** object and placed at the point indicated by the **Point** object. The **BitmapData** with the copied pixels is assigned to a **Bitmap** object and displayed on the Stage **O**.

TIP If you want to copy the entire source image, the easiest way to indicate this is to use the source **BitmapData** object's **rect** property as the second parameter, like this: **sourceImage.rect.** Any **BitmapData** object's **rect** property contains a **Rectangle** object whose size and boundaries match those of the **BitmapData** object.

TIP To place the copied pixels at the top-left corner of the destination image, use the **topLeft** property of the destination **BitmapData** object's **rect** property for the third parameter, like this: **destImage.rect.topLeft.**

```
var srcBitmapData:Daisies = new Daisies(320, 212);
var destBitmapData:BitmapData = new BitmapData(290, 212, false, 0xff0000);

var cropping:Rectangle = new Rectangle(75, 35, 103, 126);
var destBitmapDataPoint:Point = new Point(43, 43);

destBitmapData.copyPixels(srcBitmapData, cropping, destBitmapDataPoint);
var myBitmap:Bitmap = new Bitmap(destBitmapData);
addChild(myBitmap);
```

Rectangle object

Point object

srcBitmapData

destBitmapData

Test Movie mode

O The final code (top) copies a cropped portion of the original image and places it at a point 43 pixels over and 43 pixels down from the top-left corner of the destination image.

To copy one color channel of an image onto another image:

1. Continue working with the same document from the previous task.

2. In the line with the **copyPixels()** method call, change the method **copyPixels()** to **copyChannel()**.

   The **copyChannel()** method works like the **copyPixels()** method except that it copies only one of the source image's color channels (red, green, blue, or alpha) onto a single channel of the destination image.

   This is similar to the command in some image-manipulation programs that allows you to separate an image into its component channels.

3. Inside the parentheses of the **copyChannel()** method call, add two additional parameters after the three parameters that are currently there ⓟ. These two parameters are as follows:

   sourceChannel: A **Number** indicating which color channel should be copied from the source image. The value must be 1 (red), 2 (green), 4 (blue), or 8 (alpha).

   destChannel: A **Number** indicating the color channel in the destination image into which the copied pixels should be placed. The possible values are the same as for the **sourceChannel** parameter (1, 2, 4, or 8).

4. Test your movie.

   This time, instead of copying the entire image, only one of the color channels is copied onto the destination image.

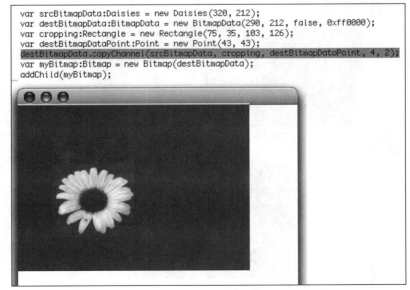

```
var srcBitmapData:Daisies = new Daisies(320, 212);
var destBitmapData:BitmapData = new BitmapData(290, 212, false, 0xff0000);
var cropping:Rectangle = new Rectangle(75, 35, 103, 126);
var destBitmapDataPoint:Point = new Point(43, 43);
destBitmapData.copyChannel(srcBitmapData, cropping, destBitmapDataPoint, 4, 2);
var myBitmap:Bitmap = new Bitmap(destBitmapData);
addChild(myBitmap);
```

ⓟ The **copyChannel()** method works like the **copyPixels()** method, but it copies only a single color channel from the source image onto a single channel of the destination image. Here the blue channel (4) of the source image has been copied into the green channel (2) of the destination image.

TIP The copied color channel is still only one of four channels in the destination image. Any color that was already present in the other channels of the destination image will be used together with the copied channel to determine the actual color displayed. If you want the destination image to show only the copied channel, create the destination image as solid black, which has a value of 0 in all color channels.

TIP For an interesting effect, try using the same image as the source and destination, and copy one channel (for example, red) into a different channel (such as green). Depending on the selected color channels and the brightness of the colors in the original image, this can create a muted effect or a wildly vivid one.

TIP To create a grayscale representation of a single color channel from the source `BitmapData` object, call the `copyChannel()` method three times. Use the same source channel for all three method calls, and use a different destination channel (1, 2, and 4) in each. For example, to create a grayscale image of the red channel, copy channel 1 to destination channel 1, copy channel 1 to destination channel 2, and finally, copy channel 1 to destination channel 4.

To blend an image onto another image:

1. As in previous tasks, create two `BitmapData` objects that will be blended together into a single image.

   The source image will be combined onto the destination image. The dimensions of the destination image will be used for the final image.

2. Declare and instantiate a `Rectangle` object with parameters indicating the portion of the source image to copy onto the destination image.

   If you want the entire source image to be used, remember that you can use the `rect` property for the `Rectangle` object.

3. Declare and instantiate a `Point` object with parameters indicating the x- and y-coordinates where the source image should be placed in the destination image.

   If you want to position the image at the top-left corner of the destination object, remember that you can use the `rect.topLeft` property for the `Point` parameter.

4. On a new line, enter the name of the destination `BitmapData` object followed by a period; then enter the method `merge()`.

5. Inside the parentheses of the `merge()` method, enter seven parameters to control how the `BitmapData` objects will be blended together **Q**.

Continues on next page

```
var srcBitmapData:Surfer1 = new Surfer1(500, 800);
var destBitmapData:Surfer2 = new Surfer2(500, 800);
destBitmapData.merge(srcBitmapData,srcBitmapData.rect,
                destBitmapData.rect.topLeft, 128, 128, 128, 128);
```

Q To use the `merge()` method, you must create two `BitmapData` objects and define the source rectangle and destination points. In this example, the source rectangle is the entire dimension of the source image (using the `rect` property), and the destination point is the top-left corner (using the `rect.topLeft` property). Entering **128** for the `merge()` method's final four (multiplier) parameters creates an even blend between the two `BitmapData` objects.

The first three parameters, **sourceBitmap**, **sourceRect**, and **destPoint**, are equivalent to those parameters in the **copyPixels()** and **copyChannel()** methods, as explained in the previous tasks.

The last four parameters are multiplier numbers between 0 and 255, which control the balance of the colors between the two images. Each parameter represents the color balance of a single channel (in the order red, green, blue, and alpha). The larger the value, the more the balance favors the source image. For instance, entering **255** for all the values shows only the source image. For an even blend between the two images, enter **128** for each parameter.

6. Enter the remaining script to create a **Bitmap** object, and assign the destination **BitmapData** object to its **bitmapData** property.

7. To see the resulting image, call **addChild()** to put the **Bitmap** object on the display list.

When you test your movie, you see a new image composed of the two original images blended together .

```
var srcBitmapData:Surfer1 = new Surfer1(500, 800);
var destBitmapData:Surfer2 = new Surfer2(500, 800);
destBitmapData.merge(srcBitmapData,srcBitmapData.rect,
               destBitmapData.rect.topLeft, 128, 128, 128,128);

var myBitmap:Bitmap = new Bitmap(destBitmapData);
addChild(myBitmap);
```

R Using the **merge()** method, the two surfer images are blended together. The destination image determines the size constraints.

Using Filters on Bitmap Images

Previously, you learned how filters can be applied to movie clips to add visual interest. The same filters can be applied to bitmap graphics as well, using the **BitmapData** class's **applyFilter()** method. There are a few important differences between applying filters to a **BitmapData** object versus **DisplayObject**s like movie clips.

First, with **DisplayObject**s, you use the **filters** property, which you can use to layer multiple filters at a time. Second, the filters are just an enhancement; they can be added or removed at any time without altering the underlying object. However, when a filter is applied to a **BitmapData** object, the object (that is, the information it contains about pixels and color values) is directly modified; there is no way to undo the change or remove a filter from a **BitmapData** object.

However, you have a greater degree of control over the end result when you apply a filter to a **BitmapData** object. Because the filter modifies the pixels of the **BitmapData** object directly, any rotation, scaling, or other transformations applied to the **BitmapData** object are reflected in the filtered result.

The **applyFilter()** method takes four parameters. The first three parameters are the source bitmap, the source rectangle, and the destination point; these are the same three parameters you used in the **copyPixels()** method and the related methods you learned about in the previous tasks. The fourth parameter is the filter object that is to be applied to the **BitmapData** object.

To apply a filter to a bitmap image:

1. Using any of the techniques described previously, create your source **BitmapData** object (the one that contains the bitmap to which the filter will be applied).

2. On the next line, declare and instantiate a destination **BitmapData** object, into which the output of the filter operation will be placed **A**.

   If you don't need to preserve the original image, you can use the source **BitmapData** object as the destination object as well.

   Whether you're using the source **BitmapData** object or a new **BitmapData** object as the destination object, there are a few important details to keep in mind—see the Tips following this task.

3. As you did in previous tasks, create a **Rectangle** object to define the region of the source bitmap to which the filter will be applied and a **Point** object defining the point where the result will be placed within the destination **BitmapData** object.

   If you want the entire image to be filtered and positioned to fill the entire source **BitmapData** object, remember that you can use the **rect** property for the **Rectangle** object and the **rect.topLeft** property for the **Point** property.

4. On the following line, declare and instantiate the filter object that will be used to alter the bitmap. Enter parameters in the constructor function to set the filter's properties, or set the properties directly **B**.

5. On a new line, enter the name of your destination **BitmapData** object followed by a period, and then enter **applyFilter()**.

6. Enter as parameters for the **applyFilter()** method the name of your source **BitmapData** object, the name of your source **Rectangle** object, the name of your destination **Point** object, and the name of your filter object **C**.

```
var srcBitmapData:Daisies = new Daisies(320, 212);
var destBitmapData:BitmapData = new BitmapData(320, 212);
```

A A source bitmap (which will be filtered) and a destination bitmap (where the filter's result will be placed) are created.

```
var srcBitmapData:Daisies = new Daisies(320, 212);
var destBitmapData:BitmapData = new BitmapData(320, 212);

var myBlur:BlurFilter = new BlurFilter(15, 15);
```

B A new **BlurFilter** object is created.

```
var srcBitmapData:Daisies = new Daisies(320, 212);
var destBitmapData:BitmapData = new BitmapData(320, 212);

var myBlur:BlurFilter = new BlurFilter(15, 15);
destBitmapData.applyFilter(srcBitmapData, srcBitmapData.rect,
                           destBitmapData.rect.topLeft, myBlur);
```

C In this example the filter will be applied to the entire source bitmap, and it will be placed in the top-left corner of the destination bitmap.

7. Enter the remaining script to create a **Bitmap** object, and assign the destination **BitmapData** object to its **bitmapData** property.

8. To see the resulting image, call **addChild()** to put the **Bitmap** object on the display list.

The destination **BitmapData** object, which contains a copy of the source **BitmapData** object with the filter applied to it, appears on the Stage **D**.

TIP Several of the filters (bevel, gradient bevel, glow, gradient glow, blur, and drop shadow) use alpha channel values; consequently, the destination **BitmapData** object must be able to store alpha channel values (its **transparent** property must be true). If your source **BitmapData** object doesn't have alpha channel information (its **transparent** property is false), you must create a new **BitmapData** object rather than using the source object as the destination object.

TIP Often, the output of a filter such as an outer glow or drop shadow is larger than the size of the **BitmapData** object (or the designated **Rectangle**). If the destination **BitmapData** object isn't large enough (for example, if its dimensions are identical to the source bitmap's dimensions), the filter will be cropped and may not be displayed.

To know the output size of the filter beforehand, use the **generateFilterRect()** method on the source bitmap. It takes two parameters—the cropping rectangle and the filter object that will be used—and returns a **Rectangle** object whose dimensions match the size of the output from the filter. Use those dimensions to define the size of your destination **BitmapData** object and the destination point to prevent the filter's result from being cropped.

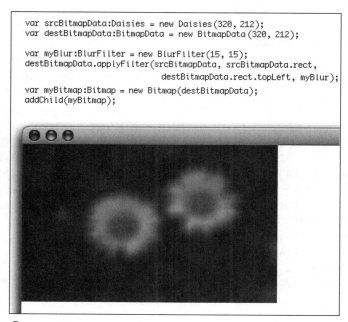

```
var srcBitmapData:Daisies = new Daisies(320, 212);
var destBitmapData:BitmapData = new BitmapData(320, 212);

var myBlur:BlurFilter = new BlurFilter(15, 15);
destBitmapData.applyFilter(srcBitmapData, srcBitmapData.rect,
                           destBitmapData.rect.topLeft, myBlur);
var myBitmap:Bitmap = new Bitmap(destBitmapData);
addChild(myBitmap);
```

D The final code (top) and the resultant image (bottom).

Putting It Together: Animating Bitmap Images

Throughout the latter part of this chapter, you've seen ways that bitmap images can be created, drawn onto, copied, combined, and changed. Putting these techniques together allow for interesting and exciting effects.

As you explore the bitmap-manipulation capabilities of Flash, chances are you'll continue to be impressed by their power and by how quickly they perform. Not only can you blend images and apply a filter effect to them, but you can also do it in real time, over and over again.

To help give your creativity a head start, the following task demonstrates how to combine the various bitmap manipulation capabilities of Flash to create an animated flame that follows the mouse pointer.

Creating animated flame

This task integrates several of the techniques you have learned about `BitmapData` objects. First, the `draw()` method copies a movie clip, the source of the fire color and shape, into a `BitmapData` object. By default, the `draw()` method copies the pixels into the top-left corner of a destination `BitmapData` object. In this case, the copied pixels will be placed at the mouse pointer, so an additional parameter is used with the `draw()` method to control the positioning. Unlike many methods that accept a `Point` object to indicate the destination point, the `draw()` method requires a `Matrix` object for that purpose.

Once the initial fire colors are drawn into the bitmap, the `copyPixels()` method animates the flame moving upward. To do this, the image is copied onto itself, but the destination point is set to (0, -3), which copies the image three pixels above its current location and creates the illusion of upward movement.

Finally, a blur filter is applied to the entire image. As the image is blurred, the orange of the flame blends with the black background, making the flame gradually blend into the black and disappear.

These three tasks—drawing the flame color, shifting the pixels upward, and blurring the image—are placed in an `Event.ENTER_FRAME` event-handler function that is called repeatedly, creating the animation.

To create an animated flame:

1. Choose Insert > New Symbol to create a new movie clip symbol that will provide the initial color and shape for the fire.

2. In symbol-editing mode, select the Oval tool and draw a small oval shape. Give the shape a radial gradient fill.

   In this example, the three gradient colors are **FFCC00** (75 percent alpha) on the left, **FF6600** (90 percent alpha) in the middle, and **FFFFFF** (0 percent alpha) on the right. These values create a radial gradient that is yellow in the center and then dark orange fading to transparent **Ⓐ**.

3. Using the Align panel, center the oval over the registration point.

4. Exit symbol-editing mode.

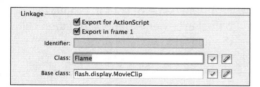

A A radial gradient with shades of yellow and orange is used to create a movie clip oval to serve as the basis of the flame.

B In the Linkage section of the Symbol Properties dialog box for the movie clip symbol, give it a class name and extend the **MovieClip** class.

5. Select your new movie clip symbol in the Library, and select Properties from the Options menu. In the Linkage section (you may have to expand the dialog box by clicking the Advanced button), identify the Library symbol with its own class name that extends the **MovieClip** class **B**.

6. Select the first keyframe, and open the Actions panel.

7. Create a new instance of your movie clip symbol in the Library.

8. On the next line, create a new instance of a **BitmapData** object with parameters for width, height, alpha, and color.

   Use the dimensions of the Stage for the width and height, false for alpha, and **0x000000** for the color, making it black **C**.

9. Next, add a listener and function to handle the **Event.ENTER_FRAME** event.

10. Inside the curly braces of the event-handler function, create a new **Matrix** object.

   A **Matrix** object contains information about transformations (position and size changes) that have been or will be applied to an object. In this case, it will define the destination position where the fire movie clip is copied into the **BitmapData** object.

Continues on next page

```
var myFlame:Flame = new Flame();
var myBitmapData:BitmapData = new BitmapData(400, 500, false, 0x000000);
```

C An instance of the gradient oval movie clip is created, and a new **BitmapData** object is created that is 400 pixels by 500 pixels and filled with black.

11. On the following line, still within the function, enter the name of the **Matrix** object and a period; then call its **translate()** method.

12. Inside the parentheses of the **translate()** method, enter two parameters separated by a comma: **mouseX** and **mouseY + 3 Ⓓ**.

The **translate()** method adds a position change to the transformations in the **Matrix** object.

The **Matrix** object is assigned the instruction to change position to the x- and y-coordinates of the mouse pointer. Whatever object the **Matrix** object is applied to will have that position change applied to it.

The extra three pixels on the y-axis compensate for the three-pixel upward motion that will be applied later to keep the flame centered on the mouse pointer.

13. On the next line, still within the event-handler function, enter the name of your **BitmapData** object and a period, and then call its **draw()** method.

14. For the parameters of the **draw()** method, enter the name of your movie clip (the color source) followed by the name of your **Matrix** object.

15. On the following line, still within the event-handler function, create a **BlurFilter** object with the parameters 2, 10, and 2, as in:

```
var myBlur:BlurFilter=new
→ BlurFilter(2,10,2);
```

This constructor creates a new **BlurFilter** object that blurs two pixels horizontally and ten pixels vertically, and has a quality setting of 2.

16. Enter the name of your **BitmapData** object and then a period, and then call the **applyFilter()** method.

```
var myFlame:Flame = new Flame();
var myBitmapData:BitmapData = new BitmapData(400, 500, false, 0x000000);

stage.addEventListener(Event.ENTER_FRAME, drawFlame);
function drawFlame(myevent:Event):void {
    var myMatrix:Matrix = new Matrix();
    myMatrix.translate(mouseX, mouseY + 3);
}
```

Ⓓ A new **Matrix** object is created, and its **translate()** method is called. The chosen parameters cause a copy of the oval movie clip to be placed at the mouse pointer's coordinates.

17. Inside the parentheses of the `applyFilter()` method, enter these four parameters **E**:

- The **BitmapData** object
- The **BitmapData** object's **rect** property
- The **BitmapData** object's **rect.topLeft** property
- The **BlurFilter** object

18. On the next line, create a **Point** object with parameters 0 and -3, as in **var myPoint:Point=new Point(0,-3)**.

This point will be used by the `copyPixels()` method to copy the image over itself three pixels higher than before.

19. On the following line, enter the name of the **BitmapData** object and a period, and then call the **copyPixels()** method.

20. Enter the following parameters for the **copyPixels()** method **F**:

- The **BitmapData** object
- The **BitmapData** object's **rect** property
- The **Point** object

21. On a new line outside the event-handler function, create a new **Bitmap** object and assign the **BitmapData** object to the **Bitmap** object's **bitmapData** property.

Continues on next page

```
var myFlame:Flame = new Flame();
var myBitmapData:BitmapData = new BitmapData(400, 500, false, 0x000000);

stage.addEventListener(Event.ENTER_FRAME, drawFlame);
function drawFlame(myevent:Event):void {
    var myMatrix:Matrix = new Matrix();
    myMatrix.translate(mouseX, mouseY + 3);
    myBitmapData.draw(myFlame, myMatrix);
    var myBlur:BlurFilter = new BlurFilter(2, 10, 2);
    myBitmapData.applyFilter(myBitmapData, myBitmapData.rect, myBitmapData.rect.topLeft, myBlur);
}
```

E The **draw()** method is used to copy the gradient oval into the **BitmapData** object. The transformations in the **Matrix** object (a position change in this example) determine the placement of the copied pixels. A blur filter is created and applied to the **BitmapData** object. This causes the color to fade away as it moves upward.

```
var myFlame:Flame = new Flame();
var myBitmapData:BitmapData = new BitmapData(400, 500, false, 0x000000);

stage.addEventListener(Event.ENTER_FRAME, drawFlame);
function drawFlame(myevent:Event):void {
    var myMatrix:Matrix = new Matrix();
    myMatrix.translate(mouseX, mouseY + 3);
    myBitmapData.draw(myFlame, myMatrix);
    var myBlur:BlurFilter = new BlurFilter(2, 10, 2);
    myBitmapData.applyFilter(myBitmapData, myBitmapData.rect, myBitmapData.rect.topLeft, myBlur);
    var myPoint:Point = new Point(0, -3);
    myBitmapData.copyPixels(myBitmapData, myBitmapData.rect, myPoint);
}
```

F The **copyPixels()** method, using a destination **Point** object of (0, -3), copies the image onto itself, shifted three pixels upward.

22. On the next line, call the **addChild()** method to add the **Bitmap** object to the display list.

23. Test your movie.

With each passing frame, the movie clip is copied onto the bitmap at the point beneath the mouse cursor, blurred, and shifted upward three pixels, creating an interactive flame effect **G**.

```
var myFlame:Flame = new Flame();
var myBitmapData:BitmapData = new BitmapData(400, 500, false, 0x000000);

stage.addEventListener(Event.ENTER_FRAME, drawFlame);
function drawFlame(myevent:Event):void {
    var myMatrix:Matrix = new Matrix();
    myMatrix.translate(mouseX, mouseY + 3);
    myBitmapData.draw(myFlame, myMatrix);
    var myBlur:BlurFilter = new BlurFilter(2, 10, 2);
    myBitmapData.applyFilter(myBitmapData, myBitmapData.rect,
                             myBitmapData.rect.topLeft, myBlur);

    var myPoint:Point = new Point(0, -3);
    myBitmapData.copyPixels(myBitmapData, myBitmapData.rect, myPoint);
}

var myBitmap:Bitmap = new Bitmap(myBitmapData);
addChild(myBitmap);
```

G The final code (above) and the result (below) is a flame that trails from the mouse pointer.

Controlling Sound

Incorporating sound into your Flash movie can enhance the animation and interactivity, and add excitement to even the simplest project by engaging more of the user's senses. You can play background music to establish the mood of your movie, use narration to accompany a story, or give audible feedback to interactions such as button clicks and drag-and-drop actions. Flash supports several audio formats for import, including WAV, AIFF, and MP3, which enables you to work with a broad spectrum of files. Flash also gives you the option of dynamically loading external MP3 files, providing an easy way to manage large sound files.

This chapter explores sound and its associated classes—**Sound**, **SoundChannel**, **SoundMixer**, **SoundTransform**, and **SoundEvent**. You'll learn how to play sounds from the Library dynamically without having to assign them to keyframes. You'll learn how to load sounds that reside outside your movie and how to start, stop, and adjust the sound volume or its stereo effect. You'll learn to access your sound's properties and events to time your sounds with animations or with other sounds.

In This Chapter

All these features give you the flexibility and power to integrate sounds into your movies creatively. You can create a slider bar that lets your viewers change the volume, for example, or add sounds to an arcade game that are customized to the gameplay.

Using Sounds

There are several ways you can use sounds in your Flash movie. The simplest approach is to import a sound file into Flash at authortime and manually put it on a keyframe of your Timeline when you want it to play. The sound waveform shows up on your Timeline to give you an idea of when and how long your sound plays **A**. Another way is to import a sound file into Flash at authortime and dynamically play it at runtime. Your sound file remains in your Library until you use ActionScript to play it **B**. A third way to use sound is to dynamically load and play an external sound **C**. This chapter explores the second and third ways to use sounds. They allow you to control when a sound plays, change its volume and playback through the left and right speakers dynamically, or retrieve information about the loading progress or sound playback progress with ActionScript.

Each sound that you play requires an instance of the **Sound** class. After you have a sound instance, you can use the **play()** method to play the sound. When you play an individual sound, an instance of the **SoundChannel** class is created, which provides you with properties to control the sound. One of the properties of the **SoundChannel** object is a **SoundTransform** object, which provides additional controls for volume and balance between the left and right speakers.

Sound in keyframe

A A sound placed in a keyframe on the Timeline is the simplest way to play sound and requires no ActionScript.

Sound in Library

B Imported sounds in the Library that are not placed on the Timeline can still be played at runtime with ActionScript.

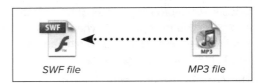

SWF file   *MP3 file*

C A separate MP3 sound file can load into a Flash (SWF) file and play at runtime using ActionScript.

Options menu

A Choose Properties from the Library options menu for each sound you want to control with ActionScript.

Playing Sounds from the Library

You can import your sound files into your Library during authortime, and use Action-Script to play them when you want at runtime. This requires that you make your sound symbols in the Library available to be called upon in ActionScript. You do this just as you did in Chapter 7, "Controlling and Displaying Graphics," when you dynamically made an instance of a movie clip or a bitmap symbol from the Library. You extend the functionality of a preexisting class to your Library symbol, so you can dynamically create new instances of it with the constructor function. In the case of a sound symbol, the **Sound** class is extended. Set the class name for your sound symbol from the Linkage section of the Symbol Properties dialog box, which is accessed from your Library.

To prepare a sound symbol for playback with ActionScript:

1. Import a sound file by choosing File > Import > Import to Library and selecting an audio file.

   Your selected audio file appears in the Library. You can import these sound formats: AIFF (Mac), WAV (Windows), and MP3 (Mac and Windows). More formats may be available if QuickTime is installed on your system.

2. Select the sound symbol in your Library.

3. From the Options menu, choose Properties **A**.

   The Symbol Properties dialog box appears.

   Continues on next page

4. Click the Advanced button. In the Linkage section of the expanded dialog box, select the Export for ActionScript check box. Leave "Export in frame 1" selected.

5. In the Class field, enter a name to identify your sound class. Leave the Base class as **flash.media.Sound** and click OK **B**.

A dialog box might appear that warns you that your class could not be found and will automatically be generated **C**. Click OK. In this example, the class name for your Library symbol is **GuitarsLoop**. This new class inherits from the **Sound** class, which means it has all the same methods and properties of the **Sound** class. Your class name will be used to create new instances of your sound. Make sure that your class name doesn't contain any periods.

To play a sound from the Library:

1. Continue with the previous task, and select the first frame of the main Timeline. Then open the Actions panel.

2. On the first line, create a new instance of your sound symbol, referencing its class name, like so:

var mySound:GuitarsLoop=new
→ GuitarsLoop()

A new instance of a **Sound** object, specifically the sound in your Library, is created.

3. Enter the name of your new sound instance followed by a period and then the method **play() D**.

Your sound instance begins to play. The sound will play through once and then stop.

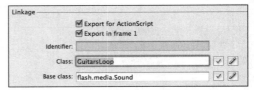

B The new class **GuitarsLoop** will be created for this SWF file. It inherits the properties and methods of the **Sound** class.

C Click OK to dismiss the warning box. It tells you that your custom class will be created for you.

```
var mySound:GuitarsLoop = new GuitarsLoop();
mySound.play();
```

D A new instance of the **GuitarsLoop** class is created and given the name **mySound**. This is an instance of the sound in your Library. Then the **play()** method plays the sound.

TIP The play() method plays the sound instance whenever it's called, even when the sound is already playing. This situation can produce multiple, overlapping sounds. To prevent overlaps of this type, use the stopAll() method of the SoundMixer class before playing the sound again. This technique ensures that a sound always stops before it plays again.

Loading and Playing External Sounds

Each time you import a sound into your Library, that sound is added to your SWF file, increasing its size. Sounds take up an enormous amount of space, even with MP3 compression, so you have to be judicious with your inclusion of sounds. One way to manage sounds so that your file stays small is to keep sounds as separate files outside your Flash movie. Use the **load()** method to bring MP3 audio files into Flash and play them only when you need them. (MP3 is the only format allowed.)

The method **load()** requires one parameter, which is a **URLRequest** object that provides the path to the MP3 file.

```
var myRequest:URLRequest = new URLRequest("music.mp3");
```

A A **URLRequest** object defines the path to the file that you want to load. In this example, the file is called music.mp3, and it resides in the same folder as the Flash movie.

```
var myRequest:URLRequest = new URLRequest("music.mp3");
var mySound:Sound = new Sound();
```

B The second line of code creates an object called **mySound**, an instance of the Sound class.

```
var myRequest:URLRequest = new URLRequest("music.mp3");
var mySound:Sound = new Sound();
mySound.load(myRequest);
mySound.play();
```

C The **load()** method loads the sound file from the location provided in the **URLRequest** object, and the **play()** method plays the sound.

To load and play an external sound:

1. Declare and instantiate a **URLRequest** object with the constructor function **new URLRequest()**. Provide the path to the MP3 file as the parameter **A**.

    The path is a string, so enclose it in quotation marks. You can load an MP3 file locally or from the Internet with an absolute URL. If the file resides in the same directory as your Flash movie, you can enter just the name of the file.

2. Declare and instantiate a **Sound** object with the constructor function **new Sound()** **B**.

3. On the next line, enter the name of your **Sound** object followed by a period. Enter the method **load()** and provide the **URLRequest** object as the parameter.

4. On the next line, enter the name of your **Sound** object followed by a period. Enter the method **play()** and provide optional parameters for the initial offset or looping **C**.

    As soon as your movie begins, it will load the MP3 file and play.

5. Save your Flash file in the same folder as the MP3 file. Test your movie.

    As soon as your movie begins, Flash uses the **URLRequest** object to find your external MP3 file, and then uses the **Sound** object to load and play it.

AAC Sound Files

You can also dynamically load and play AAC sound files by using the **NetStream** class just as you do with external videos, as described in Chapter 6, "Managing External Communication." The AAC format is an alternative to the MP3 format and is the same sound codec used in the H.264 format for F4V video files.

Controlling Sound Playback

The **play()** method of the **Sound** object can take three optional parameters. The first parameter is the offset, which is a number that determines how many milliseconds into the sound it should begin playing. You can set the sound to start from the beginning or at some later point. If you have a 20-second sound, for example, calling the method **play(10000)** makes the sound play from the middle at 10 seconds. It doesn't delay the sound for 10 seconds but begins immediately at the 10-second mark.

The second parameter is a number that determines how many times the sound loops. A setting of 2 plays the entire sound two times with no delay in between. This is useful for sounds that are specifically created where the end matches seamlessly with the beginning, so you can loop it over and over again.

The third parameter for the **play()** method takes a **SoundTransform** object, which provides control over the volume and left-right balance. You'll learn more about the **SoundTransform** object later in this chapter.

If no parameters are defined for the **play()** method, Flash plays the sound from the beginning and plays one loop.

To set the initial starting time for a sound:

Assign the first parameter of the **play()** method of your **Sound** object in milliseconds.

Your sound plays from that point (in milliseconds) forward **Ⓐ**.

To set the number of loops:

Assign the second parameter of the **play()** method of your **Sound** object to the number of times you want the sound to loop.

Your sound loops the specified number of times **Ⓑ**.

TIP Unfortunately, you have no way of telling the play() method to loop a sound indefinitely. Instead, set the second parameter to a ridiculously high number, such as 99999. An alternate approach is to create an event handler that plays the sound again when the end is detected. Sound events are discussed later in this chapter.

Stopping sounds

You stop a sound from playing by using a method of the **SoundChannel** class. When you call the **play()** method of a **Sound** object, an instance of the **SoundChannel** class is generated. There is one **SoundChannel** instance for each sound that plays.

```
var myRequest:URLRequest = new URLRequest("music.mp3");
var mySound:Sound = new Sound();
mySound.load(myRequest);
mySound.play(14000);
```

Ⓐ In this example, the **play()** method has a parameter of 14000, which makes the sound play beginning at 14 seconds.

```
var myRequest:URLRequest = new URLRequest("music.mp3");
var mySound:Sound = new Sound();
mySound.load(myRequest);
mySound.play(0,3);
```

Ⓑ In this example, the **play()** method has its first parameter set at 0 and its second parameter set at 3, which makes the sound play from the beginning and loop three times.

To assign the **SoundChannel** instance to a variable that you can later reference, use the following syntax:

```
var myChannel:SoundChannel =
→ mySound.play();
```

This statement plays the sound associated with the object called **mySound**. The returned **SoundChannel** object is put in the variable called **myChannel**. You can now stop the sound by calling the **stop()** method of the **SoundChannel** object, like so:

```
myChannel.stop();
```

To stop a sound:

1. Continue with the file you used in the earlier task, "To load and play an external sound."

2. Create a button symbol and place an instance of it on the Stage. In the Properties inspector, give it a name **C**.

   In this example, you'll assign an event handler for a mouse click on the button to stop the sound from playing.

3. Select the first frame of the main Timeline, and open the Actions panel.

4. Replace the statement with the **play()** method with this one:

   ```
   var myChannel:SoundChannel =
   → mySound.play();
   ```

   This statement plays the sound and puts the returned **SoundChannel** object of the **play()** method in a new variable (of a **SoundChannel** type) called **myChannel** **D**.

5. Create an event handler to detect a mouse click on the button on the Stage.

6. Between the curly braces of the event handler function, enter the name of your **SoundChannel** object, a period, and then the method **stop()**, like so **E**:

   ```
   myChannel.stop();
   ```

7. Test your movie.

   The external sound begins to play. When you click your button, the sound stops.

C This button instance on the Stage is named **stopbutton_btn**.

```
var myRequest:URLRequest = new URLRequest("music.mp3");
var mySound:Sound = new Sound();
mySound.load(myRequest);
var myChannel:SoundChannel = mySound.play();
```

D When the **play()** method of a **Sound** object is called, it returns a **SoundChannel** object. In this example, the **SoundChannel** object is put in the variable named **myChannel**.

```
stopbutton_btn.addEventListener(MouseEvent.CLICK, stopsound);
function stopsound(myevent:MouseEvent) {
    myChannel.stop();
}
```

E The event handler for the **stopbutton_btn** button on the Stage. The **stop()** method to stop a sound is called from the **SoundChannel** object called **myChannel**.

TIP You can also use the **stopAll()** method of the **SoundMixer** class. This stops all sounds in your Flash movie. Use the statement like so: **SoundMixer.stopAll()**.

Resuming sounds

You can keep track of the exact position of your sound playback with a **SoundChannel** property, **position**. The **position** property indicates the current position in milliseconds. This is a useful property if you want to keep track of when a sound was stopped so you can resume playback at that same position.

When a user stops a sound, you can capture the **SoundChannel position** property at that moment by putting it in a variable. Then, when the user wants to resume the sound, you can call the **play()** method of the **Sound** object and provide the number of offset seconds as the first parameter.

To resume playback of a sound:

1. Continuing with the file you used in the preceding task, place another instance of the button symbol on the Stage, and give it an instance name in the Properties inspector **F**.

   In this example, you'll assign an event handler for a mouse click on this second button to resume the sound at the point where it was stopped.

2. Select the first frame of the main Timeline, and open the Actions panel.

3. Insert a statement in your ActionScript code to declare a variable of an integer data type **G**.

   This variable will hold the current position of the sound playback. An integer is any whole number (no decimals). Since the current position is measured in milliseconds (whole numbers), an integer data type is appropriate.

F A second button instance on the Stage is named **resumebutton_btn**.

```
var myRequest:URLRequest = new URLRequest("music.mp3");
var mySound:Sound = new Sound();
mySound.load(myRequest);
var myChannel:SoundChannel = mySound.play();
var pausedposition:int;
```

G The highlighted statement declares a new variable called **pausedposition**, which will hold an integer data type.

4. In the event handler for the button that stops the sound, insert a statement before the **stop()** method, like so **H**:

```
pausedposition = myChannel.
→ position;
```

Before the sound is stopped, the current position in the playback of the sound is assigned to your variable.

5. Create another event handler to detect a mouse click on your second button on the Stage.

This event handler will resume playback of the sound.

6. Between the curly braces of the event handler for the resume function, enter the following statement **I**:

```
myChannel = mySound.play(
→ pausedposition);
```

The current position of the paused sound is used as the first parameter of the **play** method, which determines the offset point. The sound plays at the point where it was paused.

7. Test your movie.

The external sound begins to play. When you click the first button, the sound stops. When you click the second button, the sound resumes.

```
stopbutton_btn.addEventListener(MouseEvent.CLICK, stopsound);
function stopsound(myevent:MouseEvent) {
    pausedposition = myChannel.position;
    myChannel.stop();
}
```

H Before the sound stops, capture the current position in the sound and assign that value (in milliseconds) to the variable called **pausedposition**.

```
resumebutton_btn.addEventListener(MouseEvent.CLICK, resumesound);
function resumesound(myevent:MouseEvent) {
    myChannel = mySound.play(pausedposition);
}
```

I The event handler for the **resumebutton_btn** button on the Stage. The **play()** method uses the variable **pausedposition** to start playing at the point at which it stopped.

Tracking Sound Progress

You can also compare the **position** property of a sound with the total **length** of a sound to keep track of its current progress while it's playing.

position is a property of the **SoundChannel** object, and **length** is a property of the **Sound** object. However, keep in mind that the **length** property reflects the total length of the *downloaded* file. If the sound hasn't completely downloaded, the **length** property will be shorter than the actual length. To track the sound accurately, create an event handler to wait for the sound to completely download.

In the following example, you check whether the sound has been completely downloaded using the **Event.COMPLETE** event. Once the download is complete, you begin playing the sound and display the ratio of **SoundChannel position** to **Sound length** as a proportion of a horizontal bar, much like the progress bar of a preloader.

To track the sound progress:

1. Continue with the file you used in the task "To load and play an external sound."

2. Delete the last line of code (the **play()** method), and replace it with a statement that declares a **SoundChannel** object **Ⓐ**.

3. Add an event handler to the **Sound** object that detects the **Event.COMPLETE** event.

4. In the event-handler function, respond by playing the sound and adding another listener for the **Event.ENTER_FRAME** event **Ⓑ**.

   The **ENTER_FRAME** event happens at the frame rate of your movie. You can use this event to continuously monitor the progress of your sound.

```
var myRequest :URLRequest = new URLRequest("soulLoop.mp3" );
var mySound :Sound = new Sound();
mySound.load(myRequest);
var myChannel :SoundChannel;
```

Ⓐ The file called **soulLoop.mp3** is loaded by a **Sound** object called **mySound**. On the last line, a new **SoundChannel** object called **myChannel** is then declared.

```
var myRequest :URLRequest = new URLRequest("soulLoop.mp3" );
var mySound :Sound = new Sound();
mySound.load(myRequest);
var myChannel :SoundChannel;

mySound.addEventListener (Event.COMPLETE , loaded);
function loaded(myevent :Event):void {
    myChannel = mySound.play();
    stage.addEventListener (Event.ENTER_FRAME , showprogress );
}
```

Ⓑ The listener on **mySound** listens for the completion of the loading of the sound. When that happens, the sound plays and a new listener is added.

5. In the **ENTER_FRAME** event-handler function, divide the **SoundChannel position** property by the **Sound length** property and assign the fraction to the horizontal scale of a movie clip, like so **C**:

bar_mc.scaleX = myChannel.position → / mySound.length;

The **position** property measures the current location of the sound in milliseconds, and the **length** property is the total length of the song in milliseconds. The division creates a fraction that changes the width of a movie clip called **bar_mc**.

6. Create a rectangular movie clip and place it on the Stage. In the Properties inspector, name it **bar_mc**.

7. Test your movie **D**.

The **bar_mc** movie clip slowly grows to its full width as the song progresses.

```
var myRequest :URLRequest = new URLRequest ("soulLoop.mp3" );
var mySound :Sound = new Sound();
mySound.load(myRequest);
var myChannel :SoundChannel;

mySound.addEventListener (Event.COMPLETE , loaded);
function loaded(myevent :Event):void {
    myChannel = mySound.play();
    stage.addEventListener (Event.ENTER_FRAME , showprogress);
}

function showprogress(myevent :Event) {
    bar_mc.scaleX = myChannel .position / mySound.length ;
}
```

C The function called **showprogress** scales a movie clip on the Stage in proportion to the progress of the sound.

bar_mc

D The dark bar on the left is a movie clip called **bar_mc**.

Modifying Volume and Balance

Flash gives you full control of its volume and its output through either the left or right speaker, which is known as *pan control*. With this level of sound control, you can let your users set the volume to their own preferences, and you can create environments that are more realistic. In a car game, for example, you can vary the volume of the sound of cars as they approach or pass you. Playing with the pan controls, you can embellish the classic Pong game by making the sounds of the ball hitting the paddles and the walls play from the appropriate sides.

To modify the volume and balance in a sound, you must provide a third parameter in the **play()** method (recall that the first parameter determines the playback offset, and the second parameter determines the number of loops). The third parameter requires an object of the **SoundTransform** class, like so:

```
var newVolume:SoundTransform = new
→ SoundTransform();
```

Assign a new value for the **volume** property of the **SoundTransform** object, and then pass the object as the third parameter of the **play()** method, like so:

```
newVolume.volume = .5;
mySound.play(0, 0, newVolume);
```

To change the volume or pan of a sound that's already playing, you can assign the **SoundTransform** object to the **soundTransform** property of the **SoundChannel** object. For example:

```
var newVolume:SoundTransform = new
→ SoundTransform();
newVolume.volume = .5;
myChannel.soundTransform =
→ newVolume;
```

The first statement creates a new **SoundTransform** object called **newVolume**. Next, the **volume** property of the new **SoundTransform** object is changed. Finally, the **SoundTransform** object is assigned to the **soundTransform** property of the **SoundChannel** object associated with the sound that's playing.

The **SoundTransform** class has properties such as **volume** for modifying the volume and **pan** for modifying the left-right speaker balance. See **Table 8.1** for a description of these and other properties of the **SoundTransform** class.

TABLE 8.1 SoundTransform Properties

Property	Description
volume	Number (0=silent to 1=full volume)
pan	Number (−1=left to 1=right)
leftToLeft	Number(0 to 1) determining how much of the left input plays in the left speaker
leftToRight	Number(0 to 1) determining how much of the left input plays in the right speaker
rightToLeft	Number(0 to 1) determining how much of the right input plays in the left speaker
rightToRight	Number(0 to 1) determining how much of the right input plays in the right speaker

To change the volume or balance before playback:

1. Declare and instantiate a **URLRequest** object with the constructor function **new URLRequest()** and provide the path to an MP3 file as the parameter.

2. On the next line, declare and instantiate a **Sound** object with the constructor function **new Sound()**.

3. On the next line, enter the name of your **Sound** object followed by a period. Enter the method **load()** and provide the **URLRequest** object as the parameter.

   Flash loads the external MP3 file requested in the **URLRequest** object.

4. On a new line, declare and instantiate a **SoundTransform** object with the constructor function **new SoundTransform()**.

The **SoundTransform** object will provide the properties to change a sound's volume and balance.

5. On the next line, enter the name of your **SoundTransform** object followed by a period. Enter the property **volume** (to control volume level) or **pan** (to control balance) followed by an equals sign and a value **Ⓐ**.

6. On a new line, enter the name of your **Sound** object followed by a period. Enter the method **play()**. For the parameters, enter 0, 5, and then the name of your **SoundTransform** object **Ⓑ**. Assign the returned value of the **play()** method to a **SoundChannel** object.

7. Test your movie.

   The play method plays your sound, and it uses the **SoundTransform** object to modify the volume or pan.

```
var myRequest:URLRequest = new URLRequest("music.mp3");
var mySound:Sound = new Sound();
mySound.load(myRequest);

var newSetting:SoundTransform = new SoundTransform();
newSetting.volume = 0.5;
```

Ⓐ The **volume** property of this **SoundTransform** object is set to 50 percent of the full volume.

```
var myRequest:URLRequest = new URLRequest("music.mp3");
var mySound:Sound = new Sound();
mySound.load(myRequest);

var newSetting:SoundTransform = new SoundTransform();
newSetting.volume = 0.5;
var myChannel:SoundChannel = mySound.play(0, 5, newSetting);
```

Ⓑ Pass the **SoundTransform** object called **newSetting** as the third parameter in the **play()** method. This sound will play from the beginning, loop five times, and play at 50 percent of its full volume.

To change the volume or balance during playback:

1. Create a button and place an instance on the Stage. In the Properties inspector, give the button instance a name **C**.

   You will assign an event handler to a mouse click over this button that will change the volume of a sound as it plays.

2. On the first frame of the Timeline in the Actions panel, declare and instantiate a **URLRequest** object with the constructor function **new URLRequest()** and provide the path to an external MP3 file as the parameter.

3. On the next line, declare and instantiate a **Sound** object with the constructor function **new Sound()**.

4. On the next line, enter the name of your **Sound** object followed by a period. Enter the method **load()** and provide the **URLRequest** object as the parameter.

   Flash loads the external MP3 file requested in the **URLRequest** object.

5. On a new line, declare and instantiate a **SoundTransform** object with the constructor function **new SoundTransform()**.

   The **SoundTransform** object will provide the properties to change a sound's volume and balance. In this example, the **SoundTransform** object is called **newSetting**.

6. On the next line, enter the code:

   ```
   var myChannel:SoundChannel =
   → mySound.play();
   ```

   This statement plays the sound and puts the returned **SoundChannel** object of the **play()** method in a new variable (of a **SoundChannel** type) called **myChannel D**.

7. On the next line, create an event handler that detects a mouse click on the button on the Stage. Between the curly braces of the function, add the statement:

   ```
   newSetting.volume -= 0.1;
   ```

   This statement subtracts 0.1 from the **volume** property of the **SoundTransform** object each time the button is clicked.

8. On the next line, still within the function of the event handler, add the statement:

   ```
   myChannel.soundTransform =
   → newSetting;
   ```

   This statement assigns the **soundTransform** property of the sound to the settings in your

C This button instance on the Stage is named **decrease_btn**.

```
var myRequest:URLRequest = new URLRequest("music.mp3");
var mySound:Sound = new Sound();
mySound.load(myRequest);

var newSetting:SoundTransform = new SoundTransform();
var myChannel:SoundChannel = mySound.play();
```

D The external MP3 sound called music.mp3 plays.

newSetting SoundTransform object to decrease the volume level **E**.

9. Test your movie.

   The external MP3 file loads and plays. Each time the user clicks the button, the **volume** property of the **SoundTransform** object called **newSetting** decreases by 0.1. The new volume is then set while the sound still plays.

To switch the left and right speakers:

Assign the following values for a SoundTransform object:

```
leftToLeft = 0;
leftToRight = 1;
rightToRight = 0;
rightToLeft = 1;
```

Changing these properties of the **SoundTransform** object and passing it to the **soundTransform** property of the **SoundChannel** object or as the third parameter of the **play()** method redistributes the sound inputs to switch the speakers **F**.

TIP As a shortcut, you can also set the properties of a new SoundTransform object at the time you instantiate it. The first parameter in the constructor is the volume and the second is the pan. For example, var myNewSettings:SoundTransform = new SoundTransform(.5, 1); is the same as the following code:

```
var myNewSettings:SoundTransform =
new SoundTransform();
myNewSettings.volume = .5;
myNewSettings.pan = 1;
```

```
decrease_btn.addEventListener(MouseEvent.CLICK, decreaseVolume);
function decreaseVolume(myevent:MouseEvent):void {
    newSetting.volume -= 0.1;
    myChannel.soundTransform = newSetting;
}
```

E The event handler for the **decrease_btn** button on the Stage. Each time the button is clicked, the **volume** property of the **SoundTransform** object called **newSetting** decreases by 0.1. The **SoundTransform** object is assigned to the **soundTransform** property of the **SoundChannel** object to take effect.

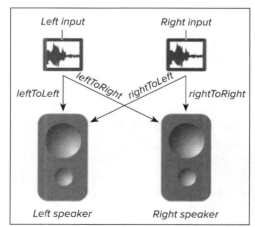

Left input   *Right input*

leftToLeft   leftToRight   rightToLeft   *rightToRight*

Left speaker   *Right speaker*

F The properties of the **SoundTransform** object that determine the distribution of sounds between the left and right speakers. The values are measured between 0 and 1.

Detecting Sound Events

You can detect when a sound finishes playing by using the **Event.SOUND_COMPLETE** event of the **SoundChannel** class. For example, consider the following script:

```
myChannel.addEventListener(
→ Event.SOUND_COMPLETE, finished);
function finished(myevent:Event):void
{
    // sound finished
}
```

In this script, when the sound associated with the **SoundChannel** object called **myChannel** is complete, Flash triggers the function called **finished** and executes any actions there.

The **Event.SOUND_COMPLETE** event lets you control and integrate your sounds in several powerful ways. Imagine creating a jukebox that randomly plays selections from a bank of songs. When one song finishes, Flash knows to load a new song. Or you could build a business presentation in which the slides are timed to the end of the narration. In the following task, the completion of the sound triggers the loading and playing of a second sound.

To detect the completion of a sound:

1. Declare and instantiate a **URLRequest** object with the constructor function **new URLRequest()** and provide the path to an MP3 file as the parameter.

2. On the next line, declare and instantiate a **Sound** object with the constructor function **new Sound()**.

3. On the next line, enter the name of your **Sound** object followed by a period. Enter the method **load()** and provide the **URLRequest** object as the parameter.

   Flash loads the external MP3 file requested in the **URLRequest** object.

Warning! Event.SOUND_COMPLETE on Windows Vista

Be aware that the **SOUND_COMPLETE** event may not work reliably on Windows Vista. You should keep your eyes (and ears) close to the Adobe Flash developer blogs for any new developments on this issue.

If you do encounter problems, one workaround would be to use the **SoundChannel** object's **position** property and the **Sound** object's **length** property to keep track of the progress of the sound (see the task "To track the sound progress").

4. On a new line enter the name of your **Sound** object followed by a period. Enter the method **play()** without any parameters. Assign the returned value to a new **SoundChannel** object **Ⓐ**.

The **play()** method plays your sound.

5. On the next line, add an event listener to the **SoundChannel** object. Listen for the **Event.SOUND_COMPLETE** event **Ⓑ**.

6. Add the function that gets triggered at the **Event.SOUND_COMPLETE** event **Ⓒ**.

When the sound finishes, the function is called. In this example, a new **Sound** object is created and loads and plays a second sound.

TIP If a sound is looping, the Event.SOUND_COMPLETE event is triggered when all the loops have finished.

TIP Keep in mind that the Event.SOUND_COMPLETE event is registered to the SoundChannel object. If you stop the sound and begin playing it again with the play() method, a *new* SoundChannel instance is generated, so your original listener will not detect the completion of the sound. You'll need to register the listener again to the new instance.

```
var myRequest:URLRequest = new URLRequest("music1.mp3");
var mySound:Sound = new Sound();
mySound.load(myRequest);
var myChannel:SoundChannel = mySound.play();
```

Ⓐ The external MP3 sound called music1.mp3 plays.

```
var myRequest:URLRequest = new URLRequest("music1.mp3");
var mySound:Sound = new Sound();
mySound.load(myRequest);
var myChannel:SoundChannel = mySound.play();

myChannel.addEventListener(Event.SOUND_COMPLETE, finished);
```

Ⓑ The event listener detects when the sound is completed and will trigger the function (not yet written here) called **finished**.

```
var myRequest:URLRequest = new URLRequest("music1.mp3");
var mySound:Sound = new Sound();
mySound.load(myRequest);
var myChannel:SoundChannel = mySound.play();

myChannel.addEventListener(Event.SOUND_COMPLETE, finished);

function finished(myevent:Event) {
    var myRequest2:URLRequest = new URLRequest("music2.mp3");
    var mySound2:Sound = new Sound();
    mySound2.load(myRequest2);
    myChannel2 = mySound2.play();
}
```

Ⓒ The function called **finished** begins playing a second sound file.

Working with MP3 Song Information

MP3 files are one of the most popular formats for storing and playing digital music. The MP3 compression gives a dramatic decrease in file size, yet the quality is maintained at near-CD levels. Another virtue of MP3 files is that they are capable of carrying simple information about the actual audio file. This *metadata* (descriptive information about data) tag was originally appended to the end of an MP3 file and called ID3 version 1. Information about the music file (such as song title, artist, album, year, comment, and genre) could be stored at the end of the song file in the ID3 tags and then detected and read by decoders.

Currently, MP3 files use ID3 version 2. One of the more notable improvements was moving the data to the beginning of the song file to better support streaming. It now also supports several new fields, such as composer, conductor, media type, copyright message, and recording date.

Flash can read the ID3v2 data of an MP3 file. Each bit of information about the song, or *tag*, corresponds to a property of the **id3** object of the **Sound** object. So, for example, **mySound.id3.TALB** refers to the album name of the MP3 file. **Table 8.2** covers all the ID3 version 2 **Sound** properties.

How do you retrieve these ID3 properties? You must first create an event handler that is triggered when available ID3 tags are present after a **play()** method is called. Using the event **Event.ID3** is the only way you can access the ID3 data.

In the following task, you'll load an external MP3 file and display the track information in the Output panel.

TABLE 8.2 ID3v2 Sound Properties

Property	Description
id3.COMM	Comment
id3.TALB	Album/movie/show title
id3.TBPM	Beats per minute
id3.TCOM	Composer
id3.TCOP	Copyright message
id3.TDAT	Date
id3.TDLY	Playlist delay
id3.TENC	Encoded by
id3.TEXT	Lyricist/text writer
id3.TFLT	File type
id3.TIME	Time
id3.TIT1	Content group description
id3.TIT2	Title/song name/description
id3.TIT3	Subtitle/description refinement
id3.TKEY	Initial key
id3.TLAN	Languages
id3.TLEN	Length
id3.TMED	Media type
id3.TOAL	Original album/movie/show title
id3.TOFN	Original filename
id3.TOLY	Original lyricists/text writer
id3.TOPE	Original artists/performers
id3.TORY	Original release year
id3.TOWN	File owner/licensee
id3.TPE1	Lead performers/soloists
id3.TPE2	Band/orchestra/accompaniment
id3.TPE3	Conductor/performer refinement
id3.TPE4	Interpreted, remixed, or otherwise modified by
id3.TPOS	Part of a set
id3.TPUB	Publisher
id3.TRCK	Track number/position in set
id3.TRDA	Recording dates
id3.TRSN	Internet radio station name
id3.TRSO	Internet radio station owner
id3.TSIZ	Size
id3.TSRC	International Standard Recording Code (ISRC)
id3.TSSE	Software/hardware and settings used for encoding
id3.TYER	Year
id3.WXXX	URL link frame

```
var myRequest:URLRequest = new URLRequest("music.mp3");
var mySound:Sound = new Sound();
mySound.load(myRequest);
mySound.play();
```

A The external MP3 sound called music.mp3 plays.

```
mySound.addEventListener(Event.ID3, gotmetadata);
function gotmetadata(myevent:Event):void {
    trace( "title=" + mySound.id3.TIT2);
}
```

B The **Event.ID3** event happens when metadata from the MP3 file is received. The property **id3.TIT2** refers to the artist's name.

To retrieve song information about an MP3 file:

1. Declare and instantiate a **URLRequest** object with the constructor function **new URLRequest()** and provide the path to an MP3 file as the parameter.

2. On the next line, declare and instanti- ate a **Sound** object with the constructor function **new Sound()**.

3. On the next line, enter the name of your **Sound** object followed by a period. Enter the method **load()** and provide the **URLRequest** object as the parameter.

   Flash loads the external MP3 file requested in the **URLRequest** object.

4. On the next line, enter the name of your **Sound** object followed by a period. Enter the method **play()** without any parameters **A**.

   The **play()** method plays your sound.

5. Add an event listener to your **Sound** object. Listen for the **Event.ID3** event as in the following:

   mySound.addEventListener(Event. ID3, gotmetadata);

   When Flash receives the ID3 metadata from the loading MP3 file, it triggers the function called **gotmetadata**.

6. Add the function called **gotmetadata** that gets triggered by the **Event.ID3** event. Between the curly braces of the function, add a trace statement that displays the ID3 property, like this **B**:

   function gotmetadata(
   → myevent:Event):void {
   trace("title=" +
   → mySound.id3.TIT2);
   }

Continues on next page

In this example, the trace action displays the title information of the MP3 song and appends it to the string **"title="**.

7. Add more trace statements within the curly braces of the function to retrieve all the ID3 information you want **C**.

8. Save your FLA file in the location where it can find your MP3 file based on the target path you entered for your **URLRequest** object.

When you test your movie in the Flash authoring environment, the Output panel displays the ID3 information **D**.

TIP Using text fields, you can have Flash dynamically display the ID3 information on the Stage (rather than in the Output panel). You'll learn more about controlling text fields in Chapter 10, "Controlling Text."

TIP When an MP3 file contains a mix of ID3v2 and ID3v1 tags, the event handler onID3 is triggered twice.

TIP To view the ID3 files of your MP3 files outside of Flash:

In Windows: Right-click the MP3 file, and select Properties > Details.

Using Mac OS X: In iTunes, select the song in your playlist, and press Cmd-I.

```
var myRequest:URLRequest = new URLRequest("music.mp3");
var mySound:Sound = new Sound();
mySound.load(myRequest);
mySound.play();

mySound.addEventListener(Event.ID3, gotmetadata);
function gotmetadata(myevent:Event):void {
    trace( "title=" + mySound.id3.TIT2);
    trace( "artist=" + mySound.id3.artist);
}
```

C The two **trace** statements display the artist's name and song title in the Output panel in test movie mode when the **Event.ID3** event occurs.

```
OUTPUT

    title=Hey Jack Kerouac
    artist=10,000 Maniacs
```

D The Output panel in Flash test movie mode.

Visualizing Sound Data

You've probably seen sound represented visually as waves or vertical spikes like mountain peaks, or perhaps even vibrating, shimmering lines and colors on a computer screen saver or a laser light show. These graphical effects are tied to different aspects of a sound; as the sound changes, so do the graphics, giving the users a direct visual representation of what they're hearing. This kind of visualization is an effective way of providing feedback that a sound is playing.

You can provide similar graphical representations of your sound in Flash. The **SoundChannel** class provides two properties, **leftPeak** and **rightPeak**, that indicate the volume levels for the left speaker and right speaker at any given moment during the sound. By continuously retrieving both properties with the **Event.ENTER_FRAME** event, or with a **Timer** object, you can display their values graphically, perhaps by scaling a vertical bar proportionately, for example.

In the following task, an external MP3 file is loaded and plays dynamically, and two rectangular movie clips change their **scaleY** properties to reflect the values of **leftPeak** and **rightPeak**.

A Two rectangular movie clips on the Stage, the left named **barleft_mc** and the right (shown selected) named **barright_mc**. Their registration points are at the bottom edge.

To visualize left and right volume levels:

1. Create a movie clip symbol of a vertical bar and place two instances on the Stage. In the Properties inspector, give each instance a different name. Make sure that the registration point for both movie clips is at the bottom edge **A**.

   These two bars will change in height to reflect the volume levels of the right and left speakers.

2. Declare and instantiate a **Sound** object with the constructor function **new Sound()**.

3. Instantiate a **URLRequest** object with the constructor function **new URLRequest()** and provide the path to an MP3 file as the parameter.

4. Enter the name of your **Sound** object followed by a period. Enter the method **load()** and provide the **URLRequest** object as the parameter.

   Flash loads the external MP3 file requested in the **URLRequest** object.

5. Call the **play()** method for your **Sound** object and assign the returned value to a new variable typed to a **SoundChannel** object, as follows:

   ```
   var myChannel:SoundChannel =
   → mySound.play();
   ```

   Flash plays the sound and a new **SoundChannel** object is created for it **B**.

Continues on next page

```
var mySound:Sound = new Sound();
var myRequest:URLRequest = new URLRequest("music.mp3");
mySound.load(myRequest);

var myChannel:SoundChannel = mySound.play();
```

B The external MP3 sound called music.mp3 plays.

6. Add an event listener to the stage that detects the **Event.ENTER_FRAME** event, like so:

   stage.addEventListener(
   → Event.ENTER_FRAME, everyframe);

   Flash triggers the function called **everyframe** at the frame rate of the Flash movie.

7. Add the function to respond to the **Event.ENTER_FRAME** event.

8. Between the curly braces of the function, enter the statements that change the movie clips, like so **C**:

   function
   everyframe(event:Event):void{
   **   barleft_mc.scaleY =**
   → myChannel.leftPeak;
   **   barright_mc.scaleY =**
   → myChannel.rightPeak;
   }

   The **leftPeak** and **rightPeak** properties of the **SoundChannel** object vary from 0 to 1. They are assigned to the **scaleY** property of the movie clips to vary their heights.

9. Make sure your external MP3 file is in the location where your Flash file can find it based on the information you provided in the **URLRequest** object. Test your movie **D**.

```
stage.addEventListener(Event.ENTER_FRAME, everyframe);
function everyframe(event:Event):void {
    barleft_mc.scaleY = myChannel.leftPeak;
    barright_mc.scaleY = myChannel.rightPeak;
}
```

C The **Event.ENTER_FRAME** event handler continuously scales both rectangular movie clips according to the sound's **leftPeak** and **rightPeak** properties.

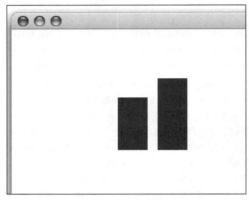

D The two rectangular movie clips move up and down synchronized to the sound.

TIP Flash provides an even more sophisticated way of looking at raw sound data with the `computeSpectrum()` method of the SoundMixer class. This method returns data for the frequency spectrum, which is the measure of the strength of the sound at each tone (where low frequencies are low-pitched tones and high frequencies are high-pitched tones). For more information and examples, look in Flash Help. Choose the category ActionScript 3.0 and Components > ActionScript 3.0 Developer's Guide > Rich Media Content > Working with sound > Accessing raw sound data.

Controlling
Information Flow

As your Flash movie displays graphics and animation and plays sounds, a lot can be happening behind the scenes that is not apparent to the viewer. Your Flash document may be tracking many bits of information, such as the number of lives a player has left in a game, a user's login name and password, or the items a customer has placed in a shopping cart. Getting and storing this information requires *variables,* which are containers for information. You've worked with variables in previous chapters when you created new instances and gave them names. You'll see how variables are essential in any Flash movie that involves complex interactivity because they let you create scenarios based on information that changes. You can modify variables and use them in *expressions*—formulas that can combine variables with other variables and values—and then test the information against certain conditions to determine how the Flash movie will unfold.

This chapter is about managing information by using variables, expressions, and conditional statements. When you understand how to get, modify, and evaluate

information, you can direct your Flash movie and change the graphics, animation, and sound in dynamic fashion.

Using Variables and Expressions

In Chapter 3, "Getting a Handle on Action-Script," you learned the basics of variables—how to declare them, assign values to them, and combine them in expressions. Now that you have more experience with variables in different contexts, this chapter takes another, more refined look at using variables and expressions in ActionScript.

You can use variables and expressions as placeholders within your ActionScript. In virtually every method that requires you to enter a parameter, you can substitute a variable or an expression instead of a fixed value. You can also use variables or expressions when you assign new values to an object's property. For example, instead of a frame number as the parameter for the basic method **gotoAndStop()**, use a variable. Changing the variable before calling the method makes Flash go to different frames according to the value of the variable.

You can also use a variable as a simple counter. Rather than taking the place of a parameter, a counter variable keeps track of how many times certain things occur for later retrieval and testing. A player's score can be stored in a variable so that Flash knows when the player reaches enough points to win the game. Or a variable can keep track of a certain state. You can set the variable **myShield = true** if a character's force field is turned on, for example, and change the variable to **myShield = false** if the force field is turned off.

```
var frameNumber:Number = 5;
```

A The variable **frameNumber** is defined to hold Number values and initialized to 5.

To initialize a variable:

In the first keyframe of the main Timeline, declare a variable using the **var** statement, entering the name of the variable and a colon, and then specifying a data type. This example uses the data type **Number**. Assign a numerical value to your variable **A**.

TIP It's important that your variable's data type be the same as the parameter or property that you want it to replace. For example, the gotoAndStop() method takes an Integer as its parameter, which represents the frame number. If you try to call the gotoAndStop() method with a variable holding a Number data type, the code may fail—not because a Number can't be used as its parameter, but because a Number allows decimals, which the gotoAndStop() method doesn't understand.

The Scope of Variables

When you initialize variables, they belong to the timeline where you create them. This is known as the *scope* of a variable. If you initialize a variable on the main Timeline, the variable is scoped to the main Timeline. If you initialize a variable inside a movie clip's timeline, the variable is scoped to that movie clip.

Think of a variable's scope as its home. Variables live on certain timelines, and if you want to use the information inside a variable, first you must find it with a target path. This process is analogous to targeting objects. To access either an object or a variable, you identify it with a target path.

Loading External Variables

You don't have to store the initial value of a variable inside your Flash movie. Flash lets you keep variables outside your Flash movie in a text document that you can load whenever you need the variables. This way, you can change the variables in the text document easily and thereby change the Flash movie without having to edit the movie. You can build a quiz, for example, with variables holding the questions and answers. Keep the variables in a text document, and when you want to change the quiz, edit the text document.

There are many ways in which data can be structured in an external document. One common way is to write variables and their values in the Multipurpose Internet Mail Extensions (MIME) URL-encoded format (or simply, URL variable format), which is a standard format that HTML forms and CGI scripts use. In the URL variable format, variables are written in the following form:

```
variable1=value1&variable2=
→ value2&variable3=value3
```

Each variable/value pair is separated from the next by a single ampersand (**&**) symbol.

```
caption1=Here's the new baby!&caption2=Our
trip to the Great Wall of China.&caption3=A
beautiful shot of the beach at sunset.
```

A Three variables and their values written in URL variable format. In this example, the variables are called **caption1**, **caption2**, and **caption3**, and are saved in a text document called data.txt.

The URLLoader and URLVariables classes

To access the variables in your external text document, use the **URLLoader** class. It provides properties, methods, and events to handle and manage incoming (and outgoing) data. It is similar to the **Loader** class that you learned about in Chapter 6, "Managing External Communication," to load in external images and SWF files. You use the method **load()** to begin loading the data from the external text document. The location of the file is provided in a **URLRequest** object.

You can test how much of the external data has loaded with the **ProgressEvent. PROGRESS** event, or define actions to take when external data finishes loading with the **Event.COMPLETE** event handler.

When the download is complete, the contents of the text file are put in the **data** property of your **URLLoader** object, where you can further process the data to get it in the correct form that you want it in with the **URLVariables** class.

To load external variables:

1. Launch a text editor, and create a new document.
2. Write your variable names and their values in the standard URL variable format **A**.
3. Save your text document in the same directory where your Flash movie will be saved.

   It doesn't matter what you name your file, but it helps to keep the name simple and to stick to a standard three-letter extension.
4. In Flash, open a new document.
5. Select the first keyframe of the root Timeline, and open the Actions panel.

6. In the Script pane, create a **URLLoader** object. Don't pass any parameters for the constructor.

7. On a new line of the Script pane, create a **URLRequest** object with the path to the text file that contains your variables.

   If your SWF file and the text file will reside in the same directory, you can enter just the text file's name, as in this example. Enclose the path or filename in quotation marks **B**.

8. On the next line, enter the name of your **URLLoader** object, and then call the method **load()**.

9. As a parameter of the **load()** method, enter the **URLRequest** object **C**.

   Flash calls the **load()** method, which loads the variable and value pairs from the external text file into the **URLLoader** object. The data comes into the **URLLoader** object's **data** property.

```
var myURLLoader:URLLoader = new URLLoader();
var myURLRequest:URLRequest = new URLRequest("data.txt");
```

B The new **URLLoader** object and the **URLRequest** object are created. The **URLRequest** object points to the external file with the variables.

```
var myURLLoader:URLLoader = new URLLoader();
var myURLRequest:URLRequest = new URLRequest("data.txt");
myURLLoader.load(myURLRequest);
```

C The **load()** method loads the data.txt file into Flash.

```
var myURLLoader:URLLoader = new URLLoader();
var myURLRequest:URLRequest = new URLRequest("data.txt");
myURLLoader.load(myURLRequest);

myURLLoader.addEventListener(Event.COMPLETE, dataOK);
function dataOK(myevent:Event):void {
    // do something with the loaded data
}
```

D The **Event.COMPLETE** event handler for the **URLLoader** object will be triggered when the loading operation completes. Nothing is written inside the event handler yet.

Receiving the loaded data

After you call the **load()** method for your **URLLoader** object, the data isn't always immediately available to the Flash Player. For instance, there is often a slight delay as the data downloads, even if the text document is local. You shouldn't try to do anything with the data until you know all of it has downloaded. You can detect when the data is completely loaded using the **Event.COMPLETE** event handler of the **URLLoader** object. Always wait for the **Event.COMPLETE** event handler to be called before attempting to use the loaded data. Typically, this means that you place the actions that use the loaded data within the event-handler function.

To detect the completion of loaded data:

1. Continuing with the file you used in the preceding task, select the first frame of the main Timeline, and open the Actions panel.

2. On a new line at the end of the current script, enter the name of your **URLLoader** object followed by a period, and then call the **addEventListener()** method to detect the **Event.COMPLETE** event.

3. On the next line, enter the function for the event handler. Between the curly braces of the function, add actions to be performed using the loaded data **D**.

   The loaded variables are added as the **data** property of the **URLLoader** object. To access a variable and its value pair, you use a **URLVariables** object, as described in the next task.

Decoding the loaded data

If your external text document contains data in the form of variable/value pairs as in the example discussed earlier, you can use the **URLVariables** object to parse the data so you can use the variables. There are several ways you can go about this. You can create a **URLVariables** object, and then call the **decode()** method and pass the **URLLoader** object's **data** property as the parameter. This will put the variables in the **URLVariables** object, as shown here:

```
var myURLVariables:URLVariables =
→ new URLVariables();
myURLVariables.decode(
→ myURLLoader.data);
```

You can also pass the **URLLoader** object's **data** property directly to the **URLVariables** object when you create it. The preceding statements can also be written as:

```
var myURLVariables:URLVariables =
→ new URLVariables(myURLLoader.data);
```

Now the loaded variables and values can be used as long as you include your **URLVariables** object in the target path, such as:

```
myURLVariables.caption1
```

Another way to access the variable/value pairs from your **URLLoader** object is to define the **dataFormat** property of the **URLLoader** object before you load the data from the text document. You can set the property like so:

```
myURLLoader.dataFormat =
→ URLLoaderDataFormat.VARIABLES;
```

Your variables would be available to you through the **data** property of the **URLLoader** object, such as:

```
myURLLoader.data.caption1
```

To decode URL-encoded data:

1. Continuing with the file you used in the preceding task, select the first frame of the main Timeline and open the Actions panel.

2. Inside the function of the **Event. COMPLETE** event handler, create a new **URLVariables** object and pass the **URLLoader.data** property to the constructor **E**.

   A new **URLVariables** object is created, and the data from the **URLLoader** object is decoded.

3. Add statements to reference and use the variables in the **URLVariables** object. In this example, the variables **caption1**, **caption2**, and **caption3** are used to assign text to three text fields on the Stage **F**.

Or

1. Continuing with the file you used in the preceding task, select the first frame of the main Timeline and open the Actions panel.

```
var myURLLoader:URLLoader = new URLLoader();
var myURLRequest:URLRequest = new URLRequest("data.txt");
myURLLoader.load(myURLRequest);

myURLLoader.addEventListener(Event.COMPLETE, dataOK);
function dataOK(myevent:Event):void {
    var myURLVariables:URLVariables = new URLVariables (myURLLoader.data);
}
```

E The **URLLoader.data** information is passed to the **URLVariables** object for handling URL-encoded information.

```
var myURLLoader:URLLoader = new URLLoader();
var myURLRequest:URLRequest = new URLRequest("data.txt");
myURLLoader.load(myURLRequest);

myURLLoader.addEventListener(Event.COMPLETE, dataOK);
function dataOK(myevent:Event):void {
    var myURLVariables:URLVariables = new URLVariables (myURLLoader.data);
    textfield1.text = myURLVariables.caption1;
    textfield2.text = myURLVariables.caption2;
    textfield3.text = myURLVariables.caption3;
}
```

textfield1

textfield2

textfield3

text field with
contents of
variables

Our trip to the Great Wall of China.

Here's the new baby!

A beautiful shot of the beach at sunset.

F The full code (top) assigns the values of each
of the variables in the external text document to
three text fields on the Stage. These text fields
are captions to images (shown as generic gray
squares). Change the external text document to
change the captions without having to open and
edit your Flash document.

```
var myURLLoader:URLLoader = new URLLoader();
var myURLRequest:URLRequest = new URLRequest("data.txt");
myURLLoader.dataFormat = URLLoaderDataFormat.VARIABLES;
myURLLoader.load(myURLRequest);
myURLLoader.addEventListener(Event.COMPLETE, dataOK);
function dataOK(myevent:Event):void {
}
```

G An alternative way of loading URL-encoded data
is to set the **dataFormat** property of your **URLLoader**
object to the string "variables" or the equivalent
constant **URLLoaderDataFormat.VARIABLES**.

```
var myURLLoader:URLLoader = new URLLoader();
var myURLRequest:URLRequest = new URLRequest("data.txt");
myURLLoader.dataFormat = URLLoaderDataFormat.VARIABLES;
myURLLoader.load(myURLRequest);
myURLLoader.addEventListener(Event.COMPLETE, dataOK);
function dataOK(myevent:Event):void {
    textfield1.text = myURLLoader.data.caption1;
    textfield2.text = myURLLoader.data.caption2;
    textfield3.text = myURLLoader.data.caption3;
}
```

H If you set the **dataFormat** of your **URLLoader**,
you can access the variables directly from the
data property.

2. Insert a new line before the **load()**
method of the **URLLoader** object. Assign
the **URLLoaderDataFormat.VARIABLES**
property to the **dataFormat** property of
the **URLLoader** object **G**.

   The **dataFormat** property determines
   how the data from the external text file
   will load. Other options include **BINARY**
   or **TEXT**. (**TEXT** is the default value.)

3. Inside the **Event.COMPLETE** event-
handler function, add statements to
reference and use the variables in the
URLLoader's **data** object. In this example, the variables **caption1**, **caption2**,
and **caption3** are used to assign text to
three text fields on the Stage **H**.

TIP The default value for the **dataFormat**
property of the URLLoader object is
URLLoaderDataFormat.TEXT.

TIP If you are loading numeric data from
external text files, you need to convert the
values into numeric values by using methods
such as **int()**, **uint()**, or **Number()**.

TIP Write your variable and value pairs in
an external text file without any line breaks
or spaces between the ampersand and equals
sign. Although you may have a harder time
reading the file, Flash will have an easier time
understanding it.

Using XML data

The previous examples showed you how to load and decode URL-encoded variables that are in the format of variable/value pairs. However, when you have more complex data, using XML is a better way to structure, read, and use the data.

XML is similar to other markup languages such as HTML, which contains information surrounded by tags that are interpreted by a computer. HTML tells the Web browser how to display information—make this text bold, put this image on the left, and so on. XML is more generic than HTML in that it lets you define information according to its content rather than its appearance. For example, you can identify one piece of information as a name and another piece of information as an address. XML also lets you order the data in an outline, or tree-like, structure. For example, the data that was loaded in the previous tasks (the caption text for three pictures on the Stage) were represented in URL-encoded format, like so:

```
caption1=Here's the new baby!&
→ caption2=Our trip to the Great
→ Wall of China.&caption3=A beautiful
→ shot of the beach at sunset.
```

In XML, you could write the same data as:

```
<slidecaptions>
<mycaption>Here's the new baby!
→ </mycaption>
<mycaption>Our trip to the Great
→ Wall of China.</mycaption>
<mycaption>A beautiful shot of the
→ beach at sunset.</mycaption>
</slidecaptions>
```

The data within the XML document is clearer and gives more opportunities to order the data. XML consists of nodes, which are the individual parts that can be arranged in a hierarchy. In the previous example, `<slidecaptions>` is the root node, with `<mycaption>` and the text values as child nodes.

In Flash, the process of loading XML data is similar to other methods of loading data: You use the **URLLoader** class and its **load()** method to start loading an XML document, and you define an **Event.COMPLETE** event handler so you know when all the data is loaded. Once the data is loaded, you can use the methods of the **XML** object to *parse*, or decode, the data and retrieve the values. Use the dot operator (.) and the array access operator ([ ]) to traverse parent and child nodes to access their properties.

Although it's beyond the scope of this book to cover XML in depth, the following example will help you understand how Flash can load simple XML data and extract the information.

To decode XML data:

1. Launch a text editor, and create a new document.

2. Write your data in XML format, as shown in **①**.

3. Save your text document in the same directory where your Flash movie will be saved.

4. In Flash, open a new document.

5. Select the first keyframe of the main Timeline, and open the Actions panel.

6. As described in the earlier tasks, create a **URLLoader** and load the external XML document. Create an event handler to detect the completion of the loading process **①**.

7. Inside the function of the **Event.COMPLETE** event handler, create a new **XML** object and pass the **URLLoader.data** property to the constructor **②**.

   Data from the external XML document is put inside the **XML** object. You can now use dot syntax to access the nodes and information in the **XML** object (here, it's called **myXML**).

Continues on next page

```
<slidecaptions>

<mycaption>Here is the new baby!</mycaption>
<mycaption>Our trip to the Great Wall of China.</mycaption>
<mycaption>A beautiful shot of the beach at sunset.</mycaption>

</slidecaptions>
```

① Data in an XML format. This is a text document that is saved in the same directory as your Flash file.

```
var myURLLoader:URLLoader = new URLLoader();
var myURLRequest:URLRequest = new URLRequest("data.xml");
myURLLoader.load(myURLRequest);
myURLLoader.addEventListener(Event.COMPLETE, dataOK);
function dataOK(myevent:Event):void {
    // do something with data
}
```

① Loading an XML document is the same as loading one in URL variables format—creating the **URLLoader** object, creating the **URLRequest** object, loading the document, and listening for the completion of the load.

```
var myURLLoader:URLLoader = new URLLoader();
var myURLRequest:URLRequest = new URLRequest("data.xml");
myURLLoader.load(myURLRequest);
myURLLoader.addEventListener(Event.COMPLETE, dataOK);
function dataOK(myevent:Event):void {
    var myXML:XML = new XML(myURLLoader.data);
}
```

② Pass the **URLLoader**'s **data** property to the new **XML** object.

8. On the next line still within the function, access the first piece of information in the **mycaption** object of the **XML** object with square brackets, and assign it to a text field on the Stage, like so:

```
textfield1.text =
→ myXML.mycaption[0];
```

The square brackets access the first item—which is the text "Here's the new baby!"—and displays it in a text field on the Stage. The square brackets are a way of accessing the contents of an **Array** or of an object that has multiple elements inside it. You'll learn more about the square brackets later in this chapter and about the **Array** object in Chapter 11, "Manipulating Information."

9. Continue accessing the rest of the information and assign the results to the text fields on the Stage **L**.

10. Create three TLF text fields on the Stage and give them names in the Properties inspector that match the names you used in your ActionScript.

11. Test your movie.

The data from the external XML document is loaded into your **URLLoader** object and then into the **XML** object. Using dots and square brackets, you can access the different information in the XML, and in this example, populate dynamic text fields for picture captions. Simply change the information in the XML document to have the changes be reflected in your Flash movie.

> **TIP** If your XML element has an attribute, as in **<mycaption fontsize="14">**, you can access its value with the @ symbol. For example, the statement **myXML.mycaption[0].@fontsize** would retrieve the value 14.

```
var myURLLoader:URLLoader = new URLLoader();
var myURLRequest:URLRequest = new URLRequest("data.xml");
myURLLoader.load(myURLRequest);
myURLLoader.addEventListener(Event.COMPLETE, dataOK);
function dataOK(myevent:Event):void {
    var myXML:XML = new XML(myURLLoader.data);
    textfield1.text = myXML.mycaption[0];
    textfield2.text = myXML.mycaption[1];
    textfield3.text = myXML.mycaption[2];
}
```

```
<slidecaptions>

<mycaption> Here is the new baby!</mycaption>
<mycaption> Our trip to the Great Wall of China.</mycaption>
<mycaption> A beautiful shot of the beach at sunset.</mycaption>

</slidecaptions>
```

XML document   myXML.mycaption[0]
                      myXML.mycaption[1]
                 myXML.mycaption[2]

L The information in the XML document can be accessed with dot operators and square brackets (array access operators).

Retrieving XML Data

The biggest challenge when using XML documents to store data is to correctly structure your XML so you can efficiently extract the data. In the task "To decode XML data," you extracted the caption data by using the array access operators (the square brackets). Each caption could be referenced by an index number in the **mycaptions** node. Let's look at something a little more complex to see how you use the array access operators to extract the data 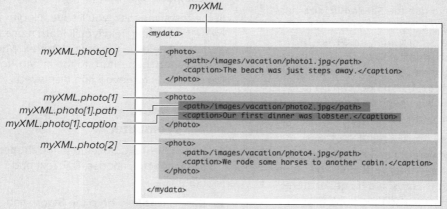 .

In this example, each slide has a path, where the image resides, and a caption, which describes the photo. To get the caption for the second photo, you drill down the hierarchy with dot syntax—first referencing the whole XML structure (**myXML**), then its second slide node (**slide[1]**), and finally the caption (**caption[0]** or just **caption** since there's only one entry). The complete path would be **myXML.slide[1].caption**.

Typically, you'll use loops (described later in this chapter) to go through all the nodes automatically to extract the data.

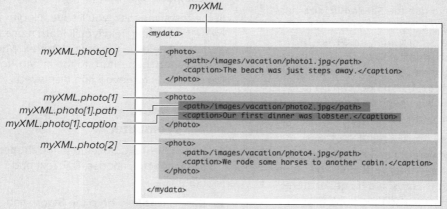

myXML

```
<mydata>

myXML.photo[0] ———— <photo>
                        <path>/images/vacation/photo1.jpg</path>
                        <caption>The beach was just steps away.</caption>
                    </photo>

      myXML.photo[1] ———— <photo>
   myXML.photo[1].path ————   <path>/images/vacation/photo2.jpg</path>
myXML.photo[1].caption ————   <caption>Our first dinner was lobster.</caption>
                           </photo>

      myXML.photo[2] ———— <photo>
                            <path>/images/vacation/photo4.jpg</path>
                            <caption>We rode some horses to another cabin.</caption>
                          </photo>

</mydata>
```

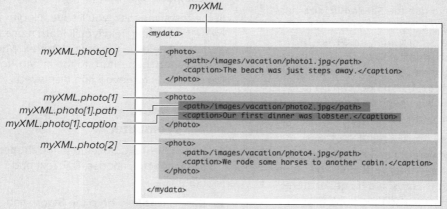 In this XML document, there are three photo nodes, each with their own path and caption nodes. If **myXML** is the name of the XML object, then information in the document can be extracted.

Storing and Sharing Information

Although variables enable you to keep track of information, they do so only within a single playing of a Flash movie. When your viewer quits the movie, all the information in variables is lost. When the viewer returns to the movie, the variables are again initialized to their starting values or are loaded from external sources.

You can have Flash remember the current values of your variables even after a viewer quits the movie, however. The solution is to use the **SharedObject** class. **SharedObject** instances save information on a viewer's computer, much like browsers save information in cookies. When a viewer returns to a movie that has saved a **SharedObject**, that object can be loaded back in and the variables from the previous visit can be used.

You can use the **SharedObject** class in a variety of ways to make your Flash site more convenient for repeat visitors. Store visitors' high scores in a game, or store their login names so they don't have to type them again. If you've created a complex puzzle game, you can store the positions of the pieces for completion at a later date; for a long animated story, you can store the user's current location; or for a site with a collection of articles, you can store information about which ones your visitor has already read.

To store information in a **SharedObject** instance, add a new property to the **SharedObject**'s **data** property object. You then store the information that you want to keep in your new property. The statement **mySharedObject.data.highscore = 200** stores the high-score information in the **SharedObject** instance. The method **getLocal()** creates or retrieves a **SharedObject**, and the method **flush()** causes the **data** properties to be written to the computer's hard drive.

In the following task, you'll save a login name from a text field (you'll learn more about text fields in the next chapter). When you quit and then return to the movie, your login name is retrieved and displayed.

To store information on a user's computer:

1. Select the Text tool, and in the Properties inspector, choose TLF Text and Editable.

2. Drag a text field onto the Stage, and give the text field the instance name **myLogin_txt Ⓐ**.

    This text field allows users to enter information via the keyboard.

Ⓐ Create a TLF text field that is editable, and give it a name in the Properties inspector.

3. Create a button, place an instance of it on the Stage, and give it an instance name in the Properties inspector.

   You'll assign actions to this button to save the information in your text field in a **SharedObject**.

4. Select the first frame of the main Timeline, and open the Actions panel.

5. In the Script pane, declare a new **SharedObject** by entering **var mySharedObject:SharedObject** followed by an equals sign.

6. On the right side of the equals sign, enter **SharedObject.getLocal("myCookie")** **B**.

   Flash looks for a **SharedObject**, and if it does not find one, it creates a **SharedObject** instance that will be stored on the user's local hard drive.

7. On the next line, create a **MouseEvent.CLICK** event handler for your button.

8. Between the curly braces of the event-handler function, enter the following:

   mySharedObject.data.loginData =
   → myLogin_txt.text

The content of your text field on the Stage is saved in a property named **loginData** in the **data** property of your **SharedObject**.

9. On the next line, enter **mySharedObject. flush()** **C**.

   Calling the **flush()** method saves all the information in the **data** property of your **SharedObject** on the viewer's computer.

TIP If the **flush()** method isn't called explicitly, the information in the **data** object of your **SharedObject** is saved automatically when the viewer quits the movie. The **flush()** method lets you choose when to save information.

TIP Many kinds of information can be stored in the **data** object of a **SharedObject**, such as numbers, strings, and even objects such as an array.

Just remember to assign the information to the **data** object of a **SharedObject**, as in:

mySharedObject.data.name = "Russell";

rather than

mySharedObject.data = "Russell";

```
var mySharedObject:SharedObject = SharedObject.getLocal("myCookie");
```

B The **getLocal()** method creates a **SharedObject** that will be stored on the user's computer.

```
var mySharedObject:SharedObject = SharedObject.getLocal("myCookie");

saveButton_btn.addEventListener(MouseEvent.CLICK, savedata);
function savedata(myevent:MouseEvent):void {
  mySharedObject.data.myLoginData = myLogin_txt.text;
  mySharedObject.flush();
}
```

C Clicking the button called **saveButton_btn** puts the contents of the text field in the **myLoginData** property of the data property of your **SharedObject** and saves it on the user's computer.

To retrieve information from a user's computer:

1. Continuing with the file you used in the preceding task, create a second button, place an instance of it on the Stage, and give it a name in the Properties inspector.

   You'll assign actions to this second button, which will retrieve **mySharedObject.data** and the most recently saved contents of your text field.

2. Select the main Timeline, and in the Actions panel, assign a **MouseEvent.CLICK** event handler to this second button.

3. Between the curly braces of the event-handler function, enter the following statement:

   ```
   myLogin_txt.text =
   → mySharedObject.data.myLoginData;
   ```

   This statement retrieves the information in **myLoginData** that was saved on the

viewer's computer in a **SharedObject**. That information is used to change the contents of your text field **D**.

4. Test your movie.

   Enter your name in the text field on the Stage, and then click the button to save the information into a **SharedObject**. Quit the movie. When you open the movie again and click the second button, your name appears in the text field because Flash retrieved the information from your previous session **E**.

To clear information on a user's computer:

Call the method **clear()** to clear information saved in a **SharedObject**.

The statement:

```
mySharedObject.clear();
```

removes all the data from the **SharedObject**.

```
var mySharedObject:SharedObject = SharedObject.getLocal("myCookie");

saveButton_btn.addEventListener(MouseEvent.CLICK, savedata);
function savedata(myevent:MouseEvent):void {
  mySharedObject.data.myLoginData = myLogin_txt.text;
  mySharedObject.flush();
}

loadButton_btn.addEventListener(MouseEvent.CLICK, loaddata);
function loaddata(myevent:MouseEvent):void {
    myLogin_txt.text = mySharedObject.data.myLoginData;
}
```

D Clicking the button called **loadButton_btn** puts the saved data into the text field for display.

E Enter your login name in the text field and click the button to save it (top). Close the Flash movie, and then open it again to return to it. When you click the second button, your login name appears again so you don't have to retype it (bottom).

Sharing information among multiple movies

Flash keeps track of a **SharedObject** saved on the viewer's computer by remembering the name of the object as well as the location of the movie in which it was created. The location of the movie is known as the **SharedObject**'s *local path*. By default, the local path is the relative path from the domain name to the filename. If your movie is at www.myDomain.com/flash/myMovie.swf, the local path is /flash/myMovie.swf. Flash lets you specify a different local path when you use the **getLocal()** method so that you can store a **SharedObject** in a different place. Why would you do this? If you have multiple movies, you can define one **SharedObject** and a common local path, allowing all the movies to access the same **SharedObject** and share its information.

Valid local paths for a **SharedObject** include the directory in which your movie sits or any of its parent directories sit. Don't include the domain name, and don't specify any other directories in the domain. Remember, you aren't telling Flash to store information on the server; you're telling Flash to store information locally on the viewer's computer (the host), and the local path helps Flash keep track of the **SharedObject**. Because local paths are relative to a single domain, a **SharedObject** can be shared only with multiple movies in the same domain.

To store information that multiple movies can share:

1. Continuing with the file that you created in the preceding task, in the Actions panel add a forward slash as the second parameter to the **getLocal()** method. Make sure the forward slash is between quotation marks **F**.

   Flash will save the **SharedObject** **mySharedObject_so** with the local path **"/"**. This entry represents the top-level directory.

2. In a new Flash document, create another text field on the Stage, and give it the name **myLogin2_txt** in the Properties inspector.

   This text field will display information stored in the **SharedObject** you created in your first movie.

Continues on next page

```
var mySharedObject:SharedObject = SharedObject.getLocal("myCookie", "/");
```

F The second parameter of the **getLocal()** method determines the local path of the **SharedObject** and its location on the viewer's computer. The single slash indicates the top-level directory of the domain where the Flash movie resides.

3. Select the first frame of the main Time-line, and open the Actions panel.

4. In the Script pane, enter the following statement:

```
var mySharedObject2:SharedObject
→ = SharedObject.getLocal(
→ "myCookie", "/");
```

Flash retrieves the **SharedObject** with the local path **"/"** from the viewer's computer. Notice that the parameter **"myCookie"** must be identical to the one used in the first Flash movie, but the **SharedObject** variable's name **mySharedObject2** can be different.

5. On a new line of the Script pane, assign the property **myLoginData** in the **data** property of the **SharedObject** to the contents of your input text field with the following statement **G**:

```
myLogin2_txt.text =
mySharedObject2.data.myLoginData;
```

This statement retrieves the **myLoginData** information from the **SharedObject** and displays it in the text field.

6. Test your movies.

Play the first movie, enter your name in the text field, click the first button to save its position in a **SharedObject**, and close the movie. Now open your second movie. Flash reads the information in the **SharedObject** created by the first movie and displays your name **H**.

```
var mySharedObject2:SharedObject = SharedObject.getLocal("myCookie", "/");
myLogin2_txt.text = mySharedObject2.data.myLoginData;
```

G In this second Flash movie, the **getLocal()** method retrieves the same **SharedObject** that was saved in the first Flash movie, because the same name and local path are given in its parameters for both movies.

H When the login name in the first Flash movie is saved (top), you can open the second Flash movie (bottom), and its text field displays the same login name. Both movies access the same **SharedObject** on the user's hard drive.

SharedObjects, Permission, and Local Disk Space

The default amount of information that Flash Player allows a single domain to store on a viewer's computer is set at 100 KB, and users can configure the amount of space they allow to be used by **SharedObject** data. When you call the **flush()** method, depending on the amount of data you're trying to store and the viewer's settings, different things happen. If the new data doesn't exceed the amount the viewer allows, the **SharedObject** is saved and **flush()** returns **true**. If the new data exceeds the allowable amount and the viewer's Flash Player is set to block requests for more space, the **SharedObject** isn't saved and **flush()** returns a value of **false**. Finally, if the **SharedObject** data exceeds the amount the user has allowed and the Flash Player isn't set to block requests for more space, a dialog box appears over the Stage asking the viewer for permission to store information . In that case, the **flush()** method returns the string "pending" or **SharedObjectFlushStatus.PENDING**. The viewer can allow the request or deny it.

Viewers can change their local storage settings at any time by right-clicking (Windows) or Ctrl-clicking (Mac) the movie and then choosing Settings from the context menu . The viewer can choose never to accept information from a particular domain or to accept varying amounts (10 KB, 100 KB, 1 MB, 10 MB, or unlimited). Local storage permission is specific to the domain (which appears in the dialog box), so future movies from the same domain can save **SharedObject**s according to the same settings.

If you know that the information you save to a viewer's computer will grow, you can request more space ahead of time by defining a minimum disk space for the **flush()** method. Calling the method **mySharedObject.flush(1000000)** saves the **SharedObject** and reserves 1,000,000 bytes (1 MB) for the information. If Flash asks the viewer to allow disk space for the **SharedObject**, it will ask for 1 MB. After the permission is given, Flash won't ask for more space until the data in that domain's **SharedObject** exceeds 1 MB or the viewer changes his local storage settings.

I Flash asks to store more information than the viewer currently allows. This request comes from local, which is the viewer's computer.

J From the Flash Player context menu (with your mouse pointer over a Flash movie, right-click for Windows or Ctrl-click for Mac), access the Settings dialog box. You can decide how much information a particular domain can save on your computer. This setting is for local, which is the viewer's computer.

Loading and Saving Files on the Hard Drive

You can get and save information on the user's local hard drive by making Flash open a file browser and having the user choose a particular file. This works well for creating more complex applications that depend on data that the user can save, modify, and retrieve, just like a word processing program or an image-editing program like Adobe Photoshop.

You can directly have your users load and save files with the **FileReference** class. The method **browse()** opens a file browser to choose a file, and the method **load()** loads in the data from a selected file. The method **save()** opens a file browser to save a file.

Event handlers for the events **Event.SELECT** and **Event.COMPLETE** are necessary to detect when a file has been selected and when the loading or saving process has been completed.

TIP The methods of the **FileReference** class can only be used if the user initiates the process (such as clicking with the mouse or pressing a key on the keyboard). This is a safeguard so that malicious Flash code cannot automatically open files on a user's hard drive or save files to the user's hard drive. Any attempt to call the methods without user interaction will result in an error.

To open the file browser to select a text file:

1. Create a button, place an instance of it on the Stage, and give it an instance name in the Properties inspector.

   You'll assign actions to this button to open the file browser to let users choose a file to load from their hard drive.

2. Select the first frame of the main Timeline, and open the Actions panel.

3. In the Script pane, declare a new **FileReference** object by entering **var myfile:FileReference** followed by an equals sign and **new FileReference().**

4. On the next line, create a **MouseEvent.CLICK** event handler for your button.

5. Between the curly braces of the event handler function, enter the following:

   myfile.browse();

   When the user clicks the button, the file browser will open **A**.

A When you click the button called **load_btn**, Flash opens the file browser (below) so the user can choose a file from the hard drive.

To load a selected text file:

1. Continue with the previous task, "To open the file browser to select a text file."

   To load a file, you must create an event handler to detect when the user selects a file.

2. On the next line, create an **Event.SELECT** event handler for your **FileReference** object.

3. Between the curly braces of the event handler function, enter the following:

   ```
   myfile.load();
   ```

   When the user selects a file from the file browser, Flash begins loading that file **B**.

To retrieve the contents of the text file:

1. Continue with the previous task, "To load a selected text file."

   To retrieve the contents of a loaded file, you must create an event handler to detect the completion of the load.

2. On the next line, create an **Event.COMPLETE** event handler for your **FileReference** object.

3. Between the curly braces of the event-handler function, enter the following:

   ```
   mytextfield_txt.text =
   → myfile.data.readUTFBytes(
   → myfile.data.length);
   ```

   When the loading process is complete, Flash reads the data in the file and puts it in a text field called **mytextfield_txt**.

   The data is in the **data** property of the **FileReference** object, but because the **data** property is a **ByteArray** object, you must use the method **readUTFBytes()** to extract the information. The **length** property refers to the total size of the file, so passing **myfile.data.length** as the parameter of **readUTFBytes()** makes Flash load the entire contents of the file **C**.

   Continues on next page

```
var myfile:FileReference = new FileReference();
load_btn.addEventListener(MouseEvent.CLICK, loadfile);
function loadfile(myevent:MouseEvent):void {
    myfile.browse();
}

myfile.addEventListener(Event.SELECT, selectfile);
function selectfile(myevent:Event):void {
    myfile.load();
}
```

B The second event handler detects when the user selects a file. When that happens, the file is loaded into Flash.

```
var myfile:FileReference = new FileReference();
load_btn.addEventListener(MouseEvent.CLICK, loadfile);
function loadfile(myevent:MouseEvent):void {
    myfile.browse();
}

myfile.addEventListener(Event.SELECT, selectfile);
function selectfile(myevent:Event):void {
    myfile.load();
}

myfile.addEventListener(Event.COMPLETE, completeloading);
function completeloading(myevent:Event):void {
    mytextfield_txt.text = myfile.data.readUTFBytes(myfile.data.length);
}
```

C The third event handler detects when the file has completely loaded into Flash. When that happens, the entire data in the file is assigned to a text field on the Stage.

4. Choose the Text tool and, in the Properties inspector, choose TLF Text and Read Only.

5. Create a text field on the Stage, and in the Properties inspector, name the text field **mytextfield_txt**.

6. Test your movie **D**.

To save a text file:

1. In a new Flash file, create a button, place an instance of it on the Stage, and give it an instance name in the Properties inspector.

You'll assign actions to this button to open the file browser to let users save a file on their hard drive.

2. Choose the Text tool and in the Properties inspector, choose TLF Text and Editable.

3. Create a text field on the Stage and name the text field **mytextfield_txt**. Select a colored border for the text field **E**.

You'll allow users to enter text in the text field, and then save the results in a file to their hard drive.

4. Select the first frame of the main Timeline, and open the Actions panel.

Text field

D In this example, the text document called sometext.txt is selected by the user (top). The contents of the text document are displayed in the text field next to the button.

Text field instance name

E Name the TLF text field on the Stage **mytextfield_txt** and choose the Editable option.

```
var myfile:FileReference = new FileReference();

save_btn.addEventListener(MouseEvent.CLICK, savefile);
function savefile(myevent:MouseEvent):void {
    myfile.save(mytextfield_txt.text);
}
```

F When the user clicks the **save_btn** button, the contents of the input text field can be saved to a file on the hard drive. The user can choose the name of the file.

G When you add a second parameter to the **save()** method, a suggested filename appears in the file browser.

5. In the Script pane, declare a new **FileReference** object by entering **var myfile:FileReference** followed by an equals sign and **new FileReference()**.

6. On the next line, create a **MouseEvent. CLICK** event handler for your button.

7. Between the curly braces of the event handler function, enter the following:

   myfile.save(mytextfield_txt.text);

   When the user clicks the button, the file browser will open, allowing the user to save the contents of the text field to a file on the hard drive **F**.

TIP If you want to prepopulate the file browser with a filename, you can provide a second parameter for the save() method. The method save(mytextfield_txt.text, "hello.txt") opens the file browser with the filename hello.txt in the Save As field **G**.

TIP The Event.COMPLETE and Event.SELECT events are triggered for both the save() and the load() methods. If the event handlers reference the same FileReference object, you will likely get an error. So, it's a good idea to have two separate FileReference objects if you are going to perform both methods.

TIP You can load and save many other kinds of files—not just text files. See the Flash Help and ActionScript 3 language reference for ways to handle other file types.

Modifying Variables

Variables are useful because you can always change their contents with updated information about the status of the movie or your viewer. Sometimes, this change involves assigning a new value to the variable. At other times, the change means adding, subtracting, multiplying, or dividing the variable's numeric values or modifying a string by adding characters. The variable `myScore`, for example, may be initialized at 0. Then, for every goal a player makes, the `myScore` variable changes in increments of 1. The job of modifying information contained in variables falls upon *operators*—symbols that operate on data.

Assignment and arithmetic operators

The assignment operator (=) is a single equals sign that assigns a value to a variable. You've already used this operator in initializing variables and creating new objects. **Table 9.1** lists the other common operators.

Operators are the workhorses of Flash interactivity. You'll use them often to perform calculations behind the scenes—adding the value of one variable to another or changing the property of one object by adding or subtracting the value of a variable, for example.

TABLE 9.1 Common Operators

Symbol	Description
+	Addition
-	Subtraction
*	Multiplication
/	Division
%	Modulo division; calculates the remainder of the first number divided by the second number. **7 % 2** results in 1.
++	Increases the value by 1. **x ++** is equivalent to **x = x + 1**.
--	Decreases the value by 1. **x --** is equivalent to **x = x - 1**.
+=	Adds a value to and assigns the result to the variable. **x += 5** is equivalent to **x = x + 5**.
-=	Subtracts a value from and assigns the result to the variable. **x -= 5** is equivalent to **x = x - 5**.
*=	Multiplies by a value and assigns the result to the variable. **x *= 5** is equivalent to **x = x * 5**.
/=	Divides by a value and assigns it to the variable. **x /= 5** is equivalent to **x = x / 5**.

To incrementally increase the value of a variable:

- Enter the name of your variable followed by two plus symbols, such as `myVariable++`.

  The value of `myVariable` increases by 1.

  or

- Enter the name of your variable followed by a plus symbol and an equals sign followed by the value of the increment, such as `myVariable += 20`.

  The value of `myVariable` increases by 20.

To incrementally decrease the value of a variable:

- Enter the name of your variable followed by two minus signs, such as `myVariable--`.

  The value of `myVariable` decreases by 1.

  or

- Enter the name of your variable followed by a minus symbol and an equals sign followed by the value of the increment, such as `myVariable -= 20`.

  The value of `myVariable` decreases by 20.

TIP To perform more complicated mathematical calculations (such as square root, sine, and cosine) or string manipulations on your variables and values, you must use the `Math` class or the `String` class. You'll learn about these objects in Chapters 10 and 11.

TIP Remember that you can always change the values of variables, but you can't change the type of data that the variables hold. So if you've created a variable to hold a number, you can't assign a string to it.

TIP The arithmetic rules of precedence (remember them from math class?) apply when Flash evaluates expressions, which means that certain operators take priority over others. The most important rule is that multiplication and division are performed before addition and subtraction. 3 + 4 * 2, for example, gives a very different result than 3 * 4 + 2.

TIP Use parentheses to group variables and operators so those portions are calculated before other parts of the expression are evaluated. (3 + 2) * 4 returns a value of 20, but without the parentheses, 3 + 2 * 4 returns a value of 11.

TIP Use the modulo division operator (%) to check whether a variable is an even or an odd number. The statement myNumber % 2 returns 0 if myNumber is even and 1 if myNumber is odd. You can use this logic to create toggling functionality. You can count the number of times a viewer clicks a light switch, for example. If the count is even, you can turn on the light; if the count is odd, you turn off the light.

Concatenating Variables and Dynamic Referencing

The addition operator (**+**) adds the values of numeric data types. But it can also put together string values. The expression **"Hello " + "world"**, for example, results in the string "Hello world". This kind of operation is called *concatenation.*

You use of concatenation to mix strings, numbers, and variables to create expressions that allow you to dynamically create and access objects or variables. For example, you can concatenate a string with a variable to make Flash go to a specified frame, depending on the current value of the variable, as in:

```
gotoAndStop("Chapter" +
→ myChapterNumber);
```

The result of the concatenation is that Flash goes to a frame labeled something like **Chapter1** or **Chapter2**, depending on the value of the variable called **myChapterNumber**. The frame label is assigned dynamically with a concatenated expression.

This kind of concatenation works because the concatenated string is used as a parameter of a method. Flash knows to resolve the expression before using it as the parameter. What happens in other cases? Consider this statement in the Script pane of the Actions panel:

```
var "myVariable" + counter = 5;
```

This statement doesn't make sense to Flash and causes an error. To construct a dynamic variable name and assign a value to that variable, you must instruct Flash to resolve (or "figure out") the left side first and then treat the result as a concatenated variable name before assigning a value to it. The way to do that is to use the array access operator.

Array access operator

To reference a variable or an object dynamically, use the *array access operators.* The array access operator is the square brackets ([ ], located on the same keys as the curly braces). It is called the array access operator because it is typically used to access the contents of an **Array** object, but it can also be used to dynamically access the contents of other objects.

What does this capability mean? Think of the main Timeline as being a **root** object; variables and objects sitting on the main Timeline are its contents. A variable **myVariable** initialized on the main Timeline can be targeted with the array access operator as follows:

```
root["myVariable"]
```

Notice that there is no dot between the object (**root**) and the square brackets. The array access operator automatically resolves concatenated expressions within the square brackets. For example, the following statement puts together a single variable name based on the value of **counter** and then assigns the numeric value of 5 to the variable:

```
root["myVariable" + counter] = 5;
```

If the value of **counter** is 7, Flash accesses the variable named **root.myVariable7** and assigns the value 5 to that variable.

Using the array access operators also enables you to call methods and change the properties of dynamically referenced objects with dot syntax. For example, you can modify an object's transparency this way:

```
root["mushroom_mc" + counter].alpha
→ = .5
```

```
root["myVariable" + counter] = 5;
```

A Flash resolves the expression in the square brackets first, so if the value of **counter** is 0, the variable called **myVariable0** will be assigned the value of 5.

```
root["myMovieClip" + counter].play();
```

B Use the array access operators to dynamically reference an object and then call one of its methods. If the value of counter is 0, the movie clip called **myMovieClip0** will begin to play.

```
root["myMovieClip" + counter].rotation = 45;
```

C Use the array access operators to dynamically reference an object and then evaluate or modify one of its properties. If the value of **counter** is 0, the movie clip called **myMovieClip0** will rotate 45 degrees clockwise.

TIP A useful method to consider when dynamically accessing objects is the method of the DisplayObject class called getChildByName(). This method returns the DisplayObject that exists with the specified name, which you can construct dynamically with an expression. For example, getChildByName("car" + counter) would return the object whose name is based on the string "car" and the value of the variable counter. Assign the returned object into a DisplayObject to manipulate, as in the following example:

```
var myObject:DisplayObject =
→ getChildByName("car" + counter);
myObject.alpha = .5;
```

If the value of **counter** is 3, the movie clip in the root Timeline named **root.mushroom_mc3** becomes 50 percent transparent. To make the movie clip play, call the designated method, like this:

```
root["myClip_mc" + counter].play()
```

To reference a variable dynamically and assign a value:

In the Script pane of the Actions panel, enter the parent of the variable followed by an opening square bracket, an expression, a closing square bracket, an equals sign, and a value.

Flash resolves the expression within the square brackets and assigns the value to the variable with that name **A**.

To reference an object dynamically and call a method:

1. In the Script pane of the Actions panel, enter the parent of the object followed by an opening square bracket, an expression, and a closing square bracket.

2. On the same line, enter a period, and then enter the method name **B**.

   Flash resolves the expression between the square brackets and calls the method on that object.

To reference an object dynamically and change a property:

In the Script pane of the Actions panel, enter the parent of the object followed by an opening square bracket, an expression, a closing square bracket, a dot, a property, an equals sign, and a value **C**.

Flash resolves the expression between the square brackets and assigns the value on the right of the equals sign to the object.

Testing Information with Conditional Statements

Variables and expressions go hand in hand with conditional statements. The information you retrieve, store in variables, and modify in expressions is useful only when you can compare it with other pieces of information. Conditional statements let you do this kind of comparison and carry out instructions based on the results. The logic of conditional statements is the same as the logic in the sentence "If abc is true, then do xyz," and in Flash, you define abc (the condition) and xyz (the consequence).

Conditional statements are in the form **if (){}**. You put a condition between the parentheses and the consequences between the curly braces. The *condition*— a statement that can be resolved to a true or false value—usually compares one thing with another. Is the variable **myScore** greater than the variable **alltimeHighScore**? Does the **bytesLoaded** property equal the **bytesTotal** property? Does the variable **myPassword** equal "Abracadabra"? These are typical examples of the types of things that are compared in conditions.

How do you compare values? You use comparison operators.

Comparison operators

A *comparison operator* evaluates the expressions on both sides of itself and returns a value of **true** or **false**. Table 9.2 summarizes the comparison operators.

When the statement is evaluated and the condition holds true, Flash performs the consequences within the **if** statement's curly braces. If the condition turns out to be false, all the actions within the curly braces are ignored **Ⓐ**.

In the following task, you'll create a graphic that moves to the right. You want to constrain the position of the graphic so it doesn't run off the Stage, so you'll construct a conditional statement to have Flash test whether the value of its *x* position is greater than 200 pixels. If it is, you'll keep its current position.

TABLE 9.2 Comparison Operators

Symbol	Description
==	Equality
===	Strict equality (value and data type must be equal)
<	Less than
>	Greater than
<=	Less than or equal to
>=	Greater than or equal to
!=	Not equal to
!==	Strict inequality

```
if (condition) {
  consequence1;
  consequence2;
  consequence3;
}
```

A If, and only if, the condition within the parentheses is true, consequence1, consequence2, and consequence3 are all performed. If the condition is false, all three consequences are ignored.

```
var myShape:Shape = new Shape();
myShape.graphics.lineStyle(1);
myShape.graphics.beginFill(0xff0000);
myShape.graphics.drawRect(100,100,50,50);
addChild(myShape);

stage.addEventListener(Event.ENTER_FRAME, moveSquare);
function moveSquare(myevent:Event):void {
    myShape.x += 5;
}
```

B The code draws a square and moves the **myShape** object continuously to the right across the Stage.

```
var myShape:Shape = new Shape();
myShape.graphics.lineStyle(1);
myShape.graphics.beginFill(0xff0000);
myShape.graphics.drawRect(100,100,50,50);
addChild(myShape);

stage.addEventListener(Event.ENTER_FRAME, moveSquare);
function moveSquare(myevent:Event):void {
    myShape.x += 5;
    if (myShape.x > 200) {
        myShape.x = 200;
    }
}
```

C Add a condition that tests the x property of **myShape** to see if its value exceeds 200. If so, Flash keeps it at 200, preventing the square from moving off the Stage.

x = 200

myShape

D The **myShape** object is limited at x = 200 because of a conditional statement.

To create a conditional statement:

1. For this example, create a **Shape** object, define a line style and fill style, and call the **drawRect()** method to draw a square.

2. Call the **addChild()** method to add the **Shape** object to the display list.

3. Create an **Event.ENTER_FRAME** event handler and, in the function of the event handler, move the position of the **Shape** to the right **B**.

   The rectangle moves to the right continuously.

4. Inside the event-handler function, after the statement that adds to the position of the rectangle, enter:

   ```
   if (myShape.x > 200) {
   }
   ```

   Flash tests to see whether the rectangle's *x* position is greater than 200.

5. Between the curly braces of the **if** statement, assign the value 200 to the **Shape**'s **x** property **C**.

   If the **x** property exceeds 200, Flash resets it to 200. This setting prevents the rectangle from moving past the 200-pixel point.

6. Test your movie **D**.

TIP A common mistake is to mix up the assignment operator (=) and the comparison operator for equality (==). The single equals sign assigns whatever is on the right side of it to whatever is on the left side. Use the single equals sign when you're setting and modifying properties and variables. The double equals sign compares the equality of two things; use it in conditional statements.

Creating a continuous-feedback button

A simple but powerful and widely applicable use of the `if` statement is to monitor the state of a `MouseEvent.MOUSE_DOWN` event and provide continuous actions as long as the mouse button is held down. An object or button that provides this kind of functionality is sometimes called a *continuous-feedback button*. When you hold down a button, for example, you can increase the sound volume (like a television remote control) until you let go. A simple event handler can't accomplish this functionality.

Creating this functionality requires that you use a Boolean variable to keep track of the state of the button. When the button is depressed, the variable is set to `true`. When the button is released or the pointer is moved away from the button, the variable is set to `false`. Within an `Event.ENTER_FRAME` handler, you can monitor the status of the variable continuously with an `if` statement. If the variable is true, the code performs an action. As long as the variable remains true (the button continues to be held down), those actions continue to be executed.

To create a continuous-feedback button:

1. Create a button symbol (or any other object that can receive `MouseEvent`s), place an instance of it on the Stage, and give it an instance name in the Properties inspector.

2. Select the first frame of the main Timeline, and open the Actions panel.

3. Declare a Boolean variable, and set its initial value to `false`.

   This will be the variable that tracks whether the button is being held down.

4. Add an event listener to your button to detect the `MouseEvent.MOUSE_DOWN` event.

5. Add the function that responds to the `MouseEvent.MOUSE_DOWN` event. Between the curly braces of the function, assign the value `true` to your variable **E**.

   The variable is set to `true` whenever the button is pressed. Note that there are no quotation marks around the word *true*, so `true` is treated correctly as a `Boolean` data type, not a string data type.

6. Add another event listener to your button to detect the `MouseEvent.MOUSE_UP` event.

7. Add the function that responds to the `MouseEvent.MOUSE_UP` event. Between the curly braces of the function, assign the value `false` to your variable **F**.

   The variable is set to `false` whenever the button is released.

8. Add another event listener to the Stage to detect the `Event.ENTER_FRAME` event.

```
var pressing:Boolean = false;
button_btn.addEventListener(MouseEvent.MOUSE_DOWN, pressdown)
function pressdown (myevent:MouseEvent):void {
    pressing = true;
}
```

E The variable `pressing` keeps track of whether the button is being pressed or released. When the button is pressed, `pressing` is set to true.

```
var pressing:Boolean = false;
button_btn.addEventListener(MouseEvent.MOUSE_DOWN, pressdown)
function pressdown (myevent:MouseEvent):void {
    pressing = true;
}

button_btn.addEventListener(MouseEvent.MOUSE_UP, letgo)
function letgo (myevent:MouseEvent):void {
    pressing = false;
}
```

F When the button is released, `pressing` is set to false.

9. Add the function that responds to the **Event.ENTER_FRAME** event. Between the curly braces of the function, enter the statement **if (){}**.

10. For the condition (between the parentheses of the **if** statement), enter the variable name followed by two equals signs and then **true**.

The condition tests whether the button is being pressed.

11. Between the curly braces of the **if** statement, choose an action as a consequence that you want to be performed as long as the button is held down **G**.

TIP You can use a shorthand way of testing whether a variable is true or false by eliminating the comparison operator (==). The **if** statement automatically tests whether its condition is true, so you can test whether a variable is true by entering the variable name within the parentheses of the **if** statement, like this:

```
if (myVariable) {
// myVariable is true
}
```

You can test whether a variable is false by preceding the variable name with an exclamation point, which means "not," like so:

```
if (!myVariable) {
// myVariable is not true
}
```

```
var pressing:Boolean = false;
button_btn.addEventListener(MouseEvent.MOUSE_DOWN, pressdown)
function pressdown (myevent:MouseEvent):void {
    pressing = true;
};

button_btn.addEventListener(MouseEvent.MOUSE_UP, letgo)
function letgo (myevent:MouseEvent):void {
    pressing = false;
};

stage.addEventListener(Event.ENTER_FRAME, continuousAction)
function continuousAction(myevent:Event):void {
    if (pressing == true){
        // add actions here
    }
}
```

```
stage.addEventListener(Event.ENTER_FRAME, continuousAction)
function continuousAction(myevent:Event):void {
    if (pressing == true){
        root.gotoAndPlay(currentFrame - 2)
    }
}
```

```
stage.addEventListener(Event.ENTER_FRAME, continuousAction)
function continuousAction(myevent:Event):void {
    if (pressing == true){
        scrollBar.y += 5;
    }
}
```

G The status of the **pressing** variable can be monitored continuously by an **if** statement inside an **Event.ENTER_FRAME** handler. This is a useful method that has wide-ranging application. For example, you can create a rewind button to control the Timeline (middle image) by subtracting a few frames from the current frame as long as the button is held down (bottom code). Another example shown in the bottom code is moving an object on the Stage as long as the button is held down.

Providing Alternatives to Conditions

In many cases, you need to provide an alternative response to the conditional statement. The **else** statement lets you create consequences when the condition in the **if** statement is false. The **else** statement takes care of any condition that the **if** statement doesn't cover.

The **else** statement must be used in conjunction with the **if** statement and follows the syntax and logic of this hypothetical example:

```
if (daytime) {
    goToWork();
} else {
    goToSleep();
}
```

Use **else** for either-or conditions—something that can be just one of two options. In the preceding example, there are only two possibilities: It's either daytime or nighttime. Situations in which the **else** statement can be useful include collision detection, true/false or right/wrong answer checking, and password verification.

For this task, you'll build an **if-else** statement to detect the keyboard input given to the question "Is the earth round?" The answer can be only right or wrong—there are no other alternatives.

To use **else** for the false condition:

1. Select the first frame of the main Timeline, and open the Actions panel.

2. Add an event listener to the Stage to detect the **KeyboardEvent.KEY_DOWN** event.

```
stage.addEventListener(KeyboardEvent.KEY_DOWN, detectText);
function detectText(myevent:KeyboardEvent):void {
    if (myevent.keyCode == 89) {
        answer_txt.text = "correct!";
    } else {
        answer_txt.text = "wrong!";
    }
}
```

A The **if** statement within the **detectText** event handler checks whether the Y key, which corresponds to the key code value of 89, is pressed. The **else** statement triggers the "wrong!" message if a key other than Y is pressed. Note how the **else** statement is commonly written in a group with the **if** statement, beginning on the same line as the ending curly brace of the **if** statement.

answer_txt text field

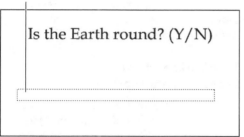

Is the Earth round? (Y/N)

B The message is displayed in a text field on the Stage.

3. On the next line, create the function that gets triggered by the **KeyboardEvent.KEY_DOWN** event.

4. Between the curly braces of the function, create an **if** statement as follows:

```
if (myevent.keyCode == 89) {
    answer_txt.text = "correct!"
}
```

The function checks to see if the key pressed matches the keycode for the Y key, and if so, a message is displayed in a text field called **answer_txt**.

5. On the same line as the closing curly brace of the **if** statement, enter **else** followed by an opening curly brace.

6. On the next line, choose another action as a response to the false condition, and then close the **else** statement with a closing curly brace, like so **A**:

```
if (myevent.keyCode == 89) {
    answer_txt.text = "correct!"
} else {
    answer_txt.text = "wrong!"
}
```

In this example, if the key pressed is Y, the correct-answer message is sent. Otherwise, the incorrect-answer message is sent. The **else** statement covers any key other than Y.

7. On the Stage, create a TLF text field and give it the name **answer_txt** in the Properties inspector.

8. Test your movie **B**.

TIP By convention, the **else** statement cuddles the closing brace of the **if** statement to show that they belong together. In the Auto Format options, however, you can change the Script pane's formatting to put the **else** statement on its own line.

Branching Conditional Statements

If you have multiple possible conditions and just as many consequences, you need to use more complicated branching conditional statements that provide functionality a single **else** statement can't. If you create an interface to a Web site or a game that requires keyboard input, for example, you need to test which keys are pressed and respond appropriately to each keypress. Flash gives you the **else if** statement, which lets you construct multiple responses, as in the following hypothetical example:

```
if (sunny) {
    bringSunglasses();
} else if (raining) {
    bringUmbrella();
} else if (snowing) {
    bringSkis();
}
```

Each **else if** statement has its own condition that it evaluates and its own set of consequences to perform if that condition returns true. Only one condition in the entire **if-else if** code block can be true. If more than one condition is true, Flash performs the consequences for the first true condition it encounters and ignores the rest. In the preceding example, even if it's both sunny *and* snowing, Flash can perform the consequence only for the sunny condition (**bringSunglasses()**) because it appears before the snowing condition. If you want the possibility of multiple conditions to be true, you must construct separate **if** statements that are independent, like the following:

```
if (sunny) {
    bringSunglasses();
}
if (raining) {
    bringUmbrella();
}
if (snowing) {
    bringSkis();
}
```

The following example uses **KeyboardEvent.KEY_DOWN** event handlers and branching conditional statements to move and rotate a movie clip according to different keypresses.

To use **else if** for branching alternatives:

1. Create a movie clip symbol, place an instance of it on the Stage, and give it an instance name in the Properties inspector. In this example, the movie clip is named **beetle_mc**.

2. Select the first frame of the main Timeline, and open the Actions panel.

3. Add an event listener to the Stage to detect the **KeyboardEvent.KEY_DOWN** event.

4. On the next line, create the function that gets triggered by the **KeyboardEvent.KEY_DOWN** event.

5. Between the curly braces of the function, create an **if** statement as follows:

```
if (myevent.keyCode ==
→ Keyboard.UP) {
    beetle_mc.rotation = 0;
    beetle_mc.y -= 30;
}
```

As in the previous task, the **if** statement checks if the key pressed on the

```
stage.addEventListener(KeyboardEvent.KEY_DOWN, detectText);
function detectText(myevent:KeyboardEvent):void {
    if (myevent.keyCode == Keyboard.UP) {
        beetle_mc.rotation = 0;
        beetle_mc.y -= 30;
    }
}
```

A If the up arrow key is pressed, this movie clip is rotated to 0 degrees and is repositioned 30 pixels up the Stage.

```
stage.addEventListener(KeyboardEvent.KEY_DOWN, detectText);
function detectText(myevent:KeyboardEvent):void {
    if (myevent.keyCode == Keyboard.UP) {
        beetle_mc.rotation = 0;
        beetle_mc.y -= 30;
    } else if (myevent.keyCode == Keyboard.LEFT) {
        beetle_mc.rotation = -90;
        beetle_mc.x -= 30;
    } else if (myevent.keyCode == Keyboard.RIGHT) {
        beetle_mc.rotation = 90;
        beetle_mc.x += 30;
    } else if (myevent.keyCode == Keyboard.DOWN) {
        beetle_mc.rotation = 180;
        beetle_mc.y += 30;
    }
}
```

B The **else if** statement provides alternatives to the first condition. The complete script has four conditions that use **if** and **else** if to test whether the up, left, right, or down arrow key is pressed. The rotation and position of the movie clip change depending on which condition holds true.

keyboard matches a particular key and executes the two statements within the curly braces to rotate and move the object.

The two statements within the **if** statement rotate the movie clip so that the head faces the top and subtract 30 pixels from its current *y* position, making it move up the Stage. Recall that the operator **-=** means "subtract this amount and assign the result to myself" **A**.

6. On the same line as the closing curly brace of the **if** statement, enter **else if** and another condition in parentheses and consequences in curly braces as in the following:

```
if (myevent.keyCode ==
→ Keyboard.UP){
    beetle_mc.rotation = 0;
    beetle_mc.y -= 30;
} else if (myevent.keyCode ==
→ Keyboard.LEFT) {
    beetle_mc.rotation = -90;
    beetle_mc.x -= 30;
}
```

7. Add two more **else if** statements in the manner described earlier to test whether **Key.DOWN** is being pressed and whether **Key.RIGHT** is being pressed. Change the rotation and position of the movie clip accordingly.

8. Test your movie.

Your series of **if** and **else if** statements tests whether the user presses the arrow keys and moves the movie clip accordingly **B**. You now have the beginnings of a game!

The switch, case, and default actions

Another way to create alternatives to conditions is to use the **switch**, **case**, and **default** statements instead of the **if** statement. These statements provide a different way to test the equality of an expression. The syntax and logic are shown in this hypothetical example:

```
switch (weather) {
    case sun :
        bringSunglasses();
        break;
    case rain :
        bringUmbrella();
        break;
    case snow :
        bringSkis();
        break;
    default :
        stayHome();
        break;
}
```

Flash compares the expression in the **switch** statement's parentheses to each of the expressions in the **case** statements. If the two expressions are equivalent, the actions after the colon are performed (for example, if **weather** is equal to **sun**, **bringSunglasses** happens). The **break** action is necessary to break out of the **switch** code block after a **case** has matched. Without it, Flash runs through all the actions. The **default** action, which is optional, provides the actions to be performed if no case matches the **switch** expression.

In the following example, you'll create the same functionality as the previous task (moving a movie clip instance around the Stage with different keypresses), but you'll use the **switch** and **case** statements instead of the **if** and **else if** statements.

To use **switch** and **case** for branching alternatives:

1. Create a movie clip symbol, place an instance of it on the Stage, and give it an instance name in the Properties inspector. In this example, the movie clip is named **beetle_mc.**

2. Select the first frame of the main Timeline, and open the Actions panel.

3. Add an event listener to the Stage to detect the **KeyboardEvent.KEY_DOWN** event.

4. On the next line, create the function that gets triggered by the **KeyboardEvent.KEY_DOWN** event.

5. Between the curly braces of the function, enter **switch** followed by a pair of parentheses with a condition inside followed by curly braces, like so:

```
switch (myevent.keyCode) {
}
```

6. Between the curly braces of the **switch** statement, add the following:

```
case Keyboard.UP :
beetle_mc.y -= 30;
beetle_mc.rotation = 0;
break;
```

The **switch** statement will compare the equality of the **myevent.keyCode** to **Keyboard.UP**, and if they are equivalent, the movie clip's position and rotation will be changed. The **break** action discontinues the current code block and makes Flash go on to any ActionScript after the **switch** statement.

7. Repeat step 6, but use different **Keyboard** properties for the case statements and different consequences **C**.

8. Test your movie.

```
stage.addEventListener(KeyboardEvent.KEY_DOWN, detectText);
function detectText(myevent:KeyboardEvent):void {
    switch (myevent.keyCode) {
        case Keyboard.UP :
            beetle_mc.y -= 30;
            beetle_mc.rotation = 0;
            break;
        case Keyboard.LEFT :
            beetle_mc.x -= 30;
            beetle_mc.rotation = -90;
            break;
        case Keyboard.RIGHT :
            beetle_mc.x += 30;
            beetle_mc.rotation = 90;
            break;
        case Keyboard.DOWN :
            beetle_mc.y += 30;
            beetle_mc.rotation = 180;
    }
}
```

C The full script to move a beetle movie clip with the arrow keys, using **switch** and **case** instead of the **if** statement.

Combining Conditions with Logical Operators

You can create compound conditions with the logical operators **&&** (**AND**), **||** (**OR**), and **!** (**NOT**). These operators combine two or more conditions in one **if** statement to test scenarios involving combinations of conditions. You can test whether somebody has entered the correct login and password, for example. Or you can test whether a draggable movie clip is dropped on one valid target or another. You can use the **NOT** operator to test whether a variable contains a valid e-mail address whose domain isn't restricted.

To test if more than one expression is true:

In the Script pane of the Actions panel, enter the **if** statement, then an open parenthesis, followed by the first expression. Enter two ampersands (**&&**) followed by your second expression and a closing parenthesis. Enter a pair of curly braces and consequences between them **Ⓐ**.

Flash checks whether both expressions on either side of the **&&** operator are true before the consequences within the curly braces are executed. Think of the **&&** operator as the word *and*.

```
if (yourAge >= 21 && yourGender == "Male") {
}
```

Ⓐ The logical **&&** operator joins these two expressions so that both must be true for the whole condition to be true.

```
if (yourAge >= 18 || parentalApproval == true) {
}
```

B The logical || operator joins these two expressions so that either must be true for the whole condition to be true.

```
if (!parentalApproval) {
}
```

C The logical ! operator can be used to check if the expression is false. If there is not parental approval, then something will happen.

To test if one of many expressions is true:

In the Script pane of the Actions panel, enter the **if** statement, then an open parenthesis, followed by the first expression. Enter two vertical bars (||) followed by your second expression and a closing parenthesis. Enter a pair of curly braces and consequences in between them **B**.

Flash checks whether one of the expressions on either side of the || operator is true before the consequences within the curly braces are executed. Think of the || operator as the word *or*.

To test if an expression is not true:

In the Script pane of the Actions panel, enter the **if** statement, then an open parenthesis, followed by the exclamation point (!), followed by an expression and a closing parenthesis. Enter a pair of curly braces and consequences between them **C**.

Flash checks whether the expression following the ! operator is false before the consequences within the curly braces are executed. Think of the ! operator as the word *not*.

TIP You can nest if statements within other if statements, which is equivalent to using the logical && operator in a single if statement. These two scripts test whether both conditions are true before setting a new variable:

```
if (yourAge >= 12){
    if (yourAge <= 20) {
        status = "teenager";
    }
}
```

or

```
if (yourAge >= 12 && yourAge <= 20) {
    status = "teenager";
}
```

Looping Statements

With looping statements, you can create an action or set of actions that repeats. For example, you may have actions repeat a certain number of times or as long as a certain condition holds true. Repeating actions are often used together with an *array,* which is a special kind of object that holds multiple values in a structured, easily accessible way. Using a looping action lets you add or retrieve the pieces of data in a particular order. You'll learn more about arrays in Chapter 11, "Manipulating Information."

In general, use looping statements to execute actions automatically a specific number of times by using an incrementing counter variable. The counter variable is used in parameters of methods called in the loop or to modify properties of objects that are created. For example, you can generate intricate patterns by duplicating dynamically drawn shapes with looping statements. Use looping statements to change the properties of a whole series of **DisplayObject**s, modify multiple sound settings, or alter the values of a set of variables.

There are three kinds of looping statements—the **while, do while**, and **for** statements—but they all accomplish the same task. The first two loop types repeat as long as a certain condition holds true. The third statement repeats using a counter variable and a condition that is checked each time the loop repeats. In this example, a new shape is drawn on the Stage and rotated in each loop, creating an overlapping, complex pattern.

To use the **while** statement to repeat a set of statements:

1. Select the first frame of the main Timeline, and open the Actions panel.

2. Declare an **int** variable named **i**, and initialize it to **0**.

   The names **i**, **j**, **k**, and so forth are often used as loop counter variables.

3. On the next line, enter **while**, then a set of parentheses and a set of curly braces.

4. In the parentheses, enter **i < 361** **Ⓐ**.

   This expression acts as a condition, like the condition of an **if** statement. As long as the condition works out to true, the actions in the curly braces of the loop will repeat, but once it's false, the Flash Player will stop looping.

5. Assign any actions that you want to run while the condition remains true (while **i** is less than 361).

   In this example, a **Shape** method is created to draw an ellipse and put it on the display list. The ellipse is rotated according to the counter variable **Ⓑ**.

```
var i:int = 0;
while (i < 361) {
}
```

Ⓐ Initialize the variable **i** and create the condition that must be true for the loop to continue. As long as the variable **i** is less than 361, this loop will run.

```
var i:int = 0;
while (i < 361) {
    var myShape:Shape = new Shape();
    myShape.graphics.lineStyle(1);
    myShape.graphics.drawEllipse(0, 0, 200, 90);
    addChild(myShape);
    myShape.x = 200;
    myShape.y = 200;
    myShape.rotation = i;
}
```

Ⓑ The **myShape** object is created and an ellipse is drawn and rotated based on the counter variable.

```
var i:int = 0;
while (i < 361) {
    var myShape:Shape = new Shape();
    myShape.graphics.lineStyle(1);
    myShape.graphics.drawEllipse(0, 0, 200, 90);
    addChild(myShape);
    myShape.x = 200;
    myShape.y = 200;
    myShape.rotation = i;
    i += 10;
}
```

C At the end of each loop, the variable **i** increases by 10. This loop will run 37 times. The pattern is formed by the combination of the **myShape** objects drawn one at a time in the loop.

```
var i:int = 0;
do {
    var myShape:Shape = new Shape();
    myShape.graphics.lineStyle(1);
    myShape.graphics.drawEllipse(0, 0, 200, 90);
    addChild(myShape);
    myShape.x = 200;
    myShape.y = 200;
    myShape.rotation = i;
    i += 10;
} while (i < 361);
```

D The equivalent **do while** statement.

```
for (var i:int = 0; i < 361; i += 10) {
    var myShape:Shape = new Shape();
    myShape.graphics.lineStyle(1);
    myShape.graphics.drawEllipse(0, 0, 200, 90);
    addChild(myShape);
    myShape.x = 200;
    myShape.y = 200;
    myShape.rotation = i;
}
```

E The equivalent **for** loop. You can read the statements in the parentheses this way: Start my counter at 0; before each loop, check the condition, and as long as it's smaller than 361, perform the loop actions; after each loop, add 10 to my counter and repeat. The **for** loop is the most efficient way of making loops.

6. On the next line, enter **i += 10** or the equivalent statement **i = i + 10**.

   Each time the loop runs, the variable **i** will increase by an increment of 10. When it exceeds 361, the condition that the **while** statement checks at each pass will become false, and Flash will end the loop **C**.

The **do while** statement

The **do while** statement is similar to the **while** statement except that the condition is checked at the end of the loop rather than the beginning. This means the actions in the loop are always executed at least once. The script in the preceding task can be written with the **do while** statement, as shown in **D**.

The **for** statement

The **for** statement provides built-in places to define a counter variable, condition, and operation to increment or decrement the counter, so you don't have to write separate statements. The three statements that go in the parentheses of the **for** statement are **init**, where you can initialize a counter variable; **condition**, which is the expression that is tested before each iteration of the loop; and **next**, which defines a statement to increment or decrement the counter variable. The preceding task's script can be written with a **for** loop, as shown in **E**.

> **TIP** Don't use looping statements to build continuous routines to check a certain condition over time. Real-time testing should be done using an **if** statement in an Event.ENTER_FRAME event handler or from a TIMER event. When Flash executes looping statements, the display remains frozen, and no mouse or keyboard events can be detected.

Continues on next page

TIP With the while and do while statements, make sure the statement that modifies the variable checked in the condition is inside the curly braces. If it isn't, the condition will never be met, and Flash will be stuck executing the loop infinitely. Fortunately, Flash warns you about this problem when it detects a problem in your script that causes it to stall **F**.

TIP Note that the statements within the parentheses of the for statement are separated by semicolons, *not* by commas.

The for..in loop and for each..in loop

Two other kinds of loops, called the for..in loop and the for each..in loop, are used specifically to look through the properties of an object or elements of an array and to look through the values of those properties or elements. You don't need to use a counter variable as you do for the other kinds of loops. Instead, you use a variable called an *iterator*, which is assigned a new value each time the loop repeats.

The built-in properties for objects (the ones that come with the preexisting classes) are hidden from the for..in and the for each..in loop—only properties that you define or elements of an **Array** are available.

To use the for..in loop to reference properties of an object:

In the Script pane of the Actions panel, enter the code as follows:

```
for (var iterator:String in
myObject) {
    // do something with iterator
    trace (iterator);
}
```

You can name the iterator variable anything you want and target any object you want. Flash goes through each property or element inside the object (here, called **myObject**) and returns the name of that property in your iterator variable. So, if **myObject** contained the properties **name** and **age**, the trace statement would return **name** and **age**. You can also put the iterator in square brackets for dynamic property access.

To use the for each..in loop to reference values of an object:

In the Script pane of the Actions panel, enter the code as follows:

```
for each (var iterator:String in
→ myObject) {
    // do something with iterator
    trace (iterator);
}
```

You can name the iterator variable anything you want and target any object you want. In the for each..in loop, the iterator can be typed to any data type, not just a **String** (for example, if you are looping through an array and you know you've only added **int** variables to the array, you can type the iterator as **int**). Flash goes through each property or element inside the object (here, called **myObject**) and returns the *value* of that property in your iterator variable. This loop is useful to automatically go through the elements of an **Array** object or of an **XML** object to access the data.

```
Error: Error #1502: A script has executed for longer than the default
timeout period of 15 seconds.
    at Untitled_fla::MainTimeline/frame1()
```

F This warning dialog box appears when you inadvertently cause an infinite loop.

10

Controlling Text

Like graphic elements, text can be *dynamic*, meaning that you can update the text during playback by changing what characters are displayed as well as how they appear entirely with ActionScript.

Flash Professional CS5 introduces a new and powerful way of working with text, called the Text Layout Framework, or TLF text. You can create layouts with sophisticated typographic control using TLF text. For example, you can make text flow around photos, you can easily create multiple columns, or you can create vertical and right-to-left running text for foreign language support. The older way of working with text, known as Classic text, is still available, and is still a great way to work with text when you don't need the fine control that TLF text allows.

This chapter explores some of the many possibilities of how ActionScript can control both Classic and TLF text. You'll learn to create, format, display, and even analyze text and control the information exchange between your Flash movie and your audience.

In This Chapter

Understanding TLF and Classic Text

TLF stands for Text Layout Framework, and it is the new text engine for Flash Player 10. TLF text supports fine typographic controls—for example, for text that flows around photos or for multicolumn text fields. The sophisticated controls over text are available to you in both the Properties inspector and through ActionScript.

When you choose the Text tool, the Properties inspector provides you with several options for text. You can choose either TLF Text or Classic Text **Ⓐ**. Classic text is the older way of creating text. Although Classic text doesn't support many of the new layout features, you can still dynamically create, modify, and display Classic text. Creating TLF text with ActionScript requires a little more coding. The trade-off is yours to decide; the choice to use TLF text or Classic text should be made based on the level of control your project requires, and the amount of ActionScript you're willing to tackle.

TLF text has three main options: Read Only, Selectable, and Editable **Ⓑ**. All three options enable you to control the text with ActionScript. The options determine what kind of interaction you want your viewers to have with the text:

- **Read Only.** Choose the Read Only option if you want your text to be for display only. The viewer cannot select or edit the text.

- **Selectable.** Choose the Selectable option if you want your viewer to be able to select the text for copying and pasting. However, the viewer cannot delete or edit the text.

- **Editable.** Choose the Editable option if you want your viewer to be able to select, delete, or edit the text. For example, if you want to create a text field for a login and a password, choose the Editable option.

Classic Text also has additional options: Static, Dynamic, and Input **Ⓒ**. These options determine whether the text can be controlled by ActionScript, and whether the text can be selected and edited by the viewer:

- **Static.** Choose the Static Text option if you want your text to be for display only. You cannot control the text with ActionScript and the viewer cannot select or edit the text.

- **Dynamic.** Choose the Dynamic Text option if you want to be able to control the text with ActionScript and allow the viewer to select the text for copying and pasting.

- **Input.** Choose the Input Text option if you want to be able to control the text with ActionScript and allow the viewer be able to select or edit the text.

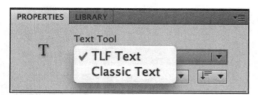

A You have two options for text. TLF text uses the latest text engine in Flash Player 10. Classic text is the older, but still useful, method.

B The options for TLF text determine how the user can interact with the text.

C The options for Classic Text determine how the user can interact with the text as well as whether you can control the text with ActionScript.

D TLF text depends on an external ActionScript library, which is published as a SWZ file next to your SWF file.

The TLF Text ActionScript library

TLF text depends on a specific external ActionScript library to function properly. When you test or publish a movie that contains TLF text, an additional Text Layout SWZ file is created next to your SWF file. The SWZ file is the external ActionScript library that supports TLF text **D**.

How does your SWF file normally find this ActionScript library? When a SWF file that contains TLF text is playing from the Web, the SWF looks for the library in a couple of locations. First, the SWF looks for the library on the local computer it is playing on, where the library is usually cached from normal Internet usage. The SWF also looks on Adobe's site for the library file, and if that fails, it looks in the same directory as the SWF.

You should always keep the SWZ file with your SWF file so the TLF text features work properly when you test your movies locally. You should also have the SWZ file accompany your SWF file when you upload it to your Web server, just to be safe.

Although it's not recommended, you can merge the required ActionScript library (the SWZ file) with your Flash project. When they are merged, you won't have to maintain the separate SWZ file, but the size of your published SWF file will be significantly larger.

To merge the TLF text library:

1. Choose File > Publish Settings. Click the Flash tab and choose Settings for ActionScript 3.0 .

or

Click the Edit button next to Action-Script settings in the Properties inspector.

The Advanced ActionScript 3.0 settings dialog box appears.

2. Click on the Library path tab; then click on the arrow next to the textLayout.swc listing in the display window.

The arrow points downward, expanding the information about the TLF text feature. Notice that the Link Type shows that the Flash file depends on a runtime shared library, and that the URL for the library is on Adobe's site. That is where your Flash file looks for the ActionScript library when it plays on the Web **F**.

3. In the Runtime Shared Library Settings section, choose "Merged into code" for the Default linkage **G**.

The Link Type changes to Merged into code **H**. The current Flash file will merge the TLF Text ActionScript library into the published SWF file.

E Choose ActionScript 3.0 Settings to see the TLF Text ActionScript library sharing options.

F The Link Type for the textLayout.swc indicates that the ActionScript library is shared (and external to your final, published SWF).

G Choose "Merged into code" if you want to merge the TLF Text ActionScript library with your final, published SWF.

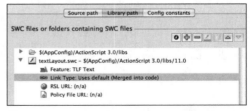

H The Link Type for the textLayout.swc indicates that the ActionScript library is merged.

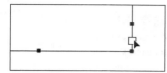

A Click the white square at the bottom right of the text field.

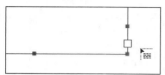

B The icon of a text field indicates that you can define the next linked text field.

First text field

Second text field

C Drag out a second text field.

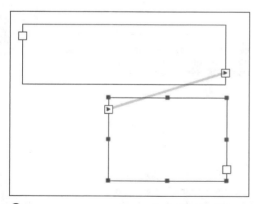

D The two text fields are linked, and they behave as one container.

Creating Wrapping Text

New in Flash Professional CS5 is the ability to create *threaded* text fields using TLF text. What this means is that individual text fields can be linked to each other on the Stage so that text that doesn't fit in one text field can overflow to the next linked text field. By linking together many different-sized text fields, you can make text wrap around objects (such as photos or animations) on the Stage for more complex and visually interesting layouts.

To create wrapping text:

1. Choose the Text tool in the Tools panel, and in the Properties inspector, choose TLF Text.

2. Click on the Stage and drag out a text field.

   A single text field is placed on the Stage.

3. Click the white box on the lower-right corner of your text field **A**.

   Your cursor changes to an icon of the corner of a text field indicating that you can define the top-left corner of the next linked text field **B**.

4. Click and drag a second text field on the Stage or just click on the Stage to define a second text field at the same size as the first **C**.

   The second text field is linked to the first. Blue lines indicate the linkage **D**.

Continues on next page

5. Continue adding additional linked text fields and enter text to wrap your text around any objects on the Stage **E**.

The linked text fields behave as a single container. As you add, delete, and edit text, the contents reflow to fit. You can select all (Edit > Select All), and the contents of all the linked text boxes will be selected.

To edit the text fields:

- Resize any of the text fields by clicking and dragging on the control squares around the blue bounding box **F**.

  If a particular text field is too small to fit its contents, and is not linked to another text field to allow the overflow, a red cross appears in the white box at the lower right of the text field to indicate that text is being cut off.

- Move any of the linked text fields to new locations on the Stage **G**.

  The linkages remain even after text fields are rearranged.

E Three linked text fields wrap text around a graphic element.

F Drag the square control points around the bounding box to change the dimensions of any text field. Here, the text field is becoming taller.

G The flow of text through the text fields maintains its order despite rearranging the text fields.

H The broken link icon indicates that you can break the link to the current text field (the one below the cursor).

I The link icon indicates that you can establish a link to the current text field (the one below the cursor).

To delete a linked text field:

Select the text field and press Delete on the keyboard.

The selected text field is deleted, but the remaining linkages are maintained. For example, if you had three linked text fields, and you deleted the second one, then the first text field would now be linked to the third.

To insert a linked text field:

Click on the white box at the lower right of a linked text field and drag out another text field on an empty part of the Stage.

A new text field is inserted between the existing linked text fields, and the text reflows to fill the new container.

To break or create new text field linkages:

Click on the white box at the lower right of a linked text field and hover over another text field.

If the second text field is linked to the first, your mouse pointer changes to a broken link icon, indicating that you can click on it to break the existing link **H**.

If the second text field is not linked, your mouse pointer changes to an intact link icon, indicating that you can click on it to create a new link to it **I**.

Creating Multicolumn Text

With TLF text, you can easily control how the text fills its individual text field. For example, you can make the text flow in multiple columns, control the spacing in between columns (called the *gutter*), and even change the padding between the text and the bounding box.

The options for creating multicolumn text and changing related properties are in the Container and Flow section of the Properties inspector.

To create multicolumn text:

Select a TLF text field on the Stage and change the value of the Columns field in the Container and Flow section of the Properties inspector .

The selected text field automatically makes the contents of the text field flow in multiple columns .

TIP The maximum number of columns you can set in the Properties inspector is 10. However, you can have more columns by changing the `columnCount` property of the text field with ActionScript, described later in this chapter.

A Enter an integer for the number of columns; there are two columns for this text field.

Lorem ipsum dolor sit amet, consectetur adipiscing elit. Maecenas ut sapien nec massa fermentum cursus id vitae erat. Sed ac nisi nec elit porta accumsan. Etiam vitae risus est. Ut sodales venenatis arcu, ac eleifend justo tincidunt in. Nam feugiat commodo magna.

B A two-column text field.

C A The column gutters value is set at 40 pixels.

40 pixels

Lorem ipsum dolor
sit amet,
consectetur
adipiscing elit.
Maecenas ut
sapien nec massa
fermentum cursus
id vitae erat. Sed

ac nisi nec elit
porta accumsan.
Etiam vitae risus
est. Ut sodales
venenatis arcu, ac
eleifend justo
tincidunt in. Nam
feugiat commodo

D The space between the two columns is 40 pixels.

Constrain the padding values

E The Left, Right, Top, and Bottom values are at 10 pixels.

10 pixels   10 pixels

Lorem ipsum
dolor sit amet,
consectetur
adipiscing elit.
Maecenas ut
sapien nec
massa fermentum

cursus id vitae
erat. Sed ac nisi
nec elit porta
accumsan. Etiam
vitae risus est. Ut
sodales venenatis
arcu.

F There is a 10-pixel space between the text and the outer bounding box.

To change the column spacing:

Select a TLF text field on the Stage and change the value of the column gutters field in the Container and Flow section of the Properties inspector **C**.

The spacing between columns changes based on the pixel value of the column gutters field. All columns are spaced uniformly **D**.

To add spacing around the columns:

Select a TLF text field on the Stage and change the Padding values in the Container and Flow section of the Properties inspector. Change the L (left), R (right), T (top), or B (bottom) values independently, or click the Link icon to constrain the spacing around all sides of the text uniformly **E**.

The spacing between the text and its bounding box (the blue outline) changes based on the pixel values of the Padding fields **F**.

Controlling Text Field Contents

You can control the contents of any text field with ActionScript, giving you the power to dynamically respond to your viewer based on changing conditions in your movie. A scoreboard, for example, can be continuously updated to display the most recent score in a game. Or a calculator can display the results of a custom monthly mortgage on a real estate site.

The property that determines a text field's contents is the **text** property. Text fields of Classic text (Dynamic or Input) or TLF text can be given instance names in the Properties inspector. Once named, use the **text** property in ActionScript to reference the contents of the text field.

Classic text and TLF text are two different ActionScript classes. Text fields of Classic text are instances of the **TextField** class. Text fields of TLF text are instances of the **TLFTextField** class. However, both classes use the **text** property to control their contents.

The following task demonstrates how you can access the contents of one editable text field and assign new contents to another. When viewers enter the temperature in Celsius in an editable text field and press the Tab key, Flash will convert the value to Fahrenheit and display it in a read-only text field.

To control the contents of text fields:

1. Choose the Text tool in the Tools panel, and in the Properties inspector, choose TLF Text and Editable.

2. Drag out a text field on the Stage and in the Properties inspector, enter an instance name **Ⓐ**.

   This first text field will accept a temperature in Celsius.

3. Create a second text field, but make this one TLF Text and Read Only.

4. In the Properties inspector, enter an instance name **Ⓑ**.

   This second text field will display the temperature in Fahrenheit.

5. Select the first frame of the main Timeline, and open the Actions panel.

6. On the first line of the Script pane, add a listener to detect a **KeyboardEvent.KEY_DOWN** event on your editable text field.

Instance name

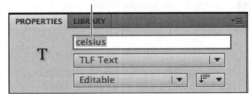

Ⓐ The instance name for this editable text field is celsius.

Instance name

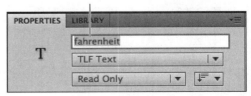

Ⓑ The instance name for this read-only text field is fahrenheit.

7. On the next line, add the function that responds to the **KeyboardEvent.KEY_DOWN** event. Within the curly braces of the function, add an **if** statement to check if the key that is pressed is the Tab key **C**.

8. As the consequence of the **if** statement, perform calculations on the contents of the editable text box (Celsius), and assign the result to a variable that holds **Number** data, as in the following:

```
var conversion:Number = (9 / 5) *
→ Number(celsius.text) + 32;
```

Notice that you must explicitly convert the **text** property of the text field to a number when doing calculations.

9. Next, convert the result to a **String** and assign it to the contents of the second text field, as in the following **D**:

```
fahrenheit.text = String(
→ conversion);
```

10. Test your movie.

When the user enters a number in the editable text field and presses the Tab key, Flash takes the contents and converts them into a Fahrenheit number. It then puts that number in the contents of the second text field to be displayed **E**.

```
celsius.addEventListener(KeyboardEvent.KEY_DOWN, doConversion);
function doConversion(myevent:KeyboardEvent):void {
    if (myevent.keyCode == Keyboard.TAB) {

    }
}
```

C This event handler detects when the Tab key is pressed within the text field called celsius.

```
celsius.addEventListener(KeyboardEvent.KEY_DOWN, doConversion);
function doConversion(myevent:KeyboardEvent):void {
    if (myevent.keyCode == Keyboard.TAB) {
        var conversion:Number = (9 / 5) * Number(celsius.text) + 32;
        fahrenheit.text = String(conversion);
    }
}
```

D The contents of the read-only text field (**fahrenheit.text**) are assigned the correct value from the editable text field (**celsius.text**) when the Tab key is pressed. Use **Number()** and **String()** to convert the data to numbers or text.

Celsius 25 ⎯⎯⎯ *Editable text field*

Fahrenheit 77 ⎯⎯⎯ *Read-only text field*

E The user can convert Celsius to Fahrenheit.

Embedding Fonts and Device Fonts

Normally when you include static or read-only text in Flash, all the font outlines are included in the final SWF. However, for any text that may be edited during runtime, you should embed the fonts. Because the user can enter any kind of text in editable text fields, you need to include those characters in the final SWF to ensure that text appears as you expect it, with the same font that you've chosen in the Properties inspector.

To embed fonts, choose Text > Font Embedding, or click the Embed button in the Character section of the Properties inspector. The Font Embedding dialog box that appears ❶ shows you what fonts you are currently using, and provides options for you to select specific characters of the font you want included.

❶ The Font Embedding dialog box. Fonts appear on the left, and options for embedding select character ranges appear on the right.

Be aware that embedding fonts dramatically increases the size of your exported SWF file, because the information needed to render the fonts is included. Keep the file size down by embedding only the characters your viewers use in the text field.

❶ Device fonts appear at the top of your Character Family pull-down menu.

Another way to maintain small file sizes and eliminate the potential problem caused by viewers not having the matching font is to use *device fonts*. Device fonts are grouped at the top of your Family pull-down menu in the Character section of the Properties inspector ❶. The three device fonts are **_sans**, **_serif**, and **_typewriter**. These options find the fonts on a viewer's computer that most closely resemble the specified device font. The following are the corresponding fonts for the device fonts:

On the Mac:

- **_sans** maps to Helvetica.
- **_serif** maps to Times.
- **_typewriter** maps to Courier.

In Windows:

- **_sans** maps to Arial.
- **_serif** maps to Times New Roman.
- **_typewriter** maps to Courier New.

Displaying HTML

Flash can display HTML-formatted text in Classic text (Input or Dynamic) or in TLF text. This means you can integrate HTML content inside your Flash movie, maintaining the styles and hyperlinks.

Displaying HTML works a little differently, depending on whether you are using Classic text (Input or Dynamic) or TLF text. For Classic text (Input or Dynamic), you must select the Render as HTML option in the Properties inspector and use the **htmlText** property of a text field. When you mark up text with HTML tags and assign the text to the **htmlText** property, Flash interprets the tags and preserves the formatting, including image and anchor tags.

The following common HTML tags are supported by Classic text (Input or Dynamic):

- **<a>**: Anchor tag to create hot links with **href**, **target**, and **event** attributes
- **<b>**: Bold style
- **
**: Line break
- **<font>**: Font style with **color**, **face**, and **size** attributes
- **<img>**: Image tag with **src**, **width**, **height**, **align**, **hspace**, **vspace**, **id**, and **checkPolicyFile** attributes
- **<i>**: Italics style

- **<li>**: List item style
- **<p>**: Paragraph style with **left**, **right**, **center**, and **justify** attributes
- **<span>**: For use with CSS text styles
- **<textformat>**: For use with Flash's **TextFormat** class
- **<u>**: Underline style

For TLF text, you can also assign HTML-formatted text to the **htmlText** property of a text field. However, only a subset of the tags listed above are supported (refer to Help > ActionScript 3.0 Reference for the Flash Platform > TLFTextField > htmlText), and embedding images are handled in a much different, more sophisticated approach that involves the interaction of additional classes. Later in this chapter, you'll learn to import HTML-formatted text and embed inline images for TLF Text.

In this task, you'll load HTML-formatted text from an external document into a Classic Text dynamic text field.

To load and display HTML in a Classic Text dynamic text field:

1. Open a text-editing application or a WYSIWYG HTML editor, and create your HTML document **Ⓐ**.

2. Save the file in the same directory where you'll create your Flash document.

Continues on next page

```
<html><body><p><b>This is an HTML page</b></p><p>This contains
<i>simple</i> HTML tags that <font face="Arial">Flash</font>
can understand. Flash will display HTML formatted text
when the HTML option is selected in Dynamic Text in the
Property Inspector.</p><p><font face="Courier">a href</font>
will also work to create links to Web sites! For example, if
you <font color="#0000FF"><u><a href="http://www.adobe.com">
click here</a></u></font>, you will be sent to Adobe's Web
site.</p>You can also insert images, just like in normal HTML,
like this <img src="logo.jpg"></body></html>
```

Ⓐ The HTML text is saved as a separate document.

3. In Flash, select the Text tool, and in the Properties inspector, choose Classic Text and Dynamic Text.

4. Drag out a large text field that nearly covers the Stage.

5. In the Properties inspector, give the text field an instance name and click the Render as HTML button **B**. Also, make sure that Multiline is selected in the Paragraph section.

   The Render as HTML button lets Flash know to treat the contents of the text field as HTML-formatted text. Multiline allows multiple text lines.

6. Select the first frame of the main Timeline, and open the Actions panel.

7. Create a new **URLLoader** and a new **URLRequest** object and provide the path to the HTML page, like so:

   ```
   var myURLLoader:URLLoader = new
   → URLLoader();
   var myURLRequest:URLRequest = new
   → URLRequest("mypage.html");
   ```

   If your HTML page is in the same folder as your Flash movie, you can just enter the filename, as in this example. You can either load a local file or one that's on the Internet.

8. On the next available line, call the **load()** method for your **URLLoader** object with the **URLRequest** object as its parameter.

9. On the next lines, create an **Event. COMPLETE** event handler to detect the completion of the loading process **C**.

Render as HTML

B Enter display as the instance name for your dynamic text field, and click the Render as HTML button.

```
var myURLLoader:URLLoader = new URLLoader();
var myURLRequest:URLRequest = new URLRequest("mypage.html");
myURLLoader.load(myURLRequest);
myURLLoader.addEventListener(Event.COMPLETE, dataOK);
function dataOK(myevent:Event):void {

}
```

C The external HTML document called "mypage. html" is automatically loaded. When the load is complete, the function called **dataOK** will get triggered.

```
var myURLLoader:URLLoader = new URLLoader();
var myURLRequest:URLRequest = new URLRequest("mypage.html");
myURLLoader.load(myURLRequest);
myURLLoader.addEventListener(Event.COMPLETE, dataOK);
function dataOK(myevent:Event):void {
    display.htmlText = myURLLoader.data;
}
```

D The data property of the **myURLLoader** object, which contains the HTML text, is assigned to the **htmlText** property of the display text field.

Dynamic text field

This is an HTML page

This contains *simple* HTML tags that Flash can understand. Flash will display HTML formatted text when the HTML option is selected in Dynamic Text in the Property Inspector. a href will also work to create links to Web sites! For example, if you click here, you will be sent to Adobe's Web site. You can also insert images, just like in normal HTML, like this

E The dynamic text field displays the HTML-formatted text, including hyperlinks and embedded images.

10. Between the curly braces of the event-handler function, assign the **data** property of your **URLLoader** object to the **htmlText** property of the dynamic text field **D**:

```
display.htmlText =
→ myURLLoader.data;
```

When the load is complete, the contents of the text file are assigned to the dynamic text field. The **htmlText** property displays HTML-tagged text correctly, as would a browser.

11. Test your movie.

The text in the external text file is loaded into the **data** property of the **URLLoader** object. When the file has completely loaded, Flash assigns the information to the **htmlText** property of the dynamic text. The dynamic text field displays the information, preserving all the style and format tags **E**.

TIP Because only a limited number of HTML tags are supported by text fields, you should do a fair amount of testing to see how the information displays. When Flash doesn't understand a tag, it ignores it.

TIP The anchor tag (<a>) normally appears underlined and in a different color in browser environments. In Flash, however, the hot link is indicated only by the pointer changing to a finger. To create the underline and color style for hot links manually, apply the underline tag (<u>) and the font-color tag (<font color="#0000FF">).

TIP The HTML tags override any style settings you assign in the Properties inspector for your dynamic text. If you choose red for your dynamic text, when you display HTML text in the field the <font color> tag will modify the text to a different color.

TIP The <img src> tag supports PNG, JPEG, GIF, and SWF files. So, you can even load in an external Flash movie to play within a dynamic text field!

To display HTML directly in a dynamic text field:

1. In Flash, select the Text tool, and in the Properties inspector, choose Classic Text and Dynamic Text.

2. Drag out a large text field that nearly covers the Stage.

3. In the Properties inspector, give the text field an instance name and click the Render as HTML button. Also make sure the Multiline is selected in the Paragraph section.

   The Render as HTML button lets Flash know to treat the contents of the text field as HTML-formatted text.

4. Enter HTML text within the dynamic text field **F**.

5. Select the first frame of the main Timeline, and open the Actions panel.

6. Assign the current contents of the dynamic text field (the **text** property) to its **htmlText** property as in the following:

   ```
   display.htmlText = display.text;
   ```

   When you test your movie, the current contents of your text field will be rendered as HTML-formatted text **G**.

TIP If you simply need to add a hyperlink in some fixed text, you can do so from the Properties inspector. In a Classic Text static text field, select the words you want hyperlinked, and enter the URL in the Link field in the Options section of the Properties inspector. In a TLF text field, enter the URL in the Link field in the Advanced Character section of the Properties inspector.

Dynamic or input text field

```
<font size = '+3'>Itinerary for our class trip to
Long Island</font><br /><b>Monday = </b>Cape Santa
Maria<br /><b>Tuesday = </b>Columbus Point<br
/><b>Wednesday</b> = Crooked Island
Caves<br><b>Thursday</b> = Deadman's Cay Caves<br
/><b>Friday</b> = Montauk Point<br /></p>
```

F Enter HTML code directly in a dynamic or input text field.

```
Itinerary for our class trip to Long Island
Monday = Cape Santa Maria
Tuesday = Columbus Point
Wednesday = Crooked Island Caves
Thursday = Deadman's Cay Caves
Friday = Montauk Point
```

G At runtime, Flash correctly displays all the HTML code in the text field.

Modifying Text Field Appearances

When you drag a text field on the Stage with the Text tool and name it in the Properties inspector, you're creating an instance of the **TextField** or **TLFTextField** class.

The instance name identifies the text field for targeting purposes. When you can target the text field, you can evaluate or change its many properties. These properties determine the kind and display of the text field. You've already used the **text** property to retrieve and assign the contents of text fields and the **htmlText** property to render HTML-formatted text. There are many other properties, including **columnCount**, which defines the number of columns in a TLF text field, or **borderColor**, which determines the color of the TLF text field's border. In addition, since the **TextField** and **TLFTextField** classes are subclasses of the **DisplayObject** class, they share the same properties to control general appearance on the Stage, such as **rotation**, **alpha**, **x**, **y**, **z**, **scaleX**, **scaleY**, **scaleZ**, and so on.

Refer to the ActionScript 3.0 Reference for the Flash Platform in Help for the extensive list of properties of the **TextField** and **TLFTextField** classes. In this task, you'll explore some of these properties.

To modify the properties of a text field:

1. In Flash, select the Text tool, and in the Properties inspector, choose TLF Text.

2. Drag out a text field on the Stage.

3. In the Properties inspector, give the text field an instance name.

4. Select the first frame of the main Timeline, and open the Actions panel.

5. In the Script pane, enter the instance name of your text field followed by a period, and then enter a property. For this example, choose **textColor**, and enter an equals sign.

6. After the equals sign, enter **0xff0000**.

   The completed statement changes the color of the text to red **A**.

7. Repeat steps 5 and 6, choosing different properties and values to modify your text field **B**.

TIP To modify the font, font size, and other characteristics of the text, you must use the **TextFormat** class for Classic text or the **TextLayoutFormat** class for TLF text, which is discussed later in this chapter.

TIP If you modify the properties **alpha** and **rotation**, you should embed the font outlines for your text field. If you don't, the text may not be rendered correctly.

TIP The properties x and y refer to the top-left corner of the text field.

TIP The properties **width** and **height** change the pixel dimensions of the text field but don't change the size of the text inside the text field. The properties **scaleX, scaleY,** and **scaleZ**, on the other hand, scale the text.

```
mytext.textColor = 0xff0000;
```

A Change the property **textColor** for the text field named **mytext**. In this example, the **textColor** property of the text field **mytext** is set to red.

```
mytext.textColor = 0xff0000;
mytext.background = true;
mytext.backgroundColor = 0x225566;
mytext.border = true;
mytext.borderColor = 0x99ff77;
mytext.rotationY = 45;
mytext.width = 200;
mytext.height = 150;
mytext.columnCount = 2;
mytext.columnGap = 10;
mytext.multiline = true;
mytext.wordWrap = true;
```

B The script modifies many properties of the text field **mytext**, resulting in the text below. Note that text can be affected by properties for formatting as well as general appearances such as transformations in 3D space. The text was already in the text field on the Stage at authortime.

Generating Text Dynamically: Classic vs. TLF Text

So far in this chapter, you've been controlling and modifying text fields that you've created on the Stage with the Text tool during authortime.

However, if you want to have text appear in your movie based on a viewer's interaction, you must be able to create a text field during runtime. When you generate text dynamically, you still have full control over its formatting, style, and many other characteristics.

The process of dynamically creating text varies, depending on if you want to work with Classic or TLF text. For Classic text, you generate text fields with the **TextField** class and modify them with the **TextFormat** class. For TLF text, you can use the **TLFTextField** class and the **TextLayoutFormat** class, but for complex layouts, your text content as well as its formatting, display, and control are separated in different classes such as **TextFlow**, **ContainerController**, **TextConverter**, and **SpanElement**.

Creating Classic Text

To create a Classic text field, use the **TextField** class constructor function, like so:

```
var myTextField:TextField = new
→TextField();
```

This statement creates a new **TextField** instance that you can now fill with text. You can also change the appearance of the text field and add it to the display list to make it visible to the viewer. To assign contents to your new **TextField** object, assign a string to its **text** property, as in **mytextfield.text = "Hello"**. Make the text visible by calling the **addChild()** method, as in:

```
stage.addChild(mytextfield);
```

To create a Classic text field:

1. Select the first frame of the main Time-line, and open the Actions panel.

2. Declare a variable using the **var** statement, and assign it the data type **TextField**. Enter an equals sign and then **new TextField()**. Don't pass any parameters to the constructor.

   Your statement looks something like:

   ```
   var mytextfield:TextField = new
   →TextField();
   ```

3. On the next lines, add content to your **TextField** object by assigning a string to its **text** property.

4. Finally, add the **TextField** object to the display list.

   A text field is created and displayed, with its default properties **A**.

TIP The default size of a dynamically generated **TextField** object is 100 pixels wide by 100 pixels tall.

```
var mytextfield:TextField = new TextField();
mytextfield.text = "Welcome to Flash!";
stage.addChild(mytextfield);
```

Welcome to Flash!

A This code creates a new instance from the **TextField** class, adds text, and displays the instance on the Stage. The dynamically generated text field is positioned at the registration point of its parent, here shown at the top-left corner of the Stage. The default format for a dynamically created text field is black 12-point Times New Roman (Windows) or Times (Mac).

The Default Classic Text Field Appearance

When you create a Classic text field dynamically, it has the following default properties:

```
type = dynamic
selectable = true
embedFonts = false
multiline = false
restrict = null
displayAsPassword = false
maxChars = null
wordWrap = false
background = false
autoSize = none
border = false
alwaysShowSelection = false
autoSize = none
antiAliasType = "normal"
```

The text field also has the following default format properties (which you can change with a **TextFormat** object):

```
font = Times New Roman (Windows)
font = Times (Mac)
leftMargin = 0
rightMargin = 0
size = 12
indent = 0
textColor = 0x000000
leading = 0
bold = false
url = ""
target = ""
italic = false
underline = false
bullet = false
align = "left"
```

To remove a text field:

Call the **removeChild()** method and use the text field as its parameter, as in:

```
removeChild(myTextField);
```

The **TextField** object is removed from the display list and disappears from the Stage or from its **DisplayObjectContainer**.

TIP You can use removeChild() to take away a text field generated dynamically or one that was created at authortime with the Text tool.

Modifying Classic text fields

The **TextFormat** class controls character and paragraph formatting, and can be used to modify a text field.

To change the formatting of a text field, first create a new instance of the **TextFormat** class, like so:

```
var myTF:TextFormat = new
⇥TextFormat();
```

Then assign values to the properties of your **TextFormat** object:

```
myTF.size = 48;
```

Finally, call the **setTextFormat()** method for your text field. This method is a method of the **TextField** class, not of the **TextFormat** class:

```
mytextfield.setTextFormat(myTF);
```

This statement applies the formatting that you define in the **TextFormat** object to the text in the text field. In this example, it changes the size of the text in the text field **mytextfield** to 48 points.

For the full list of **TextFormat** properties, refer to the ActionScript 3.0 Reference for the Flash Platform in Help.

To modify the formatting of a Classic text field:

1. Create a Classic text field, either by generating one with ActionScript with the **TextField** class or by creating one on the Stage with the Text tool.

   In this example, you'll create a text field dynamically **B**.

2. Declare a **TextFormat** object using the **var** statement followed by an equals sign and then the constructor function **new TextFormat()**.

   A new **TextFormat** object is created.

3. On the next lines, enter the name of your **TextFormat** object, followed by a period, then a property name, an equals sign, and a value. For example:

   ```
   myTF.size = 48;
   myTF.color = OxFF0000;
   myTF.italic = true;
   ```

   These three statements assign new values for the size, color, and the italics style **C**.

4. On a new line, enter the name of your text field followed by a period. Then call the **setTextFormat()** method and pass your **TextFormat** object as the parameter **D**.

   The **TextFormat** object provides the information about all the formatting of the text, and the **setTextFormat()** method applies those changes.

```
var mytextfield:TextField = new TextField();
mytextfield.text="Welcome to Flash!";
stage.addChild(mytextfield);
```

B Create a new text field from the **TextField** class, assign text, and add it on the Stage.

```
var mytextfield:TextField = new TextField();
mytextfield.text="Welcome to Flash!";
stage.addChild(mytextfield);

var myTF:TextFormat=new TextFormat();
myTF.size=48;
myTF.color=0xFF0000;
myTF.italic=true;
```

C Instantiate a **TextFormat** object called **myTF**, and assign new values for its size, color, and italics style.

```
var mytextfield:TextField = new TextField();
mytextfield.text="Welcome to Flash!";
stage.addChild(mytextfield);

var myTF:TextFormat=new TextFormat();
myTF.size=48;
myTF.color=0xFF0000;
myTF.italic=true;

mytextfield.setTextFormat(myTF);
```

D Call the **setTextFormat()** method and pass the **TextFormat** object to make the formatting changes.

```
var mytextfield:TextField = new TextField();
mytextfield.text="Welcome to Flash!";
stage.addChild(mytextfield);

var myTF:TextFormat=new TextFormat();
myTF.size=48;
myTF.color=0xFF0000;
myTF.italic=true;

mytextfield.width=600;
mytextfield.height=200;

mytextfield.setTextFormat(myTF);
```

Welcome to Flash!

E The new formatting applies to the entire text field. The width and height properties expand the text field to accommodate the text, but do not change the actual size of the text itself.

5. Be sure to change the **width** and **height** properties of the text field to accommodate the text.

6. Test your movie.

    Flash creates a **TextFormat** object. The properties of the object are passed through the **setTextFormat()** method and modify the existing contents of the text field **E**.

TIP The **setTextFormat()** method changes the formatting of existing text only, so you should already have text in your text field to see the changes. If you add more text after **setTextFormat()** is called, that text will have its original formatting.

TIP You can pass two additional, optional parameters for the **setTextFormat()** method if you want to modify only a span of characters in your text field. The first parameter is the required name of your **TextField** object, the second is the beginning position of the span, and the third is the ending position of the span. The position of each character is numbered with an index starting at 0. So the statement **mytextfield.setTextFormat(myTF, 12, 24)** formats just the characters beginning at index 12 and up to, but not including, index 24.

Embedding and applying fonts

When you want to format a Classic text field with a particular font, you use the **font** property of the **TextFormat** object to provide the name of the font. However, you must do two additional things: First, you must set the **embedFonts** property of the text field to **true**. Second, you must make the font available to the exported SWF by putting it in the Library and marking it in the Linkage options of the Symbol Properties dialog box.

To modify the font of a Classic text field:

1. In the Library, choose New Font from the Options menu **F**.

   The Font Embedding dialog box appears.

2. In the Font Embedding dialog box, choose a font from the pull-down menu **G**.

3. Click the ActionScript tab.

4. In the Linkage section, select Export for ActionScript. Leave the base class as **flash.text.Font**. Click OK **H**.

   Flash may warn you that it can't find a definition for the class. Click OK to dismiss the dialog box. Flash will export the font and include it in your SWF so you can reference it from ActionScript. Your embedded font appears in your library **I**.

5. Select the first frame of the Timeline, and open the Actions panel.

6. On the first line of the Script pane, create a new **TextField** object and add it to the Stage.

7. On the next line, assign some text to the **text** property of your **TextField** object.

F Choose New Font from the Library Options menu.

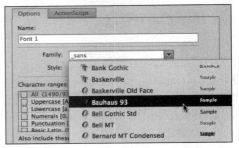

G Choose the font you want from the pull-down menu.

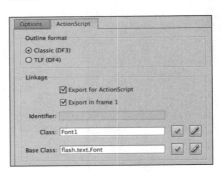

H The ActionScript tab of the Font Embedding dialog box. Select the Export for ActionScript box and leave the Base class as **flash.text.Font**.

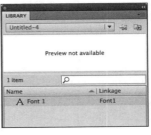

I The font appears in your library.

```
var mytextfield:TextField = new TextField();
stage.addChild(mytextfield);
mytextfield.text = "New fonts!";
mytextfield.embedFonts = true;
```

J The property **embedFonts** must be true if you want to embed fonts for a dynamically generated text field.

```
var mytextfield:TextField = new TextField();
stage.addChild(mytextfield);
mytextfield.text = "New fonts!";
mytextfield.embedFonts = true;

var myTF:TextFormat = new TextFormat();
myTF.font = "Bauhaus 93";
```

K Assign the new font to the font property of your **TextFormat** object. The font is the name that appears in the pull-down menu in your Properties inspector; here it's called "Bauhaus 93." Be sure to use quotation marks around your font name.

```
var mytextfield:TextField = new TextField();
stage.addChild(mytextfield);
mytextfield.text = "New fonts!";
mytextfield.embedFonts = true;

var myTF:TextFormat = new TextFormat();
myTF.font = "Bauhaus 93";

mytextfield.setTextFormat(myTF);
```

L The last step is to use the **setTextFormat()** method and pass your **TextFormat** object. Be sure that you've already assigned text to your text field.

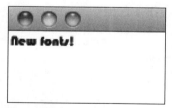

M The text is displayed in the specified font (Bauhaus 93).

8. On the following line, assign the value **true** to the **embedFonts** property of your **TextField** object **J**.

9. On the next line, create a new **TextFormat** object.

10. On the following line, enter the name of your **TextFormat** object, a period, the property **font**, an equals sign, and then the name of your font as it appears in your Properties inspector. Make sure you put quotation marks around the font name.

   Note that the **font** property takes a string value. This is not the name of your font symbol in the Library, nor is it the class name in the Linkage properties. It is the name of the font that appears in the Font field of the Font Symbol Properties dialog box, which is identical to the one that appears in the pull-down menu of fonts in the Properties inspector **K**.

11. On a new line, enter the name of your text field and a dot, and then call the **setTextFormat()** method and pass the **TextFormat** object as the parameter **L**.

12. Test your movie.

   The font symbol in your Library is marked for export into your SWF and is available to be referenced by Action-Script. Flash creates a **TextFormat** object and assigns the font outline to its **font** property. When the **setTextFormat()** method is called, the font is applied to the text field **M**.

TIP Setting the antialiasing of your text field to an advanced setting may help with the rendering and appearance of embedded fonts. Use the statement:

```
mytextfield.antiAliasType =
→ AntiAliasType.ADVANCED;
```

Creating TLF Text Fields

Using TLF text gives you more sophistication over the typography and layout, but it comes with an added price. The low-level and nuanced control over all the details of your text comes with a proportionately larger set of ActionScript code to handle those details.

The simplest way to use TLF text is to create a new text field with the **TLFTextField** class and add it to the Stage. Assign contents to the text field with its **text** property, just as you would do with Classic text:

```
var mytextfield:TLFTextField =
→ new TLFTextField();
stage.addChild(mytextfield);
mytextfield.text = "hello world";
```

However, that's where the similarities between Classic and TLF text ends. TLF text differs from Classic text in that all the text is managed through another class called **TextFlow**. To format a TLF text field, you put the contents of your TLF text field into a **TextFlow** object, and then assign a **TextLayoutFormat** object to the **format** property of your **TextFlow** object, much like this:

```
var mytextflow:TextFlow =
→ new TextFlow();
mytextflow = mytextfield.textFlow;
var myformat:TextLayoutFormat =
→ new TextLayoutFormat();
myformat.fontSize = 14;
mytextflow.format = myformat;
```

Finally, you must call a method, **updateAllControllers()**, to make the formatting take effect:

```
mytextflow.flowComposer.
→ updateAllControllers();
```

To create TLF text:

1. In the Actions panel, enter an **import** statement to include the code for the **TLFTextField** class:

   ```
   import fl.text.TLFTextField;
   ```

2. Create a new instance of a **TLFTextField** and add it to the Stage:

   ```
   var mytextfield:TLFTextField =
   → new TLFTextField();
   stage.addChild(mytextfield);
   ```

3. Assign text to your text field's **text** property, and modify any other properties to change its appearance Ⓐ.

```
import fl.text.TLFTextField;

var mytextfield:TLFTextField = new TLFTextField();
stage.addChild(mytextfield);
mytextfield.text = "Incy Wincy spider climbing up

mytextfield.width = 200;
mytextfield.height = 50;
mytextfield.multiline = true;
mytextfield.wordWrap = true;
mytextfield.columnCount = 2;
mytextfield.columnGap = 20;
```

```
Incy Wincy              spout
spider climbing
up the water
```

Ⓐ This code creates a new instance from the **TLFTextField** class, assigns text, and adds the instance to the Stage. The dynamically generated text field is positioned at the registration point of its parent, here shown at the top-left corner of the Stage. The text field has some of its properties modified: the text displays in two columns.

```
import fl.text.TLFTextField;
import flashx.textLayout.formats.TextLayoutFormat;
import flashx.textLayout.elements.TextFlow;

var mytextfield:TLFTextField = new TLFTextField();
stage.addChild(mytextfield);
mytextfield.text = "Incy Wincy spider climbing up the water spout";

mytextfield.width = 200;
mytextfield.height = 50;
mytextfield.multiline = true;
mytextfield.wordWrap = true;
mytextfield.columnCount = 2;
mytextfield.columnGap = 20;

var myformat:TextLayoutFormat = new TextLayoutFormat();
myformat.textIndent = 0;
myformat.color = 0x336633;
myformat.fontFamily = "Lucida handwriting, _sans";
myformat.fontSize = 12;
```

B The highlighted portion of the code shows the **TextLayoutFormat** object and some formatting properties. You can specify the font family in quotation marks, with alternative font families separated by commas.

```
import fl.text.TLFTextField;
import flashx.textLayout.formats.TextLayoutFormat;
import flashx.textLayout.elements.TextFlow;

var mytextfield:TLFTextField = new TLFTextField();
stage.addChild(mytextfield);
mytextfield.text = "Incy Wincy spider climbing up the water spout";

mytextfield.width = 200;
mytextfield.height = 50;
mytextfield.multiline = true;
mytextfield.wordWrap = true;
mytextfield.columnCount = 2;
mytextfield.columnGap = 20;

var myformat:TextLayoutFormat = new TextLayoutFormat();
myformat.textIndent = 0;
myformat.color = 0x336633;
myformat.fontFamily = "Lucida handwriting, _sans";
myformat.fontSize = 12;

var mytextflow:TextFlow = new TextFlow();
mytextflow = mytextfield.textFlow;
mytextflow.format = myformat;

mytextflow.flowComposer.updateAllControllers();
```

C The full code to create a **TLFTextField** and format it with a **TextLayoutFormat** object. You must use the **TextFlow** object to format the text and to call the **updateAllControllers()** method.

Incy Wincy spider climbing up   the water spout

D The text displays according to the formatting in the **TextLayoutFormat** object. Compare this text with the example with default formatting in **A**.

To format TLF text:

1. Continue with the previous task.

2. In the Actions panel, enter an **import** statement to include the code for the **TextLayoutFormat** and **TextFlow** class:

   ```
   import flashx.textLayout.formats.
   → TextLayoutFormat;
   import flashx.textLayout.elements.
   → TextFlow;
   ```

3. Instantiate a **TextLayoutFormat** object and assign new formatting properties **B**.

   The **TextLayoutFormat** object holds all the formatting information.

4. Create a **TextFlow** object and assign the **textFlow** property of your **TLFTextField** to the new **TextFlow** object.

5. Assign the **TextLayoutFormat** object to the **format** property of your **TextFlow** object.

6. Finally, call the **updateAllControllers()** method on the **flowComposer** of your **TextFlow** object. The full code can be seen here **C**.

   The text is modified according to the formatting properties in the **TextLayoutFormat** object **D**.

Getting Text into the TextFlow

Creating text with a **TLFTextField** object allows you to work with only a single block of text and hides much of the complexity and possibilities behind the TLF text engine. If you're going to use TLF text extensively, you'll want to start with the **TextFlow** object to manage your text rather than the **TLFTextField**.

The **TextFlow** object holds and organizes all your text content. It allows for many different kinds of text content, which can be highly structured, like an outline. The hierarchy lets you organize your overall *story* into paragraphs and individual elements such as pieces of text, inline graphics, or links. The **TextFlow** object is a complicated beast! The **TextFlow** object is organized like so: The **TextFlow** object can contain a div element or a paragraph element. A div element can contain another div element or more paragraph elements. A paragraph element can contain a span element (some text), an inline graphic element (an image), a link element (a hyperlink), and other less common elements. **Ⓐ** shows the hierarchy of elements within the **TextFlow** object.

There are several approaches to get text into the **TextFlow** object. One approach is to use the **TextConverter** class to import text. Another is to define each element of the **TextFlow** hierarchy.

Using the TextConverter

If you have a block of text, use the **TextConverter** class to import the text into your **TextFlow** object. Use the **importToFlow()** method of the **TextConverter** class to specify a specific string and to indicate its format. There are three formats. The string could be just regular text, it could be HTML-formatted text, or it could be structured in a **TextFlow** hierarchy, marked up with div, paragraph, and span elements. If text is marked up in this manner, it is known to be in Text Layout markup format. When you use the **TextConverter** class, make sure you use the **import** statement to include the code in your final published SWF as follows:

```
import flashx.textLayout.conversion.
→ TextConverter;
```

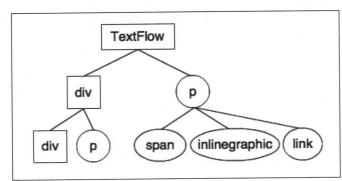

Ⓐ The structure of the **TextFlow** object. The **TextFlow** object can contain a div element or a paragraph element. The div element can contain another div element or a paragraph element. The paragraph element can contain a span (text), inline graphic (image), or link element (hyperlink).

To import plain text into the TextFlow:

In the Actions panel, enter the following script:

```
import flashx.textLayout.conversion.
→TextConverter;
var mystring:String = "Hello world";
var mytextflow:TextFlow = new
→TextFlow();
mytextflow = TextConverter.
→importToFlow(mystring,
→TextConverter.PLAIN_TEXT_FORMAT);
```

You define your text in a variable that holds String data, and then instantiate a new **TextFlow** object. The last line converts the contents of **mystring** from plain text and puts it into the **TextFlow** object.

To import HTML text into the TextFlow:

In the Actions panel, enter the following script:

```
import flashx.textLayout.conversion.
→TextConverter;
var mystring:String = "Hello
→<a href='http://www.adobe.com'>
→Adobe</a>";
var mytextflow:TextFlow = new
→TextFlow();
mytextflow = TextConverter.
→importToFlow(mystring,
→TextConverter.
→TEXT_FIELD_HTML_FORMAT);
```

You define your HTML-formatted text in a variable that holds String data, and then instantiate a new **TextFlow** object. The last line converts the contents of **mystring** from HTML text and puts it into the **TextFlow** object. The HTML format will be preserved.

To import Text Layout markup text into the TextFlow:

In the Actions panel, enter the following script:

```
import flashx.textLayout.conversion.
→TextConverter;
var mystring:String = "<TextFlow
→xmlns='http://ns.adobe.com/
→textLayout/2008'><p><span>Hello
→world</span></p></TextFlow>";
var mytextflow:TextFlow = new
→TextFlow();
mytextflow = TextConverter.
→importToFlow(mystring,
→TextConverter.TEXT_LAYOUT_FORMAT);
```

You define your Text Layout markup text in a variable that holds String data. The root node is **TextFlow** with a required namespace attribute. This is a simple example that contains a paragraph element and a span element inside of it. The last line converts the contents of **mystring** from Text Layout markup text and puts it into the **TextFlow** object.

Using the FlowElements

To get text into a **TextFlow** object, you can also define each element separately and add them to the **TextFlow** hierarchy. The elements of a **TextFlow** hierarchy are classes on their own, and part of a larger collection called **FlowElements**. Create new instances of a **SpanElement**, **DivElement**, **ParagraphElement**, **InlineGraphicElement**, and so on, and use **addChild()** to assign them as children of the **TextFlow**.

If you are defining different elements, make sure you use the **import** statement to include the code in your final published SWF as follows:

```
import flashx.textLayout.elements.*
```

To assign a Span element to the TextFlow:

In the Actions panel, enter the following script:

```
import flashx.textLayout.elements.*
var myparagraphelement:
→ ParagraphElement =
→ new ParagraphElement();
var myspanelement:SpanElement =
→ new SpanElement();
myspanelement.text = "Hello world";
myparagraphelement.addChild(
→ myspanelement);
var mytextflow:TextFlow = new
→ TextFlow();
mytextflow.addChild(
→ myparagraphelement);
```

In this example, a paragraph element and a span element are created. Some text is assigned to the span element. The span element is added to the paragraph element, which is added to the **TextFlow** object **B**.

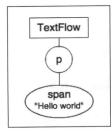

B In this example, the text "Hello world" is assigned to a span element, which is attached to a paragraph element, which is attached to the **TextFlow** object.

To assign an InlineGraphic element to the TextFlow:

In the Actions panel, enter the following script:

```
import flashx.textLayout.elements.*
var mysquare:Sprite=new Sprite();
mysquare.graphics.beginFill(
→ 0x000000);
mysquare.graphics.drawRect(0,0,20,20);
var myparagraphelement:
→ ParagraphElement =
→ new ParagraphElement();
var myinlinegraphicelement:
→ InlineGraphicElement =
→ new InlineGraphicElement();
myinlinegraphicelement.source =
→ mysquare;
```

C In this example, the black square image is assigned to the inline graphic element, which is attached to a paragraph element, which is attached to the `TextFlow` object.

```
myparagraphelement.addChild(
→ myinlinegraphicelement);
var mytextflow:TextFlow =
→ new TextFlow();
mytextflow.addChild(
→ myparagraphelement);
```

In this example, first a small black square is created. Then, a paragraph element and an inline graphic element are created. The square called **mysquare** is assigned as the **source** for the inline graphic element. Finally, the inline graphic element is added to the paragraph element, which is added to the **TextFlow** object **C**.

TIP Remember that a `SpanElement`, `InlineGraphicElement`, or `LinkElement` can't be added to a `TextFlow` directly. They must be a child of a `ParagraphElement`, and the `ParagraphElement` must be a child of the `TextFlow` object.

TIP Notice that the dynamically generated square for the inlinegraphic element did not have to be added to the Stage. In the TLF text model, a controller will eventually add all the contents of the `TextFlow` to a container and make it visible.

TLF Text Containers and Controllers

After you've assigned text to your **TextFlow** object, how do you display it on the Stage? If you wanted to wrap your **TextFlow** contents around a photo, you'd need to create multiple *containers* for the text. Text from one container flows into another, just like threaded text fields that you create with the Text tool on the Stage.

You define a container by simply creating a rectangular **Sprite** on the Stage (see Chapter 7, "Controlling and Displaying Graphics," for more about creating a **Sprite**). You can have just a single container, or multiple containers. However, each container must have its own *controller*. A controller defines the size of the container and manages its contents (text, links, and inline graphics). The controller is created from the **ContainerController** class.

After you have your containers and controllers, you must hook up each controller to your **TextFlow** object with **addController()**, which is done through the **flowComposer**. Finally, use the command **updateAllControllers()** via the **flowComposer**, which makes the text flow into the containers, updating any formatting or content changes, and rendering each line of text.

It helps to visualize the process and relationships **Ⓐ** between the objects at work: the containers (**Sprite**), controllers (**ContainerController**), and the text content (**TextFlow**).

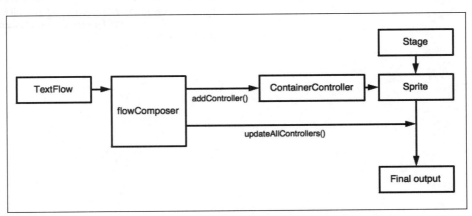

Ⓐ The model and processes that manage TLF text. The **TextFlow** object (at far left) holds all your content. You put **Sprite** objects on the Stage as containers for your content (at far right). The **ContainerController** and **flowComposer** control the flow of the content into the containers for the final output to the viewer.

To display TextFlow content:

1. Open the Actions panel, and import the necessary ActionScript code for TLF text as follows:

```
import flashx.textLayout.
→ container.*;
import flashx.textLayout.
→ elements.*
import flashx.textLayout.
→ conversion.TextConverter;
```

2. Open the Actions panel, and create a **TextFlow** object. Assign content to the **TextFlow** object in any of the ways described in the previous section, "Getting Text into the TextFlow" **B**.

3. On the next line, create a **Sprite** object and add it to the Stage **C**.

   The **Sprite** object will act as the container for your text.

4. Next, create a **ContainerController** object. The three parameters for the constructor are the **Sprite** object, the width, and the height:

```
var mycontainercontroller:
→ ContainerController =
→ new ContainerController(
→ mysprite,200,100);
```

In this example, the **ContainerController** defines the container as 200 pixels wide and 100 pixels high.

5. Now add the controller to your **TextFlow** object via the **flowComposer**:

```
mytextflow.flowComposer.
→ addController(
→ mycontainercontroller);
```

Continues on next page

```
import flashx.textLayout.container.*;
import flashx.textLayout.elements.*;
import flashx.textLayout.conversion.TextConverter;

var mystring:String = "Hello world";
var mytextflow:TextFlow = new TextFlow();
mytextflow = TextConverter.importToFlow(mystring, TextConverter.PLAIN_TEXT_FORMAT);
```

B In this example, the plain text "Hello world" is imported into the **TextFlow**.

```
var mysprite:Sprite = new Sprite();
stage.addChild(mysprite);
```

C Create a **Sprite** object for your container.

6. Finally, call the `updateAllControllers()` method via the `flowComposer`:

```
mytextflow.flowComposer.
→ updateAllControllers();
```

This example has only one controller and one container, but if you did have multiple containers and controllers, this single statement would update them all. The full code and results appear in **D**.

That's a lot of code for just a simple text display! But you can use the same model for more complex layouts. In the next task, you'll have text that flows through two containers.

To display TextFlow content in multiple containers:

1. Continue with the previous task. You'll add an additional container and controller to see how your text flows into both.

2. In the Actions panel, create a second **Sprite** and add it to the Stage **E**.

Each new container requires another **Sprite** object.

```
import flashx.textLayout.container.*;
import flashx.textLayout.elements.*;
import flashx.textLayout.conversion.TextConverter;

var mystring:String = "Hello world";
var mytextflow:TextFlow = new TextFlow();
mytextflow = TextConverter.importToFlow(mystring, TextConverter.PLAIN_TEXT_FORMAT);

var mysprite:Sprite = new Sprite();
stage.addChild(mysprite);

var mycontainercontroller:ContainerController = new ContainerController(mysprite, 200, 100);
mytextflow.flowComposer.addController(mycontainercontroller);
mytextflow.flowComposer.updateAllControllers();
```

Hello world

D The full code makes the **TextFlow** content flow into its container and displays it on the Stage. The container is 200 pixels wide by 100 pixels high, and, by default, is positioned at the upper-left corner of the Stage.

```
var mysprite:Sprite = new Sprite();
var mysprite2:Sprite = new Sprite();
stage.addChild(mysprite);
stage.addChild(mysprite2);
```

E The second **Sprite** object is created and added to the Stage.

```
var mycontainercontroller:ContainerController = new ContainerController(mysprite, 100, 50);
var mycontainercontroller2:ContainerController = new ContainerController(mysprite2, 50, 150);

mysprite2.x = 120;
mysprite2.y = 50;
```

F A second **ContainerController** is added for the second **Sprite** object, and makes it 50 pixels wide and 150 pixels high. The **Sprite** is positioned in a different location on the Stage. The controller for the first sprite has also been changed to 100 pixels wide and 50 pixels high.

3. Create a second **ContainerController** and specify the second **Sprite**, its width, and height. Also, position the **Sprite**s on the Stage where you want by assigning new x and y values **F**.

Each new container requires another controller.

4. Now add the second controller to your **TextFlow** object via the **flowComposer**. The full code should look similar to **G**.

5. Test your movie **H**.

The contents of your **TextFlow** object flows through two containers.

> **TIP** The order in which you add the **ContainerControllers** to the **TextFlow** determines the order that the text flows through the containers.

```
import flashx.textLayout.container.*;
import flashx.textLayout.elements.*;
import flashx.textLayout.conversion.TextConverter;

var mystring:String = "Star Light Star bright, The first star I see tonight, I wish I may, I
var mytextflow:TextFlow = new TextFlow();
mytextflow = TextConverter.importToFlow(mystring, TextConverter.PLAIN_TEXT_FORMAT);

var mysprite:Sprite = new Sprite();
var mysprite2:Sprite = new Sprite();
stage.addChild(mysprite);
stage.addChild(mysprite2);

var mycontainercontroller:ContainerController = new ContainerController(mysprite, 100, 50);
var mycontainercontroller2:ContainerController = new ContainerController(mysprite2, 50, 150);

mysprite2.x = 120;
mysprite2.y = 50;

mytextflow.flowComposer.addController(mycontainercontroller);
mytextflow.flowComposer.addController(mycontainercontroller2);

mytextflow.flowComposer.updateAllControllers();
```

G The full script, with new text content flowing through two containers.

H The **TextFlow** content flows into separate containers— the first is a 100x50 pixel area, and the second is 50x150 pixel area to its lower right.

Formatting the TextFlow

There are two ways to format your text. First, you can use the **TextLayoutFormat** class and create a group of formatting properties like so:

```
var myformat:TextLayoutFormat =
→ new TextLayoutFormat();
myFormat.color = 0x336633;
myFormat.fontFamily = "Arial";
myFormat.fontSize = 14;
```

Refer to the Flash Help > ActionScript 3.0 Reference for the Flash Platform for a full list and explanation of all the formatting properties you can control. Next, you assign the **TextLayoutFormat** object to the **format** property of the **TextFlow** object:

```
mytextflow.format = myformat;
```

In this example, the entire contents of the **TextFlow** object called **mytextflow** is formatted to display in 14 point green Arial.

You can also just apply the **TextLayoutFormat** object to certain elements of the **TextFlow** object. Recall that the **TextFlow** is structured hierarchically with different elements. For example, if you have several span elements, you can just modify the formatting of one of them by assigning its **format** property to the **TextLayoutFormat** object:

```
myspan:SpanElement =
→ new SpanElement();
myspan.text = "some other text";
myspan.format = myformat;
```

The second way of formatting the **TextFlow** content is to add the formatting properties to the Text Layout markup itself. For example, when you define Text Layout markup text to import with the **TextConverter** class, you can add attributes to any of the nodes:

```
var mystring:String = "<TextFlow
→ xmlns='http://ns.adobe.com/
→ textLayout/2008'><p><span color=
→ '0x336633' fontFamily='Arial'
→ fontSize='14'>Hello world</span>
→ </p></TextFlow>";
```

This example modifies the text "Hello world" to display in 14 point green Arial.

Formatting the FlowElements

You can also format the individual **FlowElement**s (span, paragraph, and so on) by assigning new formatting properties directly on the **FlowElement** itself, and not through its **format** property. For example, this statement changes the font size of this span element:

```
myspan.fontSize = 14;
```

However, if you apply a **TextLayoutFormat** object to this span element's **format** property, the previous formatting will be wiped out, and if you don't redefine its **fontSize** property, it will remain undefined.

```
var myformat:TextLayoutFormat = new TextLayoutFormat();
myformat.color = 0xff0000;
myformat.fontFamily = "Marker felt";
myformat.fontSize = 14;
```

A A new **TextLayoutFormat** object holds formatting properties for color, font, and font size.

```
var myformat:TextLayoutFormat = new TextLayoutFormat();
myformat.color = 0xff0000;
myformat.fontFamily = "Marker felt";
myformat.fontSize = 14;

mytextflow.format = myformat;
```

B The **TextLayoutFormat** object is assigned to the **format** property of the **TextFlow** object.

Star Light Star
bright, The first
star I see tonight,

I wish I
may, I
wish I
might,
Have the
wish I
wish
tonight.

C The text is modified with 14 point red Marker felt font. Compare this example to the unformatted example in **H** in the previous section.

To format TextFlow content with the TextLayoutFormat:

1. Continue with the task, "To display TextFlow content in multiple containers."

2. In the Actions panel, make sure you provide the **import** statement for the code for the **TextLayoutFormat** class, as follows:

   import flashx.textLayout.
   ↳ formats.TextLayoutFormat;

3. Instantiate a **TextLayoutFormat** object and assign new formatting properties **A**.

4. Assign the **TextLayoutFormat** object to the **format** property of either your **TextFlow** object or individual **FlowElement** objects **B**.

   Assigning the **TextLayoutFormat** object to the **format** property of the **TextFlow** object modifies its entire contents **C**. Assigning the **TextLayoutFormat** object to the **format** property of a **FlowElement** object modifies just that single element. Make sure that the **updateAllControllers()** method is the last statement in your ActionScript code so the formatting works.

To format TextFlow content in the Text Layout markup:

Assign formatting properties in the particular nodes of your Text Layout markup.

If you assign properties at the root node (in the **<TextFlow>** tag, then the entire contents of the **TextFlow** will be modified. If you assign properties in the individual nodes (**<span>**, for example), then only those nodes will be modified.

Making Text Selectable or Editable

In addition to all the powerful text layout and formatting tools, you can allow the viewer to interact with the text. You can make the text selectable so viewers can copy it, or you can make it editable, so viewers can also paste, delete, modify, or add their own text.

Enabling text to be selectable or editable differs, depending on whether you're working with TLF text (**TextFlow** objects) or Classic text (**TextField** objects). If you're working with TLF text, you'll enlist the help of the **SelectionManager** or the **EditManager** class. If you're working with Classic text, you'll be modifying the properties of the **TextField** object.

To make TLF text selectable:

Assign a new **SelectionManager** object to the **interactionManager** property of your **TextFlow**, as in the following:

```
import flashx.textLayout.edit.
↦ SelectionManager;
mytextflow.interactionManager =
↦ new SelectionManager();
```

The **import** statement includes the necessary code for the **SelectionManager**. The **SelectionManager** makes your **TextFlow** selectable, so your user can select and copy the text but not modify it 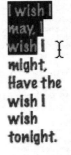. You also have access to many of the methods of the **SelectionManager**, which handles additional functions dealing with making and detecting selections.

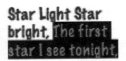

🅐 Viewers can click in the containers and select text. Notice how the selection spans multiple containers.

```
Twinkle, twinkle
little star, how I
wonder how you
                    are. Up
                    above..I
```

B Viewers can delete the contents and enter their own. In this example, the viewer is entering a new nursery rhyme, which flows through the same two containers.

To make TLF text editable:

Assign a new **EditManager** object to the **interactionManager** property of your **TextFlow**, as in the following:

```
import flashx.textLayout.edit.
→ EditManager;
mytextflow.interactionManager =
→ new EditManager();
```

The **import** statement includes the necessary code for the **EditManager**. The **EditManager** makes your **TextFlow** editable, so your user can select, copy, paste, delete, or add text **B**. You also have access to many of the methods of the **EditManager**, which handles additional editing functions.

To make Classic text selectable:

Assign the **selectable** property of a **TextField** to **true**, as in the following:

```
var mytextfield:TextField =
→ new TextField();
mytextfield.selectable = true;
```

To make Classic text editable:

Assign the **type** property of a **TextField** to **TextFieldType.INPUT**, as in the following:

```
var mytextfield:TextField =
→ new TextField();
mytextfield.type =
→ TextFieldType.INPUT;
```

Detecting Text Focus

Sometimes it's useful to be able to detect when a user is interacting with text on the Stage—you may want to know when they've placed their mouse cursor in a text field so you can provide additional relevant feedback, or you may want to know when they've moved off a particular text field.

You can detect when a text field is *focused*, or active, by listening for the **FocusEvent.FOCUS_IN** event. There can only be one focused object, whether it is a text field or a button or any other interactive object on the Stage. The focus is changed when the user presses the Tab key to move to the next interactive object, or if the user uses the mouse to click on another interactive object. You can detect when the user moves away from a text field with the event **FocusEvent.FOCUS_OUT**.

The **FocusEvent** events can be used for either **TextFlow** objects or for **TextField** objects.

To detect the focus of a text field:

1. Create text on the Stage, either with the Text tool in authortime, or with Action-Script during runtime. Make sure the text is selectable.

   In this example, a TLF text editable text field is placed on the Stage. You will detect the focus of this text field.

Detecting Text Selections

In addition to text focus, you can be even more specific and gather information about the actual position of your viewer's selection in a text field. For **TextField** objects, you can reference the properties **caretIndex**, **selectionBeginIndex**, and **selectionEndIndex**. The property **caretIndex** provides the position of the cursor's insertion point (known as a *caret*), **selectionBeginIndex** provides the position of the first character of a selection span, and **selectionEndIndex** provides the position of the last character of a selection span. The position of a character is represented by an integer called an index, starting with 0. So the first character is 0, the second character is 1 (including spaces), and so on.

For **TextFlow** objects, it's a little more complicated. You must first use the **SelectionManager** or the **EditManager** to enable selections. Then you can use the event **SelectionEvent.SELECTION_CHANGE** to detect when the user has made a selection. When the event is dispatched, use the event target's **selectionState.absoluteStart** to get the position of the first character of a selection span and **selectionState.absoluteEnd** to get the last character. For example:

```
mytextflow.addEventListener(SelectionEvent.SELECTION_CHANGE, selectionChanged);
function selectionChanged(e:SelectionEvent):void {
    trace(e.selectionState.absoluteStart)//beginning position
    trace(e.selectionState.absoluteEnd)//ending position
}
```

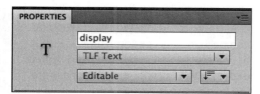

A This editable text field that is created on the Stage is named display.

```
display.addEventListener(FocusEvent.FOCUS_IN, focusdetected);
function focusdetected(myevent:FocusEvent):void {
    trace("You are in the text field!");
}
```

B Listen for the **FocusEvent.FOCUS_IN** event on the display text field.

```
display.addEventListener(FocusEvent.FOCUS_IN, focusdetected);
function focusdetected(myevent:FocusEvent):void {
    trace("You are in the text field!");
}

display.addEventListener(FocusEvent.FOCUS_OUT, focusgone);
function focusgone(myevent:FocusEvent):void {
    trace("You are out of the text field!");
}
```

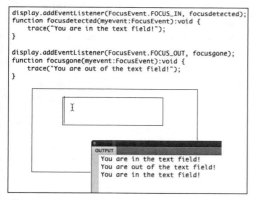

C The script detects when the text field is focused and when it goes out of focus. A message is sent to the Output panel as notice. Clicking on the Stage outside of the text field makes the text field unfocused.

2. In the Properties inspector, enter an instance name for the text field **A**.

3. Select the first frame of the Timeline, and open the Actions panel.

4. Enter the name of your text field, then a dot, and then call the **addEventListener()** method to detect the **FocusEvent.FOCUS_IN** event.

5. On the next line, create the function that will be triggered by the **FocusEvent.FOCUS_IN** event. Between the curly braces of the function, enter a **trace()** statement to provide feedback about the focused text field **B**.

   Flash detects when the text field receives focus, and when it does, displays a message in the Output panel in testing mode.

6. Create another similar event handler for the text field for the **FocusEvent.FOCUS_OUT** event and respond by displaying another message in a **trace()** statement.

7. Test your movie **C**.

When your user puts their cursor in the editable text field, the text field becomes focused, and the **FocusEvent.FOCUS_IN** event is dispatched, displaying a trace message. When your user clicks on the Stage outside the text field, it becomes unfocused, triggering the **FocusEvent.FOCUS_IN** event, and Flash traces a different message.

Analyzing Text

When you define a text field as Input (for Classic text) or Editable (for TLF text), you give your viewers the freedom to enter and edit information. Often, however, you need to analyze the text entered by the viewer before using it. You may want to tease out certain words or identify the location of a particular character or sequence of characters. If you require viewers to enter an e-mail address in an input field, for example, you can check to see whether that address is in the correct format. Or you can check a customer's telephone number, find out the area code based on the first three digits, and personalize a directory or news listing with local interests.

This kind of parsing, manipulation, and control of the information within text fields is done with the **String** class and the **RegExp** class. The **String** class is a data type that represents any sequence of characters. You can create a string simply by passing the piece of text in quotation marks to the constructor function, or more simply, by just assigning the text to a variable. The following statements are equivalent:

```
var myString:String =
→ new String("hello");
var myString:String = "hello";
```

The **String** class provides tools to search, analyze, and replace pieces of text, and compare them to patterns that you might be interested in, which are called *regular expressions*. Regular expressions (from the **RegExp** class) are patterns that you create to identify certain combinations of letters. For example, you may want to search input text for a particular person's name, or a sequence of specific numbers, or any number of character combinations. Regular expressions can be quite simple, as in **/hello/**, which matches the word "hello." But they can also be quite complex and difficult to create, and even more difficult to interpret, as in **/^\d{5}(-\d{4})?$/**, which matches a five-digit zip code with an optional dash and four-digit extension. Learning and mastering regular expressions is not an easy task. Entire books are devoted to regular expressions, but if you're willing to put in the time and effort, you'll have a powerful tool for analyzing text. This section covers regular expressions only at a basic level and looks at how Flash can detect and respond to them.

Matching text patterns with regular expressions

The first step in checking a piece of text for a matching pattern is to create the regular expression. You can do this in one of two ways. You can either use the constructor function of the **RegExp** class to define the regular expression, or you can simply declare a **RegExp** variable and assign the regular expression between two forward slashes (/). In the first approach, you provide the regular expression (in quotation marks) and a flag that modifies the regular expression. For example:

```
var myMatch:RegExp =
→ new RegExp("hello","i");
```

This statement creates a regular expression that matches the word "hello," and the second parameter (the flag) is the modifier that indicates that case should be ignored, so either uppercase or lowercase letters would match.

The second way of creating a regular expression is to simply assign it to a variable, like so:

```
var myMatch:RegExp = /hello/i;
```

In this statement, the regular expression is in between two forward slashes, and the flag immediately follows.

You learned in Chapter 3, "Getting a Handle on ActionScript," that you include special characters in a string by using the backslash (\). The backslash marks an escape sequence inside a string, so if you want to include quotation marks around the pattern "hello", you would write:

```
var myMatch:RegExp =
→ new RegExp("\"hello\"", "i");
```

or simply:

```
var myMatch:RegExp = /"hello"/i
```

Regular expressions use special codes to search for multiple characters and combinations. For example, **\d** is the code to use to search for any digit. To incorporate that code into your regular expression, you would write:

```
var myMatch:RegExp =
→ new RegExp("\\d", "g");
```

or simply:

```
var myMatch:RegExp = /\d/g;
```

The **g** flag in the previous statements is the global modifier that looks for the regular expression throughout the text, not just the first occurrence. Notice that creating regular expressions with strings and the constructor function (the first approach) is a little cumbersome because you have to use *two* backslashes—the first to escape the character and the second to indicate the code to search for any digit. For more complex regular expressions, it becomes difficult to read. For this reason, creating regular expressions by entering them between two forward slashes is the preferred method.

Table 10.1 shows you some common codes that are used to construct patterns for regular expressions. **Table 10.2** lists the various flags that you can use to modify your regular expressions.

TABLE 10.1 Common Codes for Regular Expressions

Code	Description	Example
?	Matches the previous character or group zero or one time (character is optional).	/ab?c/ matches abc or ac.
*	Matches the previous character or group zero or more times.	/ab*c/ matches abc or ac or abbbc, with b any number of times.
+	Matches the previous character or group one or more times.	/ab+c/ matches abc or abbbc, with b any number of times.
.	Matches any one character (except newline (\n) unless the **dotall** flag is set).	/a.c/ matches aac, abc, a4c, and other combinations with any middle character.
|	Or	/hi|hello/ matches hi or hello.
()	Groups the regular expression to confine scope.	/h(i|ey)/ matches hi or hey.
[ ]	Groups possible characters. A dash (–) indicates a range of characters.	/[0–9]/ matches a number from 0 to 9, /[123]/ matches 1, 2, or 3.
{n}	Matches the previous character or group exactly n times.	/a{3}bc/ matches aaabc.
{n,}	Matches the previous character or group at least n times.	/a{3,}bc/ matches aaabc, aaaabc, and other combinations where a is repeated.
{n, m}	Matches the previous character or group at least n times but no more than m times.	/a{3,4}bc/ matches aaabc and aaaabc.
\d	Matches any number.	/a\dc/ matches a1c or a2c, or other combinations where the middle character is a number.
\D	Matches any character other than a number.	/a\Dc/ matches abc but not a2c. Middle character must not be a number.
\s	Matches a whitespace character (space, tab, etc.).	/a\sc / matches a c where the middle character is a whitespace character.
\S	Matches any character other than a whitespace character.	/a\Sc/ matches abc but not a c. Middle character must not be a whitespace character.
\w	Matches any word character.	/a\wc/ matches abc but not a&c. Middle character must be a word character.
\W	Matches any character other than a word character.	/a\Wc/ matches a&c but not abc. Middle character must not be a word character.

TABLE 10.2 Flags for Regular Expressions

Flag	Description
g	Global flag, matches more than one match.
i	Ignore case flag; ignores uppercase or lowercase.
m	Multiline flag.
d	The **dotall** flag. A dot (.) can match the new line character (\n).
x	Extended flag; allows spaces to be ignored for user readability.

To create a regular expression:

1. Select the first frame of the Timeline, and open the Actions panel.

2. Enter **var**, the name of your regular expression, a colon, the **RegExp** data type, an equals sign, a forward slash, your regular expression, and finally another forward slash. Include any of the flag modifiers after the last forward slash **A**.

Your regular expression is defined.

Searching text to match a regular expression

You search text to match a regular expression with several methods. The **String** method **search()** uses a regular expression as its parameter to scan the piece of text and returns the index of the first occurrence of the matching text. The index is the position of each character in a string. If the **search()** method doesn't find a match, Flash returns a value of –1.

The **String** method **match()** also uses a regular expression as its parameter to scan the piece of text, but it returns an **Array** object containing all the occurrences of the actual matching text. If the **match()** method doesn't find a match, Flash returns a value of **null**.

```
var myMatch:RegExp = /(\w|[_.\-])+@((\w|-)+\.)+\w{2,4}+/ig;
```

A This regular expression matches a correctly formed e-mail address, with the **global** and the **ignore case** flags set.

To find the position of a pattern match in a piece of text:

1. Select the first frame of the Timeline, and open the Actions panel.

2. Create a regular expression as described in the previous task **B**.

   In this example, the regular expression **/Flash\s?\d+/ig** matches the word "Flash" followed by any series of numbers with an optional space in between. The flags ignore case and will search globally.

3. On the next line, obtain the text that you want to search. This could be text you assign to a **String** variable, text that you load in from an external document, or text from a text field.

   In this example, just assign a simple piece of text to a **String** variable **C**.

4. On the next line, enter your **String** variable, then a dot. Then call the method **search()** and pass the regular expression as its parameter. Assign the results to the **trace()** method **D**.

   The **search()** method looks through the text to find a match. It returns the position of the match in the display window in testing mode.

5. Test your movie.

To find the pattern matches in a piece of text:

1. Select the first frame of the Timeline, and open the Actions panel.

2. Create a regular expression as described in the previous task.

   In this example, the regular expression **/Flash\s?\d+/ig** matches the word "Flash" followed by any series of numbers with an optional space in between.

```
var myMatch:RegExp = /Flash\s?\d+/ig;
```

B This regular expression matches the word "Flash" and any number of digits, with an optional space in between. The **global** and **ignore case** flags are set.

```
var myMatch:RegExp = /Flash\s?\d+/ig;
var myString:String = "Is Flash 10 much better than Flash 9?";
```

C Create a sample string to test your regular expression.

```
var myMatch:RegExp = /Flash\s?\d+/ig;
var myString:String = "Is Flash 10 much better than Flash 9?";
trace(myString.search(myMatch));

OUTPUT
  3
```

D The **search()** method matches the regular expression with your string and returns the index position of the match. The word "Flash 10" matched and was located at index 3.

```
var myMatch:RegExp = /Flash\s?\d+/ig;
var myString:String = "Is Flash 10 much better than Flash 9?";
var myArray:Array = myString.match(myMatch);
```

E The **match()** method matches the regular expression with your string and returns an **Array** object containing the matched substrings.

```
var myMatch:RegExp = /Flash\s?\d+/ig;
var myString:String = "Is Flash 10 much better than Flash 9?";
var myArray:Array = myString.match(myMatch);
trace(myArray[0]);
trace(myArray[1]);
```

```
OUTPUT
  Flash 10
  Flash 9
```

F To see the matched terms, display the elements in the **Array** to the Output panel. Here, you see that two matches were found: "Flash 10" and "Flash 9".

The flags ignore case and will search globally.

3. On the next line, obtain the text that you want to search. This could be text that you assign to a **String** variable, text that you load in from an external document, or text from a text field.

   In this example, just assign a simple piece of text to a **String** variable.

4. On the next line, enter your **String** variable, then a dot. Then call the method **match()** and pass the regular expression as its parameter. Assign the results to an **Array** object **E**.

   The **match()** method looks through the text to find a match. It returns an **Array** object that contains all the occurrences of the match.

5. On the next line, enter the **trace()** method to display the elements of the **Array** object. Test your movie **F**.

   The matches are displayed in the display window in testing mode.

Greedy and Lazy Matches

Sometimes when you search for particular patterns with character repetitions (using *****, **+**, or **{ }** sequences), Flash will grab more than you actually want. For example, suppose you look for a sequence of characters that begin with "www." and end with ".com", with any number of characters in the middle using the code **.+** (match any character multiple times). If you searched the following string, "My favorite Web sites are www.adobe.com as well as www.peachpit.com", the resulting match would be "www.adobe.com as well as www.peachpit.com" because Flash first matches "www.", then marches all the way through the string because of the **.+** instructions. When it reaches the end, it backtracks and finds the ".com" match and stops. This is called a *greedy* match. To fix this problem, you need to tell Flash to match the fewest number of characters as possible. You can do so by specifying a *lazy* match, which is indicated by a question mark (**?**). If you use the code **.+?** instead of just **.+**, Flash will match the minimum number of characters until it finds the next match.

Searching and replacing text

When you find matches for your regular expression in a piece of text, you can replace the matches with another string, much like the search and replace function in a word processing application. You use the **String** class method **replace()**, which takes two parameters: one for the regular expression and another for the replacement string.

The replacement string can also include codes in it to allow parts of the pattern to be used as the replacement. **Table 10.3** lists the replacement codes. This is a powerful way to replace text. For example, you could search a text document with Web site addresses that begin with "www." and end in ".com". Once identified, you can strip them out and put them back in with HTML anchor tags around them, such as **<a href></a>**.

To replace the pattern matches in a piece of text:

1. Select the first frame of the Timeline, and open the Actions panel.

2. Create a regular expression as described in the previous task **G**.

    In this example, the regular expression **/www\..+?\.com/ig** matches any sequence of text that begins with "www." and ends with ".com". The question mark is a code to identify a lazy pattern so multiple sequences of Web sites can be identified (see the sidebar "Greedy and Lazy Matches").

TABLE 10.3 Replacement Codes

Code	Description
$&	The matched substring.
$`	The text that precedes the match. Note that the code uses the backtick key found on the same key as the tilde (the key to the left of the number 1 key).
$'	The text that follows the match. Note that the code uses the single-quote character, which is found to the left of the Enter key.
$n	The nth group match.
x	Extended flag; allows spaces to be ignored for user readability.

```
var myMatch:RegExp = /www\..+?\.com/ig;
```

G This regular expression is a simple check for a Web address beginning with "www." and ending with ".com".

3. On the next line, obtain the text that you want to search. This could be text that you assign to a **String** variable, text that you load in from an external document, or text from a text field.

In this example, just assign a simple piece of text to a **String** variable **ⓗ**.

4. On the next line, enter your **String** variable, then a dot. Then call the method **replace()** and pass the regular expression as its first parameter. For its second parameter, enter **ⓘ**:

```
"<a href=\"http://$&\">$&</a>"
```

The replacement string includes quotation marks that are escaped as well as replacement codes (**$&**) that insert the matched text at those specified points.

5. On the next line, create a new Classic text field and display the results of the replaced string **ⓙ**.

The Web site names are stripped out and put back in with HTML anchor tags around them to make them clickable in the newly generated text field **ⓚ**.

TIP The **String** class methods that you've learned in the preceding section, **search()**, **match()**, and **replace()**, don't necessarily have to always use regular expressions as parameters. You can also use these methods just with normal strings. Make sure you pass string parameters with quotation marks.

```
var myMatch:RegExp = /www\..+?\.com/ig;
var myString:String = "Visit Adobe at www.adobe.com or my website at www.RussellChun.com";
```

ⓗ Create a sample string with a few Web site addresses.

```
var myMatch:RegExp = /www\..+?\.com/ig;
var myString:String = "Visit Adobe at www.adobe.com or my website at www.RussellChun.com";
var myResult:String = myString.replace(myMatch, "<a href=\"http://$&\">$&</a>");
```

ⓘ The **replace()** method can replace the matched terms with new text. Here, it will replace the matches with anchor tags in front, then put in the matched substrings, and anchor tags behind, to automatically format it as HTML.

```
var myMatch:RegExp = /www\..+?\.com/ig;
var myString:String = "Visit Adobe at www.adobe.com or my website at www.RussellChun.com";
var myResult:String = myString.replace(myMatch, "<a href=\"http://$&\">$&</a>");

var myTextField:TextField = new TextField();
myTextField.width = 500;
myTextField.multiline = true;
myTextField.htmlText = myResult;
addChild(myTextField);
```

ⓙ The full script.

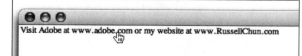

ⓚ When the **replace()** method has done its work and the results are displayed in a text field, the Web links become active.

Searching for a simple string

When you don't need to find patterns with regular expressions, you can rely on simpler methods to search for a piece of text. The methods discussed previously, the **search()**, **match()**, and **replace()** methods, can take regular strings as their parameters. Instead of searching for a pattern match, Flash searches for an exact match of the string. A few other methods work using simple strings as the search term. The **String** method **indexOf()** searches text for a character or a sequence of characters and returns the index position of its first occurrence.

To identify the position of a character or characters:

1. In the Actions panel, enter the **String** you want to search, then a dot; then call the **indexOf()** method.

2. For the parameters of the **indexOf()** method, enter a character or sequence of characters within quotation marks, a comma, and then an optional index number.

   The **indexOf()** method takes two parameters: **searchString** and **fromIndex**. The parameter **searchString** is the specific character or characters you want to identify in the **String**. The parameter **fromIndex**, which is optional, is a **Number** representing the starting position for the search within the **String**.

   Flash searches the contents of the **String** for the specified character and returns the index position of the character ❶.

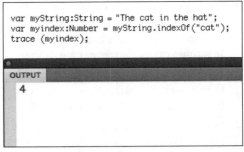

```
var myString:String = "The cat in the hat";
var myindex:Number = myString.indexOf("cat");
trace (myindex);
```

```
OUTPUT
    4
```

❶ The **indexOf()** method returns the first occurrence of the simple string search term. The word "cat" appears at index 4.

TIP The opposite of the method **indexOf()** is **charAt()**. This method returns the character that occupies the index position you specify for a string.

TIP If the character you search for with **indexOf()** occurs more than once in the string, Flash returns the index of only the first occurrence. Use the method **lastIndexOf()** to retrieve the last occurrence of the character.

TIP If Flash searches a **String** with the **indexOf()** or **lastIndexOf()** method and doesn't find the specified character, it returns a value of −1. You can use this fact to check for missing characters within a string. For example, if **indexOf("%") == −1**, you know that the percent symbol is missing from the string.

```
input.addEventListener(KeyboardEvent.KEY_DOWN, enterkey);
function enterkey(myevent:KeyboardEvent):void {
    if (myevent.keyCode == Keyboard.ENTER) {

    }
}
```

M This event handler detects when the user presses the Enter key while the text field called input has focus.

Determining a String's size

The **String** class has one property, **length**, that tells you the number of characters in the **String**. This is a read-only property that is useful for checking the relative positions of characters. Since you know the value of **length**, you can always target the last character of a **String**, which would have the index position of **length-1**.

One way you can use the **length** property is to make sure that the **length** of a Classic text input field isn't 0 (meaning that the viewer hasn't entered anything). If it is 0, you can send an error message or further instructions for the viewer. The following task demonstrates this application.

To check the length of a String:

1. Select the Text tool in the Tools panel, and choose Classic Text and Input Text.

2. Drag out a text field on the Stage and in the Properties inspector, enter an instance name.

3. Select the first frame of the main Timeline, and open the Actions panel.

4. On the first line, assign an event handler to detect the **KeyboardEvent.KEY_DOWN** event in the text field.

5. Inside the event-handler function, enter a conditional statement with the **if** statement as follows **M**:

   ```
   if (myevent.keyCode ==
   Keyboard.ENTER){
       }
   ```

   Flash checks to see if the key that is pressed is Enter.

   Continues on next page

6. Inside the **if** statement's curly braces, create another conditional statement that checks if the **length** property of the text field is 0. As the consequence, assign some text to the **text** property of the input text field as follows **N**:

```
if (input.length == 0) {
input.text = "Please enter your
→ name!";
}
```

Flash checks the **length** property of the input text field. If there is no content, the value of **length** is 0, and Flash can respond with an appropriate message.

7. Test your movie **O**.

```
input.addEventListener(KeyboardEvent.KEY_DOWN, enterkey);
function enterkey(myevent:KeyboardEvent):void {
    if (myevent.keyCode == Keyboard.ENTER) {
        if (input.length == 0) {
            input.text = "Please enter your name!";
        }
    }
}
```

N The conditional statement (highlighted) inside the event-handler function checks if the length of the text field's contents is 0, which means no information has been entered.

Please enter your name!

O If the user presses Enter without any text in the text field, this message is displayed.

Manipulating Information

The information that you store in variables, modify with expressions, and test in conditional statements often needs to be processed and manipulated by mathematical functions such as square roots, sines, cosines, and exponents. Flash can perform these calculations with the **Math** class, which lets you create formulas for complicated interactions between the objects in your movie and your viewer or for sophisticated physics in your motion. You can also turn to the **Point** class for help in geometry. Imagine modeling the correct trajectory of colliding objects to create a game of pool, simulating the effects of gravity for a physics tutorial, calculating probabilities for a card game, or generating random numbers to add unpredictable elements to your movie. All of those scenarios are possible with the **Math** and **Point** classes. Much of the information you manipulate sometimes needs to be stored in a structured manner to give you better control of your data and a more efficient way to retrieve it. You can use the **Array** class to keep track of ordered sets of data such as shopping lists, color tables, and scorecards.

In This Chapter

When the information you need depends on the time or the date, you can use the **Date** class to retrieve the current year, month, or even millisecond.

This chapter explores the variety of ways you can manipulate information with added complexity and shows you how to integrate many of the predefined classes you've learned about in previous chapters.

Making Calculations with the Math Class

The **Math** class lets you access trigono-metric functions such as sine, cosine, and tangent; logarithmic functions; rounding functions; and mathematical constants such as pi and e. **Table 11.1** summarizes the methods and properties of the **Math** class. The **Math** class has static methods and properties, which means you don't need to create an instance of the **Math** class to access them. Instead, you precede the method or property with the class name, **Math**. To calculate the square root of 10, for example, you write:

```
var myAnswer:Number = Math.sqrt(10);
```

The calculated value is put in the variable **myAnswer**.

All the **Math** class's properties are read-only values that are written in all uppercase letters. To use a constant, use syntax like this:

```
var myCircum:Number = Math.PI * 2 *
→ myRadius;
```

The mathematical constant *pi* is multiplied by 2 and the variable **myRadius**, and the result is put into the variable **myCircum**.

TABLE 11.1 Methods and Properties of the Math Class

abs(number)	Calculates the absolute value. Math.abs(-4) returns 4.
acos(number)	Calculates the arc cosine.
asin(number)	Calculates the arc sine.
atan(number)	Calculates the arc tangent.
atan2(y, x)	Calculates the angle (in radians) from the x-axis to a point on the y-axis.
ceil(number)	Rounds the number up to the nearest integer. Math.ceil(2.34) returns 3.
cos(number)	Calculates the cosine of an angle, in radians.
exp(number)	Calculates the exponent of the constant e.
floor(number)	Rounds the number down to the nearest integer. Math.floor(2.34) returns 2.
log(number)	Calculates the natural logarithm.
max(x, y)	Returns the larger of two values. Math.max(2, 7) returns 7.
min(x, y)	Returns the smaller of two values. Math.min(2, 7) returns 2.
pow(base, exponent)	Calculates the exponent of a number.
random()	Returns a random number between 0 and 1 (including 0 but not including 1).
round(number)	Rounds the number to the nearest integer. Math.round(2.34) returns 2.
sin(number)	Calculates the sine of an angle, in radians.
sqrt(number)	Calculates the square root.
tan(number)	Calculates the tangent of an angle, in radians.
E	Euler's constant e; the base of natural logarithms.
LN2	The natural logarithm of 2.
LOG2E	The base-2 logarithm of e.
LN10	The natural logarithm of 10.
LOG10E	The base-10 logarithm of e.
PI	The circumference of a circle divided by its diameter.
SQRT1_2	The square root of 1/2.
SQRT2	The square root of 2.

Calculating Angles

The angle that an object makes relative to the Stage or to another object is useful information for creating many game interactions, as well as for creating dynamic animations and interfaces based purely in ActionScript. To create a dial that controls the sound volume, for example, compute the angle at which your viewer drags the dial relative to the horizontal or vertical axis, and then change the dial's rotation and the sound volume accordingly. Calculating the angle also requires that you brush up on some of your high school trigonometry, so a review of some basic principles related to sine, cosine, and tangent is in order.

The mnemonic device *SOH CAH TOA* can help you keep the trigonometric functions straight. This acronym stands for Sine = Opposite over Hypotenuse, Cosine = Adjacent over Hypotenuse, and Tangent = Opposite over Adjacent . Knowing the length of any two sides of a right triangle is enough information to calculate the other two angles. You'll most likely know the lengths of the opposite and adjacent sides of the triangle because they represent the y- and x-coordinates of a point **B**. When you have the x- and y-coordinates, you can calculate the angle (theta) by using the following mathematical formulas:

```
tan theta = opposite / adjacent
```

or

```
tan theta = y / x
```

or

```
theta = arctan(y / x)
```

In Flash, you can write this expression by using the **Math** class this way:

```
var myTheta:Number = Math.atan(
→this.y / this.x);
```

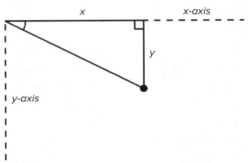

Sin theta = opposite/hypotenuse
Cos theta = adjacent/hypotenuse
Tan theta = opposite/adjacent

A The angle, theta, of a right triangle is defined by sin, cos, and tan and by the length of the three sides.

B A point on the Stage makes a right triangle with x (adjacent side) and y (opposite side).

Alternatively, Flash provides an even easier method that lets you define the Y and X positions without having to do the division. The **Math.atan2()** method accepts the Y and X positions as two parameters, so you can write the equivalent statement:

```
var myTheta:Number = Math.atan2(
→ this.y, this.x);
```

Unfortunately, the trigonometric methods of the **Math** class require and return angle values in radians, which describe angles in terms of the constant pi—easier mathematically, but not so convenient if you want to use the values to modify the **rotation** property of an object. You can convert an angle from radians to degrees, and vice versa, by using the following formulas:

```
radians = Math.PI / 180 * degrees;
degrees = radians * 180 / Math.PI;
```

The following tasks calculate the angle of the mouse pointer relative to the Stage and display the angle (in degrees) in a text field.

To calculate the angle relative to the Stage:

1. Create a TLF Read Only text field on the Stage, and give the text field an instance name in the Properties inspector.

   In this example, the text field is called **myDegrees_txt**.

2. Select the first frame of the main Timeline, and open the Actions panel.

3. Create a new instance of the **Shape** class.

   You will dynamically draw a line segment from the top-left corner of the Stage to the current position of your mouse pointer to visualize the angle.

4. On the next line, add an event listener to the Stage to detect the **Event.ENTER_FRAME** event.

5. On the next line, create the function that responds to the **Event.ENTER_FRAME** event **C**.

Continues on next page

```
var myShape:Shape = new Shape();
stage.addEventListener(Event.ENTER_FRAME, displayangle);
function displayangle(myevent:Event):void {

}
```

C The **ENTER_FRAME** event happens continuously.

6. Within the curly braces of the function, enter this statement:

```
var myRadians:Number =
→ Math.atan2(mouseY, mouseX);
```

The current mouse position is used to calculate the angle (in radians) it makes with the top of the Stage.

7. On the next line, still within the function, enter the statement:

```
var myDegrees:Number = myRadians
→ * 180 / Math.PI;
```

The angle is converted from radians to degrees and then assigned to the variable called **myDegrees**.

8. On the next line, still within the function, convert **myDegrees** to a string and assign the string to the **text** property of your dynamic text field. Concatenate the string **" degrees"** to the end of the text field **D**.

The angle (now in degrees) is displayed in the text field.

9. On the next line, still within the function, call the **clear()** method of the **graphics** property of your **Shape** object.

10. Next, assign a line style and a fill style to the **graphics** property of your **Shape** object.

```
var myShape:Shape = new Shape();
stage.addEventListener(Event.ENTER_FRAME, displayangle);
function displayangle(myevent:Event):void {
    var myRadians:Number = Math.atan2(mouseY, mouseX);
    var myDegrees:Number = myRadians * 180 / Math.PI;
    myDegrees_txt.text =  String(myDegrees) + " degrees";
}
```

D The `Math.atan2()` method calculates the angle that the mouse pointer makes with the origin (top-left corner of the Stage). The results are converted into degrees, converted into a string, and displayed in the text field called **myDegrees_txt**.

11. Next, call the **moveTo()** method to move the drawing location to **0, 0**; call the **lineTo()** method to the **mouseX** and **mouseY** position; and call another **lineTo()** method to the **mouseX** and **0** position.

The dynamic drawing methods draw line segments from the corner of the Stage to the mouse pointer and up to the top edge of the Stage, creating the triangle whose sides are used to calculate the angle.

12. Add the **Shape** object to the display list with the **addChild()** method ⓔ.

13. Test your movie.

As the viewer moves the pointer around the Stage, Flash calculates the angle that the mouse pointer makes with the x-axis of the root Timeline and displays the angle (in degrees) in the text field. The triangle is also drawn between the top-left corner of the Stage, the mouse pointer, and the x-axis ⓕ.

```
var myShape:Shape = new Shape();
stage.addEventListener(Event.ENTER_FRAME, displayangle);
function displayangle(myevent:Event):void {
    var myRadians:Number = Math.atan2(mouseY, mouseX);
    var myDegrees:Number = myRadians * 180 / Math.PI;
    myDegrees_txt.text = String(myDegrees) + " degrees";
    //
    // draw lines to show triangle
    //
    myShape.graphics.clear();
    myShape.graphics.lineStyle(1, 0x000000, 1);
    myShape.graphics.beginFill(0xff0000, .5);
    myShape.graphics.moveTo(0, 0);
    myShape.graphics.lineTo(mouseX, mouseY);
    myShape.graphics.lineTo(mouseX, 0);
    addChild(myShape);
}
```

ⓔ The lines are drawn dynamically to show the triangle whose angle is being measured.

myRadians

x

myShape dynamically drawn graphics

Mouse pointer

64.707978842971

myDegrees_txt text field

ⓕ The line between the top-left corner of the Stage and the mouse pointer makes an angle of approximately 65 degrees below the x-axis.

Rounding off decimals

So far, the returned values for your angles have had many decimal places. Often, you need to round those values to the nearest whole number (or integer) so that you can use the values as parameters in methods and properties. Use `Math.round()` to round values to the nearest integer, `Math.ceil()` to round up to the closest integer greater than or equal to the value, and `Math.floor()` to round down to the closest integer less than or equal to the value.

To round a number to an integer:

1. Continuing with the file you used in the preceding task, select the first frame of the main Timeline and open the Actions panel.

2. Select the statement that converts the angle from radians to degrees.

3. Place your pointer in front of the expression, and enter the method `Math.round()` **G**.

   Flash converts the angle from radians to degrees and then applies the method `Math.round()` to that value, returning an integer **H**.

```
var myShape:Shape = new Shape();
stage.addEventListener(Event.ENTER_FRAME, displayangle);
function displayangle(myevent:Event):void {
    var myRadians:Number = Math.atan2(mouseY, mouseX);
    var myDegrees:Number = Math.round(myRadians * 180 / Math.PI);
    myDegrees_txt.text =  String(myDegrees) + " degrees";
    //
    // draw lines to show triangle
    //
    myShape.graphics.clear();
    myShape.graphics.lineStyle(1, 0x000000, 1);
    myShape.graphics.beginFill(0xff0000, .5);
    myShape.graphics.moveTo(0, 0);
    myShape.graphics.lineTo(mouseX, mouseY);
    myShape.graphics.lineTo(mouseX, 0);
    addChild(myShape);
}
```

G The expression within the parentheses (in the highlighted statement) is rounded to the nearest integer using `Math.round()` and displayed in the text field **myDegrees_txt**.

58 degrees ——— Text field

H The text field displays the angle rounded to the nearest whole number.

Putting it together: Creating a rotating dial

You can apply the methods that calculate angles and round values to create a draggable rotating dial. The approach is to calculate the angle of the mouse's position relative to the center point of the dial and then set the **rotation** property of the dial to that angle.

To create a rotating dial:

1. Create a movie clip symbol of a dial, place an instance of it on the Stage, and give it a name in the Properties inspector.

   In this example, the name is **myDial_mc** .

2. Select the first frame of the main Timeline, and open the Actions panel.

3. Declare a **Boolean** variable named **pressing** followed by an equals sign and the value **false**.

   This variable keeps track of whether your viewer is pressing or not pressing this movie clip.

4. On the next line, create the listener that detects the **MouseEvent.MOUSE_DOWN** event over your movie clip and create the function that responds to the event.

5. Within the **MouseEvent.MOUSE_DOWN** event-handler function, enter **pressing** followed by an equals sign and then the **Boolean** value of **true** .

   The variable named **pressing** is set to **true** whenever you click on your movie clip.

6. On the next line, create the listener that detects the **MouseEvent.MOUSE_UP** event over the Stage and create the function that responds to the event.

Continues on next page

I Place a circular movie clip called **myDial_mc** on the Stage.

```
var pressing:Boolean = false;
myDial_mc.addEventListener(MouseEvent.MOUSE_DOWN, pressdown);
function pressdown(myevent:MouseEvent):void {
    pressing = true;
}
```

J Set **pressing** to **true** when the movie clip is pressed.

7. Within the **MouseEvent.MOUSE_UP** event-handler function, enter **pressing** followed by an equals sign and then the **Boolean** value of **false** **Ⓚ**.

The variable named **pressing** is set to **false** whenever you release your mouse button.

8. On a new line, create an event handler that detects the **MouseEvent.MOUSE_MOVE** event.

9. Within the **MouseEvent.MOUSE_MOVE** event-handler function, enter an **if** statement.

10. For the condition of the **if** statement, enter **pressing == true**.

11. Between the curly braces of the **if** statement, declare a new **Number** variable followed by an equals sign.

This variable will be assigned the angle between the mouse pointer and the center of the movie clip, in radians.

12. After the equals sign, enter the following expression so the full statement reads:

```
var myRadians:Number = Math.atan2(
→ (mouseY - myDial_mc.y),
→ (mouseX - myDial_mc.x));
```

Flash calculates the angle between the mouse pointer and the center of the movie clip **Ⓛ**.

```
stage.addEventListener(MouseEvent.MOUSE_UP, released);
function released(myevent:MouseEvent):void {
    pressing = false;
}
```

Ⓚ Set **pressing** to **false** when the movie clip is released.

```
stage.addEventListener(MouseEvent.MOUSE_MOVE, movedial);
function movedial(myevent:MouseEvent):void {
    if (pressing == true) {
        var myRadians:Number = Math.atan2((mouseY - myDial_mc.y), (mouseX - myDial_mc.x));

    }
}
```

Ⓛ The variable **myRadians** contains the calculated angle between the pointer and the movie clip.

13. On the next line, declare a new **Number** variable followed by an equals sign.

This variable will be assigned the angle value converted to degrees.

14. After the equals sign, enter an expression to convert radians to degrees, so the full statement reads as follows:

```
var myDegrees:Number = myRadians
→ * 180 / Math.PI;
```

15. On the next line, enter **myDial_mc.rotation**, an equals sign, the variable that holds the angle in degrees, a plus sign, and **90**.

The rotation of the movie clip is assigned to the calculated angle. The 90 degrees are added to compensate for the difference between the calculated angle and the movie clip **rotation** property. A value of 0 for **rotation** corresponds to the 12 o'clock position of an object, but a calculated arctangent angle value of 0 corresponds to the 3 o'clock position; adding 90 equalizes them 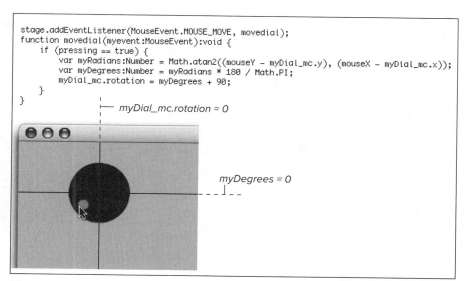.

16. Test your movie.

When users press the movie clip in the dial, they can rotate it by dragging it around its center point. When they release the mouse button, the dial stops rotating.

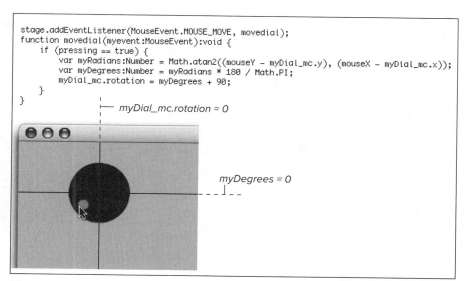

```
stage.addEventListener(MouseEvent.MOUSE_MOVE, movedial);
function movedial(myevent:MouseEvent):void {
    if (pressing == true) {
        var myRadians:Number = Math.atan2((mouseY - myDial_mc.y), (mouseX - myDial_mc.x));
        var myDegrees:Number = myRadians * 180 / Math.PI;
        myDial_mc.rotation = myDegrees + 90;
    }
}
```

— myDial_mc.rotation = 0

myDegrees = 0

M The angle is converted from radians to degrees and assigned to the variable **myDegrees**. The final statement within the **if** block modifies the rotation of the **myDial_mc** movie clip. The rotation of **myDial_mc** is set at **myDegrees** + 90 to account for the difference between the reference point of the trigonometric functions and Flash's **rotation** property.

Creating Directional Movement

To control how far an object on the Stage travels based on its angle, you can use a method of the **Point** class called **Point. polar()**. The **Point** class is a class that simply helps you with geometric manipulations by representing a location with an x- and a y-coordinate. The **Point. polar()** method is a static method, which means it is available from the class named **Point**, not from a particular instance. The **Point.polar()** method converts polar coordinates, which track position in terms of an angle and its distance from another point, to regular (Cartesian) coordinates that you're familiar with, which track position in terms of x and y.

Suppose that you want to create a racing game featuring a car that your viewer moves around a track. The car travels at a certain speed, and it moves according to where the front of the car is pointed. If you know the angle of the car and the distance that it would travel at each time interval, you can use the **Point.polar()** method to calculate its X and Y position relative to its previous position. The **Point.polar()** method takes two parameters: the first is the distance of the point from the reference point, and the second is the angle, in radians. The triangle that the polar coordinates form determines the x- and y-coordinates that the method returns as a new **Point** object **A**.

In the following task, you'll create a movie clip whose rotation can be controlled by the viewer. The movie clip has a constant velocity, so it will travel in the direction in which it's pointed, just as a car moves according to where it's steered.

A Polar coordinates describe position with angle and distance, whereas Cartesian coordinates describe position with an x- and a y-coordinate. The method **Point.polar()** takes polar coordinates and converts them into a **Point** object with the matching X and Y properties.

To create a controllable object with directional movement:

1. Create a movie clip symbol, place an instance of it on the Stage, and name it in the Properties inspector.

   In this example, the name is **car_mc**.

2. Select the first frame of the main Timeline, and open the Actions panel.

3. Create an event handler assigned to the Stage that detects the **KeyboardEvent.KEY_DOWN** event.

4. Within the **KeyboardEvent.KEY_DOWN** event-handler function, enter an **if** statement that determines whether the right arrow key is pressed. If so, add 10 degrees to the current **rotation** property of the movie clip **B**.

Whenever you press the right arrow key on the keyboard, the movie clip rotates clockwise.

5. Within the **KeyboardEvent.KEY_DOWN** event-handler function, enter another **if** statement that determines whether the left arrow key is pressed. If so, subtract 10 degrees to the current **rotation** property of the movie clip **C**.

   Whenever you press the left arrow key on the keyboard, the movie clip rotates counterclockwise.

6. On a new line, create a new event handler assigned to the Stage that detects the **Event.ENTER_FRAME** event.

Continues on next page

```
stage.addEventListener(KeyboardEvent.KEY_DOWN, rotatecar);
function rotatecar(myevent:KeyboardEvent):void {
    if (myevent.keyCode == Keyboard.RIGHT) {
        car_mc.rotation += 10;
    }
}
```

B The **car_mc** movie clip rotates 10 degrees clockwise when the right arrow key is pressed.

```
stage.addEventListener(KeyboardEvent.KEY_DOWN, rotatecar);
function rotatecar(myevent:KeyboardEvent):void {
    if (myevent.keyCode == Keyboard.RIGHT) {
        car_mc.rotation += 10;
    }
    if (myevent.keyCode == Keyboard.LEFT) {
        car_mc.rotation -= 10;
    }
}
```

C The **car_mc** movie clip rotates 10 degrees counterclockwise when the left arrow key is pressed.

7. Within the **Event.ENTER_FRAME** event-handler function, enter the following statement:

```
var radians:Number = Math.PI / 180
→ * (car_mc.rotation - 90);
```

This expression converts the angle of the movie clip to radians. Notice that you have to subtract 90 degrees from the value of **rotation** to get the equivalent angle for polar coordinates **D**.

8. On the next line, still within the **Event.ENTER_FRAME** event-handler function, enter the following expression:

```
var newSpot:Point = Point.polar(
→ 5, radians);
```

The **Point.polar()** method takes the distance that the car travels (in this case, 5 pixels) and its angle (in the variable called **radians**), and returns a new **Point** object that contains the equivalent x- and y-coordinates. The x- and y-coordinates can be represented with the properties **newSpot.x** and **newSpot.y**.

D The angle of the car is converted into radians (top). The **rotation** property of a movie clip begins from the vertical axis and increases in the clockwise direction (left). Values for radian angles begin from the horizontal axis and increase in the counterclockwise direction (right).

9. On the next line, still within the **Event.ENTER_FRAME** event-handler function, add the new x- and y-coordinates to the current coordinates of the movie clip, as follows :

```
car_mc.x += newSpot.x;
car_mc.y += newSpot.y;
```

10. Test your movie.

When the user presses the left or right arrow key, the rotation of the movie clip changes. The X and Y positions change continuously as well and are calculated from the angle of the movie clip and the constant distance it travels using the **Point.polar()** method. The movie clip moves according to where the nose of the car is pointed **F**.

```
stage.addEventListener(Event.ENTER_FRAME, movecar);
function movecar(myevent:Event):void {
    var radians:Number = Math.PI / 180 * (car_mc.rotation - 90);
    var newSpot:Point = Point.polar(5, radians);
    car_mc.x += newSpot.x;
    car_mc.y += newSpot.y;
}
```

E The x- and y-coordinates of the resulting **Point** object called **newSpot** are added to the existing position of the **car_mc** movie clip to make it move in the right direction and by the appropriate amount.

F The car moves according to where its nose is pointing.

Calculating Distances

The **Point** class can also be used to calculate the distance between two objects. This technique can be useful for creating novel interactions among interface elements—graphics, buttons, or sounds—whose reactions depend on their distance from the viewer's pointer, for example. You can also create games that involve interactions based on the distance between objects and the player. A game in which the player uses a net to catch goldfish in an aquarium, for example, can use the distance between the goldfish and the net to model the behavior of the goldfish. Perhaps the closer the net comes to a goldfish, the quicker the goldfish swims away.

The distance between any two points is calculated by the **Point.distance()** method, which takes two parameters: the first **Point** object and a second **Point** object. It returns a number representing the distance between the two points.

Because the **Point.distance()** method requires **Point** objects as its parameters, you can't just plug in x- and y-coordinates. You must create **Point** objects for the coordinates between which you want to find the distance.

In this example, you'll calculate the distance between the mouse pointer and another movie clip, and display the distance in a dynamic text field.

To calculate the distance between the mouse pointer and another point:

1. Create a movie clip, place an instance of it on the Stage, and give it a name in the Properties inspector.

   In this example, the name is **center_mc**.

2. Select the first frame of the main Timeline, and open the Actions panel.

3. Create an event handler to listen for the **MouseEvent.MOUSE_MOVE** event on the Stage.

```
stage.addEventListener(MouseEvent.MOUSE_MOVE, showdistance);
function showdistance(myevent:MouseEvent):void {
    var mousePt:Point = new Point(mouseX, mouseY);
}
```

A Create a new **Point** object whose X and Y properties are the same as the mouse pointer's X and Y properties.

```
stage.addEventListener(MouseEvent.MOUSE_MOVE, showdistance);
function showdistance(myevent:MouseEvent):void {
    var mousePt:Point = new Point(mouseX, mouseY);
    var centerPt:Point = new Point(center_mc.x, center_mc.y);
}
```

B Create a second **Point** object whose X and Y properties are the same as the movie clip's X and Y properties.

4. Within the `MouseEvent.MOUSE_MOVE` event-handler function, create a new **Point** object with the **mouseX** and **mouseY** properties as its X and Y properties, like so **Ⓐ**:

```
var mousePt:Point = new Point(
→ mouseX, mouseY);
```

5. On the next line, still within the function, create another **Point** object with the X and Y properties of the movie clip as the X and Y properties of the **Point** object, as follows **Ⓑ**:

```
var centerPt:Point = new Point(
→ center_mc.x, center_mc.y);
```

6. On a new line, still within the function, call the **Point.distance()** method and pass the two **Point** objects as parameters. Assign the result to a **Number** variable, like so:

```
var myDistance:Number = Point.
→ distance(mousePt, centerPt);
```

The distance between the **Point** object called **mousePt** and the **Point** object called **centerPt** is assigned to the variable **myDistance** **Ⓒ**.

Continues on next page

```
stage.addEventListener(MouseEvent.MOUSE_MOVE, showdistance);
function showdistance(myevent:MouseEvent):void {
    var mousePt:Point = new Point(mouseX, mouseY);
    var centerPt:Point = new Point(center_mc.x, center_mc.y);
    var myDistance:Number = Point.distance(mousePt, centerPt);
}
```

Ⓒ The distance between the two points is calculated from the method **Point.distance()**.

Calculating Distances and Angles in 3D

With the support for 3D in Flash, you may need to know distances and angles of objects in 3D space. You can do so with another class in the Flash geometry package called the **Vector3D** class. An object of the **Vector3D** class takes three parameters: the X position, the Y position, and the Z position, and an optional fourth parameter, which can hold information about its orientation in space. Define two **Vector3D** objects as in the following:

```
var myvector1:Vector3D = new Vector3D (myObject1_mc.x, myObject1_mc.y,
→ myObject1_mc.z);

var myvector2:Vector3D = new Vector3D (myObject2_mc.x, myObject2_mc.y,
→ myObject2_mc.z);
```

You can calculate the distance between the two objects with the static **distance()** method, like so:

```
var mydistance:Number = Vector3D.distance(myvector1, myvector2);
```

Similarly, you can use the **angleBetween()** method to calculate the angle between two **Vector3D** positions. The result is the angle in radians.

7. On the next line still within the function, round the value of **myDistance** and then convert it to a string with **String(Math.round(myDistance))**. Assign the result to the **text** property of a text field.

8. On the Stage, create a TLF Read Only text field and give it an instance name, the same name that is referenced in your ActionScript in step 7.

9. Test your movie.

   As the pointer moves around the movie clip, Flash calculates the distance between points in pixels **D**.

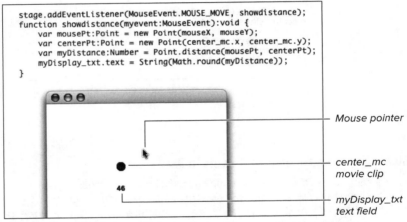

```
stage.addEventListener(MouseEvent.MOUSE_MOVE, showdistance);
function showdistance(myevent:MouseEvent):void {
    var mousePt:Point = new Point(mouseX, mouseY);
    var centerPt:Point = new Point(center_mc.x, center_mc.y);
    var myDistance:Number = Point.distance(mousePt, centerPt);
    myDisplay_txt.text = String(Math.round(myDistance));
}
```

Mouse pointer

center_mc
movie clip

myDisplay_txt
text field

D The full script is shown at the top. The text field **myDisplay_txt** displays an integer of **myDistance**.

Generating Random Numbers

When you need to incorporate random elements into your Flash movie, either for a design effect or for gameplay, you can use the **Math** class's **Math.random()** method. The **Math.random()** method generates random numbers between 0 and 1 (including 0 but *not* including 1). Typical return values are:

0.242343544598273
0.043628738493829
0.7567833408654

You can modify the random number by multiplying it or adding to it to get the span of numbers you need. If you need random numbers between 1 and 10, for example, multiply the return value of **Math.random()** by 9 and then add 1, as in the following statement:

```
Math.random() * 9 + 1;
```

You always multiply **Math.random()** by a number to get your desired range and then add or subtract a number to change the minimum and maximum values of that range.

It's important that you understand that **Math.random()** generates random numbers between 0 and 1, but it will never produce 1. So, if you need an integer, apply the **Math.round()** method to round the number down to the nearest integer, like the following statement:

```
Math.round(Math.random() * 9 + 1);
```

To generate a random integer:

1. In the Actions panel, enter **var**, then a variable name, and strictly type it to an integer data type.

2. On the same line, enter an equals sign and then the **Math.round()** method.

   The **Math.round()** method rounds any decimal number to the nearest whole number.

3. Inside the parentheses of the **Math.round()** method, enter the **Math.random()** method, multiply it by 1 less than the range of numbers you desire, and add 1, as follows:

   ```
   var myResult:int =   Math.
   →round(Math.random() * 9 + 1);
   ```

   The resulting number will be a random number between 1 and 10 Ⓐ.

TIP Be aware of when you can use decimals and when you must use integers. For example, many properties, such as the X and Y of a movie clip, can take decimal values. However, the gotoAndStop() method, which moves the playhead to a specific frame on the Timeline, must use an integer. Use the Math.round() method (or, alternatively, the Math.floor() or Math.ceil() method) to convert a decimal number to an integer before using it as a parameter in the gotoAndStop() method.

```
var myResult:int = Math.round(Math.random() * 9 + 1);
```

Ⓐ A random number between 1 and 10 is assigned to the variable called **myResult**.

Ordering Information with Arrays

When you want to store many pieces of related information as a group, you can use the **Array** class to help arrange them. Arrays are containers that hold data, just as variables do, except that arrays hold multiple pieces of data in a specific sequence. The position of each piece of data is called its index. Indexes are numbered sequentially, beginning at 0, so that each piece of data corresponds to an index, as in a two-column table **Ⓐ**. Because each piece of data is ordered numerically, you can retrieve and modify the information easily—and, most important, automatically—by referencing its index. Suppose you're building an address book of a list of your important contacts. You can store names in an **Array** so that index 0 holds your first contact, index 1 holds your second contact, and so on. By using a looping statement, you can check every entry in the **Array** automatically.

An *element* (individual item) can be accessed using the **Array** object's name followed by the element's index in square brackets, like this:

`myArray[4]`

The square brackets are known as array access operators. The previous statement accesses the data in index 4 of the array called **myArray**. The number of elements is known as the length of the **Array**; for example, the length of the **Array** in **Ⓐ** is 6.

It's useful to think of an **Array** as a set of ordered variables. You can convert the variables **myScores0**, **myScores1**, **myScores2**, and **myScores3** to a single **Array** called **myScores** of length 4 with indexes from 0 to 3. Because you have to handle only one **Array** object instead of four separate variables, using **Arrays** makes information easier to manage.

In ActionScript, the type of data that **Arrays** hold can be mixed. You can have a **Number** in index 0, a **String** in index 1, and a **Boolean** value in index 2. You can change the data in any index in an **Array** at any time. The length of **Arrays** isn't fixed, either, so they can grow or shrink to accommodate new information as needed.

Creating an **Array** involves two steps. The first is to declare an **Array** variable and use the **Array** class's constructor function to instantiate a new **Array** instance, as in this example:

`var myArray:Array = new Array();`

The second step is to fill, or *populate,* your **Array** with data. One way to populate your **Array** is to assign the data to each index in separate statements, like this:

```
myArray[0] = "Adam";
myArray[1] = "Betty";
myArray[2] = "Zeke";
```

Another way to assign the data is to put the information as parameters within the constructor function:

```
var myArray:Array = new Array
→ ("Adam", "Betty", "Zeke");
```

The latter is a more compact way of populating your **Array**, but you're restricted to entering the data in sequence.

Index	Value
0	"monitor"
1	"mouse"
2	"keyboard"
3	"CPU"
4	"modem"
5	"speakers"

A An **Array** is like a two-column table with an Index column and a corresponding Value column.

```
var myScores:Array = new Array();
```

B A new **Array** called **myScores** is instantiated.

```
var myScores:Array = new Array();
myScores[0] = 2;
myScores[1] = 3;
myScores[2] = 6;
myScores[3] = 4;
```

C This **Array** contains four elements.

To create an Array:

1. Select the first frame of the Timeline, and open the Actions panel.

2. Declare your **Array** by entering **var**, the object's name, and then **:Array**. On the same line, enter an equals sign and then the constructor **new Array().**

   Flash instantiates a new **Array B**.

3. On the next line, enter the name of your new **Array**, an index number between square brackets, and then an equals sign.

4. Enter the data you want to store in the **Array** at that index position.

5. Continue to assign more data to the **Array C**.

Two-dimensional Arrays

An **Array** has been compared to a two-column table in which the index is in one column and its contents are in a second column. But what if you need to keep track of information stored in more than one row in a table, as in a traditional spreadsheet? The solution is to nest an **Array** inside another one to create what's known as a *two-dimensional* **Array**. This type of **Array** creates two indexes for every piece of information. To keep track of a checker piece on a checkerboard, for example, you can use a two-dimensional **Array** to reference its rows and its columns **D**.

For the three rows, create three separate **Arrays** and populate them with numbers:

```
var row0:Array = new Array(1,2,3);
var row1:Array = new Array(4,5,6);
var row2:Array = new Array(7,8,9);
```

Now you can put those three **Arrays** inside another **Array**, like so:

```
var gameBoard:Array = new Array();
gameBoard[0] = row0;
gameBoard[1] = row1;
gameBoard[2] = row2;
```

To access or modify the information of a checkerboard square, first use one set of square brackets that references the row. The statement **gameBoard[2]** references the **Array** **row2**. Then, by using another set of square brackets, you can reference the column within that row. The statement **gameBoard[2][0]** accesses the number 7.

row0	1	2	3
row1	4	5	6
row2	7	8	9

D You can use a two-dimensional **Array** to map a checkerboard and keep track of what's inside individual squares. Each row is an **Array**. The rows are put inside another **Array**.

Automating Array operations with loops

Because the elements of an **Array** are indexed numerically, they lend themselves nicely to looping actions. By using looping statements such as **while**, **do while**, and **for**, you can have Flash go through each index and retrieve or assign new data quickly and automatically. To average the scores of many players in an **Array** without a looping statement, for example, you have to total all their scores and divide by the number of players, like this:

```
mySum = myScores[0] + myScores[1] +
→ myScores[2] + ...
myAverage = mySum / myScores.length;
```

(The property **length** defines the number of entries in the **Array**.)

Using a looping statement, however, you can calculate the **mySum** value quickly this way:

```
for (var i:int = 0; i <
→ myScores.length; i++) {
    mySum = mySum + myScores[i];
}

myAverage = mySum / myScores.length;
```

Flash starts at index 0 and adds each indexed entry in the **Array** to the variable **mySum** until it reaches the end of the **Array**. Then it divides the sum by the number of elements to calculate the average.

To loop through an Array:

1. Select the first keyframe of the Timeline, and open the Actions panel.

2. Declare and instantiate a new **Array** called **myScores**.

3. Populate the **myScores Array** with numbers representing scores **E**.

4. On the next line, declare an **int** variable called **mySum** and initialize it to **0**.

```
var myScores:Array = new Array();
myScores[0] = 2;
myScores[1] = 3;
myScores[2] = 6;
myScores[3] = 4;
```

E This **Array** called **myScores** contains four elements.

```
var myScores:Array = new Array();
myScores[0] = 2;
myScores[1] = 3;
myScores[2] = 6;
myScores[3] = 4;
var mySum:int = 0;
for (var i:int = 0; i < myScores.length; i++) {
}
```

F This **for** statement loops the same number of times as there are elements in the **Array myScore**.

```
var myScores:Array = new Array();
myScores[0] = 2;
myScores[1] = 3;
myScores[2] = 6;
myScores[3] = 4;
var mySum:int = 0;
for (var i:int = 0; i < myScores.length; i++) {
        mySum = mySum + myScores[i];
}
```

G The value of each element in the **Array** is added to the variable **mySum**.

```
var myScores:Array = new Array();
myScores[0] = 2;
myScores[1] = 3;
myScores[2] = 6;
myScores[3] = 4;
var mySum:int = 0;
for (var i:int = 0; i < myScores.length; i++) {
        mySum = mySum + myScores[i];
}
myAverage_txt.text = String(mySum / myScores.length);
```

H After the **for** loop, the average value of the elements in the **Array** is calculated and displayed in the text field **myAverage_txt**.

Show the average value of my array

3.75

I The final result (3.75) is displayed in the text field on the Stage.

5. On the next line, enter a **for** statement.

6. In between the parentheses of the **for** statement, enter the following:

   var i:int = 0; i < myScores.
   → **length; i++**

   Flash begins with the counter variable **i** set at the value **0**. It increases the variable by increments of 1 until the variable reaches the length of **myScores F**.

7. Between the curly braces of the **for** loop, enter **mySum** followed by an equals sign.

8. On the same line, enter **mySum + myScores[i] G**.

   Rather than using an explicit index, the value of the variable **i** will define the index (and, consequently, which element's value is retrieved and added to **mySum**).

   Flash loops through the **myScores**'s elements in turn, adding the value in each element of the **Array** to **mySum**. When the value of **i** reaches the value of **myScores.length**, Flash jumps out of the **for** loop and stops retrieving values. Therefore, the last element accessed is **myScores[myScores.length – 1]**, which is the last element of the **Array**.

9. On a new line after the ending curly brace of the **for** statement, enter **myAverage_txt.text = String(mySum / myScores_array.length) H**.

10. Create a TLF Read Only text field on the Stage with the instance name **myAverage_txt**.

11. Test your movie.

   Flash loops through the **myScores Array** to add the values in all the elements, and then it divides the total by the number of elements. The average is displayed in the text field on the Stage **I**.

The Array class's methods

The methods of the **Array** class let you sort, delete, add, and manipulate the data in an **Array**. **Table 11.2** summarizes some methods of the **Array** class. It's convenient to think of the methods in pairs: **shift()** and **unshift()**, for example, both modify the beginning of an **Array**; **push()** and **pop()** both modify the end of an **Array**; and **slice()** and **splice()** both modify the middle of an **Array**.

TABLE 11.2 Methods of the Array Object

Method	Description
concat(array1,...,arrayN)	Concatenates the specified **Array** objects, and returns a new **Array**.
join(separator)	Concatenates the elements of the **Array**, inserts the **String separator** between the elements, and returns a **String**. The default separator is a comma.
pop()	Removes the last element in the **Array**, and returns the value of that element.
push(value)	Adds a new element **value** to the end of the **Array**, and returns the new length.
shift()	Removes the first element in the **Array**, and returns the value of that element.
unshift(value)	Adds a new element **value** to the beginning of the **Array**, and returns the new length.
slice(indexA, indexB)	Returns a new **Array** beginning with element **indexA** and ending with element (**indexB - 1**).
splice(index, count, elem1,..., elemN)	Inserts or deletes elements. Set **count** to 0 to insert specified values starting at **index**. Set **count > 0** to delete the number of elements starting at and including **index**.
reverse()	Reverses the order of elements in the **Array**.
sort()	Sorts the elements of the **Array**. Numbers are sorted in ascending order, and strings are sorted alphabetically.
sortOn(fieldName)	Sorts an **Array** of objects based on the value in each element's **fieldName** (a **String**) property.
toString()	Returns a **String** with every element concatenated and separated by a comma.
indexOf(searchterm, startindex)	Searches the **Array** for the **searchterm** starting at the **startindex** and returns the first index position of the match. Returns **-1** if the **searchterm** is not found.
lastIndexof(searchterm, startindex)	Searches the **Array** for the **searchterm** starting at the **startindex** and returns the last index position of the match. Returns -1 if the **searchterm** is not found.

TABLE 11.3 Examples of Array Methods

Statement	Value of `myArray`
`var myArray:Array = new Array(2, 4, 6, 8)`	2, 4, 6, 8
`myArray.pop()`	2, 4, 6
`myArray.push(1, 3)`	2, 4, 6, 1, 3
`myArray.shift()`	4, 6, 1, 3
`myArray.unshift(5, 7)`	5, 7, 4, 6, 1, 3
`myArray.splice(2, 0, 8, 9)`	5, 7, 8, 9, 4, 6, 1, 3
`myArray.splice(3, 2)`	5, 7, 8, 6, 1, 3
`myArray.reverse()`	3, 1, 6, 8, 7, 5
`myArray.sort()`	1, 3, 5, 6, 7, 8

Table 11.3 gives examples of how some of the methods in Table 11.2 operate.

TIP It's important to note which methods of the `Array` class modify the original `Array` and which ones return a new `Array`. The methods `concat()`, `join()`, `slice()`, and `toString()` return a new `Array` or `String` and don't alter the original `Array`. The expression `var newArray:Array = originalArray.concat(8)`, for example, puts 8 at the end of `originalArray` and assigns the resulting `Array` to `newArray`. `originalArray` isn't affected. Also note that some methods modify the `Array` as well as return a specific value. These two things aren't the same. The statement `myArray.pop()`, for example, modifies `myArray` by removing the last element and also returns the value of that last element. At the end of this example, the value of `myResult` is 8, and the value of `myArray` is 2, 4, 6:

```
var myArray:Array = new Array(2, 4,
→ 6, 8);
myResult = myArray.pop();
```

TIP An easy way to remember the duties of some of these methods is to think of the elements of your `Array` as being components of a stack. (In fact, *stack* is a programming term for a type of array where the last element added is the first element retrieved.) You can think of an `Array` object as being like a stack of books or a stack of cafeteria trays on a spring-loaded holder. The bottom of the stack is the first element in an `Array`. When you call the `Array`'s `push()` method, imagine that you literally push a new tray on top of the stack to add a new element. When you call the `pop()` method, you pop, or remove, the top tray from the stack (the last element). When you shift an `Array`, you take out the bottom tray (the first element) so that all the other trays shift down into new positions.

Keeping Track of Objects with Arrays

Sometimes, you have to deal with multiple objects on the Stage at the same time. Keeping track of them all and performing actions to modify, test, or evaluate each one can be a nightmare unless you use **Array**s to help manage them. Imagine that you're creating a game in which the viewer has to avoid rocks falling from the sky. You can use the **hitTestObject()** method to see whether each falling-rock object intersects with the viewer. But if there are 10 rocks on the Stage, that potentially means 10 separate **hitTestObject()** statements. How do you manage these multiple operations? The answer is to put them in an **Array**. Doing so allows you to perform the **hitTestObject()** in a loop on the elements in the **Array** instead of in many separate statements.

Put an object into an **Array** just as you put any other data into the **Array**, using an assignment statement:

```
rockArray[0] = fallingRock0_mc;
rockArray[1] = fallingRock1_mc;
rockArray[2] = fallingRock2_mc;
```

These statements put the movie clip **fallingRock0_mc** in element 0 of the **Array rockArray**, the movie clip **fallingRock1_mc** in element 1, and the movie clip **fallingRock2_mc** in element 2. Now you can reference the movie clips through the **Array**. This statement changes the rotation of the movie clip called **fallingRock2_mc**:

```
rockArray[2].rotation = 45;
```

You can even call methods this way:

```
rockArray[2].hitTestPoint(mouseX,
→ mouseY, true);
```

This statement checks to see whether the **fallingRock2_mc** movie clip intersects with the mouse pointer.

The following tasks use looping statements to populate an **Array** with dynamically drawn **Sprite**s. When the **Array** is full of objects, you can perform the same action, such as modifying a property or calling **hitTestObject()**, on all the **Sprite**s by referencing the **Array**.

```
var blockArray:Array = new Array();
for (var i:int = 0; i < 15; i++) {
}
```

A A new **Array** called **blockArray** is instantiated and a **for** loop created. This loop uses a counter that begins at 0 and ends at 14, increasing by 1 with each loop.

```
var blockArray:Array = new Array();
for (var i:int = 0; i < 15; i++) {
    var block:Sprite = new Sprite();
    block.graphics.lineStyle(1);
    block.graphics.beginFill(0x000000);
    block.graphics.drawRect(0, 0, 30, 30);
}
```

B A The **Sprite** called **block** is created and a rectangle is drawn with it.

```
var blockArray:Array = new Array();
for (var i:int = 0; i < 15; i++) {
    var block:Sprite = new Sprite();
    block.graphics.lineStyle(1);
    block.graphics.beginFill(0x000000);
    block.graphics.drawRect(0, 0, 30, 30);
    block.x = Math.random() * 400;
    block.y = Math.random() * 400;
    addChild(block);
}
```

C The **Sprite** is randomly positioned on the Stage and then added to the display list to make it visible.

```
var blockArray:Array = new Array();
for (var i:int = 0; i < 15; i++) {
    var block:Sprite = new Sprite();
    block.graphics.lineStyle(1);
    block.graphics.beginFill(0x000000);
    block.graphics.drawRect(0, 0, 30, 30);
    block.x = Math.random() * 400;
    block.y = Math.random() * 400;
    addChild(block);

    blockArray[i] = block;
}
```

D The newly created **Sprite** is put in the **blockArray**.

To populate an Array with objects:

1. In the Actions panel, instantiate a new **Array** object.

   In this example, the instance name is **blockArray**.

2. On the next line, create a **for** statement.

3. With your pointer between the parentheses, enter **var i:int = 0; i < 15; i++** **A**.

   This loop will occur 15 times, starting with **i** equal to 0 and ending after **i** equals 14.

4. Inside the curly braces of the **for** statement, create a new **Sprite** object.

   In this example, the instance name for your new **Sprite** object is **block**.

5. On the next line, still within the **for** statement, call the **lineStyle()**, **beginFill()**, and **drawRect()** methods on the **graphics** property of your **Sprite** object **B**.

   Flash draws a rectangle.

6. On the next line, still within the **for** statement, change the X and Y positions of the **Sprite** object with a random number.

7. On the next line, still within the **for** statement, call the **addChild()** method to add the **Sprite** to the display list to make it visible **C**.

8. On the next line, still within the **for** statement, enter the name of the **Array** object, then the variable **i** in square brackets, followed by an equals sign. After the equals sign enter **block.** Each newly named **Sprite** object is put inside a different element of the **Array** **D**.

Accessing movie clips in an Array

Now that your **Array** is populated with **Sprites**, you can reference them easily with just the **Array**'s index value to change their properties or call their methods.

In the next task, you'll check to see whether the viewer's pointer touches any of the **Sprite** objects displayed randomly on the Stage. Instead of checking each **Sprite** with a separate **hitTestPoint()** method, you'll loop through the **Array** and check all the **Sprites** with only a few lines of ActionScript.

To reference objects inside an Array:

1. Continuing with the file you used in the preceding task, select the main Timeline and open the Actions panel.

2. On a new line after the **for** statement, create an **Event.ENTER_FRAME** event handler.

3. Inside the function for the **Event.ENTER_FRAME** event handler, create another **for** statement.

4. With your pointer between the parentheses of the **for** statement, enter **var i:Number = 0; i < 15; i++ E**.

   Your second **for** statement will have the same number of loops as your first **for** statement.

5. Inside the **for** statement, enter the conditional statement, **if**.

6. For the condition, enter the name of your array followed by **[i]** to reference each **Sprite** inside the **Array**.

7. On the same line, call the **hitTestPoint()** method with the parameters **mouseX**, **mouseY**, and **true F**.

```
stage.addEventListener(Event.ENTER_FRAME, checkhit);
function checkhit(myevent:Event):void {
    for (var i:int = 0; i < 15; i++) {

    }
}
```

E Enter the same loop statements for the **for** loop that you did for the first loop that generated the **Sprites**.

```
stage.addEventListener(Event.ENTER_FRAME, checkhit);
function checkhit(myevent:Event):void {
    for (var i:int = 0; i < 15; i++) {
        if (blockArray[i].hitTestPoint(mouseX, mouseY, true)) {

        }
    }
}
```

F Flash checks every **Sprite** inside **blockArray** to see whether the objects intersect with the mouse pointer.

8. Choose actions to perform when the mouse pointer intersects a **Sprite** object, and enter them in the curly braces of the **if** statement.

   For example, enter this expression: **blockArray[i].alpha = .3** 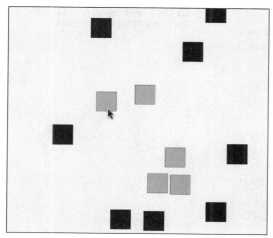.

9. Test your movie.

   When the **for** loop is performed, all the **Sprite**s inside the **Array** are tested to see whether they intersect with the pointer. Because the **for** loop is within an **Event.ENTER_FRAME** event handler, this check is done continuously. If an intersection occurs, that particular movie clip turns 30 percent opaque **H**.

```
stage.addEventListener(Event.ENTER_FRAME, checkhit);
function checkhit(myevent:Event):void {
    for (var i:int = 0; i < 15; i++) {
        if (blockArray[i].hitTestPoint(mouseX, mouseY, true)) {
            blockArray[i].alpha = .3;
        }
    }
}
```

G If Flash detects an intersection between a **Sprite** and the pointer, that particular **Sprite**'s transparency changes.

H The pointer has passed over many of the **Sprite**s, which have turned semitransparent. Use this technique to manage multiple objects that must be tested and controlled similarly.

Using the Date and Time

The **Date** class lets you retrieve the local or universal (UTC) date and time information from the clock in your viewer's computer system. Using a **Date** object, you can retrieve the year, month, day of the month, day of the week, hour, minute, second, and even millisecond. Use a **Date** object and its methods to create accurate clocks in your movie or to find information about certain days and dates in the past. You can create a **Date** object for your birthday, for example, by specifying the month, day, and year. Using methods of the **Date** class, you can retrieve the day of the week for your **Date** object that tells you what day you were born.

You first need to instantiate a **Date** object with the constructor function **new Date()**. Then you can call on its methods to retrieve specific time information. **Table 11.4** summarizes the common methods for retrieving the date and time information.

To create a clock:

1. Create a TLF Read Only text field on the Stage, and give it an instance name in the Properties inspector.

   The text field will display the time.

2. Select the first frame of the main Timeline, and open the Actions panel.

3. Enter **var**, then a name, a colon, the **Timer** data type, an equals sign, and the constructor **new Timer()**. In between the parentheses, enter **1000**.

   A new **Timer** object is created that will trigger a **TimerEvent** every 1,000 milliseconds.

4. On the next line, call the **start()** method of your **Timer** Ⓐ.

   Your **Timer** will start to count.

TABLE 11.4 Methods of the Date Class

Method	Description
getFullYear()	Returns the year as a four-digit number
getMonth()	Returns the month as a number from 0 (January) to 11 (December)
getDate()	Returns the day of the month as a number from 1 to 31
getDay()	Returns the day of the week as a number from 0 (Sunday) to 6 (Saturday)
getHours()	Returns the hour of the day as a number from 0 to 23
getMinutes()	Returns the minutes as a number from 0 to 59
getSeconds()	Returns the seconds as a number from 0 to 59
getMilliseconds()	Returns the milliseconds

```
var myTimer:Timer = new Timer(1000);
myTimer.start();
```

Ⓐ The **Timer** object is instantiated and started to fire every 1,000 milliseconds.

```
var myTimer:Timer = new Timer(1000);
myTimer.start();

myTimer.addEventListener(TimerEvent.TIMER, showtime);
function showtime(myevent:Event) {
    var myDate:Date = new Date();
}
```

B The **Date** object is instantiated.

```
var myTimer:Timer = new Timer(1000);
myTimer.start();

myTimer.addEventListener(TimerEvent.TIMER, showtime);
function showtime(myevent:Event) {
    var myDate:Date = new Date();
    var currentHour:Number = myDate.getHours();
}
```

C The current hour is assigned to the variable
currentHour.

```
var myTimer:Timer = new Timer(1000);
myTimer.start();

myTimer.addEventListener(TimerEvent.TIMER, showtime);
function showtime(myevent:Event) {
    var myDate:Date = new Date();
    var currentHour:Number = myDate.getHours();
    var currentMinute:Number = myDate.getMinutes();
    var currentSecond:Number = myDate.getSeconds();
}
```

D The current hour, minute, and second are
retrieved from the computer's clock and assigned
to different variables.

```
var myTimer:Timer = new Timer(1000);
myTimer.start();

myTimer.addEventListener(TimerEvent.TIMER, showtime);
function showtime(myevent:Event) {
    var myDate:Date = new Date();
    var currentHour:Number = myDate.getHours();
    var currentMinute:Number = myDate.getMinutes();
    var currentSecond:Number = myDate.getSeconds();
    if (currentHour > 12) {
        currentHour = currentHour - 12;
    }
}
```

E The returned value for the method **getHours()**
is a number from 0 to 23. To convert the hour to
the standard 12-hour cycle, subtract 12 for hours
greater than 12.

5. On the next line, create an event handler
   to detect the **TimerEvent.TIMER** event.

6. Within the **TimerEvent.TIMER** event-
   handler function, use the **var** statement
   to declare a **Date** object, followed by an
   equals sign, then the constructor **new
   Date()**.

   The **Date** object is instantiated **B**. If you
   don't specify any parameters in the constructor, the **Date** object is populated
   with the current date and time information. You can also specify parameters in
   the constructor to create an object that
   references a specific date and time.

7. On a new line, call the **getHours()**
   method of your **Date** object and assign
   the result to a new **Number** variable **C**.

   Flash retrieves the current hour and
   puts it in the variable **currentHour**.

8. Repeat step 7 to retrieve the current
   minute with the **getMinutes()** method
   and the current second with the
   getSeconds() method, and assign the
   returned values to variables **D**.

9. On a new line, enter the conditional
   statement, **if**.

10. For the condition, enter
    currentHour > 12.

11. On the next line inside the **if**
    statement, enter **currentHour =
    currentHour - 12 E**.

12. Place your pointer after the closing
    curly brace for the **if** statement, and
    enter the statement **else if**.

13. For the condition of the **else if** state-
    ment, enter **currentHour == 0**.

Continues on next page

14. Inside the **else if** block, enter
   currentHour = 12 .

15. On a new line after the closing curly brace
   of your **else if** statement, enter the name
   of your text field, followed by a period, the
   text property, and an equals sign.

16. After the equals sign, create an expression that concatenates the variable
   names for the hour, the minute, and
   the second with appropriate spacers
   between them .

17. Test your movie.

   The **Timer** object dispatches a
   TimerEvent.TIMER event every second,
   and the event handler detects each time
   it happens. As a response, the current
   hour, minute, and second in the 12-hour
   format are displayed in a text field.

> **TIP** Note that minutes and seconds that are
> less than 10 display as single digits, such as 1
> and 2, rather than as 01 and 02. Refine your
> clock by adding conditional statements to
> check the value of the current minutes and
> seconds and add the appropriate 0 digit.

```
var myTimer:Timer = new Timer(1000);
myTimer.start();

myTimer.addEventListener(TimerEvent.TIMER, showtime);
function showtime(myevent:Event) {
    var myDate:Date = new Date();
    var currentHour:Number = myDate.getHours();
    var currentMinute:Number = myDate.getMinutes();
    var currentSecond:Number = myDate.getSeconds();
    if (currentHour > 12) {
        currentHour = currentHour - 12;
    } else if (currentHour == 0) {
        currentHour = 12;
    }
}
```

F Because there is no 0 on a clock, have Flash
assign 12 to any hour that has the value 0.

```
var myTimer:Timer = new Timer(1000);
myTimer.start();

myTimer.addEventListener(TimerEvent.TIMER, showtime);
function showtime(myevent:Event) {
    var myDate:Date = new Date();
    var currentHour:Number = myDate.getHours();
    var currentMinute:Number = myDate.getMinutes();
    var currentSecond:Number = myDate.getSeconds();
    if (currentHour > 12) {
        currentHour = currentHour - 12;
    } else if (currentHour == 0) {
        currentHour = 12;
    }
    myDisplay_txt.text = "The time is now: \n" + currentHour + ":" + currentMinute + ":" + currentSecond;
}
```

The time is now:
9:36:43 ──────── *myDisplay_txt text field*

G The text field displays the concatenated values for the hour, minute, and second.

Date numbers and names

The values returned by the **getMonth()** and **getDay()** methods of a **Date** object are numbers instead of string data types. The **getMonth()** method returns values from 0 to 11 (0 = January), and the **getDay()** method returns values from 0 to 6 (0 = Sunday). To correlate these numeric values with the names of the months or days of the week, you need to create **Arrays** that contain this information. You can create an **Array** that contains the days of the week with the following statements:

```
var dayNames:Array = new Array();
dayNames[0] = "Sunday";
dayNames[1] = "Monday";
dayNames[2] = "Tuesday";
dayNames[3] = "Wednesday";
dayNames[4] = "Thursday";
dayNames[5] = "Friday";
dayNames[6] = "Saturday";
```

To create a calendar:

1. Create a TLF Read Only text field on the Stage, and give it an instance name in the Properties inspector.

   The text field will be used to display the date.

2. Select the first keyframe of the Timeline, and open the Actions panel.

3. Declare an **Array** object that will hold the days of the week followed by an equals sign.

4. Enter the constructor function **new Array()**.

5. In a series of statements, assign **Strings** representing the names of the days of the week as elements of your **Array** 🅗.

6. On a new line, declare a second new **Array** followed by an equals sign.

7. Enter the constructor function **new Array()**.

   This **Array** will hold the months of the year.

8. In a series of statements, assign **Strings** representing the names of the months of the year to the elements of this **Array** 🅘.

Continues on next page

```
var dayNames:Array = new Array();
dayNames[0] = "Sunday";
dayNames[1] = "Monday";
dayNames[2] = "Tuesday";
dayNames[3] = "Wednesday";
dayNames[4] = "Thursday";
dayNames[5] = "Friday";
dayNames[6] = "Saturday";
```

🅗 The Array **dayNames** contains **Strings** of all the days of the week.

```
var monthNames:Array = new Array();
monthNames[0] = "January";
monthNames[1] = "February";
monthNames[2] = "March";
monthNames[3] = "April";
monthNames[4] = "May";
monthNames[5] = "June";
monthNames[6] = "July";
monthNames[7] = "August";
monthNames[8] = "September";
monthNames[9] = "October";
monthNames[10] = "November";
monthNames[11] = "December";
```

🅘 The Array **monthNames** contains **Strings** of all the months.

9. On a new line, declare a new **Date** object followed by an equals sign.

10. Enter the constructor function **new Date()** without any parameters.

11. In a series of statements, call the **getFullYear()**, **getMonth()**, **getDate()**, and **getDay()** methods, and assign their values to new **Number** variables ❶.

12. Enter the name of your text field, followed by a period, the **text** property, and an equals sign.

13. Enter the name of the **Array** that contains the days of the week. As its index, put in the variable containing the value returned by the **getDay()** method.

    The value of this variable is a number from 0 to 6. This number is used to retrieve the correct string in the **Array** corresponding to the current day.

14. Concatenate the **Array** that contains the days of the month, and as its index put the variable containing the value returned by the **getMonth()** method call.

15. Concatenate the other variables that hold the current date and year ❶.

16. Test your movie.

    Flash gets the day, month, date, and year from the system clock. The names of the specific day and month are retrieved from the **Array** objects, and the information is displayed in the text field.

```
var myDate:Date = new Date();
var currentYear:Number = myDate.getFullYear();
var currentMonth:Number = myDate.getMonth();
var currentDate:Number = myDate.getDate();
var currentDay:Number = myDate.getDay();
```

❶ The current year, month, date, and day are retrieved from the computer's clock and assigned to new variables.

```
myDisplay_txt.text = "Today is \n" + dayNames[currentDay] + ", " +
monthNames[currentMonth] + " " + currentDate + ", " + currentYear;
```

Today is
Monday, July 5, 2010 ——————————— myDisplay_txt text field

❶ The day, month, date, and year information is concatenated and displayed in the **myDisplay_txt** text field.

Tracking elapsed time

Another way to provide time information to your viewer is to use the Flash function `getTimer()`. This function returns the number of milliseconds that have elapsed since the Flash movie started playing. You can compare the returned value of `getTimer()` at one instant with the returned value of it at another instant, and the difference gives you the elapsed time between those two instants. Use the elapsed time to create timers for games and activities in your Flash movie. You can time how long it takes for your viewer to answer questions correctly in a test or give your viewer only a certain amount of time to complete the test. Or, award more points in a game if the player successfully completes a mission within an allotted time.

Because `getTimer()` is a built-in function and not a method of an object, you call it by using the function name.

To create a timer:

1. Create a TLF Read Only text field on the Stage, and give it an instance name in the Properties inspector.

2. Select the first frame of the main Timeline, and open the Actions panel.

3. Declare a **Number** variable named **startTime**, and assign it an initial value of 0.

4. Create an event handler to detect the **MouseEvent.CLICK** event.

5. Within the **MouseEvent.CLICK** event-handler function, enter **startTime**, followed by an equals sign, then the function `getTimer()` **L**.

   Whenever the mouse button is pressed, the time that has passed since the movie started playing is assigned to the variable **startTime**.

6. On a new line, enter another event handler to detect the **Event.ENTER_FRAME** event.

7. Within the **Event.ENTER_FRAME** event-handler function, declare a **Number** variable named **currentTime**, followed by an equals sign, and then the function `getTimer()` **M**.

   Flash continuously retrieves the time that has passed since the movie started and puts that information in the variable called **currentTime**.

Continues on next page

```
var startTime:Number = 0;
stage.addEventListener(MouseEvent.CLICK, reset);
function reset(myevent:MouseEvent):void {
    startTime = getTimer();
}
```

L When the viewer clicks the mouse button, the `getTimer()` function retrieves the time elapsed since the start of the Flash movie. That time is put in the variable **startTime**.

```
stage.addEventListener(Event.ENTER_FRAME, showTime);
function showTime(myevent:Event):void {
    var currentTime:Number = getTimer();
}
```

M On an ongoing basis, the `getTimer()` function retrieves the time elapsed since the start of the Flash movie. That time is put in the variable **currentTime**.

8. On the next line still within the function, declare a **Number** variable
named **elapsedTime** followed by an
equals sign.

9. Enter **(currentTime – startTime) /
1000**.

Flash calculates the difference between
the current timer and the timer at the
instant the mouse was clicked. The
result is divided by 1,000 to convert it to
seconds **Ⓝ**.

10. On a new line, convert the value of
elapsedTime to a string and assign the
result to the **text** property of your text
field **Ⓞ**.

11. Test your movie.

Flash displays the time elapsed since
the last instant the viewer pressed the
mouse button.

> **TIP** Experiment with different event handlers
> to build a stopwatch with Start, Stop, and Lap
> buttons.

```
stage.addEventListener(Event.ENTER_FRAME, showTime);
function showTime(myevent:Event):void {
    var currentTime:Number = getTimer();
    var elapsedTime:Number = (currentTime - startTime) / 1000;
}
```

Ⓝ The variable **elapsedTime** is assigned the difference between
the two instances of time recorded in the variables **startTime** and
currentTime.

```
var startTime:Number = 0;
stage.addEventListener(MouseEvent.CLICK, reset);
function reset(myevent:MouseEvent):void {
    startTime = getTimer();
}

stage.addEventListener(Event.ENTER_FRAME, showTime);
function showTime(myevent:Event):void {
    var currentTime:Number = getTimer();
    var elapsedTime:Number = (currentTime - startTime) / 1000;
    myDisplay_txt.text = String(elapsedTime);
}
```

Time elapsed:
3.61

Ⓞ The value of **elapsedTime** is converted into a string and then
displayed in the text field **myDisplay_txt**.

Managing Content and Troubleshooting

As the complexity of your Flash movie increases with the addition of bitmaps, videos, sounds, and animations, as well as the ActionScript that integrates them, you need to keep close track of all the elements so you can make necessary revisions and bug fixes. As the project's complexity grows, you'll also find yourself working more in teams than by yourself. Fortunately, Flash provides several tools for troubleshooting, managing, and sharing assets with coworkers to make your workflow easier.

This chapter shows you how to create shared Library symbols that supply common elements to a team of Flash developers working on a project. This chapter delves into the Movie Explorer (which offers information about the organization of your movie) and the Find and Replace panel (which can help make global edits). You'll also learn to save your movie as an uncompressed XFL document. The XFL format allows the contents of your movie to be exposed so other developers can make changes quickly and efficiently.

Finally, you'll learn some strategies for making your Flash movie leaner and

faster—optimizing graphics and code, organizing your work environment, and avoiding some common mistakes—guidelines to help you become a better Flash animator and developer.

Sharing Library Symbols

Flash makes it possible for a team of animators and developers to share common Library symbols for a complex project. Each animator might be working on a separate movie that uses the same symbol—the main character in an animated comic book, for example. An identical symbol of this main character needs to reside in the Library of each movie; if the art director decides to change this character's face, a new symbol has to be copied to all the Libraries—that is, unless you create a shared Library symbol. There are two kinds of shared symbols: runtime shared symbols and authortime shared symbols.

Runtime sharing of symbols

In runtime sharing, one file provides a symbol for multiple movies to use during runtime. This simplifies the editing process and ensures consistency throughout a Flash project **A**.

Your viewers also benefit from the shared symbols because they have to download them only once. For example, a main character would be downloaded just once, for the first movie, and all subsequent movies would use that character.

Shared symbol in a Library

Separate SWF movies

A A runtime shared symbol in the Library in one SWF (top) can be used by multiple SWF files (bottom).

To create a runtime shared Library symbol, mark the symbol for "Export for runtime sharing" in the Advanced section of the Symbol Properties dialog box and give the symbol a class name so you can call on it. When you export the SWF file, the symbol will be available to other SWF movies.

Once you create a movie that shares a Library symbol, you can create other movies that use it. You do this by opening a

new Flash document and creating a symbol. In the Advanced section of the Symbol Properties dialog box, mark the symbol to "Import for runtime sharing" and enter the name and location of the source symbol as it appears in the Class field of its own Symbol Properties dialog box. At runtime, your new movie finds, imports, and uses the source symbol.

To create a runtime shared symbol:

1. In a new Flash document, create or import a symbol you want to share.

   The symbol can be a button, movie clip, font symbol, sound, or bitmap.

2. In the Library panel, select your symbol. From the Library panel's Options menu, choose Properties **B**.

   The Symbol Properties dialog box appears.

3. Click the Advanced button.

   The Symbol Properties dialog box expands, showing the Linkage and Sharing sections.

4. In the Sharing section, select the "Export for runtime sharing" option. In the URL field, enter the relative or absolute path to where the SWF file will be posted. In the Class field, enter a unique name for your symbol. Leave the Base Class field as is. Keep the "Export in frame 1" check box selected. Click OK **C**.

   Your selected symbol is now marked for export and available to be shared by other movies.

5. Export your Flash movie as a SWF file with the name and in the location you specified in the URL field of the Symbol Properties dialog box.

   This is your source file that shares its symbol.

B Choose Properties from the Library panel's Options menu.

C To mark a symbol as a shared symbol, select it for export in the Sharing section, and give a URL where it can be found. In the Linkage section, give it a name in the Class field. This shared symbol is located in the same folder as the movies that will share it. The shared symbol extends the properties and methods of the `MovieClip` class.

To use a runtime shared symbol:

1. Open a new Flash document, and create a new symbol of the kind that the source document is sharing.

   For example, say your source document is sharing a bitmap symbol. In the destination document, import another bitmap symbol. The contents of your destination symbol will be replaced by the shared symbol from the source document at runtime. The symbol in your destination movie is simply a placeholder.

2. In the Library panel, select your symbol. From the Options menu, choose Properties.

   The Symbol Properties dialog box appears.

3. If the Symbol Properties dialog box is not already expanded, click the Advanced button.

   The Symbol Properties dialog box expands, showing the Linkage and Sharing sections.

4. In the Sharing section, select the "Import for runtime sharing" option. In the URL field, enter the path to the source movie. In the Class field, enter the name for the shared symbol in the source movie (as it appears in the Class field of its own Symbol Properties dialog box). Click OK **D**.

   Your selected symbol is now marked to find the shared symbol in the source movie and import it.

Or you can do the following:

1. Open a new Flash document, and choose File > Import > Open External Library **E**. Choose the Flash file that contains the shared Library symbol.

   The Library of the Flash file that contains the shared Library symbol appears.

2. Drag the shared Library symbol into your new document's Library.

   The shared symbol appears in your destination document's Library. The symbol will automatically be marked to be imported for runtime sharing with the correct Class name and URL.

   After completing either steps 1–4 or 1–2 above, proceed with step 3.

D In the Symbol Properties dialog box, select the "Import for runtime sharing" check box, and enter the same Class name and location of the shared symbol you want to use.

E Choose File > Import > Open External Library to open the Library of the source movie that shares its symbol.

3. In your destination movie, drag an instance of the symbol onto the Stage, and use it in your movie.

4. Export your Flash movie as a SWF file, and place it in a location where it can find the source movie.

When you play the SWF file, it imports the shared symbol from the source movie. The shared symbol appears on the Stage **F**.

Continues on next page

Destination SWF at authortime   *Destination SWF at runtime*

F The destination SWF imports the shared symbol from the source SWF. The URL fields in **C** and **D** specify where the source SWF is located relative to the destination SWF. The empty symbol in the destination movie (left) imports the **kungFuMaster** shared symbol from the source SWF at runtime. As a result, the shared symbol appears in the destination SWF file (right).

When you make changes and revisions to the shared symbol in the source movie, all the destination movies that use the shared symbol are automatically updated to reflect the change.

TIP If you have many symbols in the source movie that you want to share, choose Shared Library Properties from the Library Options menu **G**. Enter the URL of the source movie's location to set the URL for all the shared symbols in the Library.

Authortime sharing of symbols

When you want to share symbols among FLA files instead of SWF files, turn to authortime sharing. Authortime sharing lets you choose a source symbol in a particular FLA file so that another FLA file can reference it and keep its symbol up to date. You have to worry about modifying only one FLA file containing the source symbol instead of multiple FLA files that contain the same symbol. Each movie stores its own copy of the common symbol. You can update the symbol to the source symbol whenever you want, or even make automatic updates before you publish a SWF file.

To update a symbol from a different Flash file:

1. Select the symbol you want to update in the Library panel. From the Options menu, choose Properties.

   The Symbol Properties dialog box appears.

2. Click Advanced.

   The Symbol Properties dialog box expands to display more options.

G Choose Shared Library Properties from the Library Options menu to set the URL path of the shared symbols.

H The Source section in the Symbol Properties dialog box contains options for authortime sharing. The selected symbol is called **kungfuMaster**.

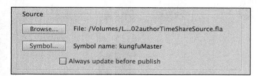

I Select the source symbol for authortime sharing.

```
Source
  Browse...   File: /Volumes/L...02authorTimeShareSource.fla
  Symbol...   Symbol name: kungfuMaster
              ☐ Always update before publish
```

J The Source section of the Symbol Properties dialog box displays the path to the authortime source symbol and the name of the source symbol.

3. In the Source section of the dialog box, click Browse **H**. Select the Flash file that contains the symbol you want to use to update your currently selected symbol. Click OK (Windows) or Open (Mac).

The Select Symbol dialog box appears, showing a list of all the symbols in the selected Flash file's Library.

4. Select a symbol, and click OK **I**.

The Select Symbol dialog box closes.

5. In the Symbol Properties dialog box that is still open, note the new source for your symbol **J**. Click OK.

The Symbol Properties dialog box closes, and your symbol is updated with the symbol you just chose for its new source. Your symbol retains its name, but its content is updated to the source symbol.

To make automatic updates to a symbol:

In the Symbol Properties dialog box, select the "Always update before publish" check box.

Whenever you export a SWF file from your Flash file, whether by publishing it or by using the Test Movie command (Control > Test Movie > in Flash Professional), Flash will locate the source symbol and update your symbol.

Runtime Sharing or Authortime Sharing?

Although they may seem similar, runtime and authortime sharing are two very different ways to work with symbols. Each approach is better suited to different types of projects and workflows. Runtime sharing is useful when multiple SWF movies can share common assets, thus decreasing symbol redundancy, file size, and download times. You publish a single SWF file holding all the common symbols that multiple SWF files can access. Authortime sharing, on the other hand, is useful for organizing your workflow *before* you publish your SWF movie. You can use authortime sharing to keep different symbols in separate FLA files. A master FLA file can reference all the symbols in the separate files and compile them into a single SWF. Working this way, you can have different members of a Flash development team work on different symbols and rely on authortime sharing to ensure that the final published movie will contain the updated symbols. Compare these two ways of sharing Library symbols in **K**.

K During runtime sharing (left), multiple SWF files can share symbols from a single common SWF file after publishing. During authortime sharing (right), multiple FLA files can provide updated symbols to a single FLA file before publishing. The single FLA file publishes a SWF file to play during runtime.

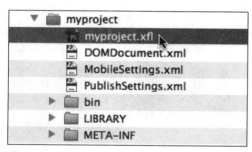

A This Flash file called **myproject** is being saved as an uncompressed document (XFL format).

B An uncompressed document (XFL format) is a folder that contains folders and files representing the contents of your Flash movie.

C Double-click the XFL file inside the folder to open your Flash file.

Saving Files in an Uncompressed Format

Flash Professional CS5 introduces a new Flash format, called the XFL format, which is an uncompressed Flash document that exposes the contents of the file so that other developers can have access and edit it. The XFL format is actually a folder with other folders inside it, and not a single document.

The contents of your file are represented by several XML files, and any assets in your Library panel are contained in the LIBRARY folder. You can edit or swap out assets from the LIBRARY folder, and all those changes will be automatically made to the FLA file.

To save a Flash file as an XFL document:

1. From the top menu, choose File > Save or File > Save As, and choose Flash CS5 Uncompressed Document **A**.

2. Choose a filename and click Save.

   Your file is saved in the XFL format, which is a folder containing all the content **B**.

To open an XFL document:

- Open the XFL folder and double-click the XFL file inside **C**.

  or

- From Flash, choose File > Open, and choose the XFL file inside the XFL folder.

  Your Flash project opens. The XFL file inside the folder doesn't contain any content—it simply provides an icon for the author to click on to open, and it points to the XML documents and assets within the other folders.

To edit an XFL document:

1. In this example, you'll swap out a bitmap in the Library panel by editing the XFL document. Save a Flash file that contains a bitmap in its library as a Flash CS5 Uncompressed Document (XFL) .

2. Open the XFL folder and the LIBRARY folder inside it **E**.

   The LIBRARY folder contains all the library assets.

3. Swap out the bitmap with another, maintaining its filename.

4. Return to your project in Flash to see the results of the substitution in the LIBRARY folder. You may have to close the file and reopen it to see the changes.

   The original Library symbol has been replaced with the new symbol **F**.

TIP When you test an XFL document, the SWF is published and saved in the same directory as the XFL folder, and *not* in the same directory as the XFL file (inside the folder).

D In this Flash file, the Library contains a few symbols and an imported JPEG image of the Grand Central Terminal in New York.

E In the LIBRARY folder inside the XFL project folder, all the symbols and the imported JPEG image are represented.

F Swapping out the image (but maintaining its filename) in the LIBRARY folder results in a clean substitution in the Flash file, both in the Library panel and on the Stage.

Tracking, Finding, and Managing Flash Elements

To manage the myriad Flash elements in your movie—symbols, text, bitmaps, ActionScript code, and so on—you can turn to the Movie Explorer panel or the Find and Replace panel. The Movie Explorer panel (Alt-F3 for Windows, Option-F3 for Mac) gives you a bird's-eye view of your Flash movie and presents its various elements in a hierarchical display. From the hierarchical display, you can quickly go to individual elements to edit them. The Movie Explorer even updates itself in real time, so as you're authoring a Flash movie, the panel displays the latest modifications. The Find and Replace panel (Ctrl-F for Windows, Cmd-F for Mac), on the other hand, lets you search your entire Flash movie for different elements, edit individual search results, and even replace multiple elements at once.

Both panels are powerful and useful tools to help you make sense of complex Flash movies. For example, to find all the instances of a movie clip, you can search for them in the Movie Explorer and have Flash display the exact scene, layer, and frame where each instance resides. You can then quickly go to those spots on the Timeline to edit the instances. If you wanted to replace all the text in your movie with a different font, you can use the Find and Replace panel to find all text of a certain font and replace that font with a new font.

The Movie Explorer panel

Use the Movie Explorer panel to provide a visual display of all your Flash elements on the Stage and on the Timeline .

Show: ——— Filtering buttons

Find: ——— Find field

Scene 1
  Layer 2
    Frame 1
  Layer 1
    Frame 1
      Actions for Frame 1
      A Left–Right Balance, <balance>, (Verdana, 10 pts)
      groove movieclip, <volumegroove_mc>
      groove movieclip, <balancegroove_mc>
      slider bar movie clip, <volume_mc>
      slider bar movie clip, <balance_mc>
      A Volume , <volume>, (Verdana, 10 pts)
  Symbol Definition(s)
    groove movieclip
      Layer 1
        Frame 1
    slider bar movie clip
      button
        Frame 1

Click to collapse or expand ——— (Layer 1)

Display ———

A A typical display in the Movie Explorer shows various elements of the movie in an expandable hierarchy.

To display different categories of elements:

From the Options menu at the right of the Movie Explorer panel, select one or more of the following :

Show Movie Elements displays all the elements in your movie and organizes them by scene. Only the current scene is displayed.

Show Symbol Definitions displays all the elements associated with symbol instances that are on the Stage.

Show All Scenes displays all the elements in your movie in all scenes.

To filter the categories of elements that are displayed:

From the row of filtering buttons at the top of the panel, select one or more to add categories of elements to display :

Show Text displays the actual contents in a text selection, the font name and font size, and the instance name for text fields.

Show Movie Clips, Buttons, and Graphics displays the symbol names of buttons, movie clips, and graphics on the Stage, as well as the instance names of movie clips and buttons.

Show ActionScript displays the Action-Script code assigned to frames (and to buttons or movie clips, if authoring in ActionScript 2.0 or earlier).

Show Video, Sounds, and Bitmaps displays the symbol names of imported video, sounds, and bitmaps on the Stage.

Show Frames and Layers displays the names of layers, keyframes, and frame labels in the movie.

Customize Which Items to Show displays a dialog box from which you can choose individual elements to display.

Go to Location
Go to Symbol Definition
Select Symbol Instances
Show in Library

Rename
Edit in Place
Edit in New Window

✓ Show Movie Elements
✓ Show Symbol Definitions
✓ Show All Scenes

Copy All Text to Clipboard

B The Options menu of the Movie Explorer panel.

Show Text

Show Movie Clips, Buttons, and Graphics

Show ActionScript

Show Video, Sounds, and Bitmaps

Show Frames and Layers

Show: A

Find:

Customize Which Items to Show

C The filtering buttons let you selectively display elements.

To find and edit elements in the display:

1. In the Find field at the top of the Movie Explorer panel, enter the name of the element you want to find **D**.

   All the elements of the movie that contain that name appear in the display list automatically as you type in the field.

2. Click the desired element to select it.

   The element is also selected on the Timeline and on the Stage. If a scene or keyframe is selected, Flash takes you to that scene or keyframe.

3. From the Options menu of the Movie Explorer panel, choose Edit in Place or Edit in New Window to go to symbol editing mode for a selected symbol.

   or

   Choose Rename from the Options menu.

   The name of the element becomes selectable so that you can edit it.

or

Double-click the desired element to modify it. Flash makes the element editable or opens an appropriate window, depending on what type of element it is:

Double-clicking a symbol (except for sound, video, and bitmaps) opens symbol-editing mode.

Double-clicking ActionScript opens the script in the Actions panel.

Double-clicking a scene or layer lets you rename it.

Double-clicking a text selection lets you edit its contents.

To find all instances of a symbol:

In the Find field of the Movie Explorer panel, enter the name of the symbol whose instances you want to find.

All instances of that symbol appear in the display **E**.

D Entering a word or phrase in the Find field displays all occurrences of that word or phrase in the Display window. Here, the instance named `circle` of the movie clip symbol `ball` has been found.

E Entering the symbol name `ball` in the Find field displays all the instances of the `ball` symbol. There are two instances listed: one called `circle` in the draggable ball layer and another called `myReferencePoint` in the stationary ball layer.

To replace all occurrences of a particular font:

1. In the Find field of the Movie Explorer panel, enter the name of the font you want to replace.

   All occurrences of that font appear in the display **F**.

2. Select all the text elements, using Shift-click to make multiple selections.

3. In the Property inspector, choose a different font and style for all text elements.

   All the selected text elements change according to your choices in the Properties inspector **G**.

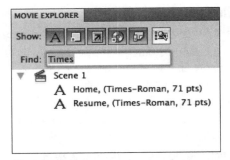

F All the occurrences of the Times font appear in the Display window.

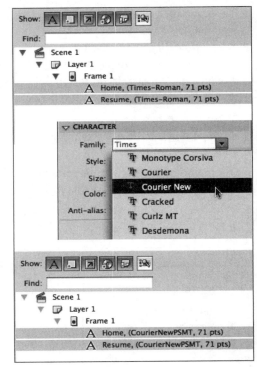

G With the Times text elements selected, choose a different font, such as Courier New (top) from the Properties inspector. Flash changes those text elements from Times to Courier New (bottom).

(H) In this Find and Replace panel, the text **gotoAndPlay** will replace **gotoAndStop** in all the ActionScript code throughout the movie.

The Find and Replace panel

Use the Find and Replace panel Edit > Find and Replace, Cmd-F for Mac, Ctrl-F for Windows) to search your whole Flash movie for various elements (text string, a font, a color, a symbol, a sound file, a video file, or an imported bitmap) and replace them with another. You can find and replace individual search results or replace all of them at once. The Find and Replace panel is particularly powerful with its text searching capabilities and options.

To find and replace text:

1. In the For pull-down menu, select Text.
2. In the Text box, enter the text that you want to find.
3. In the Replace with Text box, enter the replacement text.
4. Select the options for text searching **(H)**:

   Whole Word searches for the entire word only and won't return results if the text is part of a larger text string.

   Match Case searches for the text that exactly matches uppercase and lowercase characters.

   Regular Expressions searches for text that matches a pattern specified by a regular expression (see Chapter 10, "Controlling Text").

   Text Field Contents searches for the text in text fields.

   Frames/Layers/Parameters searches for the text in frame labels, layer names, scene names, and component parameters.

   Strings in ActionScript searches for the text in strings in ActionScript code.

   ActionScript searches for the text throughout the entire ActionScript code.

Continues on next page

5. Click Find All or Find Next.

All occurrences of that text appear in the display at the bottom if you click Find All, or just the first occurrence if you click Find Next 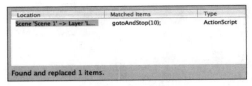.

Double-click the search result to immediately go to particular text to edit.

or

Click Replace All or Replace.

All occurrences of that text are replaced with the replacement text if you click Replace All, or just the first occurrence if you click Find Next.

To find and replace fonts:

1. In the For pull-down menu, select Font.

2. In the Search options, select Font, Style, or Size to search for particular fonts or particular styles, or to search a range of font sizes. Leave all options deselected to search for all fonts in your Flash movie.

3. In the Replace options, select Font, Style, or Size to replace all the found text with a new font, a new style, or a different font size.

4. Click Replace All.

All occurrences of the particular font, size, or style are replaced by the selected replacement font, size, or style. The results are also listed in the display at the bottom of the dialog box .

Location	Matched Items	Type
Scene 'Scene 1' -> Layer 'L...	gotoAndStop(10);	ActionScript

Found and replaced 1 items.

I One instance of the searched text was found and replaced with the new text. The results are displayed in the bottom window.

J Find all text in your movie by keeping the search restrictions unselected for font, style, and size. Replace the text with a particular font by specifying the Replace with options.

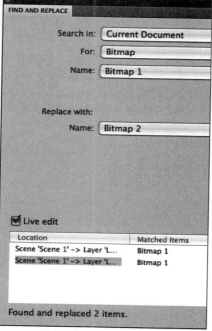

K Finding and replacing colors has additional options for replacing the colors in Text, Fills, or Strokes.

L Find and replace colors, bitmaps, symbols, sounds, or videos. In this example, all the bitmaps in the movie named Bitmap 1 were replaced by the bitmap named Bitmap 2.

To find and replace a symbol, sound, video, bitmap, or color:

1. In the For pull-down menu, select the type of element that you want to find.

2. In the Name pull-down menu, select the name of the symbol, sound, video, or bitmap (the name should be the name in the Library), or the Hex code of the color.

3. In the Replace with pull-down menu, select the name of a different symbol, sound, video, or bitmap, or another Hex code for a color. For color, you can further refine your replacements by choosing Text, Fills, or Strokes **K**.

4. Click Replace All.

   All occurrences of the particular symbol, sound, video, bitmap, or color are replaced by the selected replacement. The results are also listed in the display at the bottom of the dialog box **L**.

TIP You can only find and replace elements of the same kind. For example, you can replace one bitmap with another bitmap, but you can't replace one bitmap with a symbol.

Optimizing Your Movie

Understanding the tools you use to create graphics, animation, sound, and Action-Script is important, but it's equally important to know how best to use them to create streamlined Flash movies. After all, the best-laid designs and animations won't be appreciated if poor construction and clunky code make them too large to download or too inefficient to play easily. To streamline a Flash movie, use optimizations that keep the file size small, the animations smooth, and the revisions simple. Many factors affect the file size and performance of the final exported SWF file. Bitmaps, sounds, complicated shapes, color gradients, alpha transparencies, filters, and embedded fonts all increase the Flash file size and slow the movie's performance.

Only you can weigh the trade-offs between the quality and quantity of Flash content and the size and performance of the movie. Keep in mind the audience to whom you're delivering your Flash movies. Are you delivering content to mobile devices or to desktop computers with broadband Internet access? What is the resolution of your audience's computer screen? Knowing the answers to these questions can help you make more informed choices about what to include in your movie and how to build it.

The following strategies can help you work more efficiently and create smaller, more manageable, better-performing Flash movies.

A Well-organized layers like these are easy to understand and change.

Optimizing your authoring environment

- Use layers to separate and organize your content. For example, place all your ActionScript on one layer, all your frame labels on another layer, and all your sounds in still another layer. By using layers, you'll be able to understand and change different elements of your movie quickly **A**. Having many layers doesn't increase the size of the final exported SWF file. Lock or hide individual layers to isolate just the elements you want to work on. This will prevent you from accidentally moving or deleting other objects in the way. Use comments in keyframes as well to explain the different parts of the Timeline.

- Organize the layers on your Timeline and the symbols in your Library with folders. Just as folders on your desktop can help you group related items, folders for layers and folders for symbols will reduce clutter and make your Flash authoring environment a more manageable workspace.

- Use the **trace** statement to observe the changing values of your object's properties in your movie. The **trace** statement lets you display expressions and variables at any point during the execution of your ActionScript code.

- Avoid using scenes in your movie. Although scenes are a good organizational feature for beginners, Timelines that contain scenes are more difficult to navigate. In addition, movie clip instances aren't continuous between scenes, so they are reset from one scene to another. Instead, use labels to mark different areas of the Timeline, use movie clips to hold different parts of your animation, or load external assets as they are needed.

Optimizing bitmaps and sounds for playback performance

- Avoid animating large bitmaps. Keep bitmaps as static background elements if they're large, or make them small for tweening.

- Place streaming sounds on the main Timeline instead of within a movie clip. A movie clip needs to be downloaded in its entirety before playing. A streaming sound on the root Timeline, however, begins playing as the frames download. Better yet, keep your sound as an external asset and use ActionScript to dynamically load it.

- Use the maximum amount of compression tolerable for bitmaps and sounds. You can adjust the JPEG quality level for your exported SWF file in Publish Settings. You can also adjust the compression settings for the stream sync and event sync sounds separately, so you can keep a higher-quality streaming sound for music and narration and a lower-quality event sound for button clicks .

- Avoid using the Trace Bitmap command to create an overly complex vector image of an imported bitmap. The complexity of a traced bitmap can make the file size larger and the performance significantly slower than if you use the bitmap itself.

- Import bitmaps and sounds at the exact size or length that you want to use them in Flash. Although editing within Flash is possible, you want to import just the information you need to keep the file size small. For example, don't import a bitmap and then reduce it 50 percent to use in your movie. Instead, reduce the bitmap 50 percent first and then import it into Flash.

B The JPEG quality and audio-compression options in the Publish Settings dialog box.

C An object created with separate groups (top left) contains more information (top middle) and can produce undesirable transparency effects (top right). A single shape (bottom left) contains less information (bottom middle) and becomes transparent as one unit (bottom right).

Optimizing graphics, text, and tweening for playback performance

- Use tweening wherever you can instead of frame-by-frame animation. In an animation, Flash only has to remember the keyframes, making tweening a far less memory-intensive task.

- Avoid creating animations that have multiple objects moving at the same time or that have large areas of change. These kinds of animations tax a computer's CPU and slow the movie's performance.

- If you have a large vector graphic that isn't animated (such as a background), select the "Use runtime bitmap caching" option in the Properties inspector for the instance. This option instructs the Flash Player to not redraw the graphic's content every frame, reducing the playback computer's workload.

- Break apart groups within symbols to simplify them. Once you're satisfied with an illustration in a symbol, break the groups into shapes to flatten the illustration. Flash will have fewer curves to remember and thus will have an easier time tweening the symbol instance. Alpha effects on the instance also affect the symbol as a whole instead of the individual groups within the symbol **C**.

- Use color gradients and alpha transparencies sparingly.

- Avoid setting filters on High quality, and avoid multiple filters.

- Use the Properties inspector to change the color, tint, and brightness of instances of a single symbol instead of creating separate symbols of different colors.

Continues on next page

- Optimize curves by avoiding special line styles (such as dotted lines), by using the Pencil tool rather than the Brush tool, and by reducing the complexity of curves with Modify > Shape > Optimize or by pressing Ctrl-Alt-Shift-C for Windows or Cmd-Shift-Option-C for Mac 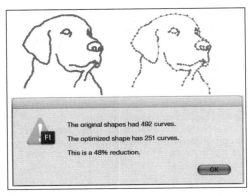.

- Use fewer font styles, and embed only the essential font outlines.

Optimizing ActionScript code

- Keep all your code in one place—preferably on the main Timeline—and keep code in just one layer.

- Use a consistent naming convention for variables, objects, and other elements that need to be identified. A consistent, simple name makes the job the variable performs more apparent.

- Use comments within your ActionScript to explain the code to yourself and to other developers who may look at your Flash document for future revisions. Use the double backslash (**//**) to comment single lines and the block comment (**/*** and ***/**) to comment multiple lines.

- Think about *modularity*. Use smaller, separate components to build your interactivity. For example, use functions to define frequently accessed tasks and keep large or common assets outside your movie but available through shared symbols and **Loader** objects. You'll reduce redundancy, save memory, and make revisions easier.

The original shapes had 492 curves.

The optimized shape has 251 curves.

This is a 48% reduction.

OK

D Complex curves and shapes can be simplified without losing their detail.

Avoiding Common Mistakes

When you're troubleshooting your Flash movie, there are a few obvious places you should look first to locate common mistakes. These problems usually involve simple but critical elements, such as overlooking quotation marks or a relative path term or forgetting to name an instance. Pay close attention to the following warning list to ensure that all your Flash movies are free of bugs:

- Be mindful of uppercase and lowercase letters. ActionScript 3 is case-sensitive, so make sure the names of your variables and objects exactly match. Flash keywords must also match in case. For example, **keyCode** isn't the same as **keycode**.

- Remember to name your movie clip, button, and text field instances in the Properties inspector. Be sure your names adhere to the naming rules explained in Chapter 3, "Getting a Handle on ActionScript."

- Double-check the target paths for your variables and objects.

- Make sure that you've completely loaded external data before you attempt to do anything with it. You must listen for the **Event.COMPLETE** before you can access the loaded object's properties, or do anything with it.

- Double-check the data types of your values. Review the Script pane to make sure quotation marks appear only around string data types. Target paths and the keyword **this** should not be within quotation marks.

Continues on next page

- Check to see whether ActionScript statements are within the correct parentheses or curly braces in the Script pane. For example, verify that statements belonging to an `if` statement or to a function statement are contained within their curly braces. Every opening parenthesis or curly brace needs a closing parenthesis or curly brace.

- Don't forget to add any dynamically generated object to the display list to make it visible. The `addChild()` method is commonly left out, especially for those users familiar with previous versions of ActionScript.

- To test simple actions and simple buttons, choose Enable Simple Frame Actions and Enable Simple Buttons from the Control menu. For more complex button events, you must choose Test Movie > in Flash Professional from the Control menu.

- Always be sure of what timeline you are working on, especially when you have embedded movie clips. Sometimes you'll add animation or code inside a movie clip symbol when you really want to add it to the main Timeline. From time to time, look at the navigation bar above the Stage to verify your current workspace (Scene 1 is the default name for the main Timeline).

- Remember that the default setting for movie clips is to play and loop. Place a `stop()` action in its first keyframe to prevent it from playing automatically, or place the action in its last keyframe to prevent it from looping.

- Do not place button symbols within button symbols. They will not work properly.

- Remember that the default setting for your Flash movie in the testing mode is to loop.

For additional help and advice about debugging your movie, check out the vast Flash resources on the Web. Begin your search at Adobe's Web site, which provides a searchable archive of tech notes, documentation, tutorials, case studies, and more. You'll also find links to other Web sites with articles, FLA source files, forums, blogs, and mailing lists. Check out the companion Web site that accompanies this book at www.peachpit.com/flashcs5vqp for more Flash links and resources.

Keyboard Key Codes

LETTERS

Letter Key	Key Code
A	65
B	66
C	67
D	68
E	69
F	70
G	71
H	72
I	73
J	74
K	75
L	76
M	77
N	78
O	79
P	80
Q	81
R	82
S	83
T	84
U	85
V	86
W	87
X	88
Y	89
Z	90

FUNCTION KEYS

Function Key	Key Code	Keyboard Class Property
F1	112	**F1**
F2	113	**F2**
F3	114	**F3**
F4	115	**F4**
F5	116	**F5**
F6	117	**F6**
F7	118	**F7**
F8	119	**F8**
F9	120	**F9**
F10	121	**F10**
F11	122	**F11**
F12	123	**F12**
F13	124	**F13**
F14	125	**F14**
F15	126	**F15**

NUMBERS AND SYMBOLS

Key	Key Code	Keyboard Class Property
0	48	
1	49	
2	50	
3	51	
4	52	
5	53	
6	54	
7	55	
8	56	
9	57	
Numpad 0	96	**NUMPAD_0**
Numpad 1	97	**NUMPAD_1**
Numpad 2	98	**NUMPAD_2**
Numpad 3	99	**NUMPAD_3**
Numpad 4	100	**NUMPAD_4**
Numpad 5	101	**NUMPAD_5**
Numpad 6	102	**NUMPAD_6**
Numpad 7	103	**NUMPAD_7**
Numpad 8	104	**NUMPAD_8**
Numpad 9	105	**NUMPAD_9**
Numpad *	106	**NUMPAD_MULTIPLY**
Numpad +	107	**NUMPAD_ADD**
Numpad Enter	108	**NUMPAD_ENTER**
Numpad –	109	**NUMPAD_SUBTRACT**
Numpad .	110	**NUMPAD_DECIMAL**
Numpad /	111	**NUMPAD_DIVIDE**
Backspace	8	**BACKSPACE**
Tab	9	**TAB**
Clear	12	
Enter	13	**ENTER**
Shift	16	**SHIFT**
Control	17	**CONTROL**
Alt	18	

NUMBERS AND SYMBOLS *(continued)*

Key	Key Code	Keyboard Class Property
Caps Lock	20	**CAPS_LOCK**
Esc	27	**ESCAPE**
Spacebar	32	**SPACE**
Page Up	33	**PAGE_UP**
Page Down	34	**PAGE_DOWN**
End	35	**END**
Home	36	**HOME**
Left arrow	37	**LEFT**
Up arrow	38	**UP**
Right arrow	39	**RIGHT**
Down arrow	40	**DOWN**
Insert	45	**INSERT**
Delete	46	**DELETE**
Help	47	
Num Lock	144	
;:	186	
=+	187	
-_	189	
/?	191	
`~	192	
[{	219	
|	220	
]}	221	
'"	222	

Index

ActionScript 3 *(continued)*

building functions to accept parameters, 116

building functions to return values, 117–118

calling methods, 110–111

capitalization, 91

case sensitivity, 91, 493

classes, 87

code hints, 97–99

Code Snippets panel, 119–122

comma (,), 91

creating block comments, 124

creating instances on Stage, 109

creating line comments, 123

creating objects, 108

curly braces ({}), 91

data types, 104–105

declaring and initializing variables, 105

editing, 101–103

escape sequences, 107

expressions, 107

`ExternalInterface` class, 195

getting information about actions, 100

initializing variables, 104–105

instances, 87

instantiating objects, 109

`int` data type, 104

methods, 88

naming instances, 110

naming variables, 106

`Number` data type, 104–105

`Object` data type, 104

objects, 87

overview of, 86

pinning scripts in, 97

properties, 88

properties of, 91

rules for naming objects, 106

semicolon (;), 91

setting formatting options, 99–100

showing earlier versions of, 96

strict typing, 104–105

`String` data type, 104–105

strings, 107

`trace()` statement, 113

`uint` data type, 104

using to animate graphics, 294–295

writing with dot syntax, 89–90

ActionScript code

adding, 95

adding via Code Snippets panel, 84

exporting, 103

importing, 103

inserting in Actions panel, 120

optimizing, 492

storing, 97

ActionScript cue points

adding from Properties inspector, 80

adding with ActionScript, 81

detecting, 83

ActionScript Script pane

adding actions in, 95

checking syntax in, 102

editing actions in, 96

Find and Replace dialog box, 102–103

finding terms in, 102–103

navigating, 95

pinning scripts in, 100

removing actions from, 96

replacing terms in, 102–103

resizing, 96

unpinning scripts in, 100

ActionScript statements, scoping, 177

`addChild()` method

including, 494

using with animated flame, 320

using with `DisplayObjectContainer` class, 232, 265–266

using with external SWF files, 200, 202

using with loaded movies, 205, 208, 210

`addEventListener()` method

using, 126

using to drag objects, 254

using to stop dragging objects, 255

addition (+) assignment operator, using, 239, 364, 366

Adobe Media Encoder

adding embedded cue points from, 79

adding video files to, 59

deleting cue points from, 79

removing video files from, 60

alpha, transforming for objects, 243–244

Alpha blend mode, described, 247

D

\d and D codes, using in regular expressions, 426
data types, checking values of, 493
Date class
  creating **myDate** object from, 109
  features of, 436
  getHours() method, 464–465
  getMinutes() method, 464–465
  methods of, 464
  numbers and names, 467
  properties of, 88
  using, 464
  using **Array** object with, 467
decimals
  vs. numbers, 453
  rounding off, 442
default statements, using, 376
degrees, converting to radians, 279
delta frames, defined, 67
device fonts, embedding, 394
digital video. *See* video
directional movement, creating, 446–449
directories
  moving up, 192
  separating with slash (/), 192
display list. *See also* graphics
  adding objects to, 263
  adding objects to top of, 265
  features of, 232
  placing instances of Library symbols in, 263
  placing objects at bottom of, 265
  removing objects from, 265
  tree hierarchy, 232
  using with Flash movies, 210
DisplayObject class
  hitTestObject() method, 258
  hitTestPoint() method, 258
DisplayObject objects. *See also* objects
  applying filters to, 251
  controlling overlapping of, 264–266
  modifying colors for, 240–245
  transform property, 240
DisplayObject properties, described, 233

distances
  calculating, 450–452
  calculating in 3D, 451
division, symbol for, 364
do while statement, using, 381
dot syntax, writing with, 89–90
double equals symbol (==)
  vs. = (assignment operator), 369
  described, 368
  using with keypresses, 155
double slash (//), using with line comments, 123
download progress. *See also* Bandwidth Profiler
  adding numeric display of, 226–227
  detecting, 222–225, 227
drag-and-drop interactivity, creating, 253
draggable masks, creating, 285–287
draggable objects
  centering, 256
  constraining, 256–257
dragging objects, 254
draw() methods
  described, 268
  using to copy image data, 300, 307
  using with animated flame, 316, 318–319
drawCircle() method, using, 280
drawPath() method, using, 281
drawRect() method, using, 281, 369
drawTriangles() method, using, 281
drop-shadow filter effect, adding dynamically, 251–252
dynamic referencing, 366–367
dynamic tweens, creating, 289–290

E

ease curves, interpreting, 15
easing
  controlling for armatures, 44–45
  in Motion Editor, 12
EditManager object, using with TLF text, 421
elements. *See* Flash elements
else if statement, using, 374, 466
else statement, using for false condition, 372–373
e-mail, preaddressing, 191
embedded video, swapping, 72. *See also* video
embedFonts property, using with Classic text, 407

I

ID3v2 sound properties, described, 338–339

if statement
  checking **true** status in, 260
  using to create continuous feedback button, 370–371
  using with cue points, 83
  using with **else if**, 374–375

images. *See* bitmap images; external images

Import Script function, using in ActionScript, 101

import statement
  using with ActionScript code, 97
  using with cue points, 82
  using with dynamic tweens, 289
  using with TLF text, 408–409

Import Video wizard, using, 70–71, 74

In point, moving for video length, 65

indexOf() method, using with **String** class, 432

inequality, symbol for, 368

information
  clearing on user's computer, 356
  default amount for storage, 359
  ordering with arrays, 454–459
  retrieving from user's computer, 356
  sharing among movies, 357
  storing for movies, 357–358
  storing on user's computer, 354–355
  testing with conditional statements, 368–371

Inkbottle tool, using with armatures, 40

instances
  creating for classes, 108
  creating for movie clips, 140
  creating on Stage, 109
  naming, 110
  using in ActionScript, 87

instantiation, process of, 108

int data type data type, using in ActionScript, 104

integers, rounding numbers to, 442

interpolation method, using with fills and gradients, 275

intersection, detecting between objects, 259

inverse kinematics. *See also* animating in 3D
  with movie clips, 33
  overview, 33
  with shapes, 39

invisible buttons, creating, 137–138. *See also* animated buttons; buttons
  "invisible" movie clip, creating, 181–182

J

JavaScript
  innerHeight window property, 199
  innerWidth window property, 199
  opening custom windows with, 197–199
  openwindow function, 198
  using to control window parameters, 195–196
  window properties, 195

JavaScript functions, passing parameters to, 195

joint constraints, position of, 43

joint rotation
  constraining, 42
  enabling, 42–43

joint style parameter, explained, 271

joint translation, options for, 42

JPEG quality settings, accessing, 490

K

key code values, using, 154

keyboard events
  in ActionScript 2, 156
  described, 168
  detecting, 153
  key code values, 154

keyboard key codes
  function keys, 495
  letter keys, 495
  numbers and symbols, 496

KeyboardEvent object
  creation of, 126
  dispatching, 154
  properties, 153

keyframe distance, setting for video compression, 67

keyframes. *See also* property keyframes
  Clear Pose command, 35
  creating in **Hit** state, 137–138
  defining for buttons, 142
  frames between, 67
  inserting for titles, 27
  intermediate, 30–31
  roving and non-roving, 7

Q

quotation mark (") character, escape sequence for, 107

R

\r sequence, character associated with, 107
radians, converting degrees to, 279
radio buttons, described, 179
random numbers, generating, 453
Rectangle object, using with draggable objects, 256–257
rectangles
    creating, 281
    filling with color, 304
regions, filling with color, 305–306
regular expressions
    codes for, 426
    creating, 427
    flags for, 426
    matching text patterns with, 425–427
    searching text to match, 427
    using **match()** method with, 429
relative path
    example of, 175–176
    linking with, 192
relative values, assigning, 238
replace() method, using with **String** class, 431
Replace options, using in Movie Explorer panel, 485–486
resizable property in JavaScript, described, 195
Resize Video setting, choosing for video compression, 66
resume() method
    using with motion tweens, 289
    using with NetStream object, 219
RGB code, displaying in Color Mixer panel, 240
root keyword, using with current timeline, 175
_root property, using with loaded movies, 211
rotating dial, creating, 443–445
rotating objects, 22–23
rotation
    changing for objects, 235
    isolating for nodes, 35
rotation DisplayObject properties
    assigning values to, 239
    described, 233

using, 235–236
rotation property, using with directional movement, 448
Round() option, using with **joint style**, 271
rounding
    numbers to integers, 442
    off decimals, 442
run() method, calling, 90
runtime armature, making, 45
runtime shared symbols. *See also* symbols
    versus authortime sharing, 478
    creating, 473
    features of, 472–473
    using, 474–476

S

\s and S codes, using in regular expressions, 426
sandbox, explained, 203
scale mode, using with paths, 270
scenes, avoiding in movies, 489
scope of variables, explained, 117, 345
scoping ActionScript statements, 177
Screen blend mode, described, 247
Script pane. *See* ActionScript Script pane
scripts, pinning and unpinning, 100. *See also* ActionScript
scrollbars property in JavaScript, described, 195
searching and replacing text, 427–428, 430–431
security features
    accessing, 194
    encountering, 193, 203
Selection tool
    using with armatures, 39–40
    using with motion tweens, 6
selections, converting to symbols, 50
semicolon (;), using in ActionScript, 91
Shader blend mode, described, 247
shape behavior, refining with Bind tool, 41
shape changes, simplifying, 30–31
shape hints, using, 28–29
Shape instance, creating for straight line, 268
Shape object
    creating, 267
    drawing and displaying on **Stage**, 270
    using with dynamic buttons, 151–152

text strings. *See* strings
Text tool
    using to animate titles, 26–27
    using with text fields, 392
TextConverter, using, 410
TextField object, default size of, 402
TextFlow content
    displaying, displaying, 415–417
    formatting in Text Layout markup, 419
TextFlow object
    assigning **InlineGraphicElement** to, 412–413
    assigning span element to, 412
    formatting, 418–419
    getting text into, 411
    importing HTML text into, 411
    importing plain text into, 411
    importing Text Layout markup text into, 411
    using, 410
TextFormat object, declaring, 404
TextLayoutFormat object, using, 418–419
theta of right triangle, defining, 438
this keyword, using, 175, 493
threaded text fields, explained, 387
time elapsed, tracking, 469
Timeline
    of movie clips, 139
    moving poses on, 35
    navigation methods, 169
    x- and y-coordinates of, 235
timelines
    identifying, 494
    navigating with movie clips, 170
    in relative mode, 175
    retrieving frame labels on, 185–186
    using frame labels with, 183–186
    using **parent** keyword with, 176
    using **root** keyword with, 175
    using **this** keyword with, 175–176
timer
    creating, 469–470
    detecting end of, 167
    events, 168
    using with continuous actions, 165–166
Timer object, using with clock, 464, 466
titles, animating, 26–27

TLF (Text Layout Framework)
    described, 22
    Editable option, 384
    Read Only option, 384
    Selectable option, 384
TLF text. *See also* Classic text; text
    adding spacing around columns, 391
    changing column spacing, 391
    vs. Classic Text, 401
    containers, 414–417
    controllers, 414–417
    creating, 408
    creating multiple columns, 390–391
    formatting, 409
    making editable, 421
    making selectable, 420
TLF text fields
    modifying properties of, 400
    properties for, 399
TLF text library
    merging, 386
    overview of, 385
    SWZ files, 385
TLFTextField object, using, 410
toggle functionality, adding to buttons, 180
toolbar property in JavaScript, described, 195
top property in JavaScript, described, 195
Trace Bitmap command, avoiding, 490
trace statement
    displaying returned values with, 118
    using, 111, 113
    using in authoring environment, 489
    using with frame labels, 185
    using with MP3 files, 340
Track as Menu Item option, using with pull-down menus, 147
transform DisplayObject property, described, 233
transform property, using with **DisplayObject** objects, 240
transformations, global vs. local, 24
transparency
    changing for movie clips, 245
    changing for objects, 237
triangle object, removing from display list, 265
triangles, calculating angles of, 438

Video Properties dialog box, opening, 215–216
video streams, detecting status of, 221
video symbol, using with external video, 215–216
visual properties, changing, 233
volume and balance, modifying, 333–335
volume levels, visualizing left and right, 341–342

W

\w and W codes, using in regular expressions, 426
Web addresses, loading in windows, 192
Web browsers
  connecting to, 188
  testing movies in, 193
Web sites
  Help topics, 203
  linking to, 188–190
  opening in windows, 193
while statement, using, 380–381
width property
  described, 195
  using with LoaderInfo object, 207
window parameters, controlling via JavaScript, 195–196
windows, opening with JavaScript, 197–199
with action, using to target objects, 177–178
wrapping text. See also text; TLF (Text Layout Framework)
  breaking text field linkages, 389

creating, 387–389
creating text field linkages, 389
deleting linked text fields, 389
editing text fields, 388
inserted linked text fields, 389

X

x- and y-coordinates, timeline considerations, 235
x DisplayObject property, described, 233
x-axis, navigating in 3D space, 22–23
XFL documents
  editing, 480
  opening, 479
  saving Flash files as, 479
XML data
  decoding XML data, 351–352
  receiving, 353
  using with external variables, 350

Y

y DisplayObject property, described, 233
y-axis, navigating in 3D space, 22–23
yellow highlight, hiding for buttons, 150

Z

z DisplayObject property, described, 233
z-axis, navigating in 3D space, 22–23
Zoom item, enabling in ContextMenu instance, 159